Recent Advances in Nutrition for Disease Prevention and Sports Performance Enhancement

Recent Advances in Nutrition for Disease Prevention and Sports Performance Enhancement

Editor

Pedro L. Valenzuela

MDPI • Basel • Beijing • Wuhan • Barcelona • Belgrade • Manchester • Tokyo • Cluj • Tianjin

Editor
Pedro L. Valenzuela
Research Institute,
Hospital 12 de Octubre
("imas12", PaHerg Group)
Madrid
Spain

Editorial Office
MDPI
St. Alban-Anlage 66
4052 Basel, Switzerland

This is a reprint of articles from the Special Issue published online in the open access journal *Nutrients* (ISSN 2072-6643) (available at: https://www.mdpi.com/journal/nutrients/special_issues/nutri_disease_prevention_sports_enhancement).

For citation purposes, cite each article independently as indicated on the article page online and as indicated below:

LastName, A.A.; LastName, B.B.; LastName, C.C. Article Title. *Journal Name* **Year**, *Volume Number*, Page Range.

ISBN 978-3-0365-7702-9 (Hbk)
ISBN 978-3-0365-7703-6 (PDF)

Contents

Pedro L. Valenzuela
Recent Advances in Nutrition for Disease Prevention and Sports Performance Enhancement
Reprinted from: *Nutrients* **2023**, *15*, 1170, doi:10.3390/nu15051170 1

Huiwen Xu, Lucas Jurado-Fasoli, Lourdes Ortiz-Alvarez, Francisco J. Osuna-Prieto, Isabelle Kohler, Xinyu Di, Ramiro Vilchez-Vargas, et al.
Plasma Levels of Omega-3 and Omega-6 Derived Oxylipins Are Associated with Fecal Microbiota Composition in Young Adults
Reprinted from: *Nutrients* **2022**, *14*, 4991, doi:10.3390/nu14234991 3

Jerônimo P. Martins, Lucia C. Silva, Matheus S. Nunes, Gabriel Rübensam, Jarbas R. Oliveira, Rodrigo B. M. Silva and Maria M. Campos
Combined Effects of Exercise and Phytoanabolic Extracts in Castrated Male and Female Mice
Reprinted from: *Nutrients* **2021**, *13*, 1177, doi:10.3390/nu13041177 15

Alessio Bellini, Andrea Nicolò, Ilenia Bazzucchi and Massimo Sacchetti
The Effects of Postprandial Walking on the Glucose Response after Meals with Different Characteristics
Reprinted from: *Nutrients* **2022**, *14*, 1080, doi:10.3390/nu14051080 49

Javier S. Morales, Pedro L. Valenzuela, Adrián Castillo-García, Javier Butragueño, David Jiménez-Pavón, Pedro Carrera-Bastos and Alejandro Lucia
The Exposome and Immune Health in Times of the COVID-19 Pandemic
Reprinted from: *Nutrients* **2022**, *14*, 24, doi:10.3390/nu14010024 61

Alejandro Martínez-Rodríguez, Javier Sánchez-Sánchez, Manuel Vicente-Martínez, María Martínez-Olcina, Laura Miralles-Amorós and Juan Antonio Sánchez-Sáez
Anthropometric Dimensions and Bone Quality in International Male Beach Handball Players: Junior vs. Senior Comparison
Reprinted from: *Nutrients* **2021**, *13*, 1817, doi:10.3390/nu13061817 91

Alejandro Gomez-Bruton, Jorge Marin-Puyalto, Borja Muñiz-Pardos, Angel Matute-Llorente, Juan Del Coso, Alba Gomez-Cabello, German Vicente-Rodriguez, et al.
Does Acute Caffeine Supplementation Improve Physical Performance in Female Team-Sport Athletes? Evidence from a Systematic Review and Meta-Analysis
Reprinted from: *Nutrients* **2021**, *13*, 3663, doi:10.3390/nu13103663 105

Liang-Yu Su, Wen-Ching Huang, Nai-Wen Kan, Te-Hsuan Tung, Linh Ba Phuong Huynh and Shih-Yi Huang
Effects of Resveratrol on Muscle Inflammation, Energy Utilisation, and Exercise Performance in an Eccentric Contraction Exercise Mouse Model
Reprinted from: *Nutrients* **2023**, *15*, 249, doi:10.3390/nu15010249 129

Yoko Tanabe, Naoto Fujii and Katsuhiko Suzuki
Dietary Supplementation for Attenuating Exercise-Induced Muscle Damage and Delayed-Onset Muscle Soreness in Humans
Reprinted from: *Nutrients* **2022**, *14*, 70, doi:10.3390/nu14010070 145

Jana Daher, Moriah Mallick and Dalia El Khoury
Prevalence of Dietary Supplement Use among Athletes Worldwide: A Scoping Review
Reprinted from: *Nutrients* **2022**, *14*, 4109, doi:10.3390/nu14194109 165

Berta Moreno, Santiago Veiga, Antonio J. Sánchez-Oliver, Raúl Domínguez and Esther Morencos
Analysis of Sport Supplement Consumption by Competitive Swimmers According to Sex and Competitive Level
Reprinted from: *Nutrients* **2022**, *14*, 3218, doi:10.3390/nu14153218 . . . . **181**

nutrients

MDPI

Editorial

Recent Advances in Nutrition for Disease Prevention and Sports Performance Enhancement

Pedro L. Valenzuela [1,2]

[1] Research Institute of the Hospital 12 de Octubre ("Imas12", PaHerg Group), 28041 Madrid, Spain; pedro.valenzuela92@gmail.com; Tel.: +34-91-779-2713
[2] Department of Systems Biology, University of Alcalá, 28871 Madrid, Spain

Citation: Valenzuela, P.L. Recent Advances in Nutrition for Disease Prevention and Sports Performance Enhancement. *Nutrients* **2023**, *15*, 1170. https://doi.org/10.3390/nu15051170

Received: 14 February 2023
Accepted: 15 February 2023
Published: 26 February 2023

The important role of nutrition on both health and sports performance, and particularly its joint association with physical exercise, is becoming increasingly clear in recent years. The present Special Issue, entitled "Recent Advances in Nutrition for Disease Prevention and Sports Performance Enhancement" reflects the great progress that is being made in this field, including different studies that address important topics related to nutrition from an integrative and multi-domain perspective.

On the one hand, we find studies focused on the role of nutrition for disease prevention. Xu et al. find an association between the plasma levels of oxylipins (i.e., the oxidation products of polyunsaturated fatty acids such as omega-3 and omega-6) on the fecal microbiota composition of young adults [1], which can have important implications for metabolic health [2]. Using a mouse model subjected to castration to accelerate sarcopenia features (e.g., loss of muscle mass and function), Martins et al. provide preliminary evidence on the effects that some phytoanabolic extracts obtained from Eurasian plants can have, particularly in combination with resistance training, on different indicators such as body composition, physical function, skeletal muscle/adipose tissue histology, and other biochemical indicators (e.g., cytokines, blood cholesterol) [3]. Moreover, Bellini et al. assessed the effect of postprandial walking on glycemic responses in healthy adults, finding that a 30-min postprandial brisk walking session improved the glycemic response after meals with different carbohydrate content and macronutrient composition [4]. The findings by Bellini et al. might be of clinical relevance, particularly given the potential detrimental effect of postpandrial hyperglycemia for cardiometabolic health [5]. Finally, a review article by Morales et al. summarizes the role of not only nutrition but also other components of the so-called "exposome" (e.g., physical activity, body weight, smoking status, sleep habits) on immune health, which is a timely topic particularly if considering situations such as the recent COVID-19 pandemic [6].

On the other hand, in this Special Issue, we find other studies more related to advances in the context of sports. Martinez-Rodriguez et al. report the body composition and anthropometric characteristics of 36 male players of the Spanish National Beach Handball Team, a sport that has received little attention to date in scientific research [7]. Focusing on the field of sports supplements and using a meta-analytical approach (18 studies included), Gomez-Bruton et al. report that acute caffeine supplementation improves team sport performance in female athletes, as reflected by increases in different outcomes such as specific team-sport skills as well as on countermovement jump height or total body impacts [8]. Additionally, focused on the field of sports supplements, Su et al. explored the effects of different doses of resveratrol on performance during a downhill running test to exhaustion (which was designed to provoke high levels of exercise-induced muscle damage) as well as on different markers of inflammation and energy metabolism [9]. Of note, high-dose resveratrol increased the time to exhaustion during the downhill running test and reduced the levels of pro-inflammatory markers such as tumor necrosis factor-α. It also enhanced the mRNA expressions of sirtuin 1, glucose transporter 4, AMP-activated protein kinase α1, and AMP-activated protein kinase α2 [9]. This preliminary evidence suggests, therefore, that resveratrol supplementation (in this case, for 4 weeks) might enhance exercise performance and attenuate inflammation after exercise-induced muscle damage. In the same line, Tanabe et al. also review the role of different dietary supplements with potential anti-inflammatory or antioxidant effects (e.g., curcumin, tart cherry juice, beetroot juice, quercetin, and isothiocyanate) for attenuating exercise-induced muscle damage and the associated delayed-onset muscle soreness, highlighting the potential beneficial effect of some of them but also the need for well-controlled studies [10]. It seems, therefore, reasonable that many athletes consume supplements with the aim of improving their performance, as summarized in the scoping review by Daher et al., who also highlight the need for rigorous research in this field (e.g., trying to homogenize factors such as the definition of dietary supplements or the definition of use) [11]. This is indeed the topic of the study by Moreno et al., who analyzed a sample of 102 male and female competitive swimmers and concluded that 86.9% of them had consumed sports supplements, with caffeine, sports drinks/bars, and vitamin C being among the most widely consumed and with no differences between genders or performance level [12].

Great advances are being made in the field of nutrition, which can lead to improvements in both the general health of the population and the performance of athletes. More high-quality evidence is needed on all the topics mentioned above, but hopefully these and other studies will lead the way and open new fields of research.

Conflicts of Interest: The author declares no conflict of interest.

References

1. Xu, H.; Jurado-Fasoli, L.; Ortiz-Alvarez, L.; Osuna-Prieto, F.J.; Kohler, I.; Di, X.; Vilchez-Vargas, R.; Link, A.; Plaza-Díaz, J.; Gil, A.; et al. Plasma Levels of Omega-3 and Omega-6 Derived Oxylipins Are Associated with Fecal Microbiota Composition in Young Adults. *Nutrients* **2022**, *14*, 4991. [CrossRef]
2. Fan, Y.; Pedersen, O. Gut microbiota in human metabolic health and disease. *Nat. Rev. Microbiol.* **2021**, *19*, 55–71. [CrossRef]
3. Martins, P.; Silva, L.C.; Nunes, M.S.; Rübensam, G.; Oliveira, J.R.; Silva, R.B.M.; Campos, M.M. Combined Effects of Exercise and Phytoanabolic Extracts in Castrated Male and Female Mice Jerônimo. *Nutrients* **2021**, *13*, 1177. [CrossRef]
4. Bellini, A.; Nicolò, A.; Bazzucchi, I.; Sacchetti, M. The Effects of Postprandial Walking on the Glucose Response after Meals with Different Characteristics. *Nutrients* **2022**, *14*, 1080. [CrossRef]
5. Ceriello, A.; Genovese, S. Atherogenicity of postprandial hyperglycemia and lipotoxicity. *Rev. Endocr. Metab. Disord.* **2016**, *17*, 111–116. [CrossRef]
6. Morales, J.S.; Valenzuela, P.L.; Castillo-García, A.; Butragueño, J.; Jiménez-Pavón, D.; Carrera-Bastos, P.; Lucia, A. The exposome and immune health in times of the COVID-19 pandemic. *Nutrients* **2022**, *14*, 24. [CrossRef]
7. Martínez-Rodríguez, A.; Sánchez-Sánchez, J.; Vicente-Martínez, M.; Martínez-Olcina, M.; Miralles-Amorós, L.; Sáncez-Sáez, J.A. Anthropometric Dimensions and Bone Quality in International Male Beach Handball Players: Junior vs. Senior Comparison. *Nutrients* **2021**, *13*, 1817. [CrossRef]
8. Gomez-Bruton, A.; Marin-Puyalto, J.; Muñiz-Pardos, B.; Matute-Llorente, A.; Del Coso, J.; Gomez-Cabello, A.; Vicente-Rodriguez, G.; Casajus, J.A.; Lozano-Berges, G. Does acute caffeine supplementation improve physical performance in female team-sport athletes? Evidence from a systematic review and meta-analysis. *Nutrients* **2021**, *13*, 3663. [CrossRef]
9. Su, L.Y.; Huang, W.C.; Kan, N.W.; Tung, T.H.; Huynh, L.B.P.; Huang, S.Y. Effects of Resveratrol on Muscle Inflammation, Energy Utilisation, and Exercise Performance in an Eccentric Contraction Exercise Mouse Model. *Nutrients* **2023**, *15*, 249. [CrossRef]
10. Tanabe, Y.; Fujii, N.; Suzuki, K. Dietary Supplementation for Attenuating Exercise-Induced Muscle Damage and Delayed-Onset Muscle Soreness in Humans. *Nutrients* **2022**, *14*, 70. [CrossRef] [PubMed]
11. Daher, J.; Mallick, M.; El Khoury, D. Prevalence of Dietary Supplement Use among Athletes Worldwide: A Scoping Review. *Nutrients* **2022**, *14*, 4109. [CrossRef] [PubMed]
12. Moreno, B.; Veiga, S.; Sánchez-Oliver, A.J.; Domínguez, R.; Morencos, E. Analysis of Sport Supplement Consumption by Competitive Swimmers According to Sex and Competitive Level. *Nutrients* **2022**, *14*, 3218. [CrossRef]

nutrients

MDPI

Article

Plasma Levels of Omega-3 and Omega-6 Derived Oxylipins Are Associated with Fecal Microbiota Composition in Young Adults

Huiwen Xu [1,2,†], Lucas Jurado-Fasoli [1,3,†], Lourdes Ortiz-Alvarez [1,2], Francisco J. Osuna-Prieto [1,4], Isabelle Kohler [5,6], Xinyu Di [7], Ramiro Vilchez-Vargas [8], Alexander Link [8], Julio Plaza-Díaz [2,9,10], Angel Gil [2,10,11,12], Patrick C. N. Rensen [13], Jonatan R. Ruiz [1,10,*] and Borja Martinez-Tellez [1,13,14,*]

1 PROFITH (PROmoting FITness and Health through Physical Activity) Research Group, Sport and Health University Research Institute (iMUDS), Department of Physical and Sports Education, Faculty of Sport Sciences, University of Granada, 18071 Granada, Spain
2 Department of Biochemistry and Molecular Biology II, School of Pharmacy, University of Granada, 18071 Granada, Spain
3 Department of Physiology, Faculty of Medicine, University of Granada, 18071 Granada, Spain
4 Department of Analytical Chemistry, Faculty of Sciences, University of Granada, 18071 Granada, Spain
5 Division of BioAnalytical Chemistry, Amsterdam Institute of Molecular and Life Sciences (AIMMS), Vrije Universiteit Amsterdam, 1081 Amsterdam, The Netherlands
6 Center for Analytical Sciences Amsterdam, 1081 Amsterdam, The Netherlands
7 Department of Systems Biomedicine and Pharmacology, Leiden Academic Centre for Drug Research (LACDR), Leiden University, 2300 Leiden, The Netherlands
8 Department of Gastroenterology, Hepatology and Infectious Diseases, Otto-von-Guericke-University Magdeburg, 39106 Magdeburg, Germany
9 Children's Hospital of Eastern Ontario Research Institute, Ottawa, ON K1H 8L1, Canada
10 Instituto de Investigación Biosanitaria, ibs.Granada, 18014 Granada, Spain
11 CIBEROBN, Biomedical Research Networking Center for Physiopathology of Obesity and Nutrition, Carlos III Health Institute, 28029 Madrid, Spain
12 Institute of Nutrition and Food Technology, Center of Biomedical Research, University of Granada, 18071 Granada, Spain
13 Department of Medicine, Division of Endocrinology, and Einthoven Laboratory for Experimental Vascular Medicine, Leiden University Medical Center, 2300 Leiden, The Netherlands
14 Department of Education, Faculty of Education Sciences and SPORT Research Group (CTS-1024), CERNEP Research Center, University of Almería, 04120 Almería, Spain
* Correspondence: ruizj@ugr.es (J.R.R.); b.martinez-tellez@lumc.nl (B.M.-T.)
† These authors contributed equally to this work.

Citation: Xu, H.; Jurado-Fasoli, L.; Ortiz-Alvarez, L.; Osuna-Prieto, F.J.; Kohler, I.; Di, X.; Vilchez-Vargas, R.; Link, A.; Plaza-Díaz, J.; Gil, A.; et al. Plasma Levels of Omega-3 and Omega-6 Derived Oxylipins Are Associated with Fecal Microbiota Composition in Young Adults. *Nutrients* **2022**, *14*, 4991. https://doi.org/10.3390/nu14234991

Academic Editor: Toshifumi Ohkusa

Received: 25 October 2022
Accepted: 21 November 2022
Published: 24 November 2022

Abstract: Pre-clinical studies suggest that circulating oxylipins, i.e., the oxidation products of polyunsaturated fatty acids (PUFAs), modulate gut microbiota composition in mice, but there is no information available in humans. Therefore, this study aimed to investigate the relationship between omega-3 and omega-6 derived oxylipins plasma levels and fecal microbiota composition in a cohort of young adults. 80 young adults (74% women; 21.9 ± 2.2 years old) were included in this cross-sectional study. Plasma levels of oxylipins were measured using liquid chromatography-tandem mass spectrometry. Fecal microbiota composition was analyzed by V3-V4 16S rRNA gene sequencing. We observed that plasma levels of omega-3 derived oxylipins were positively associated with the relative abundance of *Clostridium cluster IV* genus (*Firmicutes* phylum; rho ≥ 0.415, $p \leq 0.009$) and negatively associated with the relative abundance of *Sutterella* genus (Proteobacteria phylum; rho ≥ -0.270, $p \leq 0.041$), respectively. Moreover, plasma levels of omega-6 derived oxylipins were negatively associated with the relative abundance of *Acidaminococcus* and *Phascolarctobacterium* genera (*Firmicutes* phylum; all rho ≥ -0.263, $p \leq 0.024$), as well as *Sutterella, Succinivibrio*, and *Gemmiger* genera (*Proteobacteria* phylum; all rho ≥ -0.263, $p \leq 0.024$). Lastly, the ratio between omega-6 and omega-3 oxylipins plasma levels was negatively associated with the relative abundance of *Clostridium* cluster IV genus (*Firmicutes* phylum; rho = -0.334, $p = 0.004$) and *Butyricimonas* genus (*Bacteroidetes* phylum; rho = -0.292, $p = 0.014$). In conclusion, our results show that the plasma levels of omega-3 and omega-6 derived oxylipins are associated with the relative abundance of specific fecal bacteria genera.

Keywords: gut microbiota; inflammation; intestinal alkaline phosphatase; microbiome; PUFAs

1. Introduction

Chronic diseases, such as type 2 diabetes and cardiovascular diseases, usually accompany low-grade chronic inflammation [1–3]. The rising prevalence of such diseases is believed to be driven by an unbalanced diet, which is often characterized by a low intake of omega-3 polyunsaturated fatty acids (PUFAs) and a high intake of omega-6 PUFAs [4,5].

Omega-3 and omega-6 PUFAs can be oxidized into oxylipins by lipoxygenases (LOXs), cyclooxygenases (COXs), and the cytochrome P450 (CYP450) family enzymes [6,7]. Oxylipins are the primary mediators of the PUFA-related effects through their binding to G protein-coupled receptors (GPCRs) or peroxisome proliferator-activate receptors (PPARs) [6,7]. Generally, omega-3 derived oxylipins exert anti-inflammatory and pro-resolutive actions since both eicosapentaenoic acid (EPA) and docosahexaenoic acid (DHA) decrease the synthesis of pro-inflammatory mediators and increase the production of anti-inflammatory mediators (e.g., prostaglandins of the three series, leukotrienes of the five series, resolvins, protectins and maresins) [8,9]. In contrast, omega-6 derived oxylipins typically increase inflammation by acting as pro-inflammatory mediators (e.g., prostaglandins of the two series and leukotrienes of the four series) [9,10].

The gut microbiota is composed of microorganisms that colonize the gastrointestinal tract, where bacteria are the most abundant [11]. In humans, the gut microbiota is mainly composed of five phyla: Bacteroidetes, Firmicutes, Proteobacteria, Actinobacteria and Verrucomicrobia [12,13]. The gut microbiota is involved in the maintenance of the gut barrier permeability [14,15] and regulation of the intestinal inflammatory status through specific bacteria, their interaction with intestinal cell receptors and their secreted metabolites (e.g., short chain fatty acids) [16,17]. Interestingly, the composition of gut microbiota and metabolite production can be modified by dietary intake (e.g., nitrogenous compounds, carbohydrates, fatty acids, fiber) [18]. The specific dietary intake of PUFAs, concretely omega-3 PUFAs, increases *Bacteroidetes:Firmicutes* ratio and the diversity and counts of commensal bacteria (i.e., *Akkermansia muciniphila*, *Lactobacillus* and *Bifidobacterium*) [19]. In this sense, dietary patterns with a high content of omega-3 and a low content of omega-6 PUFAs (e.g., Mediterranean Diet) could have a positive influence on the health status of humans via the modulation of the gut microbiota partially due to the positive effects of these PUFAs in the intestinal immunity [19,20]. Therefore, studying the relationship between the primary mediators of PUFAs effects (e.g., oxylipins) with gut microbiota composition is of clinical interest.

A recent study showed that FAT-1 transgenic mice, which can convert omega-6 to omega-3 PUFAs, had a higher relative abundance of Firmicutes, Bacteroides, and Actinobacteria phyla in comparison to wild-type (WT) mice [21]. On the other hand, FAT-2 transgenic mice, which can transform monounsaturated fatty acids into omega-6 PUFAs, showed a distinct gut microbiota composition compared to FAT-1 mice [21]. Specifically, FAT-2 mice were characterized by a depletion of the *Bifidobacteriaceae* family (*Actinobacteria* phylum) vs. WT mice [22]. This study demonstrated that omega-6 and omega-3 PUFAs levels influence gut microbiota composition and their secreted metabolites, influencing intestinal permeability, reducing the inflammatory status and ultimately affecting the risk of chronic disease [22]. In addition, gut microbiota dysbiosis induced by a typical cafeteria diet altered the plasma profile of oxylipins in obese rats [23]. We, therefore, hypothesize that plasma levels of omega-3 and omega-6 derived oxylipins are associated with gut microbiota composition. In the present study, we investigated the association between omega-3 and omega-6 derived oxylipins plasma levels and fecal microbiota composition in young adults.

2. Materials and Methods

2.1. Participants

The participants were part of the ACTIBATE study [24], an exercise-based randomized controlled trial (ClinicalTrials.gov ID: NCT02365129) designed to evaluate the effect of exercise training on brown adipose tissue activity. Participants were recruited via advertisements in electronic media and leaflets. All participants reported being sedentary (less than 20 min of moderate/vigorous physical activity on less than three days per week) and had a stable body weight over the preceding three months (<3 kg change). The exclusion criteria were being pregnant, smoking, taking any medication, including antibiotics, and having an acute or chronic disease. The study protocol was designed following the Declaration of Helsinki. All participants gave their informed consent and were approved by the Ethics Committee on Human Research of the University of Granada (n°.924) and Servicio Andaluz de Salud (Centro de Granada, CEI-Granada).

In the present study, only participants with baseline data for plasma oxylipins and fecal microbiota composition available were included (80 young adults; $n = 59$ women; 21.9 ± 2.2 years old).

2.2. Determination of Plasma Levels of Oxylipins

Blood samples were collected between 8:00–9:00 AM after 10 h overnight fasting. All blood samples were immediately centrifuged to obtain plasma aliquots (obtained with Vacutainer® Hemogard™ tubes, containing the potassium salt of ethylenediaminetetraacetic acid as an anticoagulant) and stored at −80 °C. Plasma levels of omega-3 and omega-6 oxylipins were measured with a targeted metabolomics approach using liquid chromatography-tandem mass spectrometry (LC-MS/MS), with a method validated according to the Food and Drug Administration (FDA) bioanalytical method validation guidelines [25].

With this targeted LC-MS/MS approach, the relative quantification of oxylipins derived from the conversion of the omega-3 PUFAs α-linolenic acid (ALA), eicosapentaenoic acid (EPA), and docosahexaenoic acid (DHA); as well as omega-6 PUFAs linoleic acid (LA), dihomo-γ-linolenic acid (DGLA), arachidonic acid (AA), and adrenic acid (AdrA) was performed. The oxylipins detected by this method and the internal standards used are listed in Table S1. The ratio between the peak area of each oxylipin and the peak area of its respective internal standard was used for the relative quantitation. All the data from omega-3 derived oxylipin species were summed; the same was performed for omega-6 derived oxylipins (Table S2). Additionally, the plasma omega-6/omega-3 oxylipins ratio was calculated by dividing the sum of plasma omega-6 derived oxylipins peak area ratio by the sum of plasma omega-3 derived oxylipins peak area ratio. The methodology is described in detail in the supplementary material.

2.3. Fecal Collection and DNA Extraction

Fecal samples were stored in a 60-mL sterile plastic container, transported in a portable cooler to the research center and stored at −80 °C until DNA extraction. DNA extraction and purification were performed with a QIAamp DNA Stool Mini Kit (QIAGEN, Barcelona, Spain), according to the manufacturer's instructions. Concentration and quality were determined with a NanoDrop ND1000 spectrophotometer (Thermo Fisher Scientific, DE, Waltham, Massachusetts, USA).

DNA was amplified by PCR targeting the V3 and V4 hypervariable regions of the bacterial 16S rRNA gene. The amplicons were sequenced in a MiSeq (Illumina, San Diego, CA, USA), using the Illumina MiSeq paired-end sequencing system (2 × 300 nt) (Illumina, San Diego, CA, USA). We used the "dada2" package version 1.10.1 in R software [26] for merging and filtering raw sequences (FastQ files). Ribosomal Data Project (RDP) [27] was used to assign the phylotypes to their specific taxonomic affiliation (from phylum to genus). The methodology is described in detail in the supplementary material.

2.4. Anthropometry and Body Composition

The SECA model 799 electronic column scale and stadiometer (SECA, Hamburg, Germany) were used to measure the height and weight of study participants wearing standard clothes without shoes. A dual-energy X-ray absorptiometry scan (Hologic Discovery Wi Marlborough, MA) was used to measure body composition, i.e., lean and fat mass. The body mass index (BMI) was calculated as weight/height^2.

2.5. Dietary Assessment

The dietary assessment is explained in detail elsewhere [28–30]. The EvalFINUT® software was used to assess dietary intake (energy and nutrient intake) from three 24 h dietary recalls [28–30]. The 24 h dietary recalls were undertaken on three separate days (i.e., two weekdays and one weekend) during face-to-face interviews by qualified and trained dietitians. Two dieticians independently introduced the data from all interviews in the software. The food frequency consumption was assessed using a food frequency questionnaire (FFQ) [31], in which participants answered how often they had consumed each food item over the last three months, using commonly used portion size.

2.6. Statistical Analysis

Sample size estimation and power calculation were based on the primary outcome of the ACTIBATE study [24]. The current study is based on a secondary analysis using its baseline data. Therefore, no specific power calculation or sample size estimation was developed for the present study.

The descriptive parameters are presented as mean and standard deviation. First, data normality was checked using the D'Agostino & Pearson test. Due to the non-normal distribution of plasma levels of oxylipins and parameters of fecal microbiota composition, all analyses were conducted using non-parametric tests.

To investigate the relationship between the sum of omega-3 and omega-6 derived oxylipins and the omega-6/omega-3 oxylipin ratio with fecal microbiota composition at phylum and genus taxonomy levels, we employed Spearman correlation analysis by using "psych" and "corrplot" packages in R software. Volcano plots were used to depict these correlations using GraphPad Prism software (GraphPad Software, San Diego, CA, USA, version 8.0.0). Then, to examine the relationship between plasma levels of each omega-3 and omega-6 oxylipin and specific bacterial microbiota, we used Spearman correlation analysis, using "psych" and "corrplot" in R software. Heatmap plots were used to represent these correlations using the "Gplot" package in R software. Lastly, partial Spearman correlations were adjusted for BMI, total PUFAs, and fish intake. The level of significance was set at $p < 0.05$.

3. Results

3.1. Characteristics of the Study Participants

Table 1 shows the descriptive characteristics of the study participants (74% women; 21.9 ± 2.2 years old).

Table 1. Characteristics of the study participants.

	N	Mean	±	SD
Sex (women, %)	80		59 (73.8%)	
Age (years)	80	21.9	±	2.2
		Body composition		
Lean mass (kg)	80	41.0	±	8.9
Fat mass (kg)	80	36.3	±	7.8
Body mass index (kg/m^2)	80	24.7	±	4.7

Table 1. *Cont.*

	N	Mean	±	SD
	Dietary intake			
Energy (kcal/day)	80	1920	±	489
PUFAs (g/day)	80	13	±	5
Fish (servings/week)	77	5	±	3
	Total plasma levels of derived-oxylipins (peak area ratio)			
Omega-3	80	172.8	±	65.6
ALA	80	12.0	±	5.1
EPA	80	19.0	±	10.3
DHA	80	141.7	±	54.6
Omega-6	80	99.5	±	27.8
LA	80	28.6	±	10.6
DGLA	80	1.0	±	0.5
AA	80	66.4	±	22.2
AdrA	80	1.0	±	0.6
Omega-6/omega-3 oxylipin ratio	80	0.6	±	0.1
	Fecal microbiota composition (phylum, %)			
Actinobacteria	80	1.6	±	1.6
Bacteroidetes	80	39.6	±	9.0
Firmicutes	80	48.8	±	9.7
Proteobacteria	80	6.5	±	4.8
Verrucomicrobia	80	2.3	±	4.3

Data are presented as mean and standard deviation (SD), otherwise stated. Total oxylipins in each group from the individual peak area ratio of each oxylipin; AA: arachidonic acid; AdrA: adrenic acid; ALA: α-linolenic acid; DHA: docosahexaenoic acid; DGLA: dihomo-γ-linolenic acid; EPA: eicosapentaenoic acid; LA: linoleic acid; PUFAs: polyunsaturated fatty acids.

3.2. The Plasma Levels of Omega-3 Oxylipins Are Associated with the Relative Abundance of Clostridium Cluster IV and Sutterella Genera

At the phylum level, we found no association between the sum of plasma levels of omega-3 oxylipins with fecal microbiota composition (all $p > 0.05$; Figure 1A–D). However, at the genus level, the total plasma levels of both omega-3 and DHA-derived oxylipins (Table S3) were positively associated with the relative abundance of *Clostridium cluster IV* (*Firmicutes* phylum; rho ≥ 0.415, $p \leq 0.009$; Figure 1E,H). Moreover, the total plasma levels of omega-3, ALA-, EPA-, and DHA-derived oxylipins were negatively associated with the relative abundance of the *Sutterella* genus (*Proteobacteria* phylum; rho ≥ -0.270, $p \leq 0.041$; Figure 1E–H).

The plasma levels of the individual omega-3 oxylipins DPA, DHA, 8-HDoHE, 13-HDoHE and 19,20-DiDHPA, were positively associated with the relative abundance of *Clostridium cluster IV* genus (all rho ≥ 0.314, $p \leq 0.018$; Figure S1A). Conversely, the plasma levels of ALA, EPA, 5-HEPE, DHA, 4-HDoHE and 19,20-DiDHPA were negatively associated with the relative abundance of the *Sutterella* genus (all rho ≥ -0.338, $p \leq 0.042$; Figure S1B). These associations remained significant after adjusting for BMI, PUFAs, and fish intake (Tables S3 and S4).

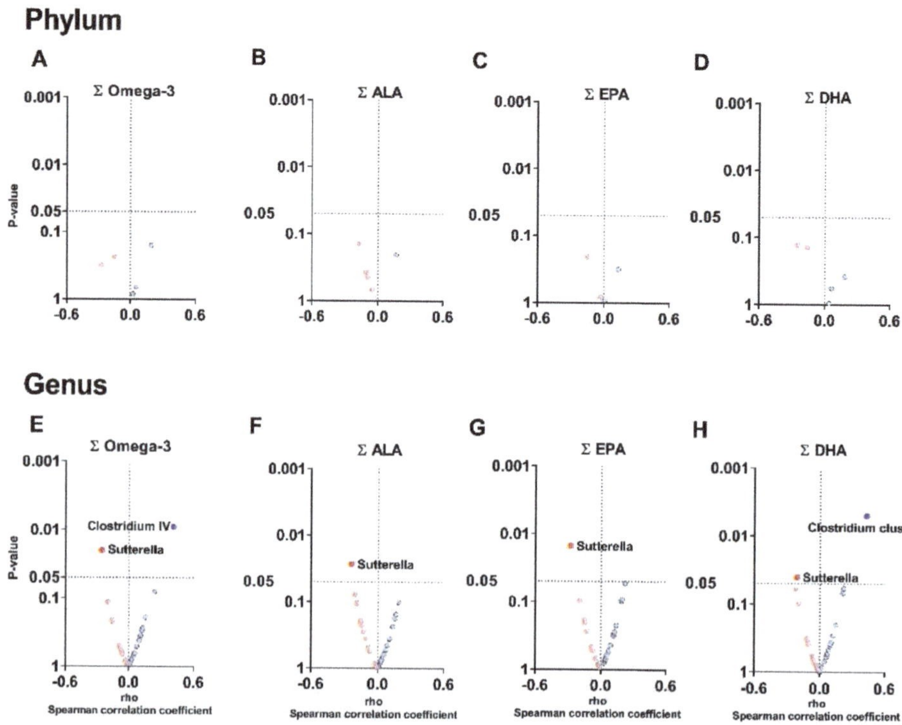

Figure 1. Volcano plots show associations between plasma levels of omega-3 oxylipins and the relative abundance of fecal microbiota composition at the phylum and genus levels. Total omega-3 (**A**,**E**), ALA- (**B**,**F**), EPA- (**C**,**G**), and DHA- (**D**,**H**) derived oxylipins were computed from the individual peak area ratio of each oxylipin within each group. The X-axis represents Spearman's correlation coefficients, whereas the Y-axis represents the p values of the correlations. Only significant associations ($p < 0.05$) were annotated with the name of the phylum or genus. Blue dots represent positive associations, whereas red dots represent negative associations. Abbreviations: ALA: α-linolenic acid; DHA: docosahexaenoic acid; EPA: eicosapentaenoic acid.

3.3. The Plasma Levels of Omega-6 Oxylipins Are Negatively Associated with the Relative Abundance of Genera Belonging to Firmicutes and Proteobacteria Phyla

At the phylum level, the total plasma levels of omega-6, LA- and DGLA-derived oxylipins were negatively associated with the relative abundances of *Bacteroidetes* (all rho ≥ -0.274, $p \leq 0.040$; Figure 2A–C), whereas the total plasma levels of AdrA-derived oxylipins were negatively associated with the relative abundance of *Proteobacteria* (rho = -0.284, $p = 0.013$; Figure 2E). However, the total plasma levels of LA-derived oxylipins were positively associated with the relative abundance of *Verrucomicrobia* phylum (rho = 0.255, $p = 0.022$; Figure 2B). At the genus level, we found that the total plasma levels of omega-6, LA-, and DGLA-derived oxylipins were negatively associated with the relative abundance of Acidaminococcus and *Phascolarctobacterium* genera (*Firmicutes* phylum; all rho ≥ -0.326, $p \leq 0.034$; Figure 2F–H). We also observed that the total plasma levels of omega-6, DGLA-, AA-, and AdrA-derived oxylipins levels were negatively associated with the relative abundance of *Sutterella, Succinivibrio,* and *Gemmiger* genera (*Proteobacteria* phylum; all rho ≥ -0.258, $p \leq 0.042$; Figure 2F–J). Similarly, the total plasma levels of DGLA-derived oxylipins were negatively associated with the relative abundance of the *Odoribacter* genus (*Bacteroidetes* phylum; rho = -0.246, $p = 0.028$; Figure 2H).

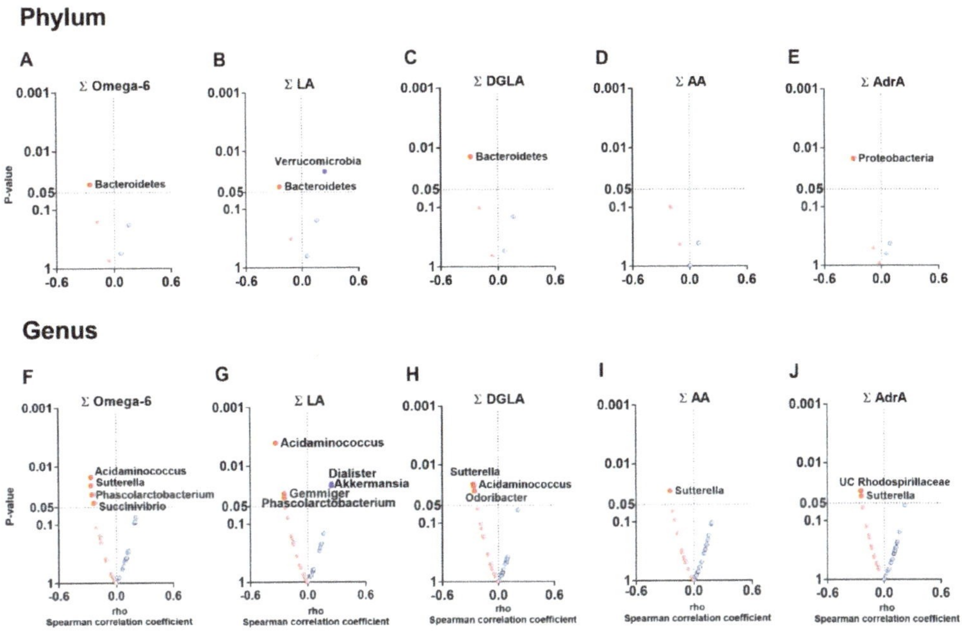

Figure 2. Volcano plots showing associations between the plasma levels of omega-6 oxylipins and the relative abundance of fecal microbiota composition at phylum and genus levels. Total omega-6 (**A**,**F**), LA- (**B**,**G**), DGLA- (**C**,**H**), AA- (**D**,**I**), and AdrA- (**E**,**J**) derived oxylipins groups were computed from the individual area peak ratio of each oxylipins group. The X-axis represents Spearman's correlation coefficients, whereas the Y-axis represents the *p* values of the correlations. Only significant correlations ($p < 0.05$) were annotated with the name of the phylum or genus. Blue dots represent positive correlations, whereas red dots represent negative correlations. Abbreviations: AA: arachidonic acid; AdrA: adrenic acid; DGLA: dihomo-γ-linolenic acid; LA: linoleic acid; UC: unclassified.

The plasma levels of individuals omega-6 oxylipins LA, DGLA, AA, 5-HETE and AdrA, were negatively associated with the relative abundance of the *Sutterella* genus (all rho ≥ -0.313, $p \leq 0.027$; Figure S1B). All these associations remained significant after adjusting for BMI, PUFA, and fish intake (Tables S3 and S4).

3.4. The Plasma Omega-6/Omega-3 Oxylipin Ratio Is Negatively Associated with the Relative Abundance of Clostridium Cluster IV and Butyricimonas Genera

At the phylum level, we found no associations between the omega-6/omega-3 oxylipin ratio in plasma and fecal microbiota composition (all $p > 0.05$; Figure 3A). On the other hand, at the genus level, the omega-6/omega-3 oxylipin ratio was negatively associated with the relative abundance of *Clostridium cluster IV* (*Firmicutes* phylum; rho = −0.334, $p = 0.004$; Figure 3B) and *Butyricimonas* genera (*Bacteroidetes* phylum; rho = −0.292, $p = 0.014$; Figure 3B) independently of BMI, PUFA, and fish intake (Table S3).

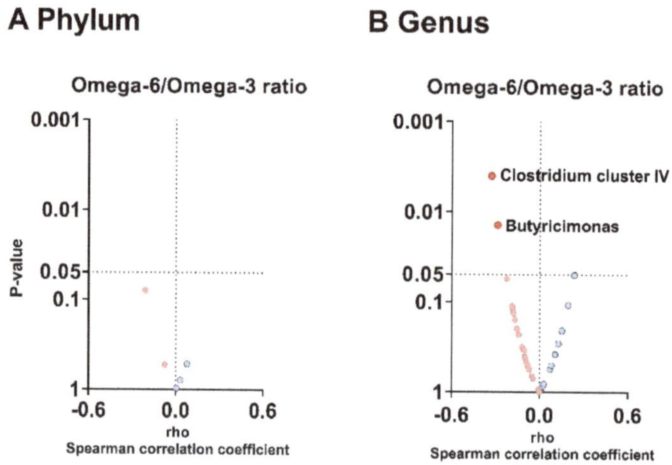

Figure 3. Volcano plots showing the associations between the omega-6/omega-3 oxylipin ratio in plasma and the relative abundance of fecal microbiota composition at the phylum (**A**) and genus levels (**B**). The X-axis represents Spearman's correlation coefficients, whereas the Y-axis represents the p values of the correlations. Only significant correlations ($p < 0.05$) were annotated with the name of the phylum or genus. Blue dots represent positive correlations, whereas red dots represent negative correlations.

4. Discussion

In the present study, we show that plasma levels of oxylipins are linked to the fecal microbiota composition of young adults. Specifically, plasma levels of omega-3 derived oxylipins were positively associated with the relative abundance of *Clostridium* cluster IV and negatively associated with the relative abundance of *Sutterella* genera. Additionally, plasma levels of omega-6 derived oxylipins were negatively associated with the relative abundance of several genera. In contrast, the ratio of omega-6/omega-3 oxylipins in plasma was negatively associated with the relative abundance of *Clostridium* cluster IV and *Butyricimonas* genera. These findings suggest that the plasma levels of omega-3 and omega-6 derived oxylipins may modulate the relative abundance of gut microbiota composition, or vice versa, in young adults.

We found that the plasma levels of omega-3 derived oxylipins and the omega-6/omega-3 oxylipin ratio in plasma are positively and negatively associated, respectively, with the relative abundance of *Clostridium* cluster IV genus, which is composed of *Clostridium*, *Eubacterium*, *Ruminococcus*, and *Anaerofilum* genera. Similarly, the *FAT-1* mice, capable of transforming omega-6 into omega-3 PUFAs, also showed a higher relative abundance of *Clostridium* cluster IV genus compared to WT mice [21]. The *Clostridium* cluster IV genus bacteria have been shown to exert anti-inflammatory effects and maintain intestinal health via the production of short-chain fatty acids, such as butyrate [32]. These findings suggest that higher plasma levels of omega-3 derived oxylipins could improve systemic and intestinal health through an increased relative abundance of *Clostridium* cluster IV genus, which produces butyrate and ultimately enhances intestinal barrier function and immunity [33]. In contrast, gut microbiota influences the production of omega-6 oxylipins, conferring host resistance to high-fat diet-induced obesity and adipose tissue inflammation in mice [34]. The above-mentioned pre-clinical studies are confirmed in the present human cohort, reinforcing the clinical benefits of omega-3 PUFAs, specifically its oxylipins, on human health.

Additionally, we identified that plasma levels of omega-3 and omega-6 oxylipins are negatively associated with the relative abundance of the *Sutterella* genus in feces. In line with these results, rats consuming a diet rich in the omega-6 PUFA LA for 10 weeks showed a decrease in the relative abundance of the *Sutterella* genus [35]. In contrast, daily oral supplementation with omega-3 PUFAs (i.e., 4 g of EPA and DHA) for eight weeks increased the relative abundance of *Sutterellaceae* family in feces of in middle-aged healthy humans [36]. After a wash-out period of eight weeks, the relative abundance of the *Sutterellaceae* family returned to baseline levels [36]. These studies show that supplementing omega-3 or omega-6 PUFAs can modulate the relative abundance of the specific bacteria in the gut. This effect might be explained by the direct effects of dietary PUFAs in the intestine since PUFAs and their downstream oxylipins can modify the fatty acid composition of the intestinal brush border membrane, increasing the intestinal alkaline phosphatase (IAP) activity in the small intestine [37,38]. Thus, we hypothesize that oxylipins could modulate IAP activity similarly to their PUFA precursors. In this regard, both supplementation of omega-3 PUFAs [21] and overproduction of omega-6 PUFAs [39] have been shown to induce the release of IAP from enterocytes, either through the modulation of resolvins (i.e., distal mediators of the anti-inflammatory/pro-resolution cascade derived from omega-3 oxylipins) [40] or the increase in the relative abundance of certain bacteria (e.g., *Sutterella* genus [22] that can produce lipopolysaccharides [LPS]). IAP dephosphorylates LPS [41], preventing LPS from binding to Toll-like receptor-4 (TLR4) [41], consequently avoiding the activation of the inflammatory cascade [41]. Since gut microbiota could contribute to the levels of oxylipins in response to inflammation [23], we hypothesize that plasma oxylipins could translocate to the gut lumen, as with other inflammatory mediators. Therefore, the relationship observed between omega-3 and omega-6 oxylipins plasma levels and the relative abundance of the *Sutterella* genus could be partially explained by the modulation of IAP activity in humans. Although this hypothesis is based on pre-clinical studies, it should be explored in future studies specifically designed. However, our results describe the relationship between the omega-3 and omega-6 oxylipins with these specific bacteria for the first time in humans. Since oxylipins are the primary mediators of PUFAs physiological effects, mainly in regulating the inflammatory and immune response, our results are of great clinical interest.

Limitations and Strengths

This study shows the following limitations: the cross-sectional study design does not allow to establishment a cause-effect relationship. Our results should be interpreted with caution due to the lack of specific sample size and power calculation for the current study. The analyses were not controlled for false discovery rate (FDR) since this approach is hypothesis-generating, and adjusting for FDR might overcorrect potentially meaningful findings. Lastly, while these results generate new hypotheses, further research is needed to elucidate the direction of the crosstalk between plasma levels of oxylipins and fecal microbiota since plasma oxylipins might influence fecal microbiota composition and vice versa. On the other hand, two major strengths in this study are: (i) we performed DNA sequencing with one of the latest technologies (*Illumina* platform) and using the DADA2 program that uses amplicon sequence variants instead of operational taxonomic units [42]; and (ii) RDP conducted the annotation step until the genus taxon, a methodology with an annotation error less than 10% [43].

5. Conclusions

Our study reveals that plasma omega-3 oxylipins are positively associated with the relative abundance of *Clostridium cluster* IV genus. In contrast, plasma levels of omega-3 and omega-6 oxylipins are negatively associated with the relative abundance of the *Sutterella* genus in fecal samples of young adults. These results may suggest that plasma levels of omega-3 and omega-6 oxylipins modulate human gut microbiota composition. Based on the well-known influence of omega-3 and omega-6 oxylipins on human health, our results suggest that these oxylipins may be involved in regulating the gut barrier function in humans. However, future studies should address the influence of omega-3 and omega-6 supplementation in gut microbiota health, as well as the effect of different probiotics on the regulation of oxylipins in the plasma and the gut barrier.

Supplementary Materials: The following supporting information can be downloaded at: https://www.mdpi.com/article/10.3390/nu14234991/s1, Table S1: Overview of the labelled internal standards used in the LC-MS/MS method. Table S2: Overview of the detected omega-3 and omega-6 oxylipins, including the variability observed in QC samples (expressed using RSD). Analytes showing an RSD < 30% in the QC samples were kept for further analysis. Table S3: Partial Spearman correlation between total omega-3 and omega-6 oxylipins and the relative abundance of fecal microbiota composition at the genus level. Table S4: Partial Spearman correlation between plasma levels of individual omega-3 and omega-6 oxylipins and the relative abundance of fecal microbiota composition at the genus level. Figure S1: Spearman correlations between plasma levels of individual omega-3 (Panel A) and omega-6 (Panel B) oxylipins and the abundance relative of Clostridium IV and Sutterella genera [44–46].

Author Contributions: H.X., L.J.-F., A.G., P.C.N.R., J.R.R. and B.M.-T. contributed to the study conception and design. H.X., L.J.-F., L.O.-A., F.J.O.-P., I.K., X.D., R.V.-V., A.L. and J.P.-D. performed material preparation and data collection. H.X., L.J.-F. and B.M.-T. performed the statistical analysis. J.R.R. and B.M.-T. have the primary responsibility for the final content. All authors have read and agreed to the published version of the manuscript.

Funding: The study was supported by the Spanish Ministry of Economy and Competitiveness via Fondo de Investigación Sanitaria del Instituto de Salud Carlos III (PI13/01393) and PTA 12264-I, Retos de la Sociedad (DEP2016- 79512-R), and European Regional Development Funds (ERDF), by the Spanish Ministry of Education (FPU16/05159, FPU16/02828, FPU17/01523 and FPU19/01609), the Fundación Iberoamericana de Nutrición (FINUT), the University of Granada Plan Propio de Investigación 2016-Excellence actions: Unit of Excellence on Exercise and Health (UCEES), AstraZeneca HealthCare Foundationand by the Junta de Andalucía, Consejería de Conocimiento, Investigación y Universidades (ERDF, SOMM17/6107/UGR), the Chinese Scholarship Council (CSC, No. 201707060012 to XD), Fundación Alfonso Martin Escudero, and Maria Zambrano fellowship by the Ministerio de Universidades y la Unión Europea –NextGenerationEU (RR_C_2021_04). AL is supported by the funds of the European Commission through the "European funds for regional development" (EFRE) as well as by the regional Ministry of Economy, Science and Digitalization of Saxony-Anhalt as part of the Autonomy in old Age "(AiA) research group for "LiLife" Project (Project ID: ZS/2018/11/95324).

Institutional Review Board Statement: The study protocol and experimental design were applied by the last revised ethical guidelines of the Declaration of Helsinki. The study was approved by the Ethics Committee on Human Research of the University of Granada (no. 924) and the Servicio Andaluz de Salud (Centro de Granada, CEI-Granada).

Informed Consent Statement: Informed consent was obtained from all subjects involved in the study.

Data Availability Statement: The data supporting this study's findings are available from the corresponding author upon reasonable request, as the study consists of a high number of participants and outcomes and requires specific knowledge for data interpretation.

Acknowledgments: This study is part of a PhD thesis conducted within the Biomedicine Doctoral Studies Program of the University of Granada, Spain. The authors would like to thank the Data Integration Center of University Medicine Magdeburg team for local data-analysis solutions supported by MIRACUM and funded by the German Federal Ministry of Education and Research (BMBF) (FKZ 01ZZ1801H).

Conflicts of Interest: The authors declare no conflict of interest.

References

1. Hotamisligil, G. Inflammation and Metabolic Disorders. *Nature* **2006**, *444*, 860–867. [CrossRef]
2. Ruiz-Núñez, B.; Pruimboom, L.; Dijck-Brouwer, D.A.J.; Muskiet, F.A.J. Lifestyle and Nutritional Imbalances Associated with Western Diseases: Causes and Consequences of Chronic Systemic Low-Grade Inflammation in an Evolutionary Context. *J. Nutr. Biochem.* **2013**, *24*, 1183–1201. [CrossRef]
3. Nathan, C.; Ding, A. Nonresolving Inflammation. *Cell* **2010**, *140*, 871–882. [CrossRef] [PubMed]
4. Leaf, A.; Weber, P.C. A New Era for Science in Nutrition. *Am. J. Clin. Nutr.* **1987**, *45*, 1048–1053. [CrossRef]

5. Simopoulos, A. The Importance of the Omega-6/Omega-3 Fatty Acid Ratio in Cardiovascular Disease and Other Chronic Diseases. *Exp. Biol. Med.* **2008**, *233*, 674–688. [CrossRef] [PubMed]
6. Yeung, J.; Hawley, M.; Holinstat, M. The Expansive Role of Oxylipins on Platelet Biology. *J. Mol. Med.* **2017**, *95*, 575–588. [CrossRef]
7. Gabbs, M.; Leng, S.; Devassy, J.G.; Monirujjaman, M.; Aukema, H.M. Advances in Our Understanding of Oxylipins Derived from Dietary PUFAs 1,2. *Adv. Nutr.* **2015**, *6*, 513–540. [CrossRef]
8. Calder, P.C. Omega-3 Fatty Acids and Inflammatory Processes. *Nutrients* **2010**, *2*, 355–374. [CrossRef] [PubMed]
9. Dyall, S.C.; Balas, L.; Bazan, N.G.; Brenna, J.T.; Chiang, N.; da Costa Souza, F.; Dalli, J.; Durand, T.; Galano, J.-M.; Lein, P.J.; et al. Polyunsaturated Fatty Acids and Fatty Acid-Derived Lipid Mediators: Recent Advances in the Understanding of Their Biosynthesis, Structures, and Functions. *Prog. Lipid Res.* **2022**, *86*, 101165. [CrossRef]
10. Robertson, R.C.; Kaliannan, K.; Strain, C.R.; Ross, R.P.; Stanton, C.; Kang, J.X. Maternal Omega-3 Fatty Acids Regulate Offspring Obesity through Persistent Modulation of Gut Microbiota. *Microbiome* **2018**, *6*, 95. [CrossRef]
11. Sekirov, I.; Finlay, B.B. Human and Microbe: United We Stand. *Nat. Med.* **2006**, *12*, 736–737. [CrossRef]
12. Arumugam, M.; Raes, J.; Pelletier, E.; Le Paslier, D.; Yamada, T.; Mende, D.R.; Fernandes, G.R.; Tap, J.; Bruls, T.; Batto, J.M.; et al. Enterotypes of the Human Gut Microbiome. *Nature* **2011**, *473*, 174–180. [CrossRef]
13. Segata, N.; Haake, S.K.; Mannon, P.; Lemon, K.P.; Waldron, L.; Gevers, D.; Huttenhower, C.; Izard, J. Composition of the Adult Digestive Tract Bacterial Microbiome Based on Seven Mouth Surfaces, Tonsils, Throat and Stool Samples. *Genome Biol.* **2012**, *13*, R42. [CrossRef] [PubMed]
14. Montalto, M.; D'Onofrio, F.; Gallo, A.; Cazzato, A.; Gasbarrini, G. Intestinal Microbiota and Its Functions. *Dig. Liver Dis. Suppl.* **2009**, *3*, 30–34. [CrossRef]
15. van de Guchte, M.; Blottière, H.M.; Doré, J. Humans as Holobionts: Implications for Prevention and Therapy. *Microbiome* **2018**, *6*, 81. [CrossRef]
16. Hill, D.A.; Artis, D. Intestinal Bacteria and the Regulation of Immune Cell Homeostasis. *Annu. Rev. Immunol.* **2010**, *28*, 623–667. [CrossRef]
17. Tomasello, G.; Mazzola, M.; Leone, A.; Sinagra, E.; Zummo, G.; Farina, F.; Damiani, P.; Cappello, F.; Geagea, A.G.; Jurjus, A.; et al. Nutrition, Oxidative Stress and Intestinal Dysbiosis: Influence of Diet on Gut Microbiota in Inflammatory Bowel Diseases. *Biomed. Pap.* **2016**, *160*, 461–466. [CrossRef] [PubMed]
18. David, L.A.; Maurice, C.F.; Carmody, R.N.; Gootenberg, D.B.; Button, J.E.; Wolfe, B.E.; Ling, A.V.; Devlin, A.S.; Varma, Y.; Fischbach, M.A.; et al. Diet Rapidly and Reproducibly Alters the Human Gut Microbiome. *Nature* **2014**, *505*, 559–563. [CrossRef]
19. Moszak, M.; Szulińska, M.; Bogdański, P. You Are What You Eat—The Relationship between Diet, Microbiota, and Metabolic Disorders—A Review. *Nutrients* **2020**, *12*, 1096. [CrossRef]
20. Fu, Y.; Wang, Y.; Gao, H.; Li, D.; Jiang, R.; Ge, L.; Tong, C.; Xu, K. Associations among Dietary Omega-3 Poly-unsaturated Fatty Acids, the Gut Microbiota, and Intestinal Immunity. *Mediat. Inflamm.* **2021**, *2021*, 8879227. [CrossRef]
21. Kaliannan, K.; Wang, B.; Li, X.-Y.; Kim, K.-J.; Kang, J.X. A Host-Microbiome Interaction Mediates the Opposing Effects of Omega-6 and Omega-3 Fatty Acids on Metabolic Endotoxemia. *Sci. Rep.* **2015**, *5*, 11276. [CrossRef]
22. Kaliannan, K.; Li, X.-Y.; Wang, B.; Pan, Q.; Chen, C.-Y.; Hao, L.; Xie, S.; Kang, J.X. Multi-Omic Analysis in Transgenic Mice Implicates Omega-6/Omega-3 Fatty Acid Imbalance as a Risk Factor for Chronic Disease. *Commun. Biol.* **2019**, *2*, 276. [CrossRef]
23. Ávila-Román, J.; Arreaza-Gil, V.; Cortés-Espinar, A.J.; Soliz-Rueda, J.R.; Mulero, M.; Muguerza, B.; Arola-Arnal, A.; Arola, L.; Torres-Fuentes, C. Impact of Gut Microbiota on Plasma Oxylipins Profile under Healthy and Obesogenic Conditions. *Clin. Nutr.* **2021**, *40*, 1475–1486. [CrossRef] [PubMed]
24. Sanchez-Delgado, G.; Martinez-Tellez, B.; Olza, J.; Aguilera, C.M.; Labayen, I.; Ortega, F.B.; Chillon, P.; Fernandez-Reguera, C.; Alcantara, J.M.A.A.; Martinez-Avila, W.D.; et al. Activating Brown Adipose Tissue through Exercise (ACTIBATE) in Young Adults: Rationale, Design and Methodology. *Contemp. Clin. Trials* **2015**, *45*, 416–425. [CrossRef] [PubMed]
25. Jurado-Fasoli, L.; Di, X.; Kohler, I.; Osuna-Prieto, F.J.; Hankemeier, T.; Krekels, E.; Harms, A.C.; Yang, W.; Garcia-Lario, J.V.; Fernández-Veledo, S.; et al. Omega-6 and Omega-3 Oxylipins as Potential Markers of Cardiometabolic Risk in Young Adults. *Obesity* **2022**, *30*, 50–61. [CrossRef]
26. R Core Team. *R: A Language and Environment for Statistical Computing, v. 4.2.2*; R Core Team: Vienna, Austria, 2019.
27. Cole, J.R.; Wang, Q.; Fish, J.A.; Chai, B.; McGarrell, D.M.; Sun, Y.; Brown, C.T.; Porras-Alfaro, A.; Kuske, C.R.; Tiedje, J.M. Ribosomal Database Project: Data and Tools for High Throughput RRNA Analysis. *Nucleic Acids Res.* **2014**, *42*, D633–D642. [CrossRef]
28. Jurado-Fasoli, L.; Amaro-Gahete, F.J.; Merchan-Ramirez, E.; Labayen, I.; Ruiz, J.R. Relationships between Diet and Basal Fat Oxidation and Maximal Fat Oxidation during Exercise in Sedentary Adults. *Nutr. Metab. Cardiovasc. Dis.* **2021**, *31*, 1087–1101. [CrossRef]
29. Jurado-Fasoli, L.; Amaro-Gahete, F.J.; Arias-Tellez, M.J.; Gil, A.; Labayen, I.; Ruiz, J.R. Relationship between Dietary Factors and S-Klotho Plasma Levels in Young Sedentary Healthy Adults. *Mech. Ageing Dev.* **2021**, *194*, 111435. [CrossRef]
30. Jurado-Fasoli, L.; Merchan-Ramirez, E.; Martinez-Tellez, B.; Acosta, F.M.; Sanchez-Delgado, G.; Amaro-Gahete, F.J.; Muñoz Hernandez, V.; Martinez-Avila, W.D.; Ortiz-Alvarez, L.; Xu, H.; et al. Association between Dietary Factors and Brown Adipose Tissue Volume/^{18}F-FDG Uptake in Young Adults. *Clin. Nutr.* **2021**, *40*, 1997–2008. [CrossRef]

31. Vioque, J.; Navarrete-Muñoz, E.-M.; Gimenez-Monzó, D.; García-de-la-Hera, M.; Granado, F.; Young, I.S.; Ramón, R.; Ballester, F.; Murcia, M.; Rebagliato, M.; et al. Reproducibility and Validity of a Food Frequency Questionnaire among Pregnant Women in a Mediterranean Area. *Nutr. J.* **2013**, *12*, 26. [CrossRef]
32. Guo, P.; Zhang, K.; Ma, X.; He, P. Clostridium Species as Probiotics: Potentials and Challenges. *J. Anim. Sci. Biotechnol.* **2020**, *11*, 24. [CrossRef]
33. Liu, H.; Wang, J.; He, T.; Becker, S.; Zhang, G.; Li, D.; Ma, X. Butyrate: A Double-Edged Sword for Health? *Adv. Nutr.* **2018**, *9*, 21–29. [CrossRef] [PubMed]
34. Miyamoto, J.; Igarashi, M.; Watanabe, K.; Karaki, S.I.; Mukouyama, H.; Kishino, S.; Li, X.; Ichimura, A.; Irie, J.; Sugimoto, Y.; et al. Gut Microbiota Confers Host Resistance to Obesity by Metabolizing Dietary Poly-unsaturated Fatty Acids. *Nat. Commun.* **2019**, *10*, 4007. [CrossRef]
35. Shrestha, N.; Sleep, S.L.; Cuffe, J.S.M.; Holland, O.J.; McAinch, A.J.; Dekker Nitert, M.; Hryciw, D.H. Pregnancy and Diet-Related Changes in the Maternal Gut Microbiota Following Exposure to an Elevated Linoleic Acid Diet. *Am. J. Physiol.-Endocrinol. Metab.* **2020**, *318*, E276–E285. [CrossRef] [PubMed]
36. Watson, H.; Mitra, S.; Croden, F.C.; Taylor, M.; Wood, H.M.; Perry, S.L.; Spencer, J.A.; Quirke, P.; Toogood, G.J.; Lawton, C.L.; et al. A Randomised Trial of the Effect of Omega-3 Polyunsaturated Fatty Acid Supplements on the Human Intestinal Microbiota. *Gut* **2018**, *67*, 1974–1983. [CrossRef]
37. Sharma, U.; Singh, S.K.; Pal, D.; Khajuria, R.; Mandal, A.K.; Prasad, R. Implication of BBM Lipid Composition and Fluidity in Mitigated Alkaline Phosphatase Activity in Renal Cell Carcinoma. *Mol. Cell. Biochem.* **2012**, *369*, 287–293. [CrossRef]
38. Stenson, W.F.; Seetharam, B.; Talkad, V.; Pickett, W.; Dudeja, P.; Brasitus, T.A. Effects of Dietary Fish Oil Supplementation on Membrane Fluidity and Enzyme Activity in Rat Small Intestine. *Biochem. J.* **1989**, *263*, 41–45. [CrossRef] [PubMed]
39. Ghosh, S.; DeCoffe, D.; Brown, K.; Rajendiran, E.; Estaki, M.; Dai, C.; Yip, A.; Gibson, D.L. Fish Oil Attenuates Omega-6 Polyunsaturated Fatty Acid-Induced Dysbiosis and Infectious Colitis but Impairs LPS Dephosphorylation Activity Causing Sepsis. *PLoS ONE* **2013**, *8*, e55468. [CrossRef] [PubMed]
40. Campbell, E.L.; MacManus, C.F.; Kominsky, D.J.; Keely, S.; Glover, L.E.; Bowers, B.E.; Scully, M.; Bruyninckx, W.J.; Colgan, S.P. Resolvin E1-Induced Intestinal Alkaline Phosphatase Promotes Resolution of Inflammation through LPS Detoxification. *Proc. Natl. Acad. Sci. USA* **2010**, *107*, 14298–14303. [CrossRef]
41. Lallès, J.-P. Intestinal Alkaline Phosphatase: Multiple Biological Roles in Maintenance of Intestinal Homeostasis and Modulation by Diet. *Nutr. Rev.* **2010**, *68*, 323–332. [CrossRef]
42. Chiarello, M.; McCauley, M.; Villéger, S.; Jackson, C.R. Ranking the Biases: The Choice of OTUs vs. ASVs in 16S RRNA Amplicon Data Analysis Has Stronger Effects on Diversity Measures than Rarefaction and OTU Identity Threshold. *PLoS ONE* **2022**, *17*, e0264443. [CrossRef] [PubMed]
43. Edgar, R. Taxonomy Annotation and Guide Tree Errors in 16S RRNA Databases. *PeerJ* **2018**, *6*, e5030. [CrossRef] [PubMed]
44. Di Zazzo, A.; Yang, W.; Coassin, M.; Micera, A.; Antonini, M.; Piccinni, F.; De Piano, M.; Kohler, I.; Harms, A.C.; Hankemeier, T.; et al. Signaling lipids as diagnostic biomarkers for ocular surface cicatrizing conjunctivitis. *J. Mol. Med.* **2020**, *98*, 751–760. [CrossRef] [PubMed]
45. Van Der Kloet, F.M.; Bobeldijk, I.; Verheij, E.R.; Jellema, R.H. Analytical error reduction using single point calibration for accurate and precise metabolomic phenotyping. *J. Proteome Res.* **2009**, *8*, 5132–5141. [CrossRef] [PubMed]
46. McMurdie, P.J.; Holmes, S. Phyloseq: An R Package for Reproducible Interactive Analysis and Graphics of Microbiome Census Data. *PLoS ONE* **2013**, *8*, e61217. [CrossRef] [PubMed]

nutrients

MDPI

Article

Combined Effects of Exercise and Phytoanabolic Extracts in Castrated Male and Female Mice

Jerônimo P. Martins [1,2], Lucia C. Silva [2,3], Matheus S. Nunes [2,4], Gabriel Rübensam [2], Jarbas R. Oliveira [1], Rodrigo B. M. Silva [2] and Maria M. Campos [1,2,4,5,*]

1 Programa de Pós-Graduação em Medicina e Ciências da Saúde, Escola de Medicina, Pontifícia Universidade Católica do Rio Grande do Sul, Porto Alegre, RS 90619-900, Brazil; jeronimo.martins@edu.pucrs.br (J.P.M.); jarbas@pucrs.br (J.R.O.)

2 Centro de Pesquisas em Toxicologia e Farmacologia, Escola de Ciências da Saúde e da Vida, Pontifícia Universidade Católica do Rio Grande do Sul, Porto Alegre, RS 90619-900, Brazil; lucia.silva.001@acad.pucrs.br (L.C.S.); matheus.nunes.002@acad.pucrs.br (M.S.N.); gabriel.rubensam@pucrs.br (G.R.); rodrigo.braccinims@gmail.com (R.B.M.S.)

3 Curso de Graduação em Fisioterapia, Escola de Ciências da Saúde e da Vida, Pontifícia Universidade Católica do Rio Grande do Sul, Porto Alegre, RS 90619-900, Brazil

4 Curso de Graduação em Odontologia, Escola de Ciências da Saúde e da Vida, Pontifícia Universidade Católica do Rio Grande do Sul, Porto Alegre, RS 90619-900, Brazil

5 Programa de Pós-Graduação em Odontologia, Escola de Ciências da Saúde e da Vida, Pontifícia Universidade Católica do Rio Grande do Sul, Porto Alegre, RS 90619-900, Brazil

* Correspondence: camposmmartha@yahoo.com

Abstract: Dry extracts from the Eurasian plants, *Ajuga turkestanica*, *Eurycoma longifolia*, and *Urtica dioica* have been used as anabolic supplements, despite the limited scientific data on these effects. To assess their actions on early sarcopenia signs, male and female castrated mice were supplemented with lyophilized extracts of the three plants, isolated or in association (named TLU), and submitted to resistance exercise. Ovariectomy (OVX) led to body weight increase and non-high-density cholesterol (HDL) cholesterol elevation, which had been restored by exercise plus *U. dioica* extract, or by exercise and TLU, respectively. Orchiectomy (ORX) caused skeletal muscle weight loss, accompanied by increased adiposity, being the latter parameter reduced by exercise plus *E. longifolia* or *U. dioica* extracts. General physical activity was improved by exercise plus herbal extracts in either OVX or ORX animals. Exercise combined with TLU improved resistance to fatigue in OVX animals, though *A. turkestanica* enhanced the grip strength in ORX mice. *E. longifolia* or TLU also reduced the ladder climbing time in ORX mice. Resistance exercise plus herbal extracts partly altered gastrocnemius fiber size frequencies in OVX or ORX mice. We provide novel data that tested ergogenic extracts, when combined with resistance exercise, improved early sarcopenia alterations in castrated male and female mice.

Keywords: ergogenic phytotherapics; *Ajuga turkestanica*; *Eurycoma longifolia*; *Urtica dioica*; resistance exercise; ovariectomy; orchiectomy; sarcopenia; aging; mice

Citation: Martins, J.P.; Silva, L.C.; Nunes, M.S.; Rübensam, G.; Oliveira, J.R.; Silva, R.B.M.; Campos, M.M. Combined Effects of Exercise and Phytoanabolic Extracts in Castrated Male and Female Mice. *Nutrients* **2021**, *13*, 1177. https://doi.org/10.3390/nu13041177

Academic Editor: Pedro L. Valenzuela

Received: 22 February 2021
Accepted: 30 March 2021
Published: 2 April 2021

Publisher's Note: MDPI stays neutral with regard to jurisdictional claims in published maps and institutional affiliations.

1. Introduction

Declining of hormonal levels in aging is a predictor factor for the onset of skeletal muscle loss and related diseases, such as sarcopenia [1–4]. Sarcopenia is characterized by a progressive reduction in muscle quantity and quality, leading to impaired movement, lessened strength, with an increased risk of injuries secondary to falls, being often associated with frailty [5,6]. Nutritional intervention and physical exercise are valuable alternatives for prevention and management of sarcopenia [5,7,8]. Various drugs and supplements have emerged to treat sarcopenia, such as antioxidant supplementation, vitamin D, ursolic acid, angiotensin-converting enzyme inhibitors, melatonin, ghrelin, dehydroepiandrosterone (DHEA), and selective androgen receptor modulators (SARMS) [9–14]. Current treatments are focused on hormone replacement therapy, which might display adverse effects including exacerbation of sleep apnea, delayed wound healing, gynecomastia, increased volume of red blood cells, higher risk of cardiovascular diseases and cancer, besides virilization in women [15,16].

Phytotherapy represents an attractive option to treat several diseases and has been used for sarcopenia prevention and maintenance of hormonal levels [17,18]. Herbal medicine involves the use of the plant alone or in combination with other plants that have complementary properties. The association of selected herbal extracts has been employed as supplements to increase muscle mass gain, based on their folk use as anabolic agents. Particularly, dry extracts obtained from the Eurasian plants *Ajuga turkestanica*, *Eurycoma longifolia*, and *Urtica dioica* have been used for this end worldwide. However, there is limited scientific evidence about their efficacy and safety, and a very few studies have investigated their effects on sarcopenia.

A. turkestanica, a plant native from Uzbekistan, is rich in ecdysteroids, including turkesterone and 20-hydroxyecdysone (20-HE). It has been used for its benefits on muscle strength, muscle pain, and heart protection [19]. A study conducted by Isenmann et al. [20] investigated the effects of a commercial product containing 100 mg of ecdysteroids on strength and muscle mass of athletes. As evidenced, there was an increase in muscle mass, and in the concentration of serum insulin growth factor-1 (IGF-1), without changes in the concentrations of luteinizing hormone, testosterone, or estradiol [20]. Noteworthy, because of the hormone-related effects, this substance became part of the monitoring program of the World Anti-Doping Agency (WADA) in 2020 for professional athletes, inside and outside competitions [21].

E. longifolia Jack, also known as Malaysian Ginseng or Tongkat Ali, is commonly found in Southeast Asia. The plant is rich in several classes of bioactive compounds, such as eurycomanone, eurycomanol, 13α(21)-epoxueurycomanone, and 13α,21-dihydroeury comanone [22,23]. A standardized extract of *E. longifolia* showed anti-adipogenic effects in animals [24] and improved several immunological parameters in humans [25]. Clinical studies have shown favorable results in the prevention of osteopenia in men and postmenopausal women [26]. In rats, *E. longifolia* led to increased serum concentrations of calcium, phosphate, and alkaline phosphatase, possibly through mechanisms related to hormonal modulation [27]. The root extract showed positive effects in increasing the sexual activity in a pre-clinical study [22], and it was able to rise hormone levels in animal [27] and clinical studies [28]. Though, another clinical study detected no benefit for the extract supplementation on resistance exercise outcomes [29].

The roots of the Eurasian plant *U. dioica* L., popularly known as stinging nettle, has been used to treat benign prostatic hyperplasia, for their anti-inflammatory effects and binding inhibition of sex hormone binding globulin (SHBG) to its receptor in prostate cells [30]. The compounds present in *U. dioica extract* include fatty acids, phenylpropanes, lignans, coumarins, triterpenes, ceramides, sterols, and lecithins [31,32]. Animals supplemented with *U. dioica* showed a reduction of adipose tissue accumulation, lower levels of fasting glucose and insulin, a decrease in HOMA-IR, and a reduction of liver triglycerides [33]. Compelling pre-clinical evidence revealed a hypoglycemic activity for the plant, and a meta-analysis carried out by Ziaie and collaborators (2019) corroborated the beneficial effects of *U. dioica* on glycemic levels. Pre-clinical in vitro and in vivo evidence also revealed the ability of *U. dioica* to inhibit 5-α-reductase activity, leading to an elevation of testosterone levels [34].

Considering the abovementioned evidence, the present study aimed to evaluate the anti-sarcopenic properties of *A. turkestanica*, *E. longifolia*, and *U. dioica* extracts, supplemented alone or in an association scheme, comparing the possible beneficial actions in castrated males and females submitted to resistance exercise.

2. Materials and Methods

2.1. Ethics and Experimental Animals

The experimental protocols used in this study followed the current Brazilian guidelines for the care and use of animals for scientific and didactic procedures, from the National Council for the Control of Animal Experimentation (MCTI-CONCEA, Brazil, 2016) [35], and were approved by the local Animal Ethics Committee (CEUA/PUCRS 8045/17). Male (weighing 18–30 g; total n = 200) and female (weighing 18–25 g; total n = 221) 12-week-old C57BL/6JUnib specific-pathogen-free mice were obtained from the Center for Experimental Biological Models (CeMBE/PUCRS). A sample size of 10–12 animals per group was determined a priori, based on previous publications using castration-related sarcopenia as the main outcome [9,36,37]. Exclusion criteria included animals that died after surgical procedures or gavage, and replacement was adopted to adjust the final sample size. The final N per group is indicated in the legend to figures and tables. Male and female mice were randomly distributed into different experimental cohorts, according to castration, climbing exercise and treatment with ergogenic plant extracts, as detailed in the next sections. A scheme showing the general study design is provided in the Supplementary Figure S1. All over the experimental time, animals were maintained in microisolator cages (maximum of 5 mice/cage), equipped with inlet/outlet air filters, under controlled temperature (22 ± 1 °C) and humidity (50–70%), under a light-dark cycle of 12 h (lights on at 7 a.m., lights off at 7 p.m.). The cages were covered with autoclaved wood chip bedding, and mice received standard pelleted chow and filtered water ad libitum. Behavioral and histological assessments were performed by an operator blinded to the experimental groups.

2.2. Surgical Castration

All the surgical procedures were performed under general anesthesia, with a mixture of xylazine (10 mg/kg) and ketamine (100 mg/kg), dosed by intraperitoneal (i.p.) route. Male and female mice were subjected to bilateral orchiectomy (ORX) or ovariectomy (OVX), respectively, according to the methodology described beforehand [9,38]. After a longitudinal incision in the dorsal skin and musculature, the testicles or the ovaries were exposed and a ligature was made for homeostasis, before surgically removing the gonads. The same procedure was carried out in the sham-operated groups (SHAM), but without ligature placement or organ removal. For pain control, the animals received acetaminophen (80 mg/kg) by oral route, for 48 h after surgery. Hereafter, the animal body weigh was monitored every week until the euthanasia.

Surgical castration was used as rodent models for inducing sarcopenia and sarcopenia-related functional changes, due to reduced levels of estrogen and testosterone, as it occurs in menopause and andropause [16,39–42].

2.3. Climbing Exercise Protocol

The resistance training was carried out by using the ladder climbing protocol. The procedures were initiated 8 weeks after ORX or OVX surgery. Sham-operated or castrated mice were subjected to a protocol of morning resistance exercise, three times a week, in a step ladder with 2-mm grids and one-meter height, with an inclination of 85 degrees. For adaptation, the animals were trained to climb the ladder for three days, one week before. On the first day, each animal was submitted to two series with three repetitions of climbing. On days 2 and 3, the training was performed in four series with three repetitions. For eight weeks, the sections of resistance exercise were performed by placing different weights in the base of the mouse tail with an adhesive tape. The initial load corresponded to 50% of the animal body weight, being progressively increased every seven days by 10%. Each section consisted of four series with 1-min resting, which were repeated three times in intervals of 2 min. The method was adapted from previous publications [43,44]. Sedentary groups of sham-operated or castrated mice were adapted in the same environment, but without any protocol of exercise. For animals submitted to resistance training, the ladder climbing time (s) was registered as the mean of three trials, as an additional measure resistance, at 16 weeks after castration (8 weeks after the onset of climbing exercise).

2.4. Treatment with Ergogenic Phytocompounds

Male and female mice from the different experimental groups, castrated or SHAM, sedentary or submitted to climbing exercise, were randomly distributed into five treatment groups that received: (i) vehicle (0.9% NaCl solution) 10 mL/kg; (ii) *Ajuga* turkestanica lyophilized extract (containing 2.5% of turkesterone) 50 mg/kg; (iii) *Eurycoma longifolia* lyophilized extract (containing eurycomanone) 200 mg/kg; (iv) *Urtica dioica* lyophilized extract 50 mg/kg (containing 0.82% of β-sitosterol); (v) a combination of the three extracts (named as TLU). The phytoanabolic extracts were administered daily by oral route, for eight weeks, beginning eight weeks after castration. The doses of the extracts were based on a series of previous publications showing efficacy and low toxicity in different experimental paradigms [34,45–59]. A scheme showing the timeline for the experimental protocols is provided in the Supplementary Figure S2. Within the figure and table legends, the following abbreviations have been used: SHAM, sham-operated; OVX, ovariectomized; ORX, orchiectomized; Exer, exercise (group submitted to exercise protocol); Sed, sedentary (that have not been submitted to exercise protocol) Turk, *Ajuga turkestanica*; Long, *Eurycoma longifolia*; Urt, *Urtica dioica*; TLU, the association of the three extracts.

2.5. Determination of Active Principles in Lyophilized Extracts

Samples were individually added in methanol (LiChrosolv, Merck, Darmstadt, Germany) at concentration of 50 mg/mL and agitated in an orbital agitator Mixer 099A (Glas-Col, LLC, Terre Haute, IN, USA) at 40 RPM, for 20 min, at room temperature (RT). Each mixture was incubated in an ultrasound bath T-14 (Thornton, São Paulo, Brazil) for 5 min, at RT and the dissolved phase was used for subsequent determinations.

Total content of phytosterols was determined by spectrophotometry, as previously described [60], using high-density cholesterol (HDL)-cholesterol (100 mg/L) as reference standard (Bioclin, Minas Gerais, Brazil) and expressing the results as milligram equivalents of HDL-cholesterol per gram of lyophilized extract (mgEq/g). Briefly aliquots of each sample were subsequently evaporated, resuspended in chloroform (Ensure, Merck, Germany), derivatized with Liebermann–Burchard reagent (LB), and read at 625 nm in a spectrophotometer (Spectramax M5, Molecular Devices, San Jose, CA, USA), using chloroform as analytical blank. LB was prepared by mixing 20 mL of ice cooled acetic anhydride (96%, J.T.Baker, Phillipsburg, NJ, USA) with 2 mL of sulfuric acid (98%, Merck, Germany).

Phytosterols were individually quantified by liquid chromatography with UV detection (LC-UV), using an Agilent LC system 1260 Infinity (Agilent Technologies, Santa Clara, CA, USA). Chromatographic separations were performed using a Zorbax Eclipse PLUS C18 RRHD 2.1 × 50 mm 1.8-µm column (Agilent, Paolo Alto, CA, USA), with 0.1% formic acid (eluent A) and 0.1% formic acid in methanol (eluent B) as the mobile phase, in gradient mode. The gradient was programmed to start with 20% of eluent B. After 2 min, eluent B was increased to 60%, remaining at this condition for 3 min. For column cleanup step, eluent B was increased to 100% for 7 min, and changed back to 20% to equilibrate the system before the next sample injection. The total time of analysis was 20 min. Ten microliters of samples were injected into the system, and the column temperature was maintained at 50 °C. The detector was operated simultaneously at 240 and 254 nm. HDL-cholesterol (Bioclin, Minas Gerais, Brazil) was used as the reference steroid for the calibration curve.

All quantified phytosterols were confirmed by liquid chromatography tandem mass spectrometry (LC-MS/MS), on an Agilent 6460 Triple Quad mass spectrometer coupled to Agilent 1290 Infinity chromatograph (Agilent, Paolo Alto, CA, USA). Phytosterol separations were performed by a similar chromatographic method as used for LC-UV analysis injecting; however, only five microliters of sample were used due to the method sensitivity. Analytes were ionized in an electrospray ionization (ESI) source and analyzed in multiple reaction monitoring mode. The ESI source was operated in positive ion mode, at 350 °C temperature, cone gas flow rate of 11 L/min, desolvation gas flow rate of 10 L/min, and a capillary volage of 3500V. The transitions (m/z) monitored were: eurycomanone (m/z 393.4 > 237.2 and 393.4 > 355.2); β-sitosterol (397.0 > 81.0 and 397.0 > 95.0); turkesterone (m/z 497.0 > 443.0 and 497.0 > 461.0).

2.6. Voluntary Locomotor Activity

Considering the motor deficits related to sarcopenia, the overall spontaneous locomotor activity of animals was assessed at 12 and 16 weeks after surgical procedures in the different experimental groups [61]. For this purpose, an automatic system comprised of an acrylic box (46 × 46 × 36 cm) with infrared sensors was used. The animals were placed in the center of the arena, with 1 min for habituation and 5 min for locomotor activity analysis. The total activity time (s), the traveled distance (cm), and the speed (mm/s) were registered. Movements were monitored on the x, y, and z-axes, which represent the height, width, and depth, respectively.

2.7. Rota-Rod Performance

The time until to fatigue was evaluated in the rota-rod apparatus, which consisted of a rod (3-cm in diameter) with five flanges, allowing the simultaneous evaluation of four mice. Mice were trained in the device 24 h before the experimental session. For training, the animals were placed in the device at a speed of 9 RPM until 60 s, and the procedure was repeated three times, with a 15-s interval. For the experimental sessions, mice were positioned in the equipment at an initial speed of 9 RPM, with an automatic gradual speed increase every 36 s, until reaching the maximal velocity of 40 RPM. The latency to fall (s) was registered as the mean of three trials, with a 15-s interval [62]. The evaluations were carried out at 12 and 16 weeks after surgical castration.

2.8. Grasping Test

This test was conducted to determine the grip strength of animals in the different experimental groups, at 12- and 16-weeks post-castration. After a gentle lifting by the tail, mice were allowed to grasp a grid positioned on an electronic balance. Animals were submitted to three trials, with a 15-s interval. The number (in grams) showed by the balance was instantly recorded, and a mean was calculated after the three trials to obtain the individual grasping strength.

2.9. Euthanasia and Sample Collection

One day after behavioral evaluations, mice were euthanized by deep isoflurane inhalation anesthesia. The blood was collected from the abdominal aorta for subsequent analysis. The following organs were sequentially collected and weighted (in g): gastrocnemius, tibialis anterior, soleus, subcutaneous adipose tissues, liver, kidney, bone, and brain.

2.10. Biochemical Analysis

The serum levels of triglycerides, total cholesterol, high-density cholesterol (HDL), non-HDL, aspartate transaminase (TGO) and alanine aminotransferase (TGP) were measured using commercial kits (Labtest, Lagoa Santa, Brazil).

2.11. Cytokine Determination

The levels of interleukin-1β (IL-1β), tumor necrosis factor (TNF), and interleukin-10 (IL-10) were measured in gastrocnemius muscle samples obtained from the different experimental groups. The cytokine levels were assessed by sandwich enzyme-linked immunosorbent assay using DuoSet kits according to the manufacturer's instructions (R&D Systems, Minneapolis, MN, USA). The results are expressed in pg/mL.

2.12. Histological Analysis of Skeletal Muscle and Adipose Tissue

After registering the wet weight, the gastrocnemius and subcutaneous inguinal adipose tissue were processed for histological assessment. Tissues were fixed in 10% formaldehyde, during 24 h. Subsequently, the samples were included in paraffin and sectioned in 5-µm slices, for staining with hematoxylin and eosin. Images were captured using a Zeiss AxioImager M2 light microscope under 400× magnification (Carl Zeiss, Gottingen, Germany) and were analyzed using NIH ImageJ 1.36b Software. Adipocyte diameter was measured by using an automated tool, whereas the muscle fiber cross-sectional areas (CSA) were measured manually, using the free-hand function, after adjusting the image scale in μm^2. The frequency size distribution of muscle or adipocyte areas were also determined. For histological analysis, 5–7 slides were evaluated from each group, in a blinded manner.

2.13. Statistical Analysis

Results are provided as the mean ± SEM. For time-course data, the areas under the curve (AUC) were calculated before statistical comparisons. The Shapiro–Wilk test was used to check data normality. Statistical analysis was performed by One-way ANOVA followed by Sidak post hoc test or by Two-way ANOVA followed by Uncorrected Fisher's LSD. Statistical tests and design of graphs were held using GraphPad Software version 8.4.3 (GraphPad Software Inc., San Diego, CA, USA).

3. Results

3.1. Analysis of Bioactive Compounds in Lyophilized Extracts

The analysis of *A. turkestanica* extract indicated a content of 7.8% regarding the total phytosterols (78.0 mgEq/g), containing 0.501 mg of turkesterone per gram, as determined by LC-UV (Figure 1C), and confirmed by LC-MS (Figure 1D). As for *E. longifolia* Jack, the extract presented 0.5% of total phytosterols (5.0 mgEq/g), with 0.009 mg of eurycomanone per gram (Figure 1E,F). The lyophilized extract of *U. dioica* presented 2.8% of total phytosterols (28.0 mgEq/g), which corresponded to 0.016 mg of β-sitosterol per gram (Figure 1G,H). HDL-cholesterol was used to determine total content of phytosterols by VIS and to estimate the concentration of each phytosterol by LC-UV (Figure 1A,B).

3.2. Castration Effects Prior to Exercise and Treatments

OVX resulted in a significant increase of body weight gain in comparison with the corresponding SHAM females, after seven weeks of surgery (Figure 2B). Differently, ORX led to body weight loss, compared with SHAM males (Figure 2D), as evaluated at the seventh week post-castration. Animals were distributed into sedentary or climbing exercise groups, and additional experimental treatment subgroups were created avoiding any significant differences when comparing the mean body weights, for either females (Figure 2B) or males (Figure 2D). Castration was confirmed by a marked reduction of uterus weight in females (Figure 2A) and the absence of testes in males (Figure 2C), as evidenced at the moment of euthanasia (16 weeks).

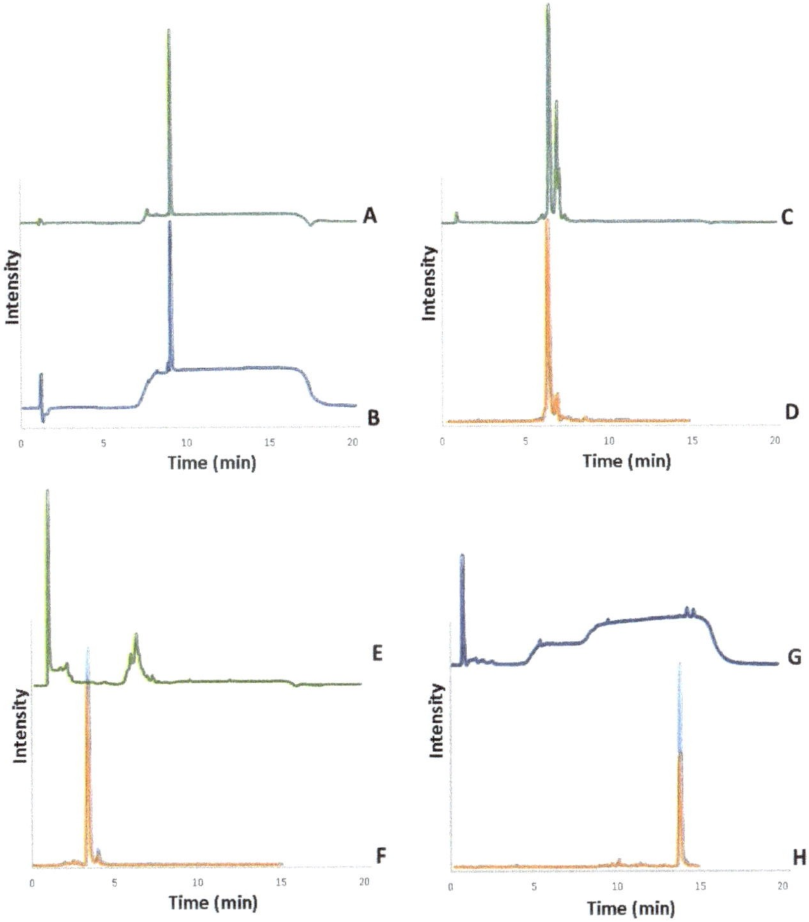

Figure 1. Identification of main active compounds in the ergogenic extracts. Cholesterol 50 mg/L (**A**) by LC-UV in 240 nm, (**B**) in 254 nm; Turkesterone (**C**) by LC-UV in 254 nm and (**D**) by LC-MS/MS with the fragments m/z 497.0 > 443.0 (light blue) and 497.0 > 461.0 (orange); Eurycomanone (**E**) by LC-UV in 254 nm and (**F**) by LC-MS/MS with the fragments m/z 391.5 > 251.1 (light blue) and 391.5 > 279.1 (orange); β-sitosterol (**G**) by LC-UV in 240 nm and (**H**) by LC-MS/MS with the fragments m/z 397.0 > 81.0 (light blue) and 397.0 > 95.0 (orange).

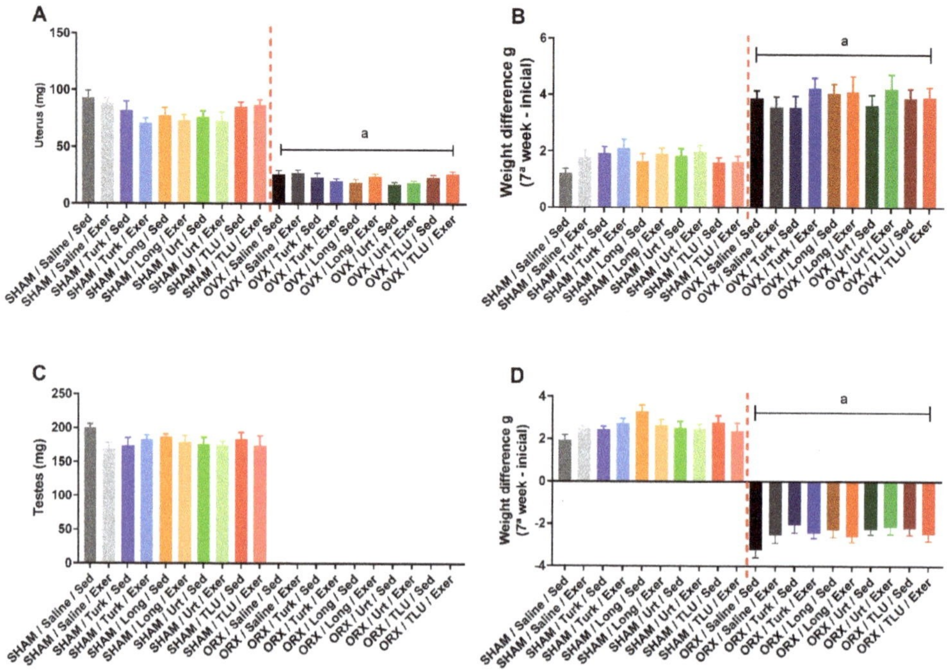

Figure 2. Effects of castration on uterus (**A**) and testes weight (**C**), 16 weeks after ovariectomy and orchiectomy, respectively, in comparison with sham-operated mice. Impacts of ovariectomy (**B**) and orchiectomy (**D**) on the body weight, 7 weeks after castration and before exercise and treatment onset. SHAM, sham-operated; OVX, ovariectomized; ORX, orchiectomized; Sed, sedentary; Exer, Exercise; Turk, Ajuga turkestanica; Long, Eurycoma longifolia; Urt, Urtica dioica; TLU, the association of the three extracts. Results are the mean ± SEM of 10 to 12 animals per group. [a] $p < 0.05$ significantly different compared to the sham-operated group (One-way ANOVA followed by Sidak post hoc test).

3.3. Changes in Body Weight after Exercise and Treatments

The body weight was monitored weekly from the time of castration until euthanasia, at 16 weeks. Time-related body weight variations over the weeks are depicted in Figure 3A,D, for females and males, respectively. The area under the curve (AUC), from 8 to 16 weeks, was calculated to assess the effects of climbing exercise and ergogenic extracts in SHAM and castrated groups. OVX triggered a significant increase of AUC in saline-treated sedentary female mice, whereas the climbing exercise was able to significantly reduce the body weight gain in OVX animals, reaching similar levels as seen in SHAM sedentary animals, irrespective of treatment with the extracts. The exercise also led to diminished body weight gain in SHAM groups, although significant differences were not observed (Figure 3B). Alternatively, the resistance exercise significantly reduced the final body weight of saline-treated SHAM females, an effect that was mirrored in the exercise groups treated with *A. turkestanica* extract or TLU. Regarding the OVX animals, only the combination of exercise and *U. dioica* extract significantly reduced the final body weight (Figure 3C).

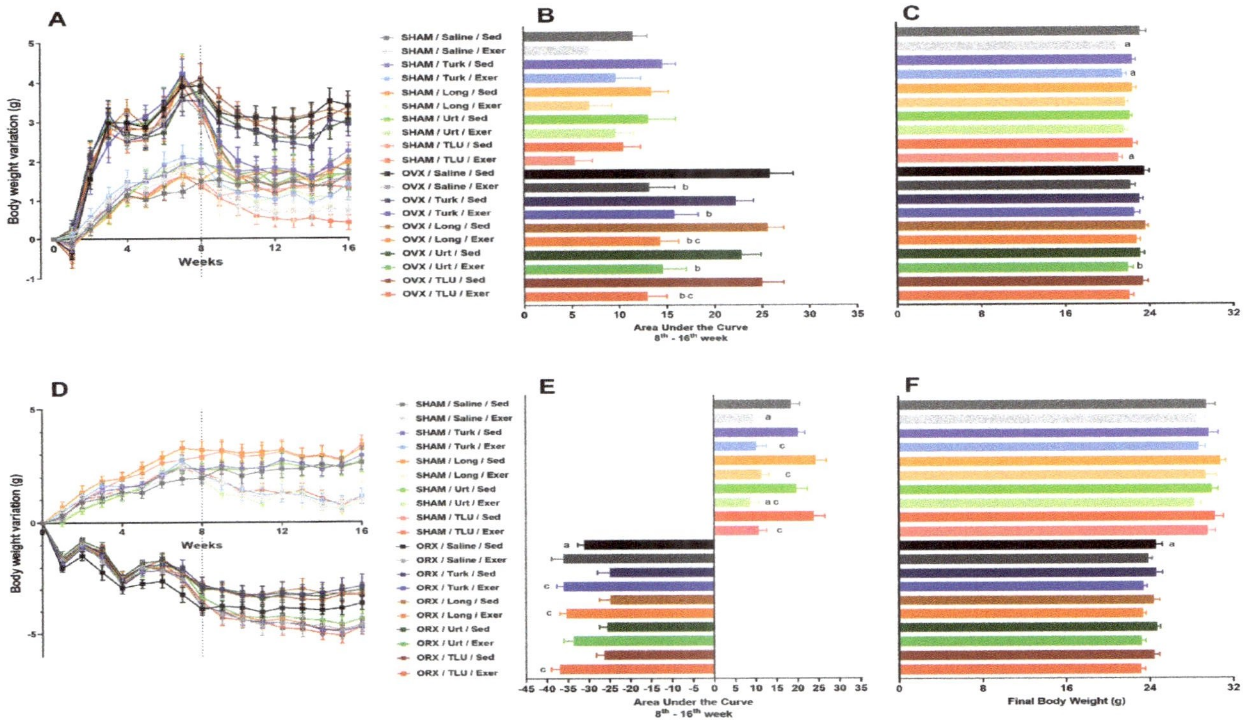

Figure 3. Changes in body weight in female (**A**) and male (**D**) mice, with treatments and exercise since castration until euthanasia. Area Under the Curve for the treatments and exercise period, from 8 to 16 weeks in females (**B**) and males (**E**). Final body weight of female (**C**) and male (**F**) mice. SHAM, sham-operated; OVX, ovariectomized; ORX, orchiectomized; Sed, sedentary; Exer, Exercise; Turk, Ajuga turkestanica; Long, Eurycoma longifolia; Urt, Urtica dioica; TLU, the association of the three extracts. Results are the mean ± SEM of 10 to 12 animals per group. [a] $p < 0.05$ significantly different compared with the sham-operated group treated with saline. [b] $p < 0.05$ significantly different compared with the castrated group treated with saline. [c] $p < 0.05$ significantly different comparing exercise to the respective sedentary group (One-way ANOVA followed by Sidak post hoc test).

SHAM male mice submitted to climbing exercise displayed a decrease of AUC body weight gain, independent on the supplementation with any extracts. ORX sedentary males presented a marked loss of body weight gain, without any beneficial effect for resistance exercise in saline-treated animals. The treatment of sedentary ORX mice with the three extracts, alone or in combination, partially reversed the body weight loss induced by castration. The combination of ergogenic extracts with exercise failed to recover the body weight loss in ORX mice (Figure 3E). Sedentary ORX animals showed a significant reduction of final body weight, when compared with sedentary saline-treated SHAM males. Either exercise or ergogenic extracts failed to recover this parameter (Figure 3F). The mean values for initial, final, and final minus initial body weight for the different experimental groups are presented in Tables 1 and 2, for females and males, respectively.

3.4. Combined Effects of Ergogenic Extracts and Exercise on Skeletal Muscle Weight

The skeletal muscle weight is an essential marker for defining muscle quantity. As indicated in Table 1, OVX did not evoke any significant alteration of gastrocnemius, tibial or soleus muscle wet weights, even when the summed weights of the three muscles were considered, in relation to the corresponding SHAM controls. For females, the treatment of sedentary OVX mice with *A. turkestanica* extract induced a significant reduction of summed wet weight of gastrocnemius, tibial and soleus, when compared with the respective saline-treated sedentary OVX group. The correction of muscle weight per body weight (in %) did not show any significant differences among the groups. Climbing exercise or supplementation with extracts failed to alter the wet weight of skeletal muscles in SHAM females (Table 1).

In males, castration significantly reduced the wet weight of the gastrocnemius, tibial and soleus muscles, which was confirmed when the total weight of the three muscles was determined. Nor exercise or the extracts significantly changed skeletal muscle mass in SHAM or ORX mice. As for the correction of muscle weight per body weight (in %), the association of climbing exercise with *U. dioica* extract increased this parameter in a significant manner (Table 2).

3.5. Adipose Depots and the Effects of Exercise and Ergogenic Extracts

In this study, the inguinal fat depots (iWAT) were evaluated as an indicative of white adipose tissue contents, whilst the interscapular fat (iBAT) was used to assess the presence of brown adipose tissue. In females, the wet weight of iWAT and iBAT, even after correction per body weight (in %), did not show any significant differences when comparing SHAM and OVX mice, regardless of exercise or administration of extracts (Table 1). As well, males did not exhibit any significant differences of iBAT (absolute weight or corrected values), when the effects of castration, resistance exercise or ergogenic extracts were evaluated (Table 2). Of note, ORX led to a marked increase of iWAT wet weight, when compared with the corresponding saline-treated SHAM group. This result was confirmed after correction of iWAT weight per body weight. ORX mice submitted to climbing exercise presented a trend toward a reduction of iWAT wet weight, but this effect was significant only in the exercise groups that had been treated with *E. longifolia* or *U. dioica* extracts. The beneficial effects of resistance exercise combined with *U. dioica* extract were also observed after analysis of iWAT weight corrected per body weight (in %) (Table 2).

Table 1. Combined effects of ergogenic extracts and exercise on body, muscle and adipose tissue weight of sham-operated and ovariectomized mice.

	SHAM										OVX									
	Saline/ Sed	**Saline/ Exer**	**Turk/ Sed**	**Turk/ Exer**	**Long/ Sed**	**Long/ Exer**	**Urt/ Sed**	**Urt/ Exer**	**TLU/ Sed**	**TLU/ Exer**	**Saline/ Sed**	**Saline/ Exer**	**Turk/ Sed**	**Turk/ Exer**	**Long/ Sed**	**Long/ Exer**	**Urt/ Sed**	**Urt/ Exer**	**TLU/ Sed**	**TLU/ Exer**
Initial Weight (g)	21.3 ± 0.6	19.8 ± 0.4 [a]	20.1 ± 0.4	20.7 ± 0.5	20.4 ± 0.3	20.7 ± 0.5	20.5 ± 0.5	20.2 ± 0.6	20.6 ± 0.3	20.5 ± 0.3	20.4 ± 0.5	20.6 ± 0.5	20.1 ± 0.5	20.8 ± 0.5	20.4 ± 0.3	20.8 ± 0.4	20.7 ± 0.3	20.3 ± 0.4	20.2 ± 0.3	20.5 ± 0.4
Final Weight (g)	23.2 ± 0.6	21.0 ± 0.4 [a]	22.4 ± 0.3	21.5 ± 0.4 [a]	22.4 ± 0.4	21.7 ± 0.3	22.1 ± 0.2	21.6 ± 0.3	22.4 ± 0.4	21.1 ± 0.4 [a]	23.5 ± 0.5	22.2 ± 0.5	23.0 ± 0.4	22.6 ± 0.5	23.6 ± 0.3	22.8 ± 0.3	23.1 ± 0.4	21.9 ± 0.5 [b]	23.4 ± 0.5	22.0 ± 0.4
Final-Initial (g)	1.8 ± 0.3	1.1 ± 0.2	2.3 ± 0.2	1.4 ± 0.4	2.0 ± 0.3	1.0 ± 0.4	1.7 ± 0.4	1.4 ± 0.4	1.8 ± 0.3	0.6 ± 0.3	3.1 ± 0.5 [a]	1.6 ± 0.5 [b]	2.9 ± 0.3	1.7 ± 0.5	3.2 ± 0.3	2.0 ± 0.2	2.9 ± 0.3	1.7 ± 0.4 [b]	3.1 ± 0.4	1.5 ± 0.3 [b c]
Gastrocnemius (mg)	116.2 ± 4.1	110.7 ± 2.6	113.4 ± 2.8	108.9 ± 3.6	107.4 ± 1.4	113.5 ± 3.5	114.6 ± 2.7	110.1 ± 4.5	110.3 ± 3.6	111.0 ± 2.5	123.5 ± 4.4	116.5 ± 2.1	109.4 ± 2.7 [b]	117.5 ± 3.3	122.6 ± 1.6	122.9 ± 1.2	116.7 ± 2.8	118.3 ± 2.6	112.4 ± 3.2	117.4 ± 3.3
Tibial (mg)	60.4 ± 2.0	56.6 ± 2.1	61.1 ± 1.6	60.3 ± 2.3	60.7 ± 2.3	62.0 ± 2.5	62.4 ± 2.3	62.3 ± 3.1	58.4 ± 2.0	56.4 ± 1.9	65.3 ± 1.5	61.1 ± 2.3	57.0 ± 4.1	59.7 ± 2.4	63.3 ± 1.9	65.9 ± 2.5	58.0 ± 3.0	61.4 ± 1.9	57.7 ± 3.2	61.8 ± 1.5
Soleus (mg)	5.7 ± 0.5	5.1 ± 0.5	5.6 ± 0.4	4.9 ± 0.4	4.5 ± 0.2	5.3 ± 0.4	5.7 ± 0.5	6.2 ± 0.8	5.0 ± 0.4	5.1 ± 0.3	5.3 ± 0.5	5.1 ± 0.7	5.9 ± 0.5	5.2 ± 0.3	6.2 ± 0.5	6.2 ± 0.5	4.9 ± 0.3	5.7 ± 0.5	6.1 ± 0.7	5.5 ± 0.4
Sum of Muscle Weight (mg)	182.3 ± 6.0	172.4 ± 4.6	180.6 ± 4.4	174.3 ± 4.9	168.2 ± 5.6	180.8 ± 6.1	182,6 ± 4.6	178.6 ± 7.7	174,9 ± 5.5	172.4 ± 4.0	194.1 ± 5.4	182.7 ± 4.0	172.3 ± 6.4 [b]	182.4 ± 5.6	192.1 ± 3.2	190.9 ± 5.8	179.5 ± 5.3	185.4 ± 3.8	175.9 ± 5.7	183.4 ± 4.5
Muscle weight over total weight (%)	0.79 ± 0.02	0.82 ± 0.02	0.82 ± 0.02	0.80 ± 0.02	0.75 ± 0.02	0.83 ± 0.02 [c]	0.82 ± 0.02	0.82 ± 0.03	0.78 ± 0.02	0.82 ± 0.01	0.81 ± 0.02	0.83 ± 0.02	0.74 ± 0.02	0.81 ± 0.02	0.81 ± 0.01	0.83 ± 0.02	0.77 ± 0.02	0.84 ± 0.01	0.75 ± 0.03	0.83 ± 0.01 [c]
iBAT (mg)	168.0 ± 11.9	182.1 ± 13.6	145.3 ± 16.6	145.4 ± 15.1	181.3 ± 10.7	133.0 ± 16.3	167.1 ± 14.6	151.3 ± 18.3	197.4 ± 15.7	161.3 ± 10.8	172.0 ± 17.4	178.5 ± 22.1	213.2 ± 26.1	188.4 ± 12.7	197.5 ± 28.6	157.5 ± 22.9	154.2 ± 28.8	139.6 ± 21.3	214.6 ± 16.1	179.2 ± 23.3
iWAT (mg)	118.7 ± 8.2	111.2 ± 7.8	107.4 ± 8.9	99.7 ± 8.2	111.5 ± 6.8	112.5 ± 6.6	106.3 ± 5.1	111.4 ± 8.6	144.6 ± 5.6	120.9 ± 5.0	143.5 ± 12.5	118.9 ± 11.8	144.4 ± 13.1	121.0 ± 11.4	139.5 ± 12.3	114.1 ± 8.7	129.2 ± 12.5	115.7 ± 9.1	163.1 ± 15.3	142.2 ± 6.1
iWAT over total weight (%)	0.51 ± 0.03	0.53 ± 0.03	0.48 ± 0.03	0.46 ± 0.03	0.50 ± 0.03	0.52 ± 0.03	0.48 ± 0.03	0.51 ± 0.04	0.65 ± 0.03	0.57 ± 0.02	0.61 ± 0.05	0.53 ± 0.04	0.62 ± 0.05	0.53 ± 0.04	0.59 ± 0.05	0.50 ± 0.03	0.056 ± 0.05	0.53 ± 0.03	0.69 ± 0.06	0.65 ± 0.02

SHAM, sham-operated; OVX, ovariectomized; Sed, sedentary; Exer, Exercise; Turk, Ajuga turkestanica; Long, Eurycoma longifolia; Urt, Urtica dioica; TLU, the association of the three extracts. Results are the mean ± SEM of 10 to 12 animals per group. [a] $p < 0.05$ significantly different compared with the sham-operated group treated with saline. [b] $p < 0.05$ significantly different compared with castrated mice treated with saline. [c] $p < 0.05$ significantly different comparing exercise to the respective sedentary group. One-way ANOVA followed by Sidak post hoc test.

Table 2. Combined effects of ergogenic extracts and exercise on body, muscle and adipose tissue weight of sham-operated and orchiectomized mice.

SHAM	Saline/Sed	Saline/Exer	Turk/Sed	Turk/Exer	Long/Sed	Long/Exer	Urt/Sed	Urt/Exer	TLU/Sed	TLU/Exer
Initial Weight (g)	27.9 ± 0.5	27.6 ± 0.6	26.8 ± 0.8	27.6 ± 0.5	27.5 ± 0.6	27.9 ± 0.9	27.3 ± 0.4	27.3 ± 0.6	26.8 ± 0.7	28.4 ± 0.5
Final Weight (g)	29.5 ± 0.8	28.6 ± 0.8	29.7 ± 0.9	28.8 ± 0.6	30.8 ± 0.5	29.4 ± 1.0	30.0 ± 0.6	28.3 ± 0.7	30.2 ± 0.8	29.6 ± 0.7
Final-Initial (g)	2.6 ± 0.3	1.0 ± 0.3 ^{a}	2.9 ± 0.4	1.1 ± 0.4 ^{ac}	3.3 ± 0.4	1.5 ± 0.3 ^{c}	2.7 ± 0.5	1.0 ± 0.2 ^{ac}	3.4 ± 0.4	1.1 ± 0.3 ^{ac}
Gastrocnemius (mg)	159.0 ± 3.0	150.1 ± 4.2	154.2 ± 4.2	158.9 ± 3.7	154.9 ± 1.3	158.0 ± 4.2	155.7 ± 1.6	150.3 ± 3.5	162.2 ± 3.3	157.3 ± 3.4
Tibial (mg)	88.2 ± 3.1	81.0 ± 1.3	83.5 ± 3.1	84.0 ± 2.9	86.0 ± 2.4	84.8 ± 3.9	90.1 ± 2.7	82.9 ± 2.6	85.5 ± 2.0	84.8 ± 3.2
Soleus (mg)	8.4 ± 0.6	7.6 ± 0.5	7.3 ± 0.3	8.3 ± 0.5	7.3 ± 0.3	7.6 ± 0.6	8.5 ± 0.5	6.9 ± 0.6	7.6 ± 0.5	7.9 ± 0.5
Sum of Muscle Weight (mg)	255.5 ± 5.3	238.7 ± 5.6	242.9 ± 7.7	256.9 ± 2.8	250.9 ± 3.9	250.3 ± 8.2	254.2 ± 4.3	240.1 ± 6.1	255.3 ± 4.8	250.1 ± 6.5
Muscle weight over total weight (%)	0.83 ± 0.01	0.85 ± 0.02	0.80 ± 0.01	0.87 ± 0.01 ^{c}	0.81 ± 0.01	0.84 ± 0.02	0.85 ± 0.02	0.85 ± 0.02	0.83 ± 0.01	0.84 ± 0.01
iBAT (mg)	178.5 ± 5.8	184.1 ± 10.0	188.0 ± 10.0	185.6 ± 7.1	189.4 ± 9.8	171.5 ± 10.6	185.3 ± 6.9	184.1 ± 8.2	185.7 ± 8.1	180.2 ± 10.0
iWAT (mg)	111.1 ± 3.86	103.5 ± 11.6	118.7 ± 8.8	106.2 ± 8.9	125.8 ± 6.9	101.5 ± 6.3	106.2 ± 9.1	107.9 ± 6.1	127.5 ± 8.4	113.9 ± 9.4
iWAT over total weight (%)	0.34 ± 0.02	0.37 ± 0.04	0.40 ± 0.03	0.37 ± 0.03	0.41 ± 0.02	0.35 ± 0.02	0.36 ± 0.03	0.39 ± 0.03	0.42 ± 0.03	0.39 ± 0.03

ORX	Saline/Sed	Saline/Exer	Turk/Sed	Turk/Exer	Long/Sed	Long/Exer	Urt/Sed	Urt/Exer	TLU/Sed	TLU/Exer
Initial Weight (g)	28.3 ± 0.6	28.5 ± 0.6	27.5 ± 0.4	28.1 ± 0.4	27.5 ± 0.5	27.9 ± 0.4	27.7 ± 0.4	27.6 ± 0.6	27.7 ± 0.5	27.8 ± 0.7
Final Weight (g)	24.6 ± 0.6	23.9 ± 0.4	24.6 ± 0.6	23.4 ± 0.3	24.4 ± 0.6	23.3 ± 0.3	24.6 ± 0.3	23.2 ± 0.4	24.41 ± 0.5	23.1 ± 0.4
Final-Initial (g)	−3.7 ± 0.3 ^{a}	−4.61 ± 0.5	−3.28 ± 0.3	−4.7 ± 0.2 ^{b}	−3.2 ± 0.5	−4.6 ± 0.3 ^{c}	−3.0 ± 0.3	−4.36 ± 0.4	−3.3 ± 0.3	−4.7 ± 0.3 ^{c}
Gastrocnemius (mg)	129.7 ± 2.4 ^{a}	132.1 ± 1.8	138.1 ± 2.7	130.9 ± 2.8	129.5 ± 2.0	130.6 ± 3.2	137.5 ± 1.4	134.0 ± 2.8	132.4 ± 2.9	126.1 ± 3.3
Tibial (mg)	69.4 ± 2.4 ^{a}	68.5 ± 2.7	72.40 ± 3.2	72.7 ± 1.8	70.6 ± 1.9	69.3 ± 2.1	76.2 ± 3.1	72.0 ± 2.1	68,0 ± 2.7	67.1 ± 2.0
Soleus (mg)	6.0 ± 0.4 ^{a}	7.1 ± 0.5	6.9 ± 0.5	6.2 ± 0.3	6.5 ± 0.5	6.6 ± 0.3	6.6 ± 0.4	6.2 ± 0.4	6.3 ± 0.4	6.3 ± 0.3
Sum of Muscle Weight (mg)	205.1 ± 4.5 ^{a}	207.7 ± 3.3	217.3 ± 5.7	209.8 ± 3.5	206.5 ± 3.6	206.5 ± 4.8	220.3 ± 3.8	212.2 ± 4.7	206.7 ± 5.3	199.5 ± 4.2
Muscle weight over total weight (%)	0.85 ± 0.01	0.87 ± 0.02	0.89 ± 0.01	0.90 ± 0.02	0.85 ± 0.02	0.89 ± 0.01	0.88 ± 0.01	0.91 ± 0.01 ^{b}	0.85 ± 0.02	0.87 ± 0.01
iBAT (mg)	179.5 ± 10.9	174.6 ± 8.1	186.1 ± 12.3	190.6 ± 10.2	183.4 ± 13.5	170.9 ± 7.7	193.7 ± 12.1	164.9 ± 10.4	177.5 ± 9.9	179.5 ± 5.6
iWAT (mg)	159.9 ± 9.3 ^{a}	127.9 ± 7.1	161.0 ± 13.1	125.7 ± 8.2	169.2 ± 16.6	128.8 ± 8.2 ^{c}	149.9 ± 8.3	122.3 ± 9.4 ^{b}	148.2 ± 8.3	130.8 ± 6.5
iWAT over total weight (%)	0.65 ± 0.03 ^{a}	0.54 ± 0.03 ^{b}	0.65 ± 0.04	0.54 ± 0.03	0.67 ± 0.06	0.58 ± 0.04	0.63 ± 0.03	0.51 ± 0.03 ^{b}	0.61 ± 0.03	0.57 ± 0.03

SHAM, sham-operated; ORX, orchiectomized; Sed, sedentary; Exer, Exercise; Turk, Ajuga turkestanica; Long, Eurycoma longifolia; Urt, Urtica dioica; TLU, the association of the three extracts. Results are the mean ± SEM of 10 to 12 animals per group. ^{a} $p < 0.05$ significantly different compared with the sham-operated group treated with saline. ^{b} $p < 0.05$ significantly different compared with castrated mice treated with saline. ^{c} $p < 0.05$ significantly different comparing exercise to the respective sedentary group. One-way ANOVA followed by Sidak post hoc test.

3.6. Exercise and Treatment with Phytoanabolic Extracts and Their Effects on Functional Parameters

Reduced hormone levels and aging-related sarcopenia likely impair muscle strength, resistance to fatigue and spontaneous locomotor behavior. SHAM females submitted to climbing exercise and treated with *A. turkestanica* extract presented an increase of grip strength when compared with their sedentary counterparts, according to the evaluation at 12 weeks (i.e., 4 weeks after intervention onset). Alternatively, there was a reduction of grip strength in OVX sedentary mice that had been treated with *U. dioica*, at the same experimental time (Figure 4A). Neither of the female groups exhibited any significant difference of grip strength at 16 weeks (Figure 4B). At 12 weeks, the protocol of resistance exercise improved the grip strength of ORX mice in all of the extract-treated groups, except in the group that received *U. dioica* supplementation (Figure 4C). The treatment with *A. turkestanica* extract improved the grip strength of ORX mice at 16 weeks, regardless of exercise training (Figure 4D).

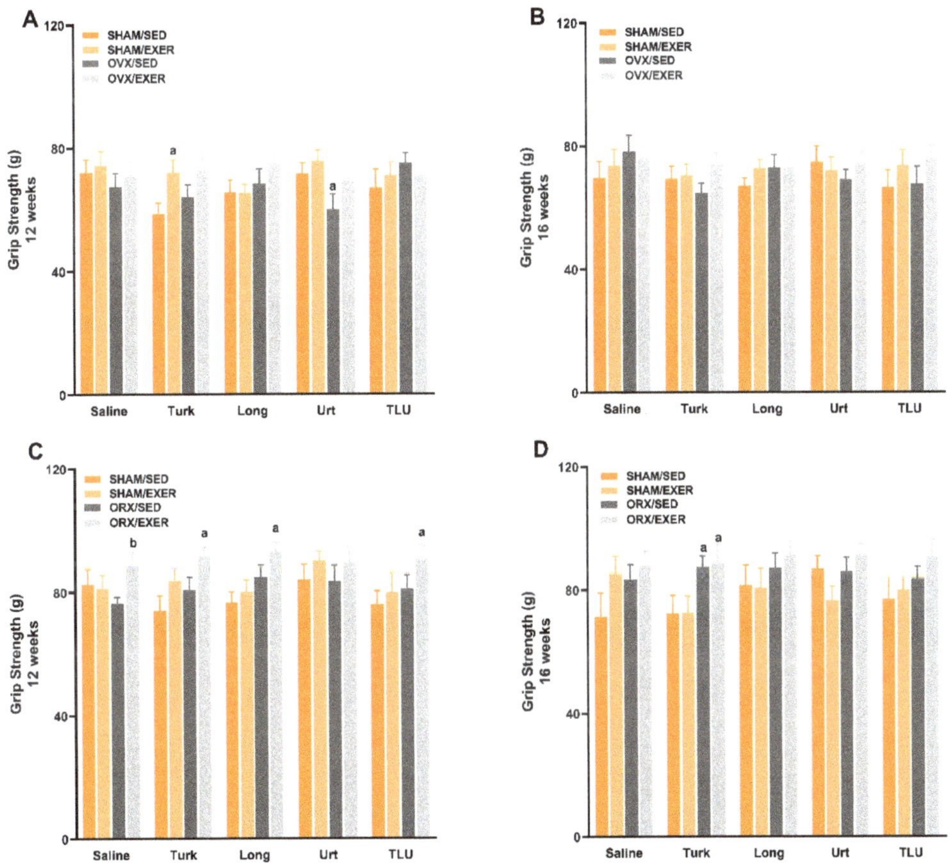

Figure 4. Grip strength assessed at 12 and 16 weeks in female ((**A**) and (**B**), respectively) and male ((**C**) and (**D**), respectively) mice. SHAM, sham-operated; OVX, ovariectomized; ORX, orchiectomized; Sed, sedentary; Exer, Exercise; Turk, Ajuga turkestanica; Long, Eurycoma longifolia; Urt, Urtica dioica; TLU, the association of the three extracts. Results are the mean ± SEM of 10 to 12 animals per group. [a] $p < 0.05$ significantly different compared with the sham-operated group. [b] $p < 0.05$ significantly different compared exercise to respective sedentary treatment (two-way ANOVA followed by Uncorrected Fisher's LSD).

By using a protocol adapted to assess fatigue resistance in the rotarod apparatus, it was possible to observe that OVX led to a reduction of resistance to fall in saline-treated sedentary mice, an effect that was restored by training exercise, at 12 weeks. However, the effects of OVX or exercise were not observed for the groups that received any of the ergogenic extracts, according to the analysis at 12 weeks (Supplementary Figure S3A). At 16 weeks, the combination of exercise and TLU greatly improved the resistance to fatigue in OVX animals, whereas the treatment with *E. longifolia* plus exercise significantly diminished this parameter (Supplementary Figure S3B). For males, no significant differences regarding the resistance to fall in the rotarod equipment were detected at 12 (Supplementary Figure S3C) or 16 weeks (Supplementary Figure S3D).

As an additional measurement of resistance, the total time spent for ladder climbing was measured in the groups submitted to resistance exercise, at 16 weeks (i.e., at the end of training and treatment protocols). The climbing time did not significantly differ when comparing SHAM and OVX females, regardless of supplementation with any extracts (Figure 5A). For males, castration significantly increased the total climbing time, and this effect was prevented by supplementation with *E. longifolia* extract or TLU, with partial effects for *A. turkestanica* extract. Nonetheless, the phytotherapics did not significantly modify the time to complete the task in SHAM males (Figure 5B).

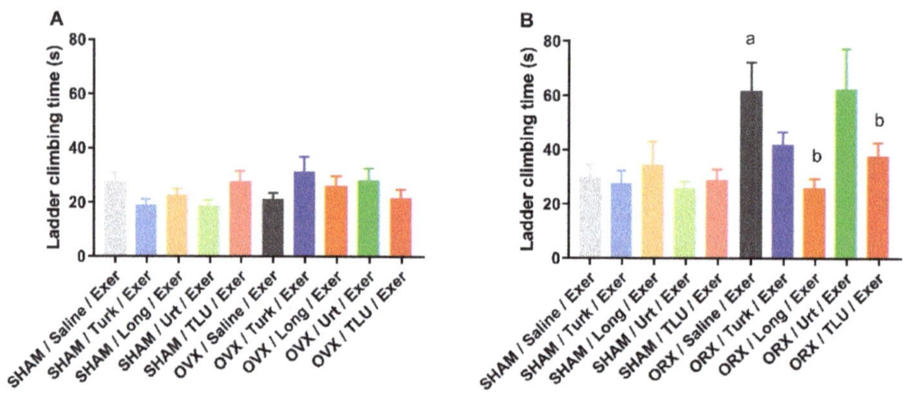

Figure 5. Total time for ladder climbing (s) assessed at 16 weeks, in females (**A**) and males (**B**). SHAM, sham-operated; OVX, ovariectomized; ORX, orchiectomized; Exer, Exercise; Turk, Ajuga turkestanica; Long, Eurycoma longifolia; Urt, Urtica dioica; TLU, the association of the three extracts. Results are the mean ± SEM of 10 to 12 animals per group. [a] $p < 0.05$ significantly different compared with the sham-operated group treated with saline. [b] $p < 0.05$ significantly different compared with the operated group treated with saline (one-way ANOVA followed by Sidak post hoc test).

As for the voluntary locomotion, the exercise training led to an overall increase of travelled distance in SHAM females (Figure 6A) and males (Figure 6B), according to the evaluation at 12 weeks. For OVX mice, the combination of resistance exercise plus *A. turkestanica*, or *U. dioica*, or TLU supplementation, significantly increased the travelled distance. The climbing exercise failed to significantly alter the travelled distance of saline- or *E. longifolia*-treated OVX mice in 12 weeks (Figure 6A). In males, resistance exercise plus supplementation with *E. longifolia*, or *U. dioica* extract enhanced the travelled distance of ORX animals. Oppositely, exercise failed to improve the travelled distance in saline- or *A. turkestanica*-treated ORX groups, with partial effects for TLU, as seen in 12 weeks (Figure 6D). Females (Figure 6C) or males (Figure 6F) displayed a time-related reduction of travelled distance from 12 to 16 weeks, without any significant effects for castration, exercise, or herbal supplementation at 16 weeks (Figure 6B,E).

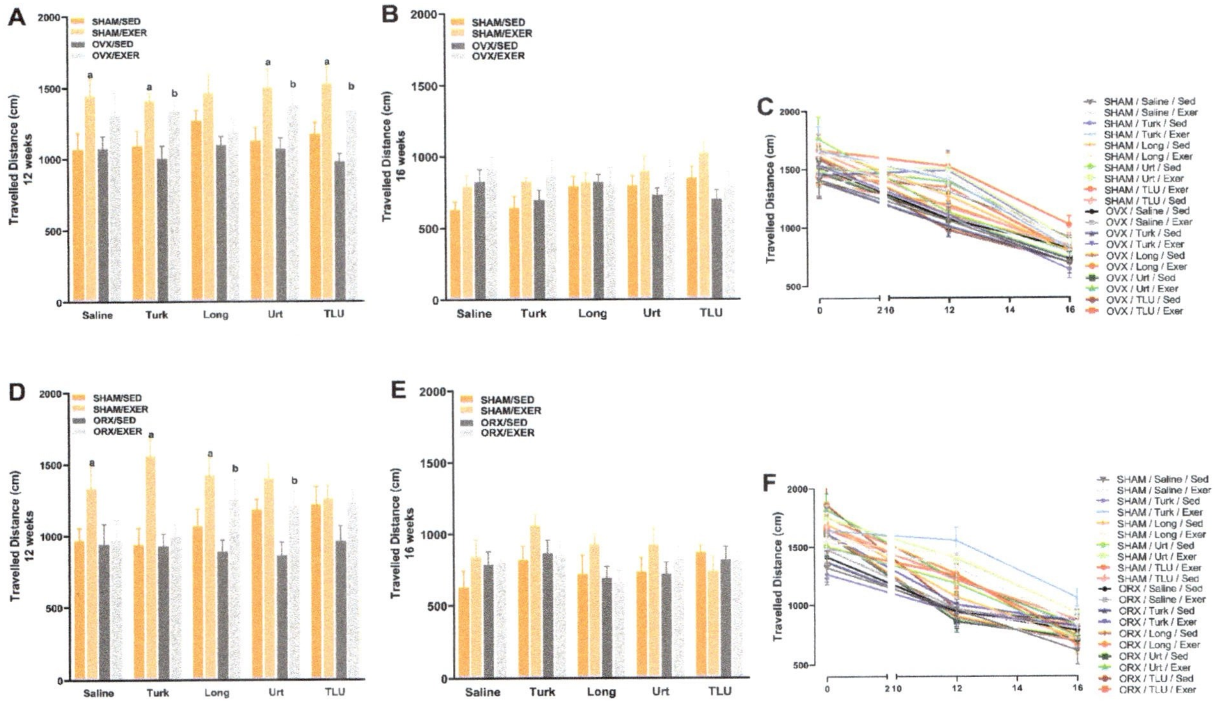

Figure 6. Assessment of spontaneous locomotor activity measured as the travelled distance for 5 min, at 12 and 16 weeks after castration in female ((**A**) and (**B**), respectively) and male mice ((**D**) and (**E**), respectively). Time-course for the travelled distance measured at three different periods: before castration, 12 and 16 weeks after castration, in female (**C**) and male mice (**F**). SHAM, sham-operated; OVX, ovariectomized; ORX, orchiectomized; Sed, sedentary; Exer, Exercise; Turk, Ajuga turkestanica; Long, Eurycoma longifolia; Urt, Urtica dioica; TLU, the association of the three extracts. Results are the mean ± SEM of 10 to 12 animals per group. [a] $p < 0.05$ significantly different compared with the sham-operated group. [b] $p < 0.05$ significantly different compared with the castrated group (two-way ANOVA followed by Uncorrected Fisher's LSD).

The analysis of speed in the open-field arena revealed general positive effects for exercise training in SHAM female (Figure 7A) or male mice (Figure 7C), as monitored at 12 weeks. In OVX animals, the association of exercise with *A. turkestanica*, or *U. dioica*, or TLU extracts significantly enhanced the speed time of females at 12 weeks (Figure 7A). At the same time-point, ORX males showed an increased speed, in groups that had been submitted to exercise training plus *E. longifolia*, or *U. dioica* extract (Figure 7C). At 16 weeks, no significant difference was observed among the experimental groups, for females (Figure 7B) or males (Figure 7D).

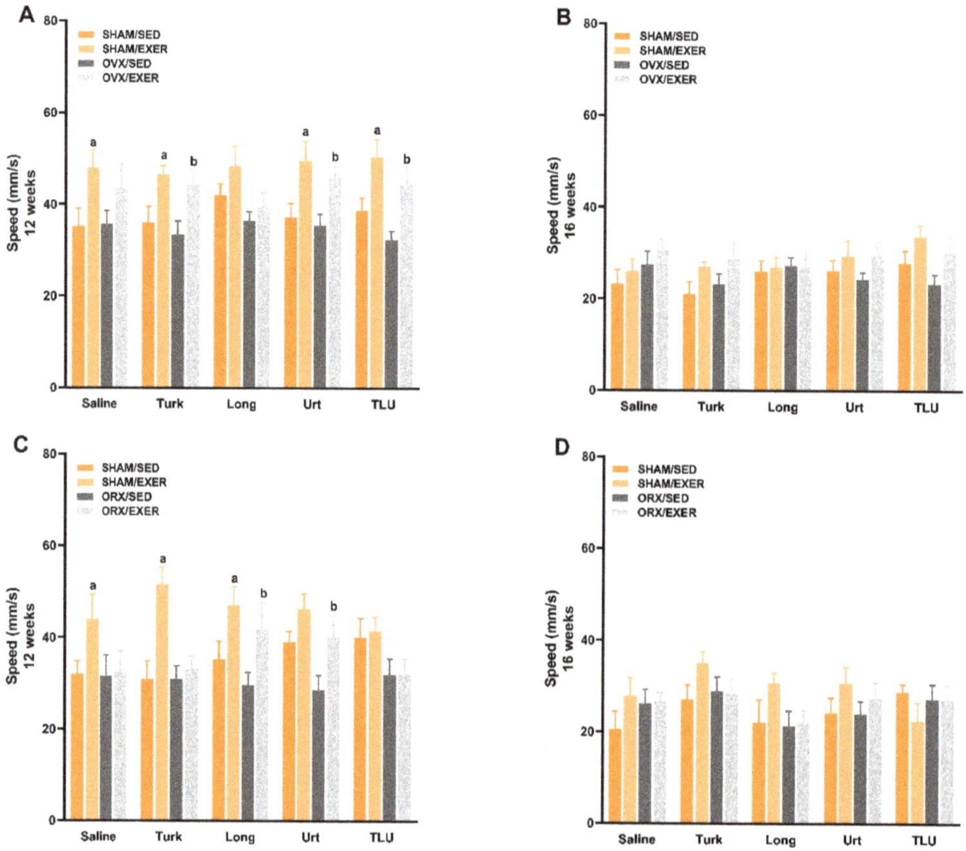

Figure 7. Assessment of spontaneous locomotor activity measured as the animal speed for 5 min, at 12 and 16 weeks after castration in female ((**A**) and (**B**), respectively) and male mice ((**C**) and (**D**), respectively). SHAM, sham-operated; OVX, ovariectomized; ORX, orchiectomized; Sed, sedentary; Exer, Exercise; Turk, Ajuga turkestanica; Long, Eurycoma longifolia; Urt, Urtica dioica; TLU, the association of the three extracts. Results are the mean ± SEM of 10 to 12 animals per group. [a] $p < 0.05$ significantly different compared with the sham-operated group. [b] $p < 0.05$ significantly different compared to the operated group (two-way ANOVA followed by Uncorrected Fisher's LSD).

Females (Supplementary Figure S4C) or males (Supplementary Figure S4F) presented a time-related reduction of activity time, independent on the experimental group, from 12 to 16 weeks. This parameter was not significantly modified by OVX or ORX, regardless of exercise or herbal supplementation, at 12 or 16 weeks, for females (Supplementary Figure S4A,B) or males (Supplementary Figure S4D,E), respectively. The combination of resistance exercise plus *A. turkestanica* extract significantly increased the activity time of SHAM male mice at 12 weeks (Supplementary Figure S4D).

3.7. Skeletal Muscle Alterations after Exercise and Treatment with Anabolic Extracts

Gastrocnemius sections from the different experimental groups were evaluated regarding the cross-sectional areas and the fiber size frequency distribution. In females, only the exercise protocol combined with *E. longifolia* extract treatment caused a significant reduction of cross-sectional area of gastrocnemius muscle in OVX mice. For the other groups, no significant differences were observed for this parameter (Figure 8A). The experimental interventions (i.e., exercise and/or herbal extracts) caused significant alterations of the fiber size frequency distribution. The fibers with 0–500 μm^2 were significantly higher in OVX mice submitted to exercise plus *E. longifolia* extract treatment, when compared with the respective sedentary group. Sedentary OVX mice treated with *A. turkestanica* extract, or OVX mice submitted to exercise plus *U. dioica* or TLU supplementation showed a reduction in the amount of fibers with 1500–2000 μm^2, when compared with saline-treated sedentary OVX animals. As for the frequency size >3000 μm^2, there was a significant higher number of fibers in sedentary OVX mice that had been treated with *E. longifolia* (Figure 8B). Representative histological images of gastrocnemius muscle in different female groups are shown in Figure 9A–T.

In males, there were no significant differences regarding the gastrocnemius cross-sectional areas, when comparing SHAM and castrated animals, despite exercise or herbal supplementation (Figure 8C). Concerning the fiber size frequency distribution, ORX mice showed a significantly higher number of fibers with 0 to 500 μm^2. SHAM males that had been trained for climbing and were treated with *E. longifolia* extract showed a significant increase of fibers with 2500–3000 and >3000 μm^2, in comparison with saline-treated sedentary SHAM males (Figure 8D). The Figure 10 provides representative histological images of gastrocnemius muscle from the 20 experimental groups composed by males.

3.8. Histological Evaluation of Adipose Tissue

To further evaluate the effects of training exercise and ergogenic extracts on adipose tissue of SHAM and castrated animals, a histological evaluation of iWAT was carried out. The assessment of average size of adipocytes did not show any significant difference when SHAM and OVX females were compared, despite a partial reduction of adipocyte diameter in mice submitted to exercise plus treatments with isolated or combined extracts (Figure 11A). Moreover, no significant differences were observed among the experimental groups, when the frequency size of adipocyte areas were evaluated separately, in either SHAM or OVX mice (Figure 11B). Representative histological images of all 20 experimental groups composed by females are depicted in Figure 12A–T. For males, there were no differences of total adipocyte areas when comparing SHAM with ORX mice, sedentary or submitted to exercise, that had been treated with saline or herbal extracts (Figure 11C). A comparison of the frequency size of adipocytes from the same experimental groups did not show any significant difference (Figure 11D). Histological images of iWAT of male mice (SHAM or ORX) are shown in Figure 13A–T.

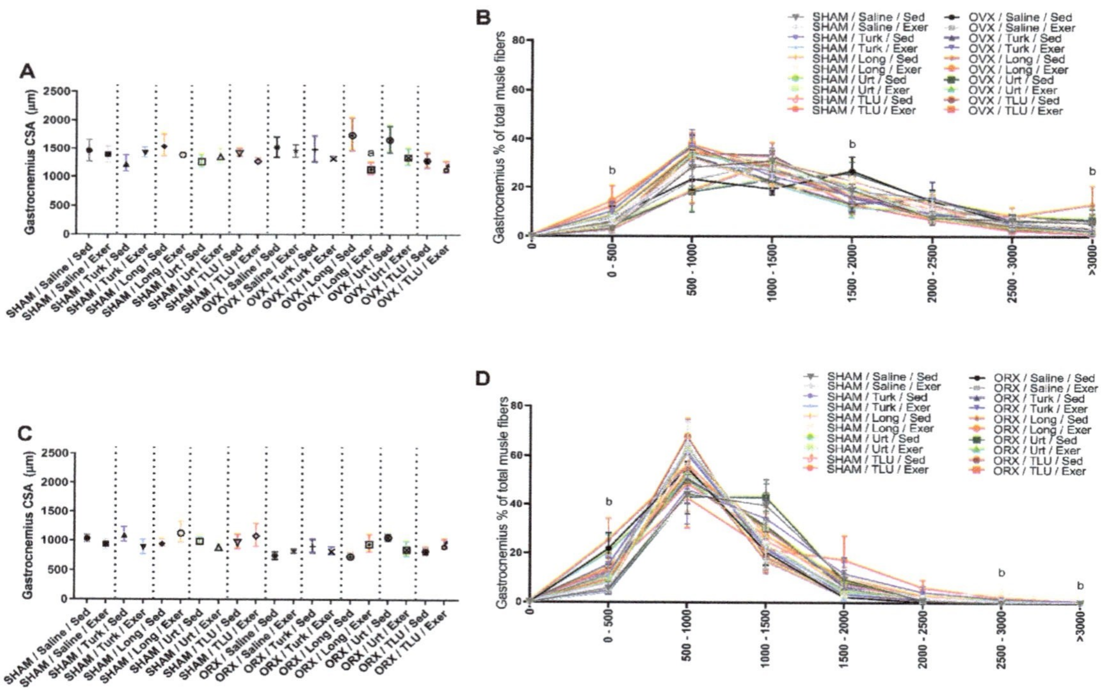

Figure 8. Average of gastrocnemius cross-sectional area of female (**A**) and male mice (**C**) castrated and sham-operated in the different treatment groups. The gastrocnemius fiber size frequency distribution of female (**B**) and male mice (**D**) castrated and sham-operated in the different treatment groups. SHAM, sham-operated; OVX, ovariectomized; ORX, orchiectomized; Sed, sedentary; Exer, Exercise; Turk, Ajuga turkestanica; Long, Eurycoma longifolia; Urt, Urtica dioica; TLU, the association of the three extracts. Results are the mean ± SEM of 5 animals per group. [a] $p < 0.05$ significantly different compared to respective sedentary treatment. [b] $p < 0.05$ when comparing the groups in each area range. (One-way ANOVA followed by Sidak post hoc test.)

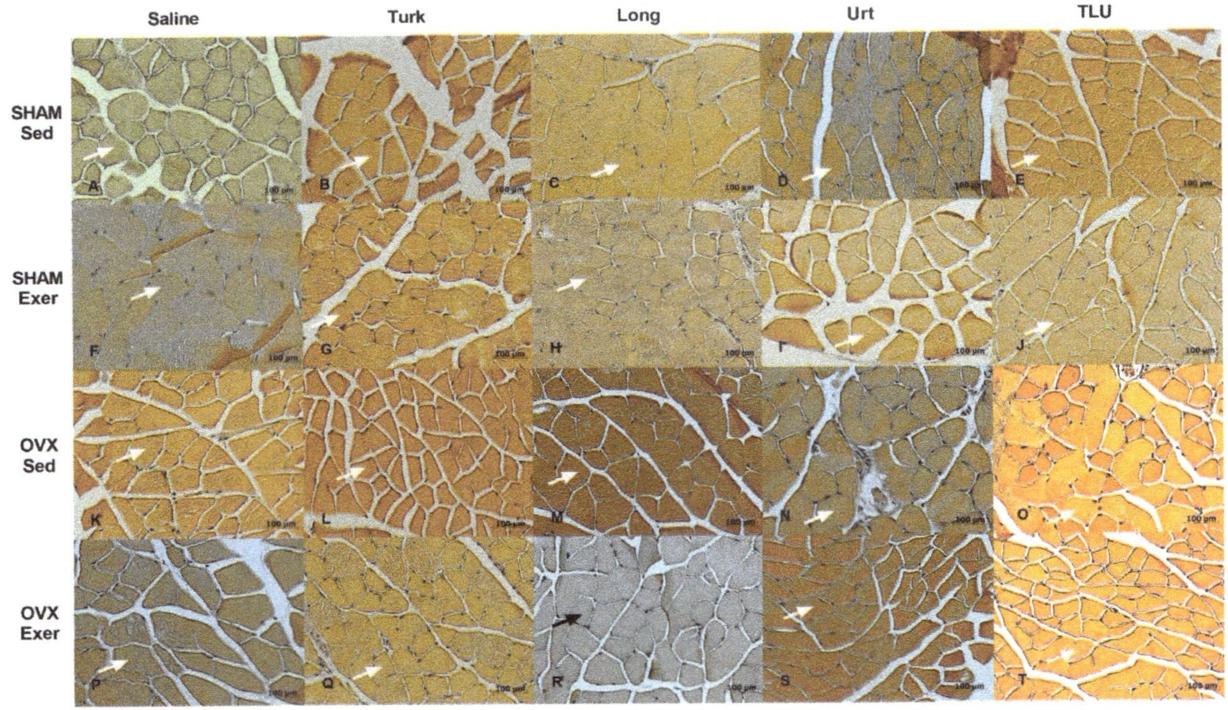

Figure 9. Representative histological images of gastrocnemius of sham-operated mice, sedentary or submitted to exercise, treated with saline (**A**,**F**), Turk 50 mg/kg (**B**,**G**), Long 200 mg/kg (**C**,**H**), Urt 50 mg/kg (**D**,**I**) or the combination of the three extracts TLU (**E**,**J**). Representative histological images of gastrocnemius of ovariectomized mice, sedentary or submitted to exercise, treated with saline (**K**,**P**), Turk 50 mg/kg (**L**,**Q**), Long 200 mg/kg (**M**,**R**), Urt 50 mg/kg (**N**,**S**) and combination of three extracts TLU (**O**,**T**). White arrow indicates gastrocnemius muscle fiber and black arrow indicates gastrocnemius muscle fiber in the group that showed a significant difference of cross-sectional areas (CSA). Turk, *Ajuga turkestanica*; Long, *Eurycoma longifolia*; Urt, *Urtica dioica*; TLU, the association of the three extracts.

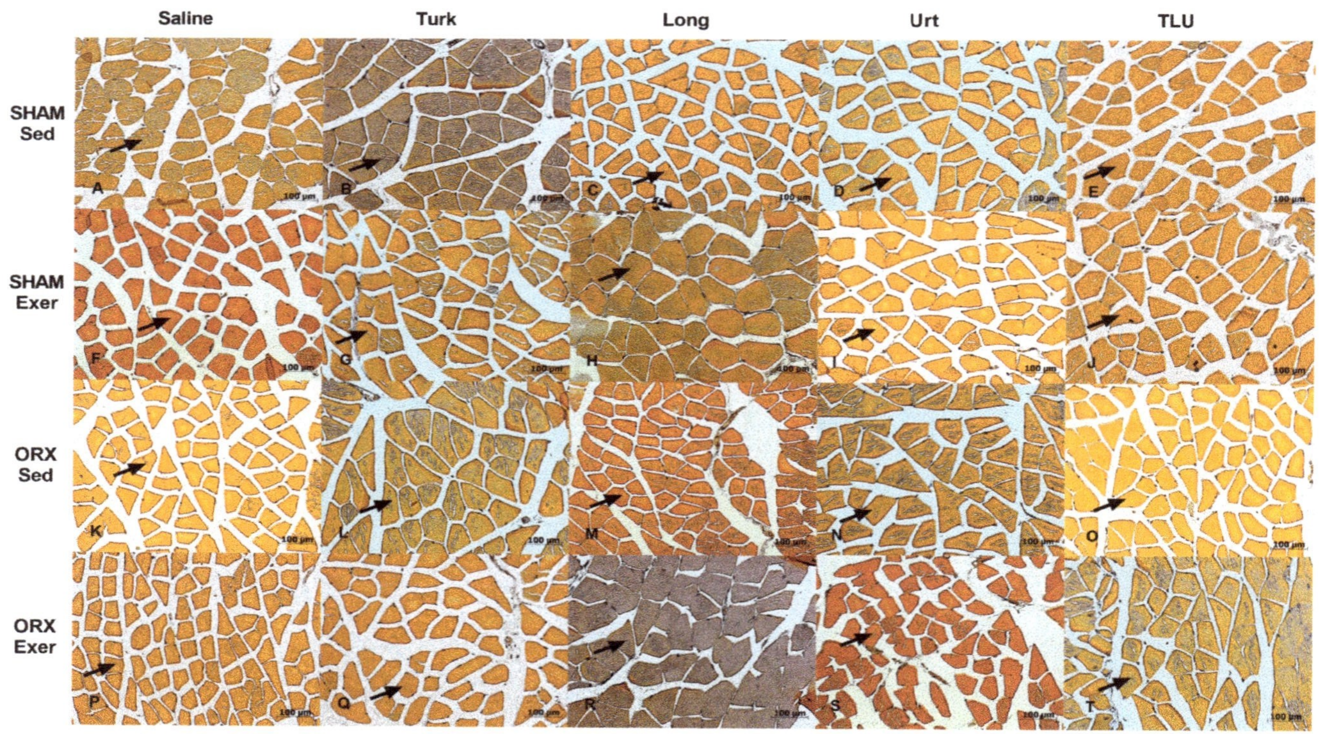

Figure 10. Representative histological images of gastrocnemius of sham-operated mice, sedentary or submitted to exercise, treated with saline (**A**,**F**), Turk 50 mg/kg (**B**,**G**), Long 200 mg/kg (**C**,**H**), Urt 50 mg/kg (**D**,**I**) or the combination of the three extracts TLU (**E**,**J**). Representative histological images of gastrocnemius of orchiectomized mice, sedentary or submitted to exercise, treated with saline (**K**,**P**), Turk 50 mg/kg (**L**,**Q**), Long 200 mg/kg (**M**,**R**), Urt 50 mg/kg (**N**,**S**) and combination of three extracts TLU (**O**,**T**). Black arrow indicates gastrocnemius muscle fiber. Turk, Ajuga turkestanica; Long, Eurycoma longifolia; Urt, Urtica dioica; TLU, the association of the three extracts.

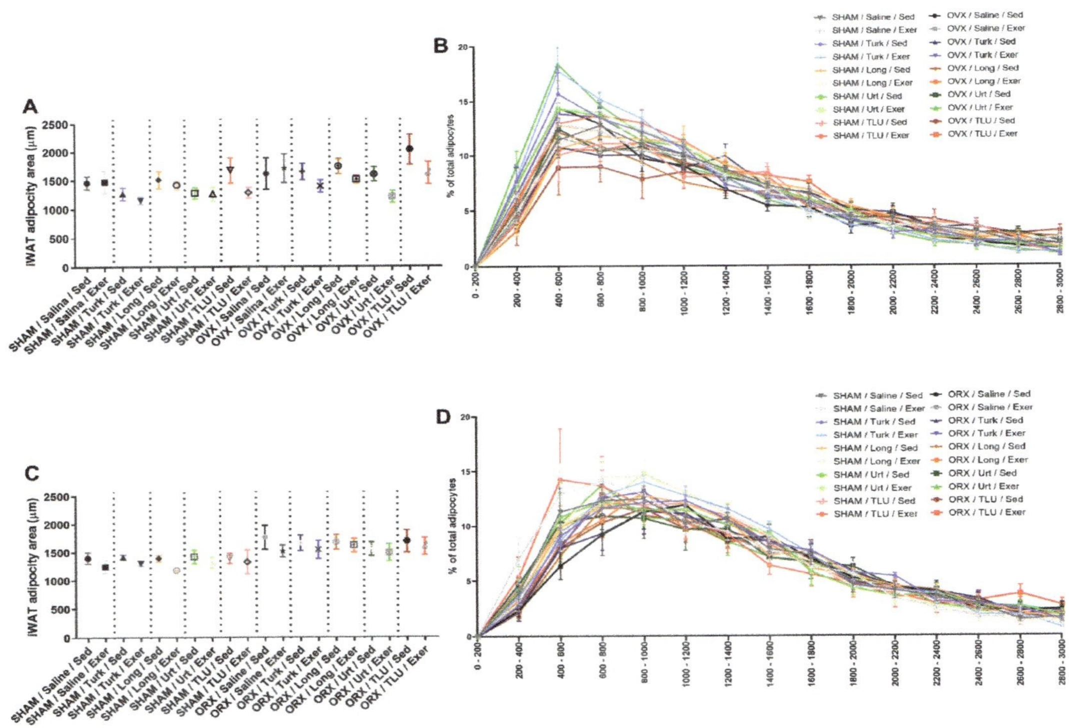

Figure 11. Average adipocyte cross-sectional area from inguinal white adipose tissue of female (**A**) and male mice (**C**) castrated or sham-operated in the different treatment groups. Adipocyte relative frequency area from inguinal white adipose tissue of female (**B**) and male mice (**D**), castrated and sham-operated, in the different treatment groups. SHAM, sham-operated; OVX, ovariectomized; ORX, orchiectomized; Sed, sedentary; Exer, Exercise; Turk, *Ajuga turkestanica*; Long, *Eurycoma longifolia*; Urt, *Urtica dioica*; TLU, the association of the three extracts. Results are the mean ± SEM of n = 5 to 7 animals per group (One-way ANOVA followed by Sidak post hoc test).

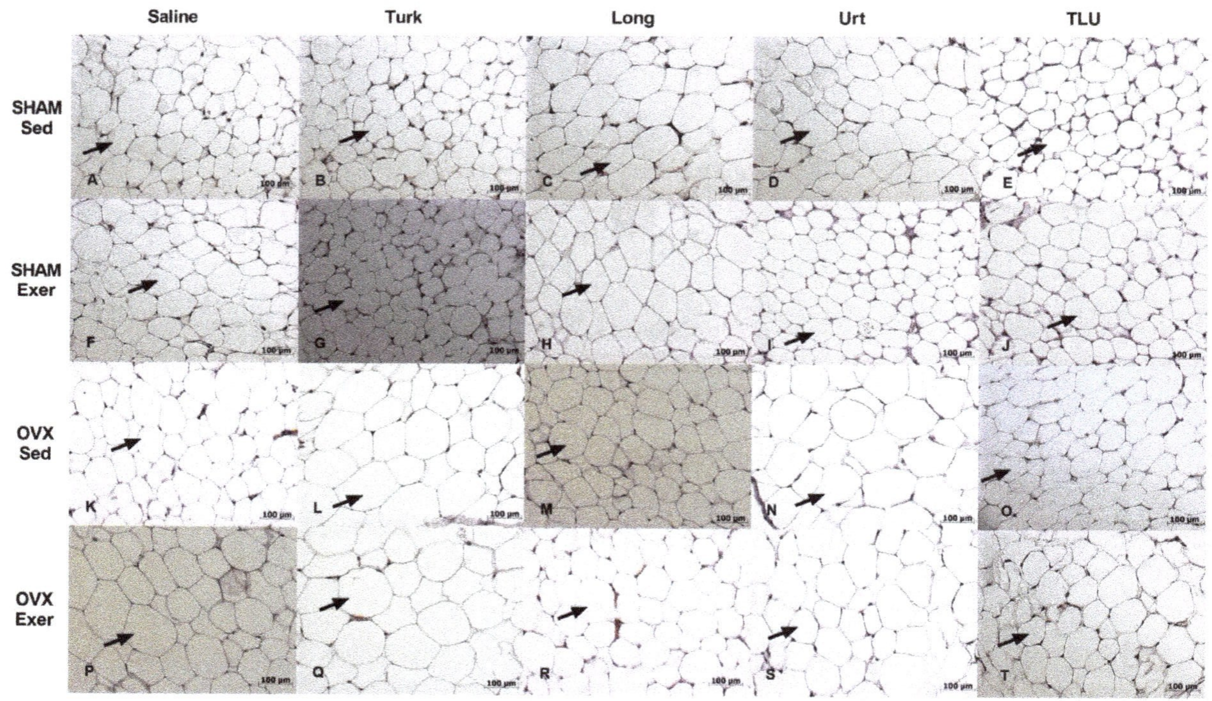

Figure 12. Representative histological images of adipocytes of inguinal white adipose tissue of sham-operated mice, sedentary or submitted to exercise, treated with saline (**A**,**F**), Turk 50 mg/kg (**B**,**G**), Long 200 mg/kg (**C**,**H**), Urt 50 mg/kg (**D**,**I**) or the combination of the three extracts TLU (**E**,**J**). Representative histological images of adipocytes inguinal white adipose tissue of ovariectomized mice, sedentary or submitted to exercise, treated with saline (**K**,**P**), Turk 50 mg/kg (**L**,**Q**), Long 200 mg/kg (**M**,**R**), Urt 50 mg/kg (**N**,**S**) and combination of three extracts TLU (**O**,**T**). Black arrow indicates adipocyte cell. Turk, *Ajuga turkestanica;* Long, *Eurycoma longifolia;* Urt, *Urtica dioica;* TLU, the association of the three extracts.

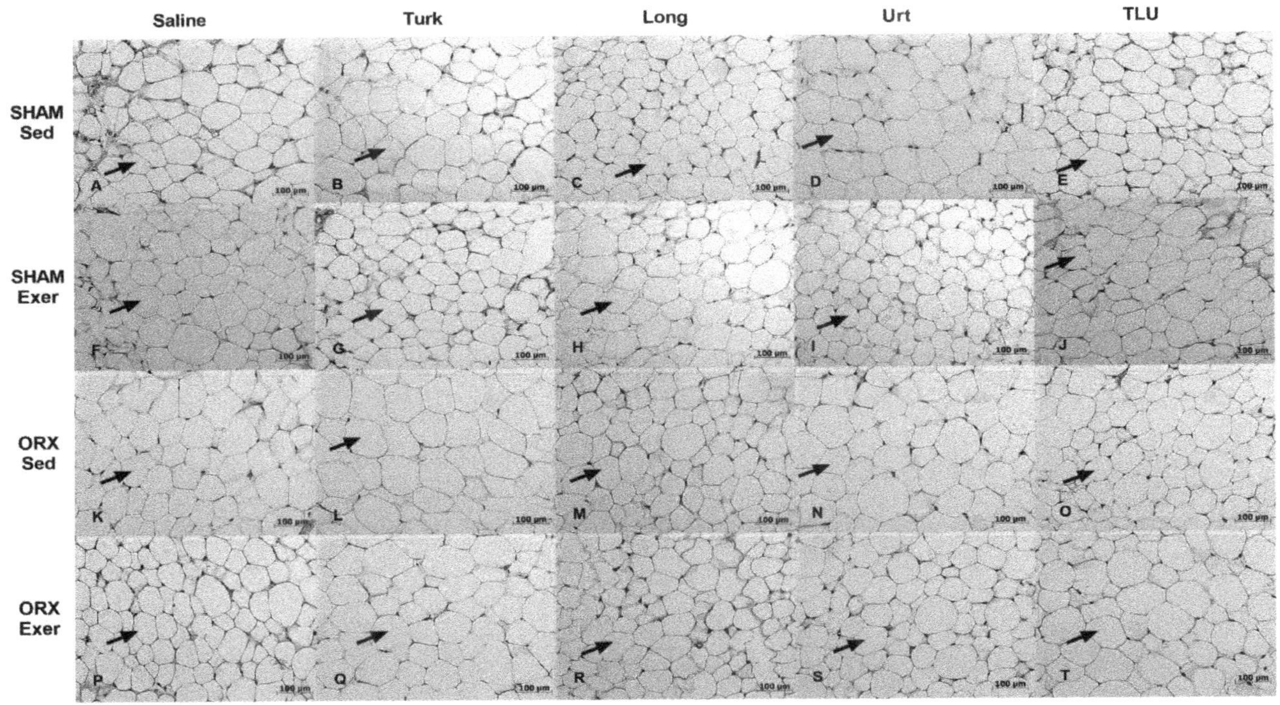

Figure 13. Representative histological images of adipocytes inguinal white adipose tissue of sham-operated mice, sedentary or submitted to exercise, treated with saline (**A**,**F**), Turk 50 mg/kg (**B**,**G**), Long 200 mg/kg (**C**,**H**), Urt 50 mg/kg (**D**,**I**) or the combination of the three extracts TLU (**E**,**J**). Representative histological images of adipocytes inguinal white adipose tissue of orchiectomized mice, sedentary or submitted to exercise, treated with saline (**K**,**P**), Turk 50 mg/kg (**L**,**Q**), Long 200 mg/kg (**M**,**R**), Urt 50 mg/kg (**N**,**S**) and combination of three extracts TLU (**O**,**T**). Black arrow indicates adipocyte cell. Turk, *Ajuga turkestanica;* Long, *Eurycoma longifolia;* Urt, *Urtica dioica;* TLU, the association of the three extracts.

3.9. Evaluation of Changes in Weights of Kidney, Liver, Brain and Bone

The weight of liver and kidneys was assessed as an indicative of possible toxicity of herbal extracts, or as a consequence of castration or resistance exercise. The training exercise led to a significant reduction of kidney wet weight, in comparison with saline-treated sedentary SHAM females. A significant decrease of kidney weight was also observed in sedentary OVX mice that received *A. turkestanica* extract, or in OVX mice submitted to exercise plus treatment with one of the extracts: *A. turkestanica, E. longifolia* or *U. dioica*, dosed isolated. The liver weight was increased in OVX mice that received *A. turkestanica* as supplementation, irrespective of climbing exercise. Brain and femur bone weights were also assessed, but no significant differences were detected when comparing the different female experimental groups (Supplementary Table S1). For males, a significant reduction of kidney and liver weights was observed in saline-treated sedentary ORX mice, when compared with SHAM-matched controls. A trend for a decrease of liver and kidney wet weights was seen in every ORX experimental group, independent on the exercise or treatment. As for femur bones and brain, no significant differences were seen regarding the male groups (Supplementary Table S2).

3.10. Biochemical and Inflammatory Parameters

In this part of the study, only saline- or TLU-treated animals distributed in the different experimental groups regarding castration and/or exercise were tested. Castrated females showed an elevation of total and non-HDL cholesterol serum levels. These alterations returned to values seen in saline-treated sedentary SHAM controls, when OVX mice were submitted to resistance exercise, regardless of treatment with TLU. The supplementation with TLU displayed a similar effect in sedentary OVX mice, restoring the total and non-HDL cholesterol levels. The serum levels of triglycerides, TGO or TGP did not significantly differ among the experimental groups composed by females (Table 3). In males, serum cholesterol (total, HDL or non-HDL), triglycerides, TGO or TGP did not present significant differences when comparing SHAM and ORX mice, sedentary or submitted to training exercise, despite the treatment with phytotherapics (Table 4). The pro-inflammatory IL-1β and TNF or the anti-inflammatory IL-10 cytokines were not detected in the gastrocnemius muscle of any experimental group of females or males (Tables 3 and 4).

Table 3. Combined effects of ergogenic extracts and exercise on biochemical and inflammatory parameters sham-operated and ovariectomized mice.

	SHAM				OVX			
	Saline/Sed	**Saline/Exer**	**TLU/Sed**	**TLU/Exer**	**Saline/Sed**	**Saline/Exer**	**TLU/Sed**	**TLU/Exer**
Cholesterol (mg/dL)	76.7 ± 8.2	87.7 ± 5.2	79.2 ± 4.4	83.3 ± 9.3	100.0 ± 6.7	85.12 ± 11.16	89.1 ± 3.2	87.1 ± 4.9
HDL (mg/dL)	51.5 ± 5.2	56.3 ± 4.3	48.7 ± 2.8	58.99 ± 2.1	59.0 ± 3.8	58.2 ± 5.7	57.5 ± 3.0	55.3 ± 3.8
Non-HDL (mg/dL)	30.4 ± 4.5	31.5 ± 2.3	30.5 ± 2.1	36.9 ± 3.6	41.0 ± 3.2 [a]	35.1 ± 2.2	31.6 ± 2.2	31.8 ± 1.8
Triglycerides (mg/DL)	67.4 ± 7.3	66.1 ± 2.2	62.2 ± 6.1	74.9 ± 5.2	74.2 ± 5.7	70.8 ± 7.5	66.0 ± 8.2	70.4 ± 5.8
TGO (U/L)	56.5 ± 14.0	61.9 ± 13.8	48.9 ± 7.9	53.6 ± 9.5	60.9 ± 12.3	63.8 ± 7.8	44.4 ± 10.4	54.8 ±13.8
TGP (U/L)	32.6 ± 3.0	58.1 ± 17.6	38.3 ± 8.2	45.3 ± 10.2	57.1 ± 5.2	39.8 ± 11.8	31.2 ± 6.7	21.6 ± 18.7
IL-1β	ND	ND	ND	ND	ND	ND	ND	ND
TNF	ND	ND	ND	ND	ND	ND	ND	ND
IL-10	ND	ND	ND	ND	ND	ND	ND	ND

SHAM, sham-operated; OVX, ovariectomized; Sed, sedentary; Exer, Exercise; Turk, Ajuga turkestanica; Long, Eurycoma longifolia; Urt, Urtica dioica; TLU, the association of the three extracts. Results are the mean ± SEM of 10 to 12 animals per group. [a] $p < 0.05$ significantly different compared with the sham-operated group treated with saline. One-way ANOVA followed by Sidak post hoc test.

Table 4. Combined effects of ergogenic extracts and exercise on biochemical and inflammatory parameters sham-operated and orchiectomized mice.

	SHAM				ORX			
	Saline/Sed	**Saline/Exer**	**TLU/Sed**	**TLU/Exer**	**Saline/Sed**	**Saline/Exer**	**TLU/Sed**	**TLU/Exer**
Cholesterol (mg/dL)	103.0 ± 7.0	109.3 ± 11.2	91.9 ± 4.4	89.4 ± 5.2	106.1 ± 8.8	96.2 ± 10.1	99.2 ± 1.9	99.4 ± 6.4
HDL (mg/dL)	69.9 ± 7.5	71.2 ± 5.8	55.0 ± 3.4	61.0 ± 6.3	62.7 ± 5.0	64.0 ± 5.8	64.6 ± 5.0	67.0 ± 4.5
Non-HDL (mg/dL)	33.1 ± 2.2	24.6 ± 2.1	36.9 ± 4.1	28.4 ± 5.6	43.4 ± 6.5	32.3 ± 5.8	34.5 ± 5.5	32.4 ± 4.4
Triglycerides (mg/DL)	103.9 ± 1.5	104.5 ± 5.2	107.4 ± 19.1	102.3 ± 10.6	98.1 ± 12.7	93.74 ± 12.12	112.1 ± 15.3	106.9 ± 13.8
TGO (U/L)	101.2 ± 11.5	78.8 ± 9.1	118.0 ± 10.4	86.8 ± 12.3	90.3 ± 19.8	84.0 ± 14.3	95.2 ± 17.3	64.0 ± 9.5
TGP (U/L)	53.0 ± 10.9	48.5 ± 6.9	35.2 ± 4.3	38.8 ± 4.5	35.33 ± 4.9	37.5 ± 7.1	38.4 ± 9.1	37.6 ± 4.7
IL-1β	ND	ND	ND	ND	ND	ND	ND	ND
TNF	ND	ND	ND	ND	ND	ND	ND	ND
IL-10	ND	ND	ND	ND	ND	ND	ND	ND

SHAM, sham-operated; ORX, orchiectomized; Sed, sedentary; Exer, Exercise; Turk, Ajuga turkestanica; Long, Eurycoma longifolia; Urt, Urtica dioica; TLU, the association of the three extracts. Results are the mean ± SEM of 10 to 12 animals per group. One-way ANOVA followed by Sidak post hoc test.

4. Discussion

In this study, we investigated the anabolic effects of *A. turkestanica*, *E. Longifolia*, and *U. dioica* extracts, administered for two months along with a protocol of resistance exercise, in castrated female and male mice. Hormonal balance is an important factor for maintaining homeostasis, and endocrine alterations can lead to disease development. Indeed, OVX and ORX have been used as rodent models for inducing sarcopenia, due to reduced levels of estrogen and testosterone, respectively [16,39–42]. In our study, according to that described previously in the literature, OVX led to an increase in body weight gain [63,64]. Even so, ORX promoted a reduction in body weight, accompanied by a decline in muscle mass and accumulation of subcutaneous fat [65,66]. Regarding the tested herbal extracts and the combination of exercise, the main findings show that: (i) the supplementation with *A. turkestanica* associated with exercise recovered the locomotor activity in OVX animals, while in sham females it showed benefits on muscle strength. (ii) In male ORX animals, *A. turkestanica* improved the muscle strength regardless of exercise, whereas the association of the extract with exercise reduced the time to ladder climbing. (iii) *E. longifolia* associated with exercise showed benefits regarding body composition, with an increase in the frequency of larger muscle fibers and a marked reduction in inguinal fat in ORX mice. Additionally, it increased the muscle strength, and the distance and speed covered, besides a reduction in the time to climb the ladder. (iv) The association of *U. dioica* with exercise reduced the final weight in OVX mice. It also increased the travelled distance and speed. (v) In ORX animals, the supplementation with *U. dioica* associated with exercise increased the percentage of muscle mass over total weight, with a reduction in inguinal adiposity. An increase in locomotor activity was also observed. (vi) TLU combined with exercise, in OVX animals, increased the voluntary locomotor activity and the time until fatigue. Furthermore, there was a reduction in non-HDL cholesterol independent on exercise. (vii) Finally, in ORX animals, TLU plus exercise reduced the time to climb the ladder and increased the muscle strength. Collectively, the present data suggests that the tested ergogenic extracts, mainly when combined with resistance exercise, improved sarcopenia alterations associated with hormonal decline, with different profiles in female and male mice.

The prophylactic or therapeutic benefits of physical activity on sarcopenia has been widely demonstrated in the literature. Several variables in the exercise protocol can interfere with the desired effect, such as type, time, frequency and intensity [67]. As described by Beckwée et al. [8], resistance exercise, performed with the use of weights, has positive results in the management of sarcopenia and has been widely indicated for sarcopenic patients [8]. In animal models, the replication of this type of exercise is complex; however, some studies proposed the use of ladder climbing associated with draping of weights in the tail, as a good alternative to reproduce resistance exercise in rodents [67]. Some studies described hypertrophy of the soleus plantaris extensor digitorum longus (EDL) and anterior tibialis muscles, considering their high recruitment in the climbing movement [68]. In our study, the resistance training exercise did not induce muscle hypertrophy in female or male SHAM mice, according to the evaluation of gastrocnemius, tibial, or soleus muscles. Corroborating our data, it was demonstrated that ladder climbing exercise led to hypertrophy of the flexor hallucis longus (FHL), without any effects on gastrocnemius or soleus muscles [69]. A possible explanation for the absence of hypertrophy is that climbing exercise primarily involves concentric, but not eccentric muscle actions, with slight or no muscle mass gain [69,70]. However, the protocol of exercise adopted by us led to increased travelled distance and speed in either female or male SHAM animals, showing its effectiveness to improve physical function, despite the absence of hypertrophy.

Considering the body composition of castrated animals, climbing exercise triggered a reduction of body weight gain in OVX mice, without changes in skeletal muscle or fat mass. In females, estrogen displays a protective role in muscle integrity and function [40]. The reduction of estrogen levels in OVX mice might preclude the effects of exercise in promoting muscle mass gain, despite the overall reduction in body weight. Accordingly, Bunratsami et al. [71] showed a slight reduction of EDL muscle weight in OVX rats, without any change in gastrocnemius—in this case, only a high dose of estrogen was able to induce muscle hypertrophy. The authors also showed that OVX led to a downregulation of ER-α and ER-β receptors in skeletal muscles [71], reinforcing the relevance of estrogen-related pathways for muscle mass gain. As for ORX males, we observed that climbing exercise potentiated the body weight decrease elicited by castration, partly by diminishing the accumulation of iWAT, without any effects on skeletal muscle weights. It has been suggested that low levels of testosterone might be associated with anabolic resistance in aged mice, impacting the muscle responsiveness to exercise, regardless of the benefits on physical function [72]. In OVX and ORX, the resistance exercise also led to improvements of functional parameters, such as muscle strength, resistance to fatigue and physical activity as seen in SHAM animals, but in this case when combined with the tested anabolic extracts. These details will be discussed for each of the three extracts in separated sections.

As a first approach, we decided to analyze the contents of the active compounds in the lyophilized extracts used in the present study. The presence of ecdysteroids, such as turkesterone and β-sitosterol, as well as eurycomanone and other quassinoids in herbal extracts, have been analyzed by using methanol for sample extraction, as it was used in the present study [73–76]. The initial screening was performed spectrophotometrically, and the identification of active compounds was carried out by LC-MS, and quantified by LC-UV [77], using HDL-cholesterol as standard [78]. The presence of turkesterone (m/z 497.0 > 443.0 and m/z 497.0 > 461.0), eurycomanone (m/z 391.5 > 251.1 and 391.5 > 279.1), and β-sitosterol (m/z 397.0 > 81.0 and 397.0 > 95.0) was confirmed by mass spectrometry, in lyophilized extracts of *A. turkestanica*, *E. longifolia*, and *U. dioica*, respectively, based on transitions previously described in literature [79–81]. Therefore, the lyophilized extracts used in our study contained the corresponding active compounds as described by the commercial supplier.

High doses of the ecdysteroid 20-HE were able to increase the muscle mass and to diminish fat depots in OVX rats, with beneficial effects on lipid metabolism [82]. In our study, the supplementation with *A. turkestanica* in sedentary OVX mice led to reduction of gastrocnemius weight, with an increased frequency of fibers with a small diameter, contrasting somewhat with literature data. However, hormone therapy in women is not likely related to an improvement in muscle mass, despite an increase in muscle strength after estrogen replacement [83,84]. In fact, in the present study, the administration of *A. turkestanica* potentiated the effects of exercise on physical activity in OVX mice, as indicated by a recovery of travelled distance and speed, what might suggest estrogen-related actions for this extract on muscle function. Our suggestion is reinforced by data showing benefits for *A. turkestanica* extract in SHAM females submitted to training exercise, regarding an increase of grip strength.

About the effects of ecdysteroids in males, it was demonstrated that ecdysterone triggers muscle hypertrophy via the activation of ER-β, without any involvement of androgen receptors [85]. Strikingly, estrogen supplementation was demonstrated to revert disuse-related muscle dystrophy in male rodents [86]. In addition, some of the effects previously attributed to testosterone have been currently linked to estrogens, and there is a positive correlation between estrogen levels and muscle strength preservation in men [87]. In our study, the treatment with *A. turkestanica* extract significantly improved the grip strength of ORX mice, independent on training exercise. Moreover, in ORX mice, the supplementation with *A. turkestanica* extract partially restored the time to perform the ladder climbing task, despite the absence of any effect on wet weight of gastrocnemius, tibial or soleus. From this series of results, it is possible to suggest that *A. turkestanica* extract plus resistance exercise differently impacted the muscle function of OVX and ORX mice, mostly favoring increased physical activity in castrated females, whereas it improved muscle strength and force in ORX males.

The effects of standardized extract of *E. longifolia* have been studied in animals and in humans, displaying a positive modulation on testosterone levels [27,28]. In ORX mice, resistance exercise plus *E. longifolia* extract supplementation showed significantly beneficial effects regarding the body composition, with an increase in the frequency of larger muscle fibers, and a marked reduction of iWAT. Supporting our data, *E. longifolia* extract presented antiadipogenic actions, via reduction of PPARγ and C/EBPα expression in the early stage of preadipocyte differentiation in vitro, an effect that was confirmed in vivo in mice [24]. The combination of exercise with *E. longifolia* supplementation also improved the functional performance of ORX mice, by increasing the grip strength and improving travelled distance and speed, with a marked reduction of time necessary to complete the ladder climbing. In SHAM males, only travelled distance and speed were improved by this strategy. It is reasonable to correlate the present findings with the beneficial effects of *E. longifolia* extract on hypogonadism. Accordingly, the active compounds of *E. longifolia*, named eurypeptide and eurycomanone, were able to modulate the biosynthesis of androgens and to reduce testosterone degradation by aromatase inhibition, respectively [27,28,54,88].

A previous publication showed that treatment with *E. longifolia* herbal extract increased the levels of progesterone and estrogen, with mild effects on bone metabolism and testosterone levels, according to the evaluation of OVX rats [27]. In our study, the supplementation with *E. longifolia* extract led to a significant increase of larger muscle fibers in sedentary OVX mice, whereas it increased the frequency of small fibers in OVX mice that had been submitted to exercise training. As for physical aspects, *E. longifolia* plus exercise failed to improve the travelled distance and speed in OVX females and impaired the resistance to fatigue in the rotarod test. The divergent effects of *E. longifolia* extract in castrated males and females might be partly explained by the sex-related differences concerning the responses of skeletal muscles cells to testosterone, with a higher sensitivity for males [86].

A very few studies have investigated the actions of *U. dioica* extract in physical function, and as far we know, there is no previous investigation regarding its effects in sarcopenia. Indeed, its main application is related to treatment of benign prostatic hyperplasia. In addition, some studies have described benefits for *U. dioica* extract for management of diabetes complications [34,57,89]. More recently, it was demonstrated that supplementation with plain *U. dioica* led to body weight loss in mice that received a high-fat diet, via modulation of genes related to lipid and glucose metabolism [33]. In our study, the association of exercise with *U. dioica* extract significantly reduced the final body weight in OVX mice, and also improved the travelled distance and speed in an open arena. Favorable effects for *U. dioica* plus exercise on physical activity were also observed in SHAM females.

Conversely, Namjou and collaborators previously described that consumption of *U. dicoica* extract had clear benefits on lipid profile in OVX rats, but not in SHAM controls [90].

In ORX mice, exercise combined with *U. dioica* was able to significantly increase the muscle weight over total body weight, with a reduction of abdominal adiposity, besides an improvement of locomotor activity. Alternatively, this intervention had minimal effects in SHAM males. It was demonstrated that *U. dioica* extract had inhibitory effects on 5α-reductase, the enzyme responsible for the conversion of testosterone in dihydrotestosterone, increasing the serum testosterone levels, without affecting the prostate weight [34]. The raise of free testosterone might explain the elevation in muscle percentage in ORX mice, that had been submitted to exercise plus *U. dicoica* supplementation.

It is well known that andropause and menopause can impact several organs [91]. Additionally, some plant extracts are known by their toxic effects on these organs [92]. Hence, the wet weights of kidneys, liver, femur bone and brain were determined in the different experimental groups of males and females. It was possible to observe that *A. turkestanica* extract reduced kidney weight, while it increased liver mass, according to assessment of sedentary or trained OVX mice. Noteworthy, protective effects for ecdysteroid compounds have been suggested before in models of liver or kidney toxicity [93]. Indeed, estrogen deficiency has been associated with hepatic steatosis [94], and turkesterone-enriched *A. turkestanica* extract might present favorable effects on this condition. For males, ORX led to a reduction of liver and kidney mass, without any effects for exercise and herbal extracts. A previous publication demonstrated that ORX induced a significant decrease of kidney weight, with a slight reduction of liver mass, in mice receiving a standard chow diet [95], supporting somewhat the present data. Overall, castration, exercise, and herbal supplementation had minor effects on organ weights and on most biochemical markers that had been analyzed, suggesting low toxicity levels.

The association of the three extracts was thought to present complementary mechanisms that could generate greater benefits in reversing sarcopenia, as described in folk medicine. In our study, TLU, in combination with resistance exercise, significantly increased the voluntary locomotor activity, and improved resistance to fatigue in OVX mice. Additionally, TLU supplementation recovered the time necessary for ladder climbing and improved the grip strength in ORX mice. Nonetheless, TLU failed to alter some of the tested body composition parameters and physical function, possibly due to the antagonistic effects of the associated extracts, as discussed beforehand.

To gain further insights into the effects of resistance exercise and TLU in castrated mice, we analyzed the serum lipids, triglycerides, besides the markers of tissue damage, namely TGO and TGP. The results did not show any variation of the analyzed biomarkers, except by an increase of total cholesterol and non-HDL cholesterol in saline-treated sedentary OVX mice. A similar alteration of cholesterol levels has been demonstrated before in OVX rats [96]. Of note, both climbing exercise and TLU supplementation, implemented alone or in combination, restored the total and non-HDL cholesterol to the levels seen in SHAM females counterparts. Based on this result, it is time to infer that exercise combined with TLU herbal therapy might also be useful for management of cardiovascular alterations in menopause, besides improving physical performance.

Either inflammatory cytokines, including TNF and IL-1β, or anti-inflammatory cytokines such as IL-10 have been implicated in sarcopenia-related frailty in humans and rodents [97]. Thus, we investigated whether the experimental interventions tested in the present study might modulate the levels of these cytokines in gastrocnemius. Any of the cytokines were undetectable in SHAM, OVX, or ORX groups, irrespective of exercise or TLU supplementation. It is possible to suggest that gains in physical activity or muscle strength observed for the combined intervention with exercise plus extracts did not rely on the modulation of inflammatory markers in skeletal muscle. Further studies are required to assess other inflammatory markers and different biological matrices.

5. Conclusions

In this study, using castrated mice, we showed that phytoanabolic extracts of the Eurasian plants *A. turkestanica*, *E. longifolia*, and *U. dioica*, or TLU, differently modulated several parameters related to hormone reduction, such as muscle mass, adiposity, muscle strength, fatigue, general locomotor activity, and lipid profile. These effects were evident when isolated or associated extracts were supplemented in combination with a training exercise protocol. In Figure 14, we provide a schematic illustration about the effects of the tested interventions on body weight variation and summed weight of skeletal muscles (gastrocnemius, soleus and tibial). In saline-treated SHAM males and females and OVX mice, it is possible to observe a trend for reduction in muscle weight, accompanied by a reduction of body weight gain, when the animals were submitted to the ladder climbing exercise. In ORX males, this profile changed, with an inverse effect for exercise on muscle mass and body weight gain. Concerning the supplementation with herbal extracts, *A. turkestanica*, *U. dioica* or TLU changed the profile of body weight gain and skeletal muscle mass in OVX mice. In ORX mice, all of the tested herbal extracts changed the relation between the two parameters in comparison with saline treatment. For sham females and males, there was a change for *E. longifolia* or *A. turkestanica* extracts, respectively. With this, it is possible to identify the importance of the association of exercise with the administration of the extracts considering the management of sarcopenia in menopause and andropause.

Considering the results presented and discussed, we highlight some important points that we identified in our study. *A. turkestanica*, combined with exercise, has a different impact in muscle function of OVX and ORX mice and appears to show better results in ladder climbing speed and muscle strength in ORX mice compared to OVX mice. When evaluating *E. longifolia* plus exercise, it is possible to correlate the results with beneficial effects on hypogonadism. Few studies have investigated the actions of *U. dioica* extract on physical function and, as far as we know, there is no previous investigation on its effects on sarcopenia. With presented results we could mention that *U. dioica* associated with exercise can have beneficial effects on body composition in castrated males and females. Finally, when the association of the extracts was carried out, interestingly, we identified that some of the positive results of the extracts used isolated in the castrated animals were maintained, while the negative results of some of the extracts were mitigated in the association.

A

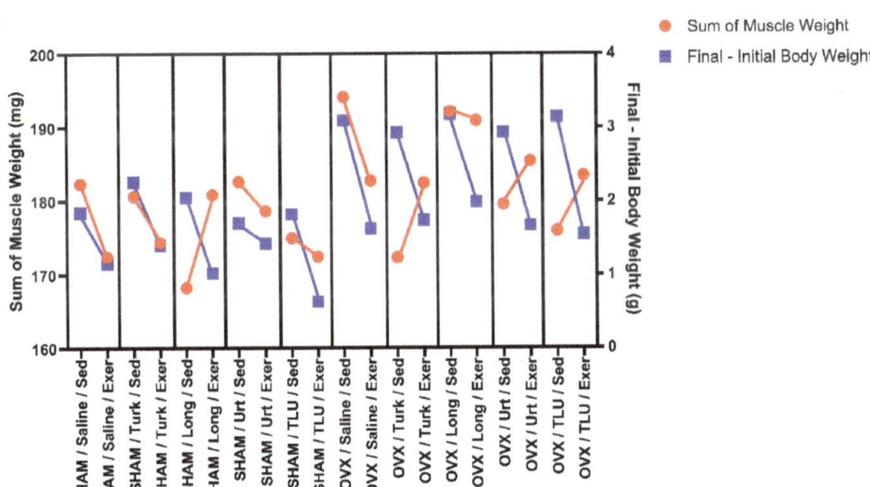

Figure 14. *Cont.*

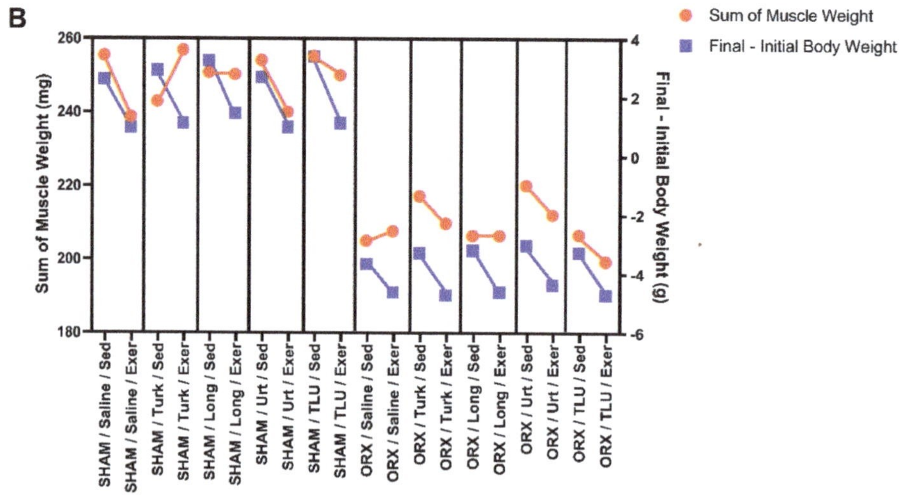

Figure 14. Scheme representing the body weight variation and the summed weight of the three muscles (gastrocnemius, tibial, and soleus) when the animals were submitted to the exercise protocol, in the different treatment groups with: saline, Turk, Long, Urt and TLU, in female sham-operated and ovariectomized mice (**A**) and male sham-operated and orchiectomized mice (**B**). SHAM, sham-operated; OVX, ovariectomized; ORX, orchiectomized; Sed, sedentary; Exer, Exercise; Turk, Ajuga turkestanica; Long, Eurycoma longifolia; Urt, Urtica dioica; TLU, the association of the three extracts.

Supplementary Materials: The following are available online at https://www.mdpi.com/article/10.3390/nu13041177/s1, Figure S1: Distribution of experimental cohorts, Figure S2: Timeline for main experimental procedures, Figure S3: Evaluation of resistance to fatigue in the Rota-rod apparatus in the different experimental groups, Figure S4: Assessment of spontaneous locomotor activity in the different experimental groups; Table S1: Effects of treatment with ergogenic extracts on the wet weight of kidney, liver, bone and brain of sham-operated or ovariectomized mice, Table S2: Effects of treatment with ergogenic extracts on the wet weight of kidney, liver, bone and brain of sham-operated or orchiectomized mice.

Author Contributions: J.P.M. and M.M.C. conceived and designed research; J.P.M., L.C.S., M.S.N., G.R., and R.B.M.S. performed experiments; J.P.M., J.R.O., R.B.M.S., and M.M.C. analyzed and interpreted results of experiments; J.P.M. prepared figures; J.P.M. and M.M.C. drafted manuscript; J.P.M., J.R.O., R.B.M.S., and M.M.C. revised and edited manuscript. All authors have read and agreed to the published version of the manuscript.

Funding: This work was supported by Coordenação de Aperfeiçoamento de Pessoal de Nível Superior (CAPES; Finance Code 001), Conselho Nacional de Desenvolvimento Científico e Tecnológico (CNPq), Fundação de Amparo à Pesquisa do Estado do Rio Grande do Sul (FAPERGS), and PUCRS. J.P.M. is a PhD student receiving scholarships from CAPES. L.C.S. and M.S.N. received grants for undergraduate students from CNPq and FAPERGS, respectively. R.B.M.S. is a recipient of pos-doctoral grants from CNPq (DTI-A). MMC and J.R.O. are researcher career awardees of CNPq.

Institutional Review Board Statement: The experimental protocols followed the current Brazilian guidelines for the care and use of animals for scientific and didactic procedures, from the National Council for the Control of Animal Experimentation (MCTI-CONCEA, and were approved by the local Animal Ethics Committee (CEUA/PUCRS 8045/17).

Informed Consent Statement: Not applicable.

Acknowledgments: We would like to thank Janaína Pasetti Nunes for her valuable technical assistance in histological processing.

Conflicts of Interest: The funders had no role in the design of the study; in the collection, analyses.

References

1. Morley, J.E. Hormones and Sarcopenia. *Curr. Pharm. Des.* **2017**, *23*, 4484–4492. [CrossRef] [PubMed]
2. Messier, V.; Rabasa-Lhoret, R.; Barbat-Artigas, S.; Elisha, B.; Karelis, A.D.; Aubertin-Leheudre, M. Menopause and sarcopenia: A potential role for sex hormones. *Maturitas* **2011**, *68*, 331–336. [CrossRef]
3. Urban, R.J.; Al, E.T. Translational studies in older men using testosterone to treat sarcopenia. *Trans. Am. Clin. Climatol. Assoc.* **2014**, *125*, 27–44. [PubMed]
4. Basualto-alarcón, C.; Varela, D.; Duran, J.; Maass, R.; Estrada, M. Sarcopenia and androgens: A link between pathology and treatment. *Front. Endocrinol.* **2014**, *5*, 217. [CrossRef]
5. Papadopoulou, S.K. Sarcopenia: A contemporary health problem among older adult populations. *Nutrients* **2020**, *12*, 1293. [CrossRef] [PubMed]
6. Cruz-Jentoft, A.J.; Bahat, G.; Bauer, J.; Boirie, Y.; Bruyère, O.; Cederholm, T.; Cooper, C.; Landi, F.; Rolland, Y.; Sayer, A.A.; et al. Sarcopenia: Revised European consensus on definition and diagnosis. *Age Ageing* **2019**, *48*, 16–31. [CrossRef] [PubMed]
7. Bowen, T.S.; Schuler, G.; Adams, V. Skeletal muscle wasting in cachexia and sarcopenia: Molecular pathophysiology and impact of exercise training. *J. Cachex Sarcopenia Muscle* **2015**, 197–207. [CrossRef] [PubMed]
8. Beckwée, D.; Delaere, A.; Aelbrecht, S.; Baert, B.; Beaudart, C.; Bruyere, O.; de Saint-Hubert, M.; Butmans, I. Exercise Interventions for the Prevention and Treatment of Sarcopenia. A Systematic Umbrella Review. *J. Nutr. Health Aging* **2019**, *23*, 494–502. [CrossRef]
9. Chisamore, M.J.; Gentile, M.A.; Dillon, G.M.; Baran, M.; Gambone, C.; Riley, S.; Schmidt, A.; Flores, O.; Wilkinson, H.; Alves, S.E. A novel selective androgen receptor modulator (SARM) MK-4541 exerts anti-androgenic activity in the prostate cancer xenograft R-3327G and anabolic activity on skeletal muscle mass & function in castrated mice. *J. Steroid Biochem. Mol. Biol.* **2016**, *163*, 88–97. [CrossRef]
10. Coss, C.C.; Jones, A.; Hancock, M.L.; Steiner, M.S.; Dalton, J.T. Selective androgen receptor modulators for the treatment of late onset male hypogonadism. *Asian J. Androl.* **2014**, 256–261. [CrossRef]
11. Sakuma, K.; Yamaguchi, A. Recent advances in pharmacological, hormonal, and nutritional intervention for sarcopenia. *Pflugers Arch. Eur. J. Physiol.* **2018**, *470*, 449–460. [CrossRef]
12. Teixeira, C.J.; Ribeiro, L.M.; Veras, K.; Araujo, L.C.; da Cunha Araujo, L.C.; Curi, R.; de Oliveira Carvalho, C.R. Dehydroepiandrosterone supplementation is not bene fi cial in the late postmenopausal period in diet-induced obese rats. *Life Sci.* **2018**, *202*, 110–116. [CrossRef]
13. Stacchiotti, A.; Favero, G.; Rodella, L.F. Impact of Melatonin on Skeletal Muscle and Exercise. *Cells* **2020**, *9*, 288. [CrossRef]
14. Tamaki, M.; Miyashita, K.; Hagiwara, A.; Wakino, S.; Inoue, H.; Fujii, K.; Fujii, C.; Endo, S.; Uto, A.; Mitsuishi, M.; et al. Ghrelin treatment improves physical decline in sarcopenia model mice through muscular enhancement and mitochondrial activation. *Endocr. J.* **2017**, *64*, S47–S51. [CrossRef]
15. Gagliano-Juca, T.; Basaria, S. Testosterone replacement therapy and cardiovascular risk. *Nat. Rev. Cardiol.* **2019**. [CrossRef]
16. Kathryn Korkidakis, A.; Reid, R.L. Testosterone in Women: Measurement and Therapeutic Use. *J. Obstet. Gynaecol. Can.* **2017**, *39*, 124–130. [CrossRef]
17. Rondanelli, M.; Miccono, A.; Peroni, G.; Guerriero, F.; Morazzoni, P.; Riva, A.; Guido, D.; Perna, S. A systematic review on the effects of botanicals on skeletal muscle health in order to prevent sarcopenia. *Evid. Based Complement. Altern. Med.* **2016**, *2016*. [CrossRef]
18. Liu, Y.; Weng, W.; Gao, R.; Liu, Y.; Monacelli, F. New Insights for Cellular and Molecular Mechanisms of Aging and Aging-Related Diseases: Herbal Medicine as Potential Therapeutic Approach. *Oxid. Med. Cell. Longev.* **2019**, *2019*. [CrossRef]
19. Luan, F.; Han, K.; Li, M.; Zhang, T.; Liu, D.; Yu, L.; Lv, H. Ethnomedicinal uses, phytochemistry, pharmacology, and toxicology of species from the genus ajuga L.: A systematic review. *Am. J. Chin. Med.* **2019**, *47*, 959–1003. [CrossRef]
20. Isenmann, E.; Ambrosio, G.; Felix, J.; Mazzarino, M.; De, X.; Zimmer, P.; Kazlauskas, R.; Goebel, C.; Botrè, F.; Diel, P.; et al. Ecdysteroids as non-conventional anabolic agent: Performance enhancement by ecdysterone supplementation in humans. *Arch. Toxicol.* **2019**, *93*, 1807–1816. [CrossRef]
21. Parr, M.K.; Ambrosio, G.; Wuest, B.; Mazzarino, M.; de la Torre, X.; Sibilia, F.; Joseph, J.F.; Diel, P.; Botrè, F. Targeting the administration of ecdysterone in doping control samples. *Forensic Toxicol.* **2020**, *38*, 172–184. [CrossRef]
22. Bhat, R.; Karim, A.A. Fitoterapia Tongkat Ali (*Eurycoma longifolia* Jack): A review on its ethnobotany and pharmacological importance. *Fitoterapia* **2010**, *81*, 669–679. [CrossRef]
23. Al-Salahi, O.; Kit-Lam, C.; Majid, A.; Al-Suede, F.; Mohammed Saghir, S.; Abdullah, W.; Ahamed, M.; Yusoff, N. Anti-angiogenic quassinoid-rich fraction from *Eurycoma longifolia* modulates endothelial cell function. *Microvasc. Res.* **2013**, *90*, 30–39. [CrossRef]
24. Balan, D.; Chan, K.; Murugan, D.; AbuBakar, S.; Wong, P. Antiadipogenic effects of a standardized quassinoids—Enriched fraction and eurycomanone from *Eurycoma longifolia*. *Phytother. Res.* **2018**, 1–14. [CrossRef]
25. George, A.; Suzuki, N.; Abas, A.B.; Mohri, K.; Utsuyama, M.; Hirokawa, K.; Takara, T. Immunomodulation in Middle-Aged Humans Via the Ingestion of Physta® Standardized Root Water Extract of *Eurycoma longifolia* Jack—A Parallel Study. *Phytother. Res.* **2016**, *635*, 627–635. [CrossRef] [PubMed]
26. Rehman, S.U.; Choe, K.; Yoo, H.H. Review on a traditional herbal medicine, *Eurycoma longifolia* Jack (Tongkat Ali): Its traditional uses, chemistry, evidence-based pharmacology and toxicology. *Molecules* **2016**, *21*, 331. [CrossRef]

27. Chinnappan, S.M.; George, A.; Ashok, G.; Choudhary, Y.K. Effect of herbal extract *Eurycoma longifolia* (Physta®) on female reproductive hormones and bone biochemical markers: An ovariectomised rat model study. *BMC Complement. Med. Ther.* **2020**, *20*, 1–9. [CrossRef]
28. Tambi, M.I.B.M.; Imran, M.K.; Henkel, R.R. Standardised water-soluble extract of *Eurycoma longifolia*, Tongkat ali, as testosterone booster for managing men with late-onset hypogonadism? *Andrologia* **2012**, *44*, 226–230. [CrossRef]
29. Chen, C.K.; Ooi, F.K.; Kasim, N.A.A.; Asari, M.A. Effects of *Eurycoma Longifolia* Jack Supplementation Combined with Resistance Training on Isokinetic Muscular Strength and Power, Anaerobic Power, and Urinary Testosterone: Epitestosterone Ratio in Young Males. *Int. J. Prev. Med.* **2019**, *10*, 118. [CrossRef]
30. Allkanjari, O.; Vitalone, A. What do we know about phytotherapy of benign prostatic hyperplasia? *Life Sci.* **2015**, *126*, 42–56. [CrossRef]
31. Dhouibi, R.; Affes, H.; Salem, M.B.; Hammami, S.; Sahnoun, Z.; Zeghal, K.M.; Ksouda, K. Screening of pharmacological uses of *Urtica dioica* and others bene fi ts. *Prog. Biophys. Mol. Biol.* **2019**. [CrossRef]
32. Ibrahim, M.; Rehman, K.; Razzaq, A.; Hussain, I.; Farooq, T.; Hussain, A.; Akash, M.S.H. Investigations of phytochemical constituents and their pharmacological properties isolated from the genus urtica: Critical review and analysis. *Crit. Rev. Eukaryot. Gene Expr.* **2018**, *28*, 25–66. [CrossRef] [PubMed]
33. Fan, S.; Raychaudhuri, S.; Kraus, O.; Shahinozzaman, M.; Lofti, L.; Obanda, D.N. Urtica dioica whole vegetable as a functional food targeting fat accumulation and insulin resistance—A preliminary study in a mouse pre-diabetic model. *Nutrients* **2020**, *12*, 1059. [CrossRef] [PubMed]
34. Nahata, A.; Dixit, V.K. Ameliorative effects of stinging nettle (*Urtica dioica*) on testosterone-induced prostatic hyperplasia in rats. *Andrologia* **2012**, 396–409. [CrossRef]
35. MCTI-CONCEA. Diretriz Brasileira para o Cuidado e a Utilização de Animais em Atividades de Ensino ou de Pesquisa Científica—DBCA. Resolução Normativa CONCEA n. 30. 2 February 2016. Available online: http://www.mctic.gov.br/mctic/export/sites/institucional/institucional/concea/arquivos/legislacao/resolucoes_normativas/Resolucao-Normativa-CONCEA-n-30-de-02.02.2016-D.O.U.-de-03.02.2016-Secao-I-Pag.-03.pdf (accessed on 29 March 2017).
36. Riedl, I.; Yoshioka, M.; St-amand, J. Concomitant modulation of transcripts related to fiber type determination and energy metabolism in skeletal muscle of female ovariectomized mice by estradiol injection. *J. Steroid Biochem. Mol. Biol.* **2010**, *122*, 91–99. [CrossRef]
37. Corazza, A.V.; Paolillo, F.R.; Groppo, F.C.; Bagnato, V.S.; Caria, P.H.F. Phototherapy and resistance training prevent sarcopenia in ovariectomized rats. *Lasers Med. Sci.* **2013**, *28*, 1467–1474. [CrossRef]
38. Zheng, W.; Hengevoß, J.; Soukup, S.; Kulling, S.; Xie, M.; Diel, P. An isoflavone enriched diet increases skeletal muscle adaptation in response to physical activity in ovariectomized rats. *Mol. Nutr. Food Res.* **2017**, *61*, 1–30. [CrossRef]
39. Collins, B.C.; Laakkonen, E.K.; Lowe, D.A. Aging of the musculoskeletal system: How the loss of estrogen impacts muscle strength. *Bone* **2019**, *123*, 137–144. [CrossRef]
40. Ikeda, K.; Horie-inoue, K.; Inoue, S. Functions of estrogen and estrogen receptor signaling on skeletal muscle. *J. Steroid Biochem. Mol. Biol.* **2019**, *191*, 105375. [CrossRef]
41. Doulamis, I.; Tzani, A.; Konstantopoulos, P.; Daskalopoulou, A.; Spinos, T.; Bletsa, E.; Mitsopoulou, D.; Spinou, M.; Brinia, M.; Palaiopanos, K.; et al. Experimental hypogonadism: Insulin resistance, biochemical changes and effect of testosterone substitution. *J. Basic Clin. Physiol. Pharmacol.* **2019**, *30*, 1–5. [CrossRef]
42. Ropelle, E.R.; Pauli, J.R.; Zecchin, K.G.; Ueno, M.; de Souza, C.T.; Morari, J.; Faria, M.C.; Velloso, L.A.; Saad, M.J.; Carvalheira, J.B. A Central Role for Neuronal Amp Activated Protein Kinase (Ampk) in Cancer-Induced Anorexia. *Endocrinology* **2007**, *148*, 5220–5229. [CrossRef]
43. Lee, S.; Khamoui, A.V.; Jo, E.; Zourdos, M.C.; Panton, L.B.; Ormsbee, M.J.; Kim, J. Effect of conjugated linoleic acids and omega-3 fatty acids with or without resistance training on muscle mass in high-fat diet-fed middle-aged mice. *Exp. Physiol.* **2017**, *11*, 1500–1512. [CrossRef]
44. Lee, S.; Barton, E.R.; Sweeney, H.L.; Farrar, R.P. Viral expression of insulin-like growth factor-I enhances muscle hypertrophy in resistance-trained rats. *J. Appl. Physiol.* **2004**, *96*, 1097–1104. [CrossRef]
45. Tashmukhamedova, M.; Almatov, K.; Syrov, V.; Sultanov, M.; Abidov, A. Comparative study of the effect of ecdysterone, turkesterone and nerobol on the function of rat liver mitochondria in experimental diabetes. *Vopr. Med. Khim.* **1986**, *32*, 24–28.
46. Syrov, V. Mechanism of the anabolic action of phytoecdisteroids in mammals. *Nauchnye Doki. Vyss. Shkoly Biol. Nauk.* **1984**, *11*, 16–20.
47. Syrov, V.; Kurmukov, A.; Sakhibov, A. Effect of turkesterone and nerobol on the activity of the protein synthesizing system of mouse liver. *Vopr. Med. Khim.* **1978**, *24*, 456–460.
48. Syrov, V.; Tashmukhamedova, M.; Khushbaktova, Z.; Mirtalipov, D.; Mamatkhanov, A. Effect of phytoecdysteroids and nerobol on parameters of carbohydrate and lipid metabolism and phospholipid spectrum of liver mitochondrial membrane in experimental diabetes mellitus of rats. *Ukr. Biokhim. Zhurnal* **1978**, *64*, 61–67.
49. Tashmukhamedova, M.; Almatov, K.; Syrov, V.; Sultanov, M.; Abidov, A. Effect of phytoecdisteroids and anabolic steroids on liver mitochondrial respiration and oxidative phosphorylation in alloxan diabetic rats. *Nauchnye Doki. Vyss. Shkoly Biol. Nauk.* **1985**, *9*, 37–39.

50. Arthur, S.T.; Zwetsloot, K.A.; Lawrence, M.M.; Nieman, D.C.; Lila, M.A.; Grace, M.H.; Howden, R.; Cooley, I.D.; Keith, M.D.; Demick, J.L.; et al. Ajuga turkestanica increases Notch and Wnt signaling in aged skeletal muscle. *Eur. Rev. Med. Pharmacol. Sci.* **2014**, *18*, 2584–2592.
51. Low, B.; Das, P.K.; Chan, K. Acute, Reproductive Toxicity and Two-generation Teratology Studies of a Standardized Quassinoid-rich Extract of *Eurycoma longifolia* Jack in Sprague—Dawley Rats. *Phytother. Res.* **2014**, *1029*, 1022–1029. [CrossRef]
52. Abdulghani, M.; Hussin, A.H.; Sulaiman, S.A.; Chan, K.L. The ameliorative effects of *Eurycoma longifolia* Jack on testosterone-induced reproductive disorders in female rats. *Reprod. Biol.* **2012**, *12*, 247–255. [CrossRef]
53. Wahab, N.A.; Mokhtar, I.N.M.; Nurul, I.W.; Halim, H.A. Basic research the effect of *Eurycoma longifolia* Jack on spermatogenesis in estrogen-treated rats. *Clinics* **2010**, *65*, 93–98. [CrossRef]
54. Ang, H.; Lee, K. Effect of *Eurycoma longifolia* Jack on libido in middle-aged male rats. *J. Basic Clin. Physiol. Pharmacol.* **2002**, *13*, 249–254. [CrossRef]
55. Ang, H.; Cheang, H. Effects of *Eurycoma longifolia* jack on laevator ani muscle in both uncastrated and testosterone-stimulated castrated intact male rats. *Arch. Pharm. Res.* **2001**, *24*, 437–440. [CrossRef]
56. Patel, S.S.; Udayabanu, M. Urtica dioica extract attenuates depressive like behavior and associative memory dysfunction in dexamethasone induced diabetic mice. *Metab. Brain Dis.* **2014**, *29*, 121–130. [CrossRef]
57. Dar, S.A.; Ganai, F.A.; Yousuf, A.R.; Balkhi, H.; Bhat, T.M.; Sharma, P.; Ahmad, S.; Ganai, F.A.; Yousuf, A.R.; Dar, S.A.; et al. Pharmacological and toxicological evaluation of *Urtica dioica*. *Pharm. Biol.* **2013**, *51*. [CrossRef]
58. Jalili, C.; Salahshoor, M.R.; Naseri, A. Protective effect of *Urtica dioica* L. against nicotine-induced damage on sperm parameters, testosterone and testis tissue in mice. *Iran. J. Reprod. Med.* **2014**, *12*, 401–408.
59. Obanda, D.N.; Ribnicky, D.; Yu, Y.; Stephens, J.; Cefalu, W.T. An extract of *Urtica dioica* L. mitigates obesity induced insulin resistance in mice skeletal muscle via protein phosphatase 2A (PP2A). *Sci. Rep.* **2016**, 1–9. [CrossRef]
60. Zheng, X.X.; Chen, R.S.; Shen, Y.; Yin, Z.Y. Phytosterols elevation in bamboo shoot residue through laboratorial scale solid-state fermentation using isolated *Aspergillus niger* CTBU. *Appl. Biochem. Biotechnol.* **2014**, *172*, 4078–4083. [CrossRef]
61. Toledo, M.; Penna, F.; Busquets, S.; Lopez-Soberiano, F.J.; Argiles, J.M. Distinct Behaviour of Sorafenib in Experimental Cachexia-Inducing Tumours: The Role of STAT3. *PLoS ONE* **2014**, *9*, e113931. [CrossRef]
62. Murphy, K.T.; Chee, A.; Trieu, J.; Naim, T.; Lynch, G.S. Importance of functional and metabolic impairments in the characterization of the C-26 murine model of cancer cachexia. *Dis. Model. Mech.* **2012**, *5*, 533–545. [CrossRef] [PubMed]
63. Lin, C.L.; Lee, M.C.; Hsu, Y.J.; Huang, W.C.; Huang, C.C.; Huang, S.W. Isolated soy protein supplementation and exercise improve fatigue-related biomarker levels and bone strength in ovariectomized mice. *Nutrients* **2018**, *10*, 1792. [CrossRef] [PubMed]
64. Counts, B.R.; Fix, D.K.; Hetzler, K.L.; Carson, J.A. The Effect of Estradiol Administration on Muscle Mass Loss and Cachexia Progression in Female ApcMin/+ Mice. *Front. Endocrinol.* **2019**, *10*, 1–16. [CrossRef] [PubMed]
65. White, J.P.; Gao, S.; Puppa, M.J.; Sato, S.; Welle, S.L.; Carson, J.A. Testosterone regulation of Akt/mTORC1/FoxO3a signaling in skeletal muscle. *Mol. Cell. Endocrinol.* **2013**, *365*, 174–186. [CrossRef]
66. Sciote, J.; Horton, M.; Zyman, Y.; Pascoe, G. Differential effects of diminished oestrogen and androgen levels on development of skeletal muscle fibres in hypogonadal mice. *Acta Physiol. Scand.* **2001**, *172*, 179–187. [CrossRef]
67. Guo, S.; Huang, Y.; Zhang, Y.; Huang, H.; Hong, S.; Liu, T. Impacts of exercise interventions on different diseases and organ functions in mice. *J. Sport Health Sci.* **2020**, *9*, 53–73. [CrossRef]
68. Krause Neto, W.; Silva, W.D.A.; Ciena, A.P.; Anaruma, C.A.; Gama, E.F. Vertical climbing for rodent resistance training: A discussion about training parameters. *Int. J. Sport Sci.* **2016**, *6*, 36–49. [CrossRef]
69. Lee, S.; Farrar, R.P. Resistance training induces muscle-specific changes in muscle mass andfunction in rat. *J. Exerc. Physiol.* **2003**, *6*, 80–87.
70. Ahtiainen, J.P.; Lensu, S.; Ruotsalainen, I.; Schumann, M.; Ihalainen, J.K.; Fachada, V.; Mendias, C.L.; Brook, M.S.; Smith, K.; Atherton, P.J.; et al. Physiological adaptations to resistance training in rats selectively bred for low and high response to aerobic exercise training. *Exp. Physiol.* **2018**, *103*, 1513–1523. [CrossRef]
71. Bunratsami, S.; Udomuksorn, W.; Kumarnsit, E.; Vongvatcharanon, S.; Vongvatcharanon, U. Estrogen replacement improves skeletal muscle performance by increasing parvalbumin levels in ovariectomized rats. *Acta Histochem.* **2015**. [CrossRef]
72. Graber, T.G.; Fandrey, K.R. Novel individualized power training protocol preserves physical function in adult and older mice. *GeroScience* **2019**, 165–183. [CrossRef]
73. Elhag, H.E.E.A.; Sulaiman, A.Z.; Ajit, A.B. A Review on the Exraction Methods of Extracts and Phytochemicals from Eurycoma longifolia. In Proceedings of the National Conference for Postgraduate Research (NCON-PGR), Universiti Malaysia, Pahang, Malaysia, 24–25 September 2016; pp. 253–259.
74. Mamatkhanov, A.U.; Yakubova, M.R.; Syrov, V.N. The technological isolation of turkesterone from the epigeal part of *Ajuga turkestanica* (Rgl.) Brig. is described, a method is proposed for the quantitative determination of turkesterone, and the results of an investigation of its biological activity. *Chem. Nat. Compd.* **1998**, *34*, 150–154. [CrossRef]
75. Chrubasik, J.E.; Roufogalis, B.D.; Wagner, H.; Chrubasik, S. A comprehensive review on the stinging nettle effect and efficacy profiles. Part II: *Urticae radix*. *Phytomedicine* **2007**, *14*, 568–579. [CrossRef]
76. Chakraborty, D.; Pal, A. *Quassinoids: Chemistry and Novel Detection Techniques*; Springer: Berlin/Heidelberg, Germany, 2013; ISBN 9783642221446.

77. Pandey, A.; Tripathi, S. Concept of standardization, extraction and pre phytochemical screening strategies for herbal drug. *J. Pharmacogn. Phytochem.* **2014**, *2*, 115–119.
78. Abidi, S.L. Chromatographic analysis of plant sterols in foods and vegetable oils. *J. Chromatogr. A* **2001**, *935*, 173–201. [CrossRef]
79. Destrez, B.; Pinel, G.; Monteau, F.; Lafont, R.; Le, B. Detection and identification of 20-hydroxyecdysone metabolites in calf urine by liquid chromatography-high resolution or tandem mass spectrometry measurements and establishment of their kinetics of elimination after 20-hydroxyecdysone administration. *Anal. Chim. Acta* **2008**, *7*, 178–184. [CrossRef]
80. Teh, C.; Murugaiyah, V.; Chan, K. Developing a validated liquid chromatography—Mass spectrometric method for the simultaneous analysis of five bioactive quassinoid markers for the standardization of manufactured batches of *Eurycoma longifolia* Jack extract as antimalarial medicaments. *J. Chromatogr. A* **2011**, *1218*, 1861–1877. [CrossRef]
81. Bataglion, G.A.; Meurer, E.C.; De Albergaria, A.C.R.; Bícego, M.C.; Weber, R.R.; Eberlin, M.N. Determination of geochemically important sterols and triterpenols in sediments using UHPLC-MS/MS. *Anal. Chem.* **2015**, *85*, 7771–7778. [CrossRef]
82. Seidlova-Wuttke, D.; Ehrhardt, C.; Wuttke, W. Metabolic effects of 20-OH-Ecdysone in ovariectomized rats. *J. Steroid Biochem. Mol. Biol.* **2010**, *119*, 121–126. [CrossRef]
83. Kenny, A.M.; Kleppinger, A.; Wang, Y.; Prestwood, K.M. Effects of Ultra-Low-Dose Estrogen Therapy on Muscle and Physical Function in Older Women. *J. Am. Geriatr. Soc.* **2005**, *53*, 1973–1977. [CrossRef]
84. Javed, A.A.; Mayhew, A.J.; Shea, A.K.; Raina, P. Association Between Hormone Therapy and Muscle Mass in Postmenopausal Women A Systematic Review and Meta-analysis. *JAMA Netw. Open* **2019**, *2*, 1–17. [CrossRef] [PubMed]
85. Parr, M.K.; Zhao, P.; Haupt, O.; Ngueu, S.T.; Hengevoss, J.; Fritzmeier, K.H.; Piechotta, M.; Schlorer, N.; Muhn, P.; Zheng, W.-Y.; et al. Estrogen receptor beta is involved in skeletal muscle hypertrophy induced by the phytoecdysteroid ecdysterone. *Mol. Nutr. Food Res.* **2014**, 1–12. [CrossRef] [PubMed]
86. Rosa-Caldwell, M.E.; Greene, N.P. Muscle metabolism and atrophy: Let's talk about sex. *Biol. Sex. Differ.* **2019**, *10*, 1–14. [CrossRef] [PubMed]
87. Russel, N.; Grossmann, M. Estradiol as a male hormone. *Eur. J. Endocrinol.* **2019**, *181*, R23–R43. [CrossRef]
88. Low, B.; Choi, S.; Abdul, H.; Kumar, P.; Chan, K. Eurycomanone, the major quassinoid in *Eurycoma longifolia* root extract increases spermatogenesis by inhibiting the activity of phosphodiesterase and aromatase in steroidogenesis. *J. Ethnopharmacol.* **2013**, 1–7. [CrossRef]
89. Ziaei, R.; Foshati, S.; Hadi, A.; Kermani, M.A.H.; Ghavami, A.; Clark, C.C.T.; Tarrahi, M.J. The effect of nettle (Urtica dioica) supplementation on the glycemic control of patients with type 2 diabetes mellitus: A systematic review and meta-analysis. *Phyther. Res.* **2020**, *34*, 282–294. [CrossRef]
90. Namjou, A.; Heidarian, E.; Rafieian-Kopaei, M. Effects of Urtica dioica hydro-alcoholic extract on blood serum glucose and lipid profiles of female Wistar rats with long-term estrogen deficiency. *Vet Res. Forum.* **2018**, *9*, 349–355. [CrossRef]
91. Horstman, A.M.; Dillon, E.L.; Urban, R.J.; Sheffi, M. The Role of Androgens and Estrogens on Healthy Aging and Longevity. *J. Gerontol. A Biol. Sci. Med. Sci.* **2012**, *67*, 1140–1152. [CrossRef]
92. Neergheen-bhujun, V.S. Underestimating the Toxicological Challenges Associated with the Use of Herbal Medicinal Products in Developing Countries. *Biomed. Res. Int.* **2013**, *2013*. [CrossRef]
93. Dinan, L.; Lafont, R. Effects and applications of arthropod steroid hormones (ecdysteroids) in mammals. *J. Endocrinol.* **2006**, *191*, 1–8. [CrossRef]
94. Quinn, M.A.; Xu, X.; Ronfani, M.; Cidlowski, J.A.; Quinn, M.A.; Xu, X.; Ronfani, M.; Cidlowski, J.A. Estrogen Deficiency Promotes Hepatic Steatosis via a Glucocorticoid Receptor-Dependent Mechanism in Mice. *Cell Rep.* **2018**, *22*, 2690–2701. [CrossRef]
95. Harada, N.; Hanaoka, R.; Horiuchi, H.; Kitakaz, T.; Mitani, T. Castration influences intestinal microflora and induces abdominal obesity in high-fat diet-fed mice. *Sci. Rep.* **2016**, 1–9. [CrossRef]
96. Morrone, M.S.; Schnorr, C.E.; Behr, G.A.; Gasparotto, J.; Bortolin, R.C.; Martinello, B.; Henkin, B.S.; Rabello, T.K.; Zanotto-Filho, A.; Gelain, D.P.; et al. Adiposity Accumulation, Serum Cholesterol Alterations, and Oxidative Stress in Ovariectomized Rats. *Oxid. Med. Cell. Longev.* **2016**, *2016*, 5719291. [CrossRef]
97. Álvarez-satta, M.; Berna-erro, A.; Carrasco-garcia, E.; Alberro, A.; Saenz-antoñanzas, A.; Vergara, I.; Otaegui, D.; Matheu, A. Relevance of oxidative stress and inflammation in frailty based on human studies and mouse models. *Aging* **2020**, *12*, 9982–9999. [CrossRef]

nutrients

Article

The Effects of Postprandial Walking on the Glucose Response after Meals with Different Characteristics

Alessio Bellini, Andrea Nicolò, Ilenia Bazzucchi and Massimo Sacchetti *

Department of Movement, Human and Health Sciences, University of Rome "Foro Italico", Piazza Lauro De Bosis 6, 00135 Rome, Italy; alessiobellini1@gmail.com (A.B.); andrea.nicolo@uniroma4.it (A.N.); ilenia.bazzucchi@uniroma4.it (I.B.)
* Correspondence: massimo.sacchetti@uniroma4.it; Tel.: +39-06-3673-3281

Abstract: We evaluated the effect of postprandial walking on the post-meal glycemic response after meals with different characteristics. Twenty-one healthy young volunteers participated in one of two randomized repeated measures studies. Study 1 (10 participants) assessed the effects of 30 min of brisk walking after meals with different carbohydrate (CHO) content (0.75 or 1.5 g of CHO per kg/body weight). Study 2 (11 participants) evaluated the effects of 30 min of brisk walking after consuming a mixed meal or a CHO drink matched for absolute CHO content (75 g). Postprandial brisk walking substantially reduced ($p < 0.009$) the glucose peak in both studies, with no significant differences across conditions. When evaluating the glycemic response throughout the two hours post-meal, postprandial walking was more effective after consuming a lower CHO content (Study 1), and similarly effective after a mixed meal or a CHO drink (Study 2), although higher glucose values were observed when consuming the CHO drink. Our findings show that a 30 min postprandial brisk walking session improves the glycemic response after meals with different CHO content and macronutrient composition, with implications for postprandial exercise prescription in daily life scenarios.

Keywords: post-meal glycemia; postprandial exercise; breakfast exercise; post-meal exercise

Citation: Bellini, A.; Nicolò, A.; Bazzucchi, I.; Sacchetti, M. The Effects of Postprandial Walking on the Glucose Response after Meals with Different Characteristics. *Nutrients* **2022**, *14*, 1080. https://doi.org/10.3390/nu14051080

Academic Editor: Pedro L. Valenzuela

Received: 28 January 2022
Accepted: 2 March 2022
Published: 4 March 2022

1. Introduction

Elevated postprandial blood glucose concentration and large glycemic excursions have been identified as better predictors of cardiometabolic disorders than fasting hyperglycemia in both healthy individuals and diabetic patients [1]. Indeed, exaggerated blood glucose spikes lead to a higher increase in oxidative stress [2], endothelial dysfunction [2,3], proinflammatory factors levels [4], and in the risk of developing cardiovascular pathologies [5] than fasting hyperglycemia. Exercise and nutrition have a fundamental role in the management of excessive elevation of post-meal glycemia [6], and previous studies have shown that postprandial exercise, also in relation to the modality it is administered, is effective in improving the glycemic response to a standard meal [6–11]. However, it is currently unclear if the prescription of postprandial exercise should take into account the characteristics of the meal and how.

Among the exercise parameters, exercise timing has a key role in improving post-meal glycemic control [7,8,12,13]. Previous studies have widely demonstrated that exercising in the period immediately after the meal provides a greater reduction in the post-meal glycemic peak compared with pre-meal exercise, especially when exercise starts before reaching peak glucose levels [8,14]. Other parameters have a lower impact on the glucose response to a meal compared with exercise timing. For instance, the modulation of exercise intensity and duration does not lead to substantial variations in postprandial glucose concentration in healthy individuals [8,15]. Likewise, aerobic, resistance, or combined exercises are similarly effective in improving the post-meal glycemic response [7,8]. Hence, moderate-intensity walking appears to be a feasible exercise option for everyone as it can easily be performed without the need for any equipment and supervision of an exercise specialist. Importantly, postprandial walking has been proven effective for improving glycemic response to different meals of the day (i.e., breakfast, lunch, and dinner) both in healthy and diabetic individuals [8,11,14,16–19].

Nutrition is another important factor to consider when attempting to improve the glycemic response to a meal. While the meal characteristics may widely vary in daily life, the studies assessing the effects of postprandial exercise on glycemia have rarely attempted to evaluate the effects of exercise after different mixed meals. A large body of research focused on the effects of postprandial exercise after the consumption of an oral glucose tolerance test (OGTT), thus inducing a different glycemic response compared with that of a mixed meal [20], which better resembles what is often consumed in daily life. When the use of a mixed meal was implemented, it was consistently shown that 30 min of step cadence paced moderate-intensity walking is effective in improving the glycemic response to a meal providing 1 g of CHO per kg of body weight [8]. However, it is currently unclear how the effectiveness of a typical postprandial walking session (e.g., 30 min of brisk walking) would change in relation to meals with different CHO content and composition.

Indeed, among the nutritional factors affecting the glycemic response to a meal, the amount of carbohydrate (CHO) provided with the meal plays an important role. Previous studies have documented a higher glycemic response with the increase in the meal CHO content [21]. The macronutrient characteristics of the meal may also have a relevant influence on the postprandial glucose response. Indeed, high-protein and/or high-fat meals induce a significant reduction in the postprandial glucose response [22–26]. In addition, whether a meal is solid or liquid should also be considered for the impact on the postprandial glycemic response, with higher glycemic excursions observed after a liquid meal compared with a solid one [27,28].

Therefore, we performed two studies aiming to determine the effects of postprandial walking on the glycemic response to meals with different characteristics. Study 1 evaluated the effects of exercise after mixed meals with different CHO content, while Study 2 assessed the effects of exercise after the consumption of meals with a different macronutrient composition (e.g., mixed meal vs. CHO drink (i.e., OGTT)), but the same amount of CHO. Collectively, findings from the two studies were expected to assess the efficacy of 30 min of postprandial brisk walking when varying some characteristics of the meal, with potential implications for implementing this simple exercise strategy in daily life.

2. Materials and Methods

2.1. Participants

Twenty-three healthy, physically active (reaching the minimum amount of physical activity recommended by the World Health Organization guidelines [29]), young and healthy adults (20–35 years old) volunteered to participate in this investigation. In total, twenty-one individuals completed all the experimental protocols of one of the two studies. More detailed information on participants' characteristics is reported in Table 1. The studies were conducted in accordance with the Declaration of Helsinki and ethical approval was provided by the Local Ethical Committee (52/2020, 11 June 2020). Written informed consent was obtained from all the volunteers involved in the study.

Table 1. Participants' characteristics of the two studies.

	Study 1	**Study 2**
Sample size (M/F)	10 (5/5)	11 (5/6)
Age (years)	25 ± 3	25 ± 2
Weight (kg)	66 ± 9	68 ± 10
Height (m)	1.70 ± 0.09	1.74 ± 0.13
BMI (kg/m^2)	22.9 ± 2.6	22.5 ± 2.3

Abbreviations: M, male; F, female; BMI, body mass index. Data are expressed as mean ± SD.

2.2. Study Overview

Volunteers performed one of the two repeated measures studies with four experimental trials per study. At the beginning of each study, a familiarization visit was performed. Subsequently, participants performed four experimental visits in a randomized order, lasting 2 h each. At least seventy-two hours of rest were considered between visits in order to avoid any residual effect of exercise [30]. In Study 1, participants consumed a breakfast differing in CHO content (i.e., 0.75 vs. 1.5 g of CHO per kg of body weight), while in Study 2 participants consumed a breakfast differing in macronutrient composition (i.e., CHO drink vs. mixed meal) with the same amount of CHO (i.e., 75 g). In each study and meal condition, after breakfast participants performed 30 min of moderate-intensity walking or remained seated for the whole experimental period. A schematic representation of the design of the two studies is shown in Figure 1.

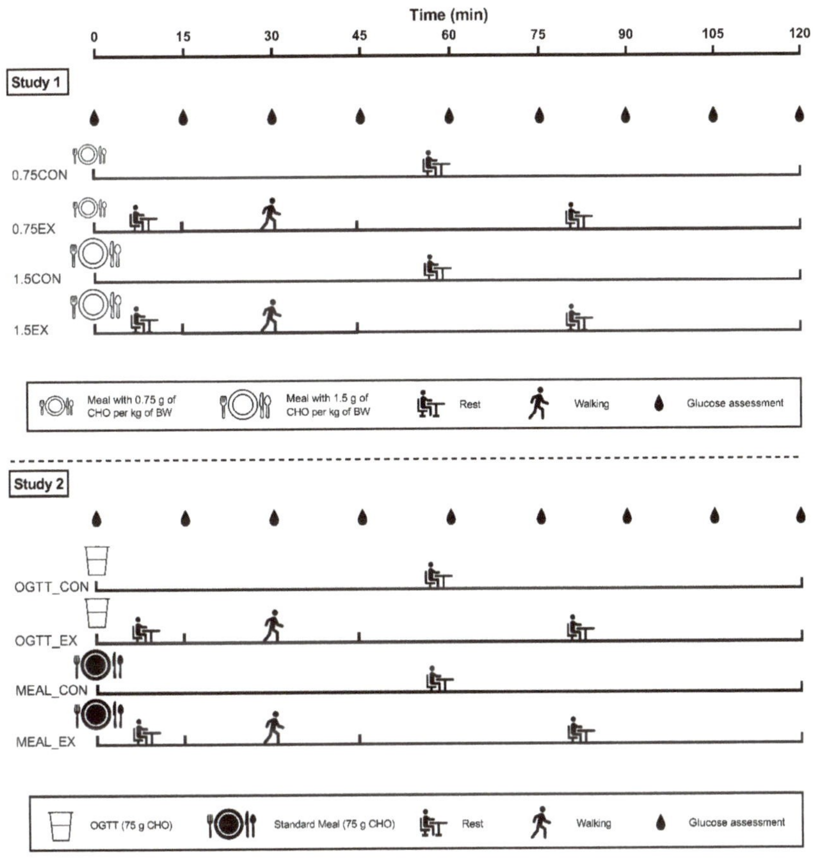

Figure 1. Graphic representation of the two studies. In Study 1, participants consumed a meal containing 0.75 g of carbohydrates (CHO) per kg of body weight (BW) (0.75CON and 0.75EX), or 1.5 g of CHO per kg of BW (1.5CON and 1.5EX). In Study 2, participants consumed 75 g of CHO alone dissolved in water (OGTT_CON and OGTT_EX) or 75 g of CHO combined with protein and fat in a solid mixed meal (MEAL_CON and MEAL_EX). For both studies, after each meal participants performed 30 min of walking started 15 min after the beginning of the meal (0.75EX, 1.5EX, OGTT_EX, and MEAL_EX) or remained seated for the whole experimental period (0.75CON, 1.5CON, OGTT_CON, and MEAL_CON). After the 30 min of walking, participants remained seated until the end of the experimental period.

2.3. Familiarization

Before the beginning of each study, volunteers participated in a familiarization session, during which all the experimental procedures adopted were explained. Participants were requested to avoid moderate-to-vigorous physical activity for the 48 h preceding each experimental visit and to abstain from caffeine and alcohol consumption since the evening before the visit. Participants were also requested to register activities performed during the 48 h and food consumed during the 24 h before the first experimental visit and to replicate them before the remaining three visits.

2.4. Study 1—The Effects of Postprandial Exercise on Glycemia after Consuming Mixed Meals with Different CHO Content

Ten participants were included in this study and completed all the visits (Table 1). Participants attended the laboratory at 08.00 a.m. after an overnight fasting (>10 h of fasting). At 09.00 a.m., participants consumed one of two meals high in CHO content, containing 0.75 g (0.75CON and 0.75EX) or 1.5 g (1.5CON and 1.5EX) of CHO per kg of body weight. The meal consisted of partially skimmed milk, rusks, and jam (Table 2). Participants were given 10 min to finish their meal. After each meal, participants remained seated until the end of the experimental session (0.75CON and 1.5CON) or performed 30 min of walking starting 15 min after the beginning of the meal (0.75EX and 1.5EX), as shown in Figure 1.

Table 2. Meal composition in the two studies.

	Study 1		Study 2	
	Meal 1	**Meal 2**	**Meal 1**	**Meal 2**
Energy intake (kcal)	276.20 ± 29.97	551.73 ± 62.57	297.00 ± 0.00	421.84 ± 0.00
CHO (g)	50.57 ± 5.76	100.77 ± 11.34	75.00 ± 0.00	75.00 ± 0.00
Protein (g)	8.57 ± 8.51	17.22 ± 4.32	0 ± 0.00	14.50 ± 0.00
Fat (g)	4.12 ± 1.23	8.28 ± 2.46	0 ± 0.00	6.78 ± 0.00
CHO (%)	73.79 ± 6.17	73.66 ± 6.05	100.00 ± 0.00	71.38 ± 0.00
Protein (%)	12.38 ± 12.37	12.45 ± 12.40	0 ± 0.00	13.82 ± 0.00
Fat (%)	13.35 ± 3.48	13.42 ± 3.42	0 ± 0.00	14.51 ± 0.00

In Study 1, Meal 1 consists in 0.75 g of carbohydrates (CHO) per kg of body weight and Meal 2 in 1.5 g of CHO per kg of body weight. In Study 2, Meal 1 consists in 75 g of CHO dissolved in water and Meal 2 in 75 g consumed in a mixed meal along with protein and fat. Data are expressed as mean ± SD.

2.5. Study 2—The Effects of Postprandial Exercise on Glycemia after Consuming Meals with Different Macronutrient Composition

Eleven participants were included in this study and completed all the visits (Table 1). As for Study 1, participants attended the laboratory at 08.00 a.m. after an overnight fasting (>10 h of fasting), and at 09.00 a.m. consumed 75 g of glucose (Yamamoto Nutrition, Italy) dissolved in 300 mL of water (as commonly done for the OGTT) or a mixed meal, providing the same amount of CHO. The mixed meal consisted of 280 mL partially skimmed milk, 44 g rusks, and 50 g jam (MEAL_CON and MEAL_EX). Detailed information on the macronutrient composition of the two meals is reported in Table 2. Participants were given 10 min to finish their meal. As for Study 1, after the meal, participants remained seated for the whole experimental period (OGTT_CON and MEAL_CON) or performed 30 min of exercise starting 15 min after the beginning of the meal (OGTT_EX and MEAL_EX) (Figure 1).

2.6. Exercise and Resting Time

Participants were invited to remain seated throughout all the visits of the two studies, except for the 30 min of exercise or for using services. While sitting they were allowed to read or use the PC, but they were asked to replicate their actions during all the visits.

The exercise was the same for the four exercise visits of the two studies (i.e., 0.75EX, 1.5EX, OGTT_EX, and MEAL_EX) (Figure 1). Specifically, it consisted of 30 min of walking, started 15 min after the beginning of the meal (09.15 a.m.), at 120 steps per minute, rhythmically established through a digital metronome (Soundbrenner, Berlin, Germany). Participants walked alone on an indoor track. The use of step cadence has been previously proposed as a valid estimate of the metabolic cost of walking [31,32]. In addition, the step cadence may also be a practical mode for prescribing exercise intensity in real life. At the end of the exercise session, participants remained seated for the remaining experimental time.

2.7. Glycemic Assessment

Capillary blood glucose measures were regularly collected and analyzed by using reactive strips and a glucometer (Contour®Next, Bayer HealthCare S.p.A., Milan, Italy). Two measures were collected and the average of the two was considered. When a difference greater than 10% between the two measures was found, a third measure was collected. Glycemia was assessed at fasting and every 15 min after the meal, until the end of the visit (Figure 1). Before each measure was performed in any of the visits, participants washed their hands in order to avoid possible alterations of the measure related to external factors.

2.8. Rating of Perceived Exertion

In both studies, during the exercise conditions (i.e., 0.75EX and 1.5EX, in Study 1, and OGTT_EX and MEAL_EX, in Study 2), perceived exertion was evaluated using the rating of perceived exertion (RPE) Borg's 6–20 scale every 15 min during the 30 min walking (i.e., 30 and 45 min from the beginning of the meal).

2.9. Statistical Analysis

Statistical analysis was performed using the software IBM SPSS statistics version 23.0 (SPSS Inc., Chicago, IL, USA). The analyses performed were identical in both studies for all variables. Data normality was checked using the Shapiro–Wilk test. The glycemic time course was compared across conditions using a two-way repeated-measures ANOVA (condition × time). In the case of significant interactions, the simple main effect of condition at each time point was analyzed using a one-way repeated-measures ANOVA. Mean blood glucose concentration at 0–120 min was also calculated and analyzed using a one-way repeated-measures ANOVA. The time-averaged positive incremental area under the curve (iAUC) was calculated at 0–60, 60–120, and 0–120 min [33]. A one-way repeated measures ANOVA was used to analyze differences between conditions for positive iAUC. RPE values were compared across conditions using a two-way repeated-measures ANOVA (condition × time).

The Greenhouse–Geisser or the Huynh–Feldt corrections were used for adjusting the degrees of freedom of the within-subject comparisons for $\varepsilon < 0.75$ and $\varepsilon > 0.75$, respectively. In the case of significant differences, the least significant differences (LSD) correction was used for the analysis of multiple comparisons. For all statistical tests, the level of significance was set at 0.05. Partial eta squared (η_p^2) effect sizes were determined, considering $\eta_p^2 \geq 0.01$ as small, $\eta_p^2 \geq 0.059$ as medium, and $\eta_p^2 \geq 0.138$ as large [34]. Values are reported as mean (±SD) in tables and in the text, and as mean (±SEM) in figures.

3. Results

3.1. Study 1—The Effects of Postprandial Exercise on Glycemia after Consuming Mixed Meals with Different CHO Content

A significant interaction (condition × time) was found when comparing the glycemic time course between conditions ($p < 0.001$, $\eta_p^2 = 0.506$). The exercise conditions significantly ($p < 0.009$) reduced the glycemic peak at 30 min (0.75EX, 5.16 ± 1.42 mmol·L^{-1} and 1.5EX, 5.17 ± 1.15 mmol·L^{-1}) compared with the control conditions (0.75CON, 6.96 ± 0.89 mmol·L^{-1} and 1.5CON, 6.70 ± 0.52 mmol·L^{-1}). At 120 min, 0.75CON (4.53 ± 0.36 mmol·L^{-1}) and 0.75EX (4.42 ± 0.25 mmol·L^{-1}) showed significantly lower values compared with 1.5CON

(5.23 ± 0.30 mmol·L^{-1}) and 1.5EX (5.01 ± 0.71 mmol·L^{-1}) ($p < 0.041$). Detailed information on the simple main effect of conditions at each time point is reported in Figure 2.

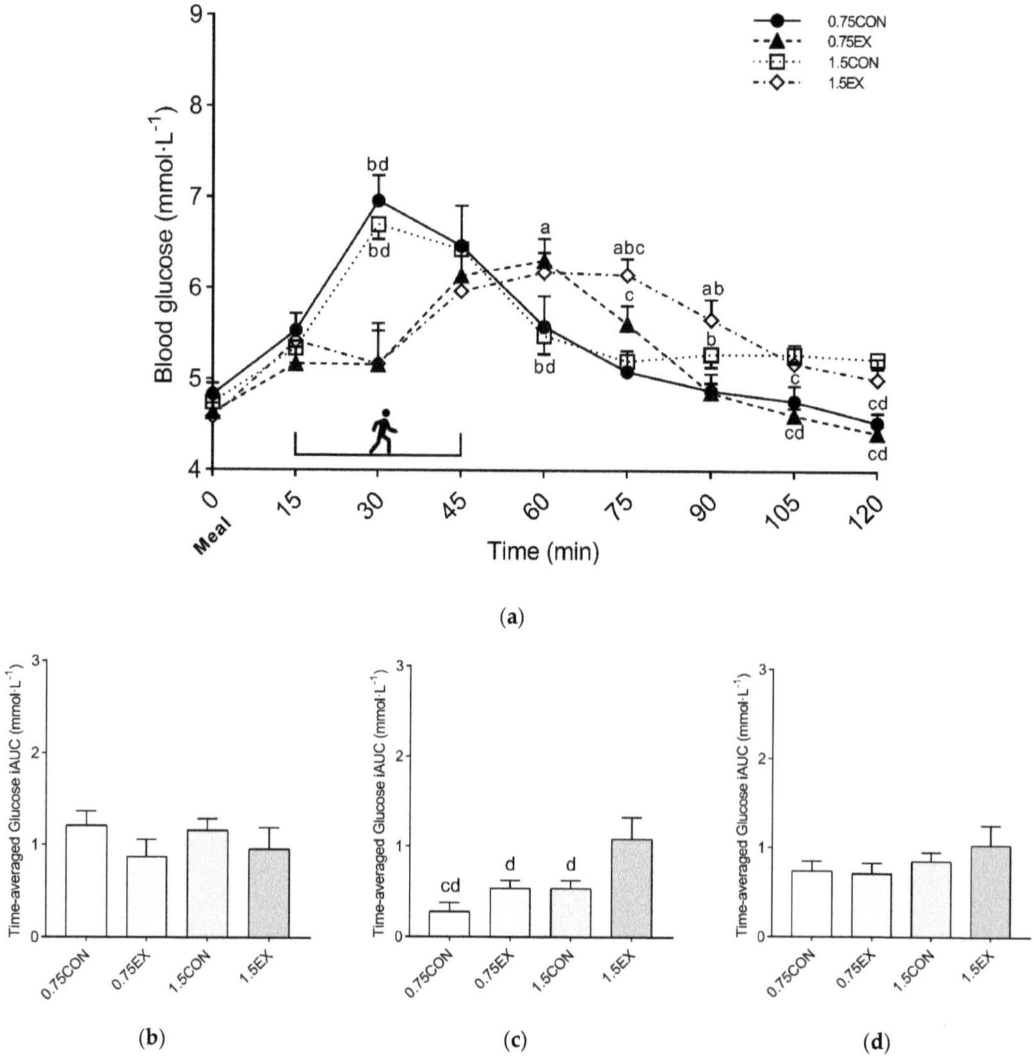

Figure 2. Glycemic time course (**a**) and time-averaged positive iAUC at 0–60 min (**b**), 60–120 min (**c**), and 0–120 min (**d**) of Study 1. Symbols: a, $p < 0.05$ vs. 0.75CON; b, $p < 0.05$ vs. 0.75EX; c, $p < 0.05$ vs. 1.5CON; and d, $p < 0.05$ vs. 1.5EX. The half-box represents the exercise sessions. Values are reported as mean (±SEM).

The analysis of the time-averaged positive iAUC did not show significant differences between conditions either at 0–60 min (0.75CON, 1.21 ± 0.49 mmol·L^{-1}; 0.75EX, 0.87 ± 0.59 mmol·L^{-1}; 1.5CON, 1.16 ± 0.41 mmol·L^{-1}; and 1.5EX, 0.96 ± 0.71 mmol·L^{-1}) or 0–120 min (0.75CON, 0.74 ± 0.11 mmol·L^{-1}; 0.75EX, 0.71 ± 0.40 mmol·L^{-1}; 1.5CON, 0.85 ± 0.30 mmol·L^{-1}; and 1.5EX, 1.03 ± 0.69 mmol·L^{-1}). Conversely, significantly higher values were found at 60–120 min for 1.5EX (1.09 ± 0.24 mmol·L^{-1}) compared with 0.75CON (0.28 ± 0.10 mmol·L^{-1}), 0.75EX (0.54 ± 0.09 mmol·L^{-1}), and 1.5EX (0.54 ± 0.09 mmol·L^{-1})

($p < 0.03$). In addition, 1.5CON showed significantly higher values compared with 0.75CON ($p = 0.048$) (Figure 2), while a statistical trend ($p = 0.063$) was found when comparing 0.75CON with 0.75EX.

No significant differences were found between conditions for 0–120 mean blood glucose concentration (0.75CON, 5.40 ± 0.57 mmol·L^{-1}; 0.75EX, 5.21 ± 0.46 mmol·L^{-1}; 1.5CON, 5.52 ± 0.30 mmol·L^{-1}; and 1.5EX, 5.48 ± 0.54 mmol·L^{-1}).

No significant differences were found across conditions for RPE either at 30 (0.75EX, 9.95 ± 2.03; 1.5EX 10.20 ± 1.30) or 45 min (0.75EX, 10.25 ± 1.99; 1.5EX 10.45 ± 1.38).

3.2. Study 2—The Effects of Postprandial Exercise on Glycemia after Consuming Meals with Different Macronutrient Composition

A significant interaction (condition × time) was found when comparing the glycemic time course between conditions ($p < 0.001$, $\eta_p^2 = 0.381$). The exercise conditions significantly ($p < 0.004$) reduced the glycemic peak at 30 min (OGTT_EX, 6.56 ± 1.07 mmol·L^{-1} and MEAL_EX, 5.99 ± 0.74 mmol·L^{-1}) compared with the control conditions (OGTT_CON, 8.17 ± 0.95 mmol·L^{-1} and MEAL_CON, 7.81 ± 0.59 mmol·L^{-1}). At 45 min, OGTT_CON (7.95 ± 1.79 mmol·L^{-1}) showed significant higher glucose values compared with OGTT_EX (6.41 ± 0.95 mmol·L^{-1}), MEAL_CON (6.66 ± 0.63 mmol·L^{-1}), and MEAL_EX (6.18 ± 0.65 mmol·L^{-1}) ($p < 0.028$). Detailed information on the simple main effect of conditions at each time point is reported in Figure 3.

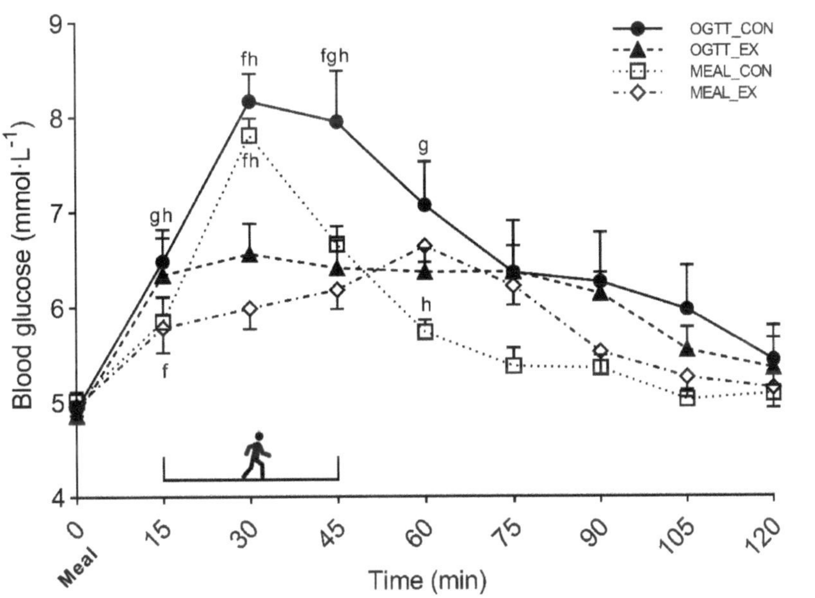

(a)

Figure 3. *Cont.*

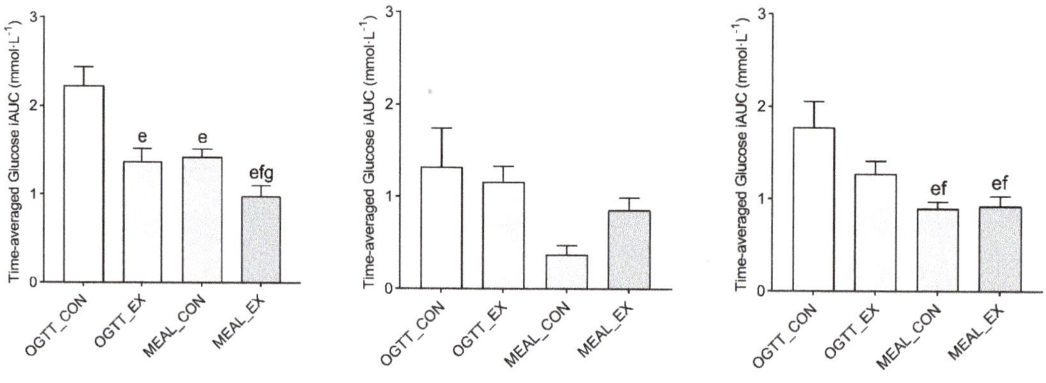

(b) (c) (d)

Figure 3. Glycemic time course (**a**) and time-averaged positive iAUC at 0–60 min (**b**), 60–120 min (**c**), and 0–120 min (**d**) of Study 2. Symbols: e, $p < 0.05$ vs. OGTT_CON; f, $p < 0.05$ vs. OGTT_EX; g, $p < 0.05$ vs. MEAL_CON; and h, $p < 0.05$ vs. MEAL_EX. The half-box represents the exercise sessions. Values are reported as mean (±SEM).

The time-averaged positive glucose iAUC showed significantly higher values at 0–60 min for OGTT_CON (2.22 ± 0.74 mmol·L^{-1}) compared with OGTT_EX (1.37 ± 0.51 mmol·L^{-1}), MEAL_CON (1.42 ± 0.32 mmol·L^{-1}) and MEAL_EX (0.98 ± 0.38 mmol·L^{-1}) ($p < 0.005$). In addition, MEAL_EX showed significantly lower glucose values compared with OGTT_EX and MEAL CON ($p < 0.034$). Significantly lower values were also found at 0–120 min in MEAL_CON (0.89 ± 0.27 mmol·L^{-1}) and MEAL_EX (0.92 ± 0.38 mmol·L^{-1}) compared with OGTT_CON (1.77 ± 0.94 mmol·L^{-1}) and OGTT_EX (1.27 ± 0.48 mmol·L^{-1}) ($p < 0.011$ and $p < 0.025$, respectively). A statistical trend was found for positive iAUC at 60–120 min ($p = 0.065$) (Figure 3).

Mean blood glucose concentration (0–120 min) was significantly lower in MEAL_CON (5.76 ± 0.28 mmol·L^{-1}) and MEAL_EX (5.74 ± 0.43 mmol·L^{-1}) compared with OGTT_CON (6.51 ± 1.05 mmol·L^{-1}) ($p < 0.036$). In addition, a statistical trend was observed between MEAL_EX and OGTT_EX (5.99 ± 0.54 mmol·L^{-1}) ($p = 0.053$).

No significant differences were found across conditions for RPE either at 30 (OGTT_EX, 10.82 ± 0.87; MEAL_EX, 11.27 ± 1.13) and 45 min (OGTT_EX, 11.18 ± 1.08; MEAL_EX, 11.68 ± 1.15).

4. Discussion

Improving the post-meal glycemic response is important for reducing cardiometabolic disorders both in healthy individuals and in patients with diabetes [1,7,12,35]. While 30 min of postprandial walking has proven to be effective in attenuating the glycemic response after a standard meal [8], less is known on its efficacy in relation to the amount of CHO provided with the meal or to its macronutrient composition. Hence, we performed two studies collectively showing that 30 min of postprandial walking is:

(i) Effective in reducing the glucose peak both when increasing the CHO content of a mixed meal and when consuming a CHO drink.
(ii) Less effective in improving the total glycemic response two hours after the meal when the CHO content of a mixed meal is relatively high.

These findings have implications for planning exercise sessions aimed at improving the postprandial glycemic response after meals with different characteristics.

The results of our two studies showed that performing 30 min of walking exercise, started immediately after the meal, effectively attenuated the glucose peak after meals with different CHO quantities and compositions. Study 1 showed that the post-meal glucose peak was similarly reduced by exercise when the amount of CHO was either 0.75 or 1.5 g per kg of body weight. This suggests that moderate-intensity exercise has an important impact on the glucose peak after the consumption of a meal with a relatively high amount of CHO in healthy individuals. Likewise, a similar reduction in the glucose peak was observed when participants performed moderate walking either after consuming an OGTT or a mixed meal, even though the latter had a greater energy intake. This attenuation of the post-meal glucose peak has implications for the reduction in the cardiometabolic disorders associated with it, as suggested by the reduction in the levels of markers associated with oxidative stress [36]. Our results extend previous findings on the effectiveness of postprandial exercise in reducing the post-meal glycemic peak [8,14,16] to meals characterized by different CHO levels and contents of macronutrients. This constitutes a step forward for suggesting the implementation of a 30 min postprandial moderate walk in daily life scenarios, where the meal content and composition may substantially vary.

Although we found a similar reduction in the glycemic peak after consuming mixed meals with two different amounts of CHO (Study 1), the CHO content of the meal moderated the effect of postprandial exercise on the glycemic response when considering the first two hours after the meal. Indeed, a substantial glycemic rebound was found after exercise when participants consumed 1.5 g of CHO per kg of body weight, with higher glycemic values observed throughout the second hour post-meal when compared with the 0.75EX condition. The extent of the glycemic rebound in the 1.5EX condition can be further appreciated when considering that the time-averaged glucose iAUC value was significantly higher than that of the other three conditions (Figure 2c). Although we did not investigate the mechanisms underlying this effect, higher glycemic values may be related to the longer release of the meal-derived glucose from the gastrointestinal system [37]. These findings suggest that when consuming a meal with a high CHO content, 30 min of postprandial continuous walking started early after the meal are sufficient to elicit a marked attenuation of the early glucose response, while it is less effective in the late postprandial phase. In this context, other exercise strategies should be considered to improve the glucose response over the entire post-meal period. For instance, previous evidence has shown the effectiveness of spreading the exercise session into shorter activity breaks over the entire postprandial period for preventing the glycemic rebound and improving the glucose iAUC response [8,38–41]. Further studies should investigate whether activity breaks may also provide a relevant stimulus for reducing the glucose levels over the two hours even when the CHO content of a meal is high.

The comparison between the effects of postprandial exercise after a mixed meal or a CHO drink matched for CHO content allowed us to gain further insight into the glycemic response both from a methodological and practical perspective. While an OGTT is often used in research to evaluate the effects of postprandial exercise on the glycemic response, it does not generally reproduce real-life conditions, hence impacting on the applicability of the study findings. We have compared the CHO drink with a mixed meal with the same absolute content of CHO, which is similar to the standard meal that we have previously used [8]. As expected, the CHO drink consumption results in a more rapid increase in glycemia and in higher glycemic values throughout the first two hours after the meal compared with the glycemic response observed after the mixed meal. The presence of fat and protein in the mixed meal may explain this difference between the OGTT and the mixed meal. Indeed, several studies have shown that the presence of these macronutrients may delay gastric emptying and attenuate the glycemic response [22,25,26]. Similarly, the greater energy intake and the semi-solid composition of the mixed meal may also have contributed to delaying gastric emptying compared with the OGTT [28]. It is also conceivable that the greater insulin secretion that usually occurs after the consumption of a mixed meal may have contributed to improving the glycemic response in that experimental condition [23]. These findings suggest caution when assessing the effect of postprandial exercise with an OGTT test, as the factors determining glycemic control may differ compared with a mixed meal, as also shown in previous studies [20,28]. From a practical perspective, this comparison allowed us to show that exercise is effective even when a CHO-only drink is consumed.

While we did not attempt to investigate the mechanisms underlying the effect of postprandial exercise on glycemic control after meals with different characteristics, the systematic manipulation of the meal has the potential to shed some light on this issue. Indeed, different meals may have different effects on the factors affecting the rate of blood glucose appearance and disappearance. This applies, for instance, to the glucose release from the gastrointestinal system [37,42,43], and to insulin-dependent glucose uptake [44]. Hence, the manipulation of the meal should be accompanied by the assessment of relevant hormonal (e.g., insulin levels) and physiological responses in future studies. An improved understanding of the mechanisms underlying the interaction between meal and exercise would further refine the prescription of postprandial exercise.

5. Conclusions

We conducted two studies assessing the efficacy of 30 min of postprandial brisk walking performed 15 min after meals with different CHO content or macronutrient composition. Study 1 showed that exercise similarly reduces the glycemic peak after mixed meals containing either 0.75 or 1.5 g of CHO per kg of body weight, while it is less effective in improving the glycemic response throughout the first two hours post meal when the amount of CHO in the meal is relatively higher. Study 2 showed that the glycemic response differs both in time course and absolute values after an OGTT or a mixed meal matched for CHO content, with similar improvements when postprandial exercise is performed.

Collectively, our findings show that 30 min of postprandial brisk walking is effective in improving the glycemic response after meals with different CHO content or macronutrient composition. These results support the implementation of walking among the tools for improving glycemic control in everyday life scenarios, where the content and composition of a meal may vary substantially. This study was performed in young, healthy individuals, and further studies are required to evaluate whether similar responses may occur in older, unfit, or individuals with metabolic disorders.

Author Contributions: Conceptualization, M.S.; investigation, A.B., A.N., I.B. and M.S.; data analysis, A.B. and A.N.; data interpretation, A.B., A.N., I.B. and M.S.; writing original draft preparation, A.B.; writing review and editing, A.B., A.N., I.B. and M.S.; funding acquisition, M.S. All authors have read and agreed to the published version of the manuscript.

Funding: Funding for the present work was provided by the University of Rome "Foro Italico".

Institutional Review Board Statement: The study was conducted in accordance with the Declaration of Helsinki, and approved by the Institutional Review Board of the University of Rome "Foro Italico" (52/2020, 11 June 2020).

Informed Consent Statement: Informed consent was obtained from all subjects involved in the study.

Data Availability Statement: The data presented in this study are available on request from the corresponding author.

Acknowledgments: The authors sincerely acknowledge Alessandra Conti for her help with technical assistance.

Conflicts of Interest: The authors declare no conflict of interest.

References

1. Ceriello, A.; Genovese, S. Atherogenicity of postprandial hyperglycemia and lipotoxicity. *Rev. Endocr. Metab. Disord.* **2016**, *17*, 111–116. [CrossRef] [PubMed]
2. Ceriello, A.; Esposito, K.; Piconi, L.; Ihnat, M.A.; Thorpe, J.E.; Testa, R.; Boemi, M.; Giugliano, D. Oscillating glucose is more deleterious to endothelial function and oxidative stress than mean glucose in normal and type 2 diabetic patients. *Diabetes* **2008**, *57*, 1349–1354. [CrossRef] [PubMed]

3. Ceriello, A.; Taboga, C.; Tonutti, L.; Quagliaro, L.; Piconi, L.; Bais, B.; Da Ros, R.; Motz, E. Evidence for an independent and cumulative effect of postprandial hypertriglyceridemia and hyperglycemia on endothelial dysfunction and oxidative stress generation: Effects of short- and long-term simvastatin treatment. *Circulation* **2002**, *106*, 1211–1218. [CrossRef]
4. Esposito, K.; Nappo, F.; Marfella, R.; Giugliano, G.; Giugliano, F.; Ciotola, M.; Quagliaro, L.; Ceriello, A.; Giugliano, D. Inflammatory cytokine concentrations are acutely increased by hyperglycemia in humans: Role of oxidative stress. *Circulation* **2002**, *106*, 2067–2072. [CrossRef] [PubMed]
5. Coutinho, M.; Gerstein, H.C.; Wang, Y.; Yusuf, S. The relationship between glucose and incident cardiovascular events. A metaregression analysis of published data from 20 studies of 95,783 individuals followed for 12.4 years. *Diabetes Care* **1999**, *22*, 233–240. [CrossRef] [PubMed]
6. Gillen, J.B.; Estafanos, S.; Govette, A. Exercise-nutrient interactions for improved postprandial glycemic control and insulin sensitivity. *Appl. Physiol. Nutr. Metab.* **2021**, *46*, 856–865. [CrossRef]
7. Chacko, E. Exercising tactically for taming postmeal glucose surges. *Scientifica* **2016**, *2016*, 4045717. [CrossRef]
8. Bellini, A.; Nicolò, A.; Bazzucchi, I.; Sacchetti, M. Effects of different exercise strategies to improve postprandial glycemia in healthy individuals. *Med. Sci. Sports Exerc.* **2021**, *53*, 1334–1344. [CrossRef]
9. Aqeel, M.; Forster, A.; Richards, E.A.; Hennessy, E.; McGowan, B.; Bhadra, A.; Guo, J.; Gelfand, S.; Delp, E.; Eicher-Miller, H.A. The effect of timing of exercise and eating on postprandial response in adults: A systematic review. *Nutrients* **2020**, *12*, 221. [CrossRef]
10. Solomon, T.P.J.; Tarry, E.; Hudson, C.O.; Fitt, A.I.; Laye, M.J. Immediate post-breakfast physical activity improves interstitial postprandial glycemia: A comparison of different activity-meal timings. *Pflugers Arch. Eur. J. Physiol.* **2020**, *472*, 271–280. [CrossRef]
11. Reynolds, A.; Venn, B. The timing of activity after eating affects the glycaemic response of healthy adults: A randomised controlled trial. *Nutrients* **2018**, *10*, 1743. [CrossRef] [PubMed]
12. Haxhi, J.; Scotto di Palumbo, A.; Sacchetti, M. Exercising for metabolic control: Is timing important. *Ann. Nutr. Metab.* **2013**, *62*, 14–25. [CrossRef] [PubMed]
13. Kanaley, J.A.; Colberg, S.R.; Corcoran, M.H.; Malin, S.K.; Rodriguez, N.R.; Crespo, C.J.; Kirwan, J.P.; Zierath, J.R. Exercise/physical activity in individuals with type 2 diabetes: A consensus statement from the American College of Sports Medicine. *Med. Sci. Sports Exerc.* **2022**, *54*, 353–368. [CrossRef] [PubMed]
14. Zhang, X.; Wongpipit, W.; Sun, F.; Sheridan, S.; Huang, W.Y.J.; Sit, C.H.P.; Wong, S.H.S. Walking initiated 20 minutes before the time of individual postprandial glucose peak reduces the glucose response in young men with overweight or obesity: A randomized crossover study. *J. Nutr.* **2021**, *151*, 866–875. [CrossRef]
15. Shambrook, P.; Kingsley, M.I.; Wundersitz, D.W.; Xanthos, P.D.; Wyckelsma, V.L.; Gordon, B.A. Glucose response to exercise in the post-prandial period is independent of exercise intensity. *Scand. J. Med. Sci. Sports* **2018**, *28*, 939–946. [CrossRef]
16. Yoko, N.; Hiroshi, Y.; Ying, J. Type and timing of exercise during lunch breaks for suppressing postprandial increases in blood glucose levels in workers. *J. Occup. Health* **2021**, *63*, e12199. [CrossRef]
17. Colberg, S.R.; Zarrabi, L.; Bennington, L.; Nakave, A.; Thomas Somma, C.; Swain, D.P.; Sechrist, S.R. Postprandial walking is better for lowering the glycemic effect of dinner than pre-dinner exercise in type 2 diabetic individuals. *J. Am. Med. Dir. Assoc.* **2009**, *10*, 394–397. [CrossRef]
18. Teo, S.Y.M.; Kanaley, J.A.; Guelfi, K.J.; Cook, S.B.; Hebert, J.J.; Forrest, M.R.L.; Fairchild, T.J. Exercise timing in type 2 diabetes mellitus: A systematic review. *Med. Sci. Sports Exerc.* **2018**, *50*, 2387–2397. [CrossRef]
19. Sacchetti, M.; Haxhi, J.; Sgrò, P.; Scotto di Palumbo, A.; Nicolò, A.; Bellini, A.; Bazzucchi, I.; di Luigi, L. Effects of exercise before and/or after a mixed lunch on postprandial metabolic responses in healthy male individuals. *Eur. J. Nutr.* **2021**, *60*, 3437–3447. [CrossRef]
20. Meier, J.J.; Baller, B.; Menge, B.A.; Gallwitz, B.; Schmidt, W.E.; Nauck, M.A. Excess glycaemic excursions after an oral glucose tolerance test compared with a mixed meal challenge and self-measured home glucose profiles: Is the OGTT a valid predictor of postprandial hyperglycaemia and vice versa? *Diabetes Obes. Metab.* **2009**, *11*, 213–222. [CrossRef]
21. Galgani, J.; Aguirre, C.; Díaz, E. Acute effect of meal glycemic index and glycemic load on blood glucose and insulin responses in humans. *Nutr. J.* **2006**, *5*, 22. [CrossRef]
22. Alssema, M.; Schindhelm, R.K.; Rijkelijkhuizen, J.M.; Kostense, P.J.; Teerlink, T.; Nijpels, G.; Heine, R.J.; Dekker, J.M. Meal composition affects insulin secretion in women with type 2 diabetes: A comparison with healthy controls. The hoorn prandial study. *Eur. J. Clin. Nutr.* **2009**, *63*, 398–404. [CrossRef] [PubMed]
23. Gentilcore, D.; Chaikomin, R.; Jones, K.L.; Russo, A.; Feinle-Bisset, C.; Wishart, J.M.; Rayner, C.K.; Horowitz, M. Effects of fat on gastric emptying of and the glycemic, insulin, and incretin responses to a carbohydrate meal in type 2 diabetes. *J. Clin. Endocrinol. Metab.* **2006**, *91*, 2062–2067. [CrossRef] [PubMed]
24. King, D.G.; Walker, M.; Campbell, M.D.; Breen, L.; Stevenson, E.J.; West, D.J. A small dose of whey protein co-ingested with mixed-macronutrient breakfast and lunch meals improves postprandial glycemia and suppresses appetite in men with type 2 diabetes: A randomized controlled trial. *Am. J. Clin. Nutr.* **2018**, *107*, 550–557. [CrossRef] [PubMed]
25. Meng, H.; Matthan, N.R.; Ausman, L.M.; Lichtenstein, A.H. Effect of prior meal macronutrient composition on postprandial glycemic responses and glycemic index and glycemic load value determinations. *Am. J. Clin. Nutr.* **2017**, *106*, 1246–1256. [CrossRef]

26. Parr, E.; Devlin, B.; Callahan, M.; Radford, B.; Blankenship, J.; Dunstan, D.; Hawley, J. Effects of providing high-fat versus high-carbohydrate meals on daily and postprandial physical activity and glucose patterns: A randomised controlled trial. *Nutrients* **2018**, *10*, 557. [CrossRef]
27. Brodovicz, K.G.; Girman, C.J.; Simonis-Bik, A.M.C.; Rijkelijkhuizen, J.M.; Zelis, M.; Bunck, M.C.; Mari, A.; Nijpels, G.; Eekhoff, E.M.W.; Dekker, J.M. Postprandial metabolic responses to mixed versus liquid meal tests in healthy men and men with type 2 diabetes. *Diabetes Res. Clin. Pract.* **2011**, *94*, 449–455. [CrossRef]
28. Lupoli, R.; Pisano, F.; Capaldo, B. Postprandial glucose control in type 1 diabetes: Importance of the gastric emptying rate. *Nutrients* **2019**, *11*, 1559. [CrossRef]
29. Bull, F.C.; Al-Ansari, S.S.; Biddle, S.; Borodulin, K.; Buman, M.P.; Cardon, G.; Carty, C.; Chaput, J.-P.; Chastin, S.; Chou, R.; et al. World Health Organization 2020 guidelines on physical activity and sedentary behaviour. *Br. J. Sports Med.* **2020**, *54*, 1451–1462. [CrossRef]
30. King, D.S.; Baldus, P.J.; Sharp, R.L.; Kesl, L.D.; Feltmeyer, T.L.; Riddle, M.S. Time course for exercise-induced alterations in insulin action and glucose tolerance in middle-aged people. *J. Appl. Physiol.* **1995**, *78*, 17–22. [CrossRef]
31. Rowe, D.A.; Welk, G.J.; Heil, D.P.; Mahar, M.T.; Kemble, C.D.; Calabró, M.A.; Camenisch, K. Stride rate recommendations for moderate-intensity walking. *Med. Sci. Sports Exerc.* **2011**, *43*, 312–318. [CrossRef] [PubMed]
32. Tudor-Locke, C.; Aguiar, E.J.; Han, H.; Ducharme, S.W.; Schuna, J.M.; Barreira, T.V.; Moore, C.C.; Busa, M.A.; Lim, J.; Sirard, J.R.; et al. Walking cadence (steps/min) and intensity in 21–40-year-olds: CADENCE-adults. *Int. J. Behav. Nutr. Phys. Act.* **2019**, *16*, 8. [CrossRef] [PubMed]
33. Narang, B.J.; Atkinson, G.; Gonzalez, J.T.; Betts, J.A. A tool to explore discrete-time data: The time series response analyser. *Int. J. Sport Nutr. Exerc. Metab.* **2020**, *30*, 374–381. [CrossRef] [PubMed]
34. Cohen, J. *Statistical Power Analysis for the Behavioral Sciences*, 2nd ed.; Lawrence Erlbaum Associates: Hillsdale, NJ, USA, 1988; ISBN 978-0-8058-0283-2.
35. Monnier, L.; Colette, C.; Owens, D.R. Glycemic variability: The third component of the dysglycemia in diabetes. Is it important? How to measure it? *J. Diabetes Sci. Technol.* **2008**, *2*, 1094–1100. [CrossRef]
36. Haxhi, J.; Leto, G.; di Palumbo, A.S.; Sbriccoli, P.; Guidetti, L.; Fantini, C.; Buzzetti, R.; Caporossi, D.; Di Luigi, L.; Sacchetti, M. Exercise at lunchtime: Effect on glycemic control and oxidative stress in middle-aged men with type 2 diabetes. *Eur. J. Appl. Physiol.* **2016**, *116*, 573–582. [CrossRef]
37. Holst, J.J.; Gribble, F.; Horowitz, M.; Rayner, C.K. Roles of the gut in glucose homeostasis. *Diabetes Care* **2016**, *39*, 884–892. [CrossRef]
38. Loh, R.; Stamatakis, E.; Folkerts, D.; Allgrove, J.E.; Moir, H.J. Effects of interrupting prolonged sitting with physical activity breaks on blood glucose, insulin and triacylglycerol measures: A systematic review and meta-analysis. *Sports Med.* **2020**, *50*, 295–330. [CrossRef]
39. Saunders, T.J.; Atkinson, H.F.; Burr, J.; MacEwen, B.; Skeaff, C.M.; Peddie, M.C. The acute metabolic and vascular impact of interrupting prolonged sitting: A systematic review and meta-analysis. *Sports Med.* **2018**, *48*, 2347–2366. [CrossRef]
40. Shambrook, P.; Kingsley, M.I.; Taylor, N.F.; Wundersitz, D.W.; Wundersitz, C.E.; Paton, C.D.; Gordon, B.A. A comparison of acute glycaemic responses to accumulated or single bout walking exercise in apparently healthy, insufficiently active adults. *J. Sci. Med. Sport* **2020**, *23*, 902–907. [CrossRef]
41. Zhang, X.; Zheng, C.; Ho, R.S.T.; Miyashita, M.; Wong, S.H.S. The effects of accumulated versus continuous exercise on postprandial glycemia, insulin, and triglycerides in adults with or without diabetes: A systematic review and meta-analysis. *Sports Med. Open* **2022**, *8*, 14. [CrossRef]
42. Morrison, D.J.; Kowalski, G.M.; Grespan, E.; Mari, A.; Bruce, C.R.; Wadley, G.D. Measurement of postprandial glucose fluxes in response to acute and chronic endurance exercise in healthy humans. *Am. J. Physiol. Endocrinol. Metab.* **2018**, *314*, E503–E511. [CrossRef] [PubMed]
43. Schiavon, M.; Hinshaw, L.; Mallad, A.; Man, C.D.; Sparacino, G.; Johnson, M.; Carter, R.; Basu, R.; Kudva, Y.; Cobelli, C.; et al. Postprandial glucose fluxes and insulin sensitivity during exercise: A study in healthy individuals. *Am. J. Physiol. Endocrinol. Metab.* **2013**, *305*, E557–E566. [CrossRef] [PubMed]
44. Sylow, L.; Kleinert, M.; Richter, E.A.; Jensen, T.E. Exercise-stimulated glucose uptake—Regulation and implications for glycaemic control. *Nat. Rev. Endocrinol.* **2017**, *13*, 133–148. [CrossRef] [PubMed]

nutrients

Review

The Exposome and Immune Health in Times of the COVID-19 Pandemic

Javier S. Morales [1,2,*], Pedro L. Valenzuela [3,4], Adrián Castillo-García [5], Javier Butragueño [6], David Jiménez-Pavón [1,2,7], Pedro Carrera-Bastos [8,9] and Alejandro Lucia [3,4,7]

1 MOVE-IT Research Group, Department of Physical Education, Faculty of Education Sciences, Universidad de Cádiz, 11519 Cadiz, Spain; david.jimenez@uca.es
2 Biomedical Research and Innovation Institute of Cádiz (INiBICA) Research Unit, Puerta del Mar University Hospital, University of Cádiz, 11009 Cadiz, Spain
3 Faculty of Sport Sciences, Universidad Europea de Madrid, 28670 Madrid, Spain; pedroluis.valenzuela@universidadeuropea.es (P.L.V.); alejandro.lucia@universidadeuropea.es (A.L.)
4 Physical Activity and Health Research Group ('PaHerg'), Research Institute of the Hospital 12 de Octubre ('imas12'), 28041 Madrid, Spain
5 Fissac—Physiology, Health and Physical Activity, 28015 Madrid, Spain; adriancastillogarcia@icloud.com
6 LFE Research Group, Department of Health and Human Performance, Faculty of Physical Activity and Sport Sciences, Polytechnic University of Madrid (UPM), 28040 Madrid, Spain; javier.butragueno@gmail.com
7 CIBER of Frailty and Healthy Aging (CIBERFES), 28029 Madrid, Spain
8 Centre for Primary Health Care Research, Lund University, Skane University Hospital, 205 02 Malmö, Sweden; pmcbastos@gmail.com
9 Faculty of Biomedical and Health Sciences, Universidad Europea de Madrid, 28670 Madrid, Spain
* Correspondence: javier.salvador@uca.es

Abstract: Growing evidence supports the importance of lifestyle and environmental exposures—collectively referred to as the 'exposome'—for ensuring immune health. In this narrative review, we summarize and discuss the effects of the different exposome components (physical activity, body weight management, diet, sun exposure, stress, sleep and circadian rhythms, pollution, smoking, and gut microbiome) on immune function and inflammation, particularly in the context of the current coronavirus disease 2019 (COVID-19) pandemic. We highlight the potential role of 'exposome improvements' in the prevention—or amelioration, once established—of this disease as well as their effect on the response to vaccination. In light of the existing evidence, the promotion of a healthy exposome should be a cornerstone in the prevention and management of the COVID-19 pandemic and other eventual pandemics.

Keywords: healthy lifestyle; environmental exposure; COVID-19; vaccines; infectious diseases

Citation: Morales, J.S.; Valenzuela, P.L.; Castillo-García, A.; Butragueño, J.; Jiménez-Pavón, D.; Carrera-Bastos, P.; Lucia, A. The Exposome and Immune Health in Times of the COVID-19 Pandemic. *Nutrients* **2022**, *14*, 24. https://doi.org/10.3390/nu14010024

Academic Editor: Francisco J. Pérez-Cano

Received: 12 November 2021
Accepted: 19 December 2021
Published: 22 December 2021

1. Introduction

After the reemergence of the Severe Acute Respiratory Syndrome (SARS) Coronavirus (SARS-CoV) in 2003, Cheng et al. [1] warned (in 2007) of the need to take measures aimed at preventing the possibility that SARS—or other viruses—returning if conditions are fit for their introduction, mutation, amplification, and transmission. In light of the more than 233 million cases and 4.7 million deaths worldwide, according to data from The Johns Hopkins University (updated as of 30 September 2021) [2], caused by the current pandemic of coronavirus disease 2019 (COVID-19), it seems clear that countries are not prepared to deal with an emergency that had already been predicted 13 years earlier. Yet, the COVID-19 pandemic is just one of the many pandemics that are likely to come in the foreseeable future [3].

Combining a healthy lifestyle with environmental exposure could be an important companion measure to vaccines and medications for the prophylaxis and treatment of future pandemics (Figure 1). The implementation of healthy lifestyles and environmental exposures can still play a key role in the context of the current COVID-19 pandemic, potentially contributing to the prevention of new cases or the improvement of the prognosis of infected patients [4–8]. These lifestyle measures will be explained in detail from Section 2 to Section 9 and mainly include performing regular physical activity, avoiding obesity, following a diet rich in fresh fruits, vegetables, polyphenols, micronutrients and fish-derived omega-3 fatty acids (e.g., the Mediterranean diet) that together can contribute to attenuate inflammation, minimizing psychosocial stress and exposure to environmental pollutants, following healthy sleeping patterns, and avoiding smoking. In this regard, a study conducted with twins revealed that, compared with genetic endowment, non-heritable factors seem to be the strongest contributors to individual variability in immune responses [9]. Indeed, various lifestyles and environmental factors cannot only modulate immune responses [10–13] but also individual response to vaccination [14].

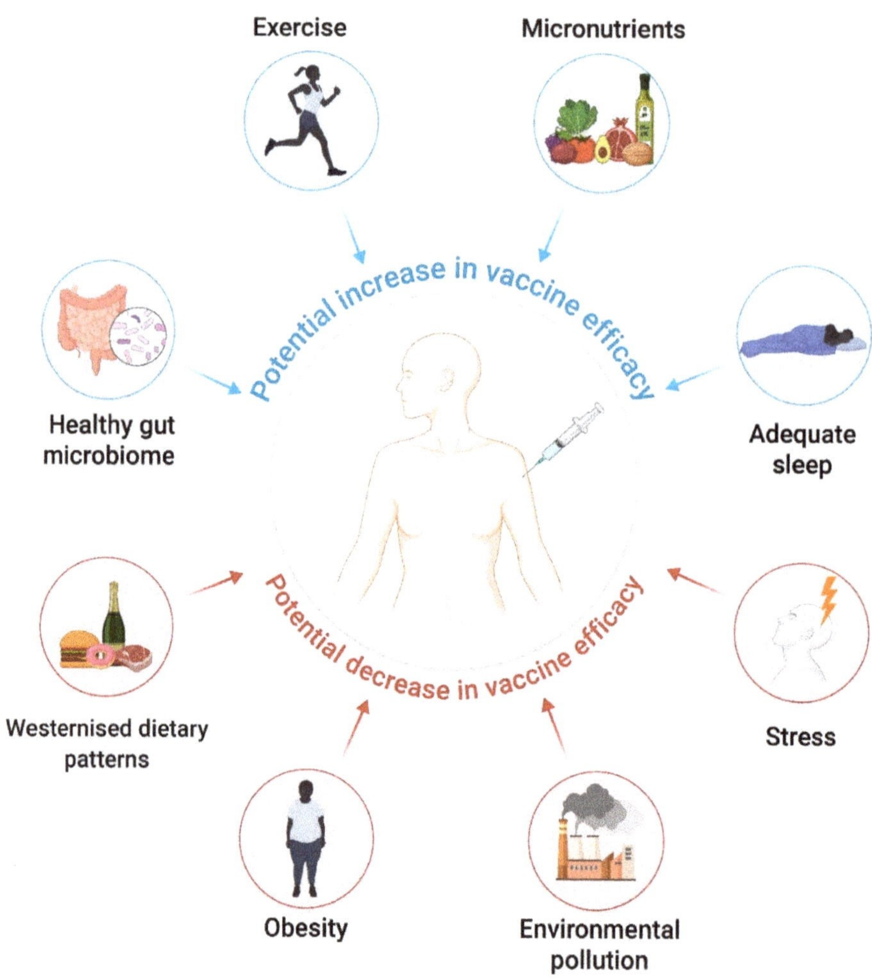

Figure 1. Summary of potential mechanisms underlying the positive and negative effects of the different exposome components on vaccine efficacy. Source: Self-elaboration based on the main results obtained in the scientific literature.

The relevance of lifestyle/environmental factors for health has been extensively evidenced [15]. However, most epidemiological studies have focused almost exclusively on single exposures. Since health status obviously depends on multiple variables [16], a more comprehensive paradigm that considers the exposure to different endogenous and environmental factors collectively is emerging, the so-called exposome. Briefly, the exposome refers to life-course exposures starting from the prenatal period onward [17]. This holistic approach might help to gain insight into the influence of lifestyle/environmental factors on human health [18–22]. The exposome encompasses two broad categories of non-genetic exposures: individual-level (physical activity, weight management, diet, stress, sleep and circadian rhythms, pollution, smoking, as well as the gut microbiome) and general exposures (climate and sunlight, environmental pollution), respectively [23]. Of interest, all these exposures can act synergistically through common mechanisms, such as the nuclear factor binding near the k light-chain gene in the B cells (NF-κB) family of transcriptional factors and the inflammasome machinery—the innate immune system receptors and sensors that regulate the activation of caspase-1 and induce inflammation in response to infectious microbes and host-derived molecules, the so-called damage-associated molecular patterns—and subsequent inflammation [24].

In the present narrative (non-systematic) review, we aim to summarize the effect of the exposome (including physical activity, weight management, diet, vitamin D and sun exposure, stress, sleep and circadian rhythms, exposure to environmental pollution, smoking, and gut microbiome) on inflammation and immune function, with a focus on the potential role of lifestyle changes in the prevention—or amelioration once established—of infectious diseases such as COVID-19, as well as their influence on the efficacy of vaccines. Our objective is to draw attention to the potential importance of complementary lifestyle-related measures in order to deal with the COVID-19 pandemic and possible future pandemics, which should be implemented along with other established measures such as vaccination and medical treatments.

2. Physical Activity

Approximately one-quarter of the population worldwide is considered physically inactive (that is, not meeting the minimum international recommendations, i.e., at least 150 or 75 min/week of moderate (such as walking) or vigorous (such as very brisk walking) aerobic activities, respectively) [25]. There is evidence that in the context of the current pandemic, preventive measures such as social distancing and forced lockdown have increased sedentary behaviors and physical inactivity [26–30]. Of relevance, physical inactivity can promote baseline inflammation and several related pathophysiologic alterations including, among others, insulin resistance, dyslipidemia, vascular endothelial dysfunction, high blood pressure, and sarcopenia [24,31]. Consistent with these effects, physical inactivity has been described as a contributor to over 35 chronic conditions [31].

Conversely, the beneficial effects of regular physical activity (PA) on immune function are well documented. Regular PA is associated with a 31% and 37% risk reduction of community-acquired infectious diseases and subsequent mortality, respectively, compared to inactive controls [32]. Physical exercise interventions can increase CD4 lymphocyte counts and salivary immunoglobulin A (IgA) concentration and decrease neutrophil counts compared to controls [32]. In fact, even just four weeks of either moderate- or high-intensity interval exercise can lead to a remarkable improvement in natural killer (NK) cell number and function (i.e., 'killing capacity') [33]. Regular exercise can also attenuate *immunosenescence* [34], that is, the progressive immune dysfunction that occurs as we age, with remodeling of lymphoid organs and a higher susceptibility to infections.

Acute bouts of exercise also provide some benefits to the immune system, stimulating the interchange of innate immune cells between lymphoid tissues and the blood compartment, while improving immunosurveillance against pathogens and decreasing systemic inflammation [35]. Indeed, muscle contractions induce the release of hundreds of molecules—mostly but not only small peptides (cytokines) collectively known as *myokines*—

from skeletal muscles (but also from other tissues, in which case they are broadly termed *exerkines*) into the bloodstream, thereby reaching other tissues and organs where they elicit myriad beneficial effects, including anti-inflammatory ones [36,37]. Thus, the beneficial effects of regular PA can be attributed, at least in part, to the accumulation of frequent, repeated 'time windows' (i.e., during exertion and in the following hours) where myokines (or *exerkines*) are being released to the blood with the subsequent salutary effects. Notably, when it is released from the working muscles and thus acts as a myokine, interleukin (IL)-6 exerts anti-inflammatory effects and can stimulate NK cells, an effect that is not observed under resting conditions. In fact, IL-6 released from other sources, such as immune cells, in a non-exercise milieu, has a pro-inflammatory role [38].

A high level of cardiorespiratory fitness (CRF), which can be achieved through regular exercise practice, has been associated with fewer days (−46%) of illness from acute respiratory infections as compared with a low level of CRF [39]. A high CRF has also been reported to positively impact the expression of immune markers that could theoretically reduce the risk of COVID-19 complications [40], particularly the so-called *cytokine storm* syndrome [40]; that is, the excessive, uncontrolled release of proinflammatory cytokines (e.g., interferon-γ, IL-1, IL-6, IL-18, tumor necrosis factor [TNF]-α) to the bloodstream that is frequently found in patients with severe disease, including COVID-19 [41]. In the same line, CRF has been reported to be independently and inversely associated with the likelihood of hospitalization for COVID-19 [42].

Physical exercise might also be beneficial in improving the efficacy of vaccines against SARS-coronavirus (CoV)-2 [32,43] and other infectious agents. Both 'acute' (i.e., a single session) or regular exercise (repeated sessions) prior to influenza vaccination are safe and can enhance the immune response to vaccination [44,45]. Edwards et al. showed that performing eccentric contractions of the deltoid and biceps brachii muscles of the non-dominant arm 6 h before influenza vaccination in the same arm improved cell-mediated response (as reflected by enhanced interferon-γ responses) in men and increased antibody responses in women [46]. A meta-analysis by Chastin et al. found that regular exercise increases antibody titers after vaccination against influenza, pneumococcal, or varicella zoster virus, respectively [32]. There is also evidence from interventional research supporting the beneficial role of regular exercise. Notably, a study with participants aged ~70 years who were previously sedentary and had poor influenza vaccine responses found that those randomized to moderate-intensity cardiovascular exercise showed marked improvements in influenza seroprotection throughout the entire influenza season compared to the control group [47]. In addition, exercise may minimize the deleterious effects of immunosenescence on vaccination efficacy by maintaining the peripheral T-cell pool and the ability of these cells to respond to novel vaccine antigens. Physically active, older adults are known to have fewer and more 'senescent' and naïve T cells, respectively, than their sedentary counterparts. Importantly, preserving a diverse pool of both functional (non-senescent) and naïve T-cells is likely to reduce infection risk, and the regular release of muscle-derived cytokines such as IL-7 and IL-15 has been purported to play important roles in the beneficial effects of exercise on immunity [34]. Furthermore, elderly women who were physically active had a better immune response after vaccination than those who were less active [48]. Although more studies are needed to confirm its efficacy, acute exertion (i.e., a single session of relatively intense exercise performed just prior to vaccination) has also been postulated as an effective strategy to increase the immune response to vaccination [44].

3. Body Weight Management

The worldwide prevalence of obesity has almost tripled since 1975, with 39% and 13% of adults now considered to have overweight and obesity, respectively [49]. Excessive adiposity, especially central adiposity—accumulation of fat in the lower torso around the abdominal area—is detrimental to health, with consistent evidence showing that overweight and obesity are associated with an increased risk of associated comorbidities—mainly, but not only, cardiovascular disease (CVD) [50]. Furthermore, obesity is overall associated with accelerated ageing and subsequent immune dysfunction, the so-called *adipaging* [51].

There is meta-analytical evidence that individuals with obesity are not only at greater risk of COVID-19 infection but also of having a worse prognosis (higher risk of severe disease and mortality) than their normal-weight peers [52–54]. Several mechanisms could contribute to the detrimental effects of obesity on immune function. Excess of adiposity, particularly around abdominal organs (i.e., visceral adipose tissue), is characterized by increased production and secretion of pro-inflammatory cytokines and other molecules, the so-called *adipocytokines* or *adipokines* [55], which could lead to low-grade chronic inflammation (LGCI) and contribute to several chronic inflammatory conditions. Excess of adiposity has been reported to exert modulatory effects on key populations of immune cells that are critical for ensuring an adequate response to SARS-CoV-2 [56]. Obesity is also associated with both a reduced number of NK lymphocytes and a lower cytotoxic capacity of these cells [57,58]. On the other hand, leptin, one of the most abundant adipokines produced by adipocytes, affects both innate and adaptive immunity [59,60]. Notably, leptin increases the production of pro-inflammatory cytokines in monocytes and macrophages [61]. Thus, a positive correlation between circulating leptin and inflammatory biomarkers (C-reactive protein [CRP], IL-6, TNF-α) has been suggested [62]. In this context, obesity is frequently associated with leptin resistance, a phenomenon traditionally attributed to impaired transport of this molecule through the blood–brain barrier that leads to increased leptin levels [63]. This, in turn, leads to the dysregulation of cytokine production, increased susceptibility to infectious diseases, autoimmune conditions, and upregulated inflammatory responses [60], and could explain why many obesity-associated comorbidities have been linked to immune dysfunction [64]. Moreover, angiotensin converting enzyme (ACE) 2 expression in adipose tissue exceeds that of the lung tissue [65]. Since ACE2 is an important entry receptor for SARS-CoV-2 [66], elevated levels of this membrane receptor, as a consequence of excess adipose tissue, could promote viral entrance into target cells and increase the risk of COVID-19 infection.

Some comorbidities linked to obesity are also associated with higher COVID-19 severity. Obesity is often associated with respiratory dysfunction, which increases the risk of hypoventilation, pulmonary hypertension, and cardiac stress, worsening COVID-19 prognosis [67]. People with obesity have impaired ventilatory mechanics, as excess adiposity causes a decrease in expiratory reserve volume, leading to lower levels of both functional residual capacity and total lung capacity [68]. Overall, these effects can lead to lower CRF levels which, as mentioned above, have been inversely associated with the risk of COVID-19 hospitalization [42].

Obese individuals show an impaired response to vaccination compared to normal-weight individuals, as a recent study with 248 healthcare workers who were vaccinated against COVID-19 with the second dose of the BNT162b2 vaccine suggests [69]. This is in line with previous evidence that obesity could decrease the immune response after vaccination against hepatitis B [70,71], rabies [72], tetanus [73], or influenza [74]. Different mechanisms might explain an obesity-induced impairment in response to vaccination. On the one hand, due to excessive adiposity, individuals with obesity could receive a lower relative vaccination dose or experience reduced absorption from the site of injection [73]. Alternatively, obesity-induced LGCI might reduce the immune response to vaccines [73].

In summary, excess adiposity can lead to a pro-inflammatory status, also known as metaflammation [75], with subsequent immune dysfunction (e.g., impaired innate and adaptative response to infectious agents and vaccines) and respiratory dysfunction, thereby worsening prognosis after virus infections. Thus, body weight management should be a key public health concern in the prevention/management of the current COVID-19 pandemic and future pandemics.

4. Diet

The westernised way of life has brought several changes to the human diet, particularly the widespread consumption of ultra-processed foods with a high content of fat, sugar, salt, and flavour additives that can cause an excess calorie intake [76]. These features contribute to obesity, which, as previously discussed, can lead to a proinflammatory status, impair immune function, and increase the risk of many chronic diseases (Figure 2).

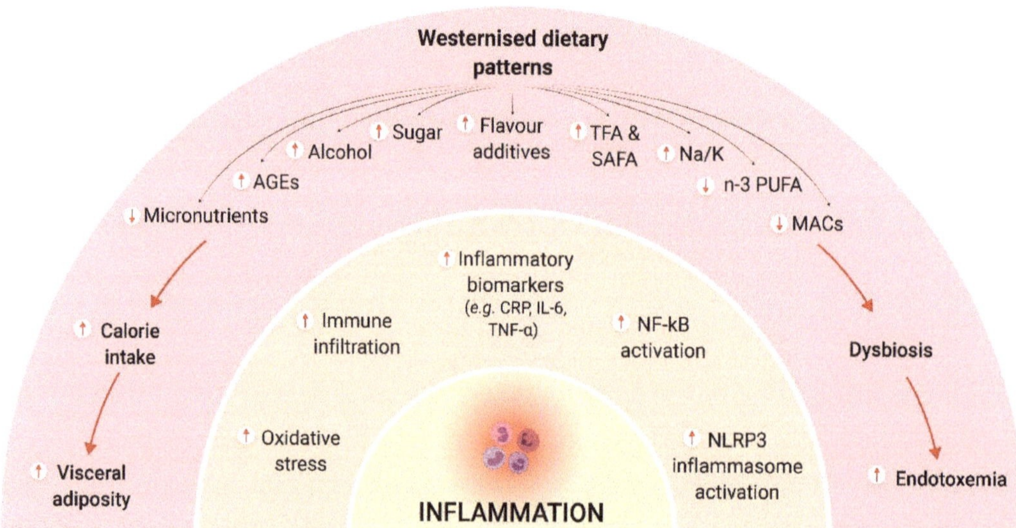

Figure 2. Summary of potential mechanisms underlying the deleterious effects of westernised dietary patterns on inflammation. Abbreviations: AGEs, advanced glycation end products; CRP, C-reactive protein; IL-6, interleukin-6; MACs, microbiota-accessible carbohydrates; NF-κB, nuclear factor-κB; PUFA, polyunsaturated fatty acids; SAFA, saturated fatty acids; TFA, trans fatty acids; TNF, tumor necrosis factor. Source: Self-elaboration based on the main results obtained in the scientific literature.

The abundance of food and the way it is consumed in Western countries has led to dietary patterns characterized by several meals per day consumed in a very long eating window. Thus, feeding periods longer than 14 h have been described in overweight individuals [77]. However, when overweight individuals with >14 h eating duration ate for only 10–11 h per day over 16 weeks, they reduced their energy intake by 20% and showed a reduction in total body weight (−3.27 kg) and body mass index (−1.15 kg/m^2) [77]. In this effect, intermittent fasting and particularly time-restricted feeding (TRF) protocols have gained popularity in recent years because they might help adults with obesity to lose weight. However, controversy exists, and in fact, meta-analytical evidence indicates no significant difference in weight loss when comparing intermittent (i.e., TRF) or continuous energy restriction interventions [78–81]. This being said, TRF might produce larger metabolic benefits even in the absence of weight loss, including increases in insulin sensitivity and decreases in blood pressure or oxidative stress [82].

Controversy also exists on the influence of TRF on inflammation. The available evidence suggests that TRF has no effects on inflammatory markers such as CRP, IL-6, or TNF-α [82–86], although it is possible that different types of TRF could produce different effects. For instance, a study conducted during the Ramadan period, 16 h fasting from sunrise to sunset throughout 29 consecutive days, showed that this type of TRF increased IL-6 levels but also induced a reduction in TNF-α and CRP [87]. Other beneficial effects of intermittent fasting could involve metabolic switching and cellular resistance stress, although the specific mechanisms remain unclear [88].

Beyond its obesogenic effect, westernized diets represent a major source of advanced glycation end products (AGEs) [89]; that is, proteins, nucleic acids, or lipids that become non-enzymatically glycated as a result of exposure to reducing sugars. Dietary AGEs are typically found in foods cooked under dry heat (such as grilling, broiling, roasting, and frying) or exposed to thermal treatments, with processed and ultra-processed foods being a major source of these compounds. A systematic review of randomized controlled trials (RCT) found that AGEs-rich diets can increase TNF-α as well as 8-isoprostane, a marker of oxidative stress [90]. There is a growing body of evidence that closely links AGEs with chronic diseases [89,91,92]. Conversely, meta-analytical evidence suggests that reducing dietary AGEs can lower circulating AGEs as well as the receptor for these compounds, which translates into a reduction in TNF-α, vascular cell adhesion molecule-1 (VCAM-1), 8-isoprostane, and leptin, respectively, together with an increase in adiponectin and sirtuin-1 [93]. Western diets typically also include high glycemic load ingredients, such as sugars and refined cereal grains. These have been shown, in mononuclear cells from healthy individuals, to increase the generation of reactive oxygen species (ROS) and activate redox-sensitive transcription factors, such as NF-κB, which upregulates the expression of various proinflammatory genes [94,95]. Other potential dietary triggers of inflammation that are present in excess in the Western diet include alcohol, salt, industrial trans fatty acids, and certain saturated fatty acids (particularly palmitic acid), all of which have been shown to cause inflammation through different mechanisms [96–99]. For instance, a high-salt diet may favour polarization of macrophages towards a pro-inflammatory (M1) phenotype, skew the balance between the proinflammatory T helper (Th)17 lymphocytes and the anti-inflammatory T regulatory (reg) cells, and may adversely change the microbiome [96], which, as will be discussed later, also affects inflammation and overall immune function. Conversely, increasing potassium intake has been shown to neutralize salt-loading-induced Th17 activation [100,101].

Giving support to the role of dietary factors in LGCI, various intervention studies have shown that hypercaloric fast-food meals (which are high in AGEs, sugars, refined grains, salt, and hydrogenated or saturated fats) increase the concentration of various proinflammatory molecules, even in lean healthy individuals [102,103]. Moreover, there is evidence associating westernised diets with increased serum CRP levels [104]. Westernised dietary patterns also tend to be low in fresh fruits and vegetables. This is relevant since a low intake of these food groups is considered one of the main diet-related risk factors according to the Global Burden of Disease Study [105,106] that estimated that poor dietary patterns were responsible for 11 million deaths worldwide (even outrunning smoking) in 2017 [105]. Interestingly, since fruits and vegetables are major sources of the so-called microbiota-accessible carbohydrates, reducing their intake can decrease the richness and diversity of the gut microbiota, which, as reviewed below, can contribute to LGCI [107,108]. Conversely, diets with a high content of fruits and vegetables have been reported to decrease circulating concentrations of TNF-α and CRP while increasing gamma-delta T lymphocytes (a group of T cells that are abundant in the gut mucosa known as 'intraepithelial lymphocytes') [109]. Foods that are rich in fruits or vegetables have also been shown to prevent or attenuate the oxidative and inflammatory stress induced by hypercaloric fast food meals [110–113]. This has mainly been attributed to their high content of several bioactive compounds involved in the regulation of genes that affect the inflammatory response and antioxidant status [114,115]. In addition, foods rich in fruits and vegetables are high in various minerals and vitamins reported to decrease oxidative stress and inflammation while improving overall immune function (i.e., potassium [100,101], magnesium [116,117], and vitamins B9 (folate [118–120]), C [121,122], and E [123]).

Other important micronutrients for immune health are zinc, copper, iron, and selenium, as well as vitamins A, B6, B12, and D. The impact of these micronutrients on viral infections has been extensively reviewed elsewhere [5,120,124,125]. As for vitamin D, it will be discussed at length in a later section. Of note, the nutritional status of zinc, copper, and selenium has been correlated with severity and mortality due to COVID-19 [126–128].

Accordingly, two observational studies found an association between zinc supplementation and better outcomes in COVID-19 hospitalized patients [129,130]. However, supplementation with high-dose zinc, vitamin C, or a combination of the two nutrients in ambulatory COVID-19 patients did not reduce the duration of symptoms compared with standard care [131]. Patients who might benefit the most from increasing the intake of these nutrients are those who are zinc and/or vitamin C-deficient [132], or have severe and critical COVID-19 since those typically present with high-grade inflammation [133], which can significantly affect the status of zinc [134] and vitamin C [135]. What seems clear is that, in times of the pandemic, it is essential to cover any nutritional deficiencies through an adequate diet and specific nutritional supplementation if applicable [136].

An optimal nutritional status can affect not only the outcome of an infection but also vaccination efficacy. Indeed, malnutrition might produce a lower antibody response to vaccination in children [137–141]. On the other hand, chronic overfeeding can cause obesity, which, as mentioned above, can lead to an impaired response to vaccination [142,143]. Interestingly, not only lean malnourished individuals but also obese people can present with multiple micronutrient deficiencies [144–146]. This is relevant because there is some evidence (albeit still limited) that zinc, copper, selenium, and iron, as well as vitamins A, B6, B9, B12, C, D, and E, might affect the immune response to various vaccines [124].

The daily consumption of five or more portions of fruits and vegetables per day has been shown, in an RCT, to improve the antibody response to Pneumovax II vaccination in healthy participants aged 65–85 years [147]. A study that included 3,042 individuals of both sexes showed that those with higher adherence to the Mediterranean diet (characterized by a high intake of fruits, vegetables, legumes, nuts, whole grains, fish and olive oil, moderate consumption of dairy products and red wine, and low consumption of red meat [148]) had 20%, 17%, 14%, 15%, and 6% lower levels of CRP, IL-6, white blood cell counts, homocysteine, and fibrinogen, than individuals with low adherence to the diet, respectively [149]. Consuming a Mediterranean diet modulated specific components of the gut microbiome of non-frail or pre-frail participants from several European countries, with microbiome changes associated with a reduction in the risk of frailty, an improvement in cognitive function, and a decrease in the circulating levels of two inflammatory markers, high-sensitivity CRP (hsCRP) and IL-17 [150]. In addition, results from the Moli-sani study including 14,586 healthy individuals showed that white blood cell and platelet counts were both inversely related to Mediterranean diet adherence [151]. Meta-analytical evidence indicates that high adherence to a Mediterranean diet attenuates inflammation and improves vascular endothelial function by increasing adiponectin and flow-mediated dilatation while decreasing hsCRP, IL-6, and intracellular adhesion molecule-1 [152]. Accordingly, adherence to the Mediterranean diet has been associated with a lower incidence (and related mortality) of CVD, cancer, and neurodegenerative conditions, as well as with all-cause mortality [153]. Even if compared to a low-fat diet, a Mediterranean diet supplemented with extra-virgin olive oil or nuts has been associated with a lower rate of major CVD events in individuals at high risk for CVD [154]. These results might be explained by the salutary—notably, antioxidant and immunomodulator—effects of certain dietary components of the Mediterranean diet. These include polyphenols [155,156] (found in fruits and vegetables, nuts, and extra virgin olive oil), micronutrients (such as magnesium [116,117], vitamins B9 [118–120], C [121,122] and E [123]), and fish-derived omega-3 fatty acids (which stimulate the resolution of inflammation by giving rise to molecules, the so-called specialized proresolving mediators) [157]. Hence, due to its antioxidant, anti-inflammatory and immunomodulatory benefits, and its protective effect against predictors of morbidity and mortality in patients with COVID-19 such as CVD, the Mediterranean diet could be a promising and relatively easy-to-apply method to attenuate the severity of SARS-CoV-2 and eventual future viral pandemics [158,159]. In fact, a study showed that adherence to the Mediterranean diet was inversely associated with COVID-19 cases and related deaths in Spain and across 23 Organization for Economic Co-operation and Development countries [160].

5. Vitamin D and Sun Exposure

While traditionally known for its role in bone metabolism and skeletal muscle function [161], vitamin D has recently gained attention as an important player in immune health [162]. Vitamin D modulates both the adaptive and innate arms of the immune system [162] and might improve the inflammatory response to viral infection [163,164]. In fact, a Mendelian randomization study with 35,833 participants showed that low levels of plasma 25-hydroxyvitamin (OH)D, a biomarker of vitamin D status, were associated with a higher risk of bacterial pneumonias during a 38-year follow-up [165]. Additionally, vitamin D deficiency has been associated with an increase in proinflammatory cytokines (TNF-α, IL-6) [166,167]. Preclinical studies have shown that vitamin D polarizes macrophages towards an anti-inflammatory phenotype, thereby reducing the secretion of proinflammatory cytokines such as IL-6 or TNF-α [168,169]. Moreover, vitamin D can polarize T CD4+ lymphocytes from a pro- (Th1/Th17) to an anti-inflammatory (Treg) phenotype, respectively [162]. Furthermore, this vitamin regulates the expression of genes that code for antimicrobial proteins in dendritic cells and macrophages [162]. A recent systematic review and meta-analysis of case-control, cross-sectional, and prospective cohort studies showed a significant and non-linear correlation between 25(OH)D levels below 37.5 nmol/L on the one hand, and risk and severity of acute respiratory tract infection on the other [170]. There is also meta-analytical evidence that vitamin D supplementation can reduce the incidence of respiratory infections and asthma exacerbations, especially in people with vitamin D deficiency [171,172].

Hence, vitamin D can affect the prognosis of COVID-19. Those European countries with lower reported plasma levels of vitamin D in the population, such as Spain and Italy (especially in older people), had the highest mortality rates from COVID-19 early in the pandemic [173,174]. In addition, vitamin D deficiency has been associated with a greater susceptibility to COVID-19 infection [175,176] and a greater risk of intensive care unit (ICU) admission in infected patients [177], with lower vitamin D levels reported for patients with a severe course of the disease [178,179]. Accordingly, there is evidence suggesting that vitamin D supplementation can have a positive effect on COVID-19 symptoms and severity. Compared with a lower dose (1000 IU), daily oral supplementation with 5000 IU of vitamin D3 for two weeks reduced the time to recovery of symptoms such as cough and gustatory sensory loss among mild-to-moderate COVID-19 patients with sub-optimal vitamin D status [180]. Further, a meta-analysis including 13 studies and 2933 patients found that vitamin D supplementation was associated with a reduced risk of adverse outcomes, ICU admission, and mortality from COVID-19 [181]. Interestingly, vitamin D supplementation was associated with improved clinical outcomes, especially when administered after the diagnosis of COVID-19 and not in patients who received vitamin D before diagnosis [181]. The benefits of vitamin D on COVID-19 complications could be due to its effects on the production of antimicrobial and antiviral proteins, as well as on the modulation of the inflammatory response, thereby preventing (or suppressing) the cytokine storm [182].

Yet there is some controversy on the potential benefits of vitamin D. A recent retrospective study determined that 25(OH)D levels above 40 nmol/L were not able to adequately predict in-hospital mortality in patients with COVID-19 [183]. A systematic review and meta-analysis found no significant effect of vitamin-D supplementation on major health-related outcomes in COVID-19 (such as mortality, ICU admission rates or need for invasive ventilation) [184]. A multi-center, double-blind, placebo-RCT trial did not find any beneficial effect on length of hospitalization among patients with COVID-19 receiving a single high oral dose of vitamin D3 (200,000 IU). This finding could also be explained by the fact that vitamin D supplementation prevents acute respiratory infections (e.g., COVID-19) when given as low-dose daily maintenance, but not as high-dose intermittent bolus [185,186].

The potential role of vitamin D on vaccine responses seems unclear [187]. Zimmerman et al. found that low vitamin D levels at baseline were associated with higher antibody titers in response to the human papillomavirus vaccine in young male adults [188]. However, a systematic review and meta-analysis failed to find a significant association between vitamin D status and the immunogenic response to influenza vaccination, although a lower seroprotective response to vaccination with some strains of influenza was observed in patients with vitamin D deficiency [189]. A placebo, double-blind RCT found no differences of serum levels of cathelicidin antimicrobial peptide (a polypeptide that is primarily stored in the lysosomes of macrophages and polymorphonuclear leukocytes), antibody titers, and ROS production 28 days after the influenza vaccine between cholecalciferol supplementation and placebo in deficient elderly persons, despite the former increasing vitamin D levels [190]. However, the supplementation group showed a reduced Th1/Th2 ratio after vaccination (coinciding with the end of the 3-month period with vitamin D supplementation) as well as low plasma levels of TNF-α and IL-6, together with higher levels of transforming growth factor-β 28 days post-vaccination [190]. Intramuscular co-administration of calcitriol, also known as 1α,25-dihydroxyvitamin D_3, the active form of vitamin D, at a site adjacent to an influenza vaccination did not enhance subsequent serum hemagglutination inhibition titers to any of the vaccine antigens compared to a placebo [191]. In a recent RCT, oral vitamin D supplementation or simulated sunlight exposure beginning three days after a hepatitis B vaccination, and achieving vitamin D sufficiency within five weeks, did not influence the response to vaccination [192]. Although more studies are needed to build stronger evidence [193], given the potential benefits of vitamin D for immune health in general and the safety of its supplementation, "there is nothing to lose and much to gain by achieving an optimal vitamin D status" in those people affected by COVID-19 [194].

Ultraviolet radiation exerts immunomodulatory effects independent of vitamin D [195]. For instance, ultraviolet radiation-induced immunosuppression is key to the development of carcinogenesis in the skin [196]. In addition to causing immune suppression, exposure to ultraviolet light induces a shift from a Th1- to a Th2-mediated response, increases regulatory T cell function, augments macrophage differentiation, and inhibits plasma cell differentiation [197]. However, the clinical implications of these effects are not entirely clear. On the one hand, the skin area that has been exposed chronically to ultraviolet radiation (such as that above the deltoid muscle) may not be an optimal site for the delivery of vaccines because their efficacy could be compromised, with unexposed sites (e.g., buttock, inside of the upper arm) being potentially more suitable [198]. Moreover, higher levels of antibody titers were found in children who received the rubella vaccine in the winter (with lower exposure to ultraviolet radiation and hence lower vitamin D levels) compared with their summer-inoculated peers [199]. This suggests that sun exposure may impair the efficacy of vaccines. By contrast, hepatitis B vaccine responses have proven to be poorer in winter than summer [192]. In cold and temperate climates, annual epidemics of influenza and the common cold occur during autumn and winter [22], when there is less sunlight and hence lower levels of vitamin D-stimulating ultraviolet radiation. Furthermore, the influenza virus is rapidly inactivated when exposed to ultraviolet radiation from sunlight [200]. Interestingly, both SARS and COVID-19 have emerged during winter months [201] and a recent study estimated that cold and dry weather, together with low levels of ultraviolet radiation, is moderately associated with higher SARS-CoV-2 transmissibility [202]. All this being said, it is too early to draw definitive conclusions on sun exposure and COVID-19.

6. Stress

The prevalence of mental health issues increased in April 2020 compared to pre-COVID-19 trends [203,204], with a recent systematic review and meta-analysis reporting that approximately one-third of the general population showed symptoms of stress during the COVID-19 pandemic [205]. Psychological stress can trigger immune dysfunction [206]. Brief episodes of stress, like the ones experienced during an exam or a first date, tend to suppress cellular immunity while preserving humoral immunity, whereas chronic stressors are associated with the suppression of both cellular and humoral measures [207]. Psychological stress has been associated in a dose-response manner with a higher risk of acute respiratory infections [208], and the link between psychological stress and several chronic conditions is well established, particularly for clinical depression, CVD, and human immunodeficiency virus/acquired immune deficiency syndrome [209]. There is meta-analytic evidence for a direct association between acute stress and inflammatory biomarkers (IL-1β, IL-6, IL-10, TNF-α) [210]. Several forms of chronic stress (such as job stress, immigration status, or poverty) have been correlated to elevated levels of hsCRP or CRP [211–213]. Conversely, there is recent meta-analytical evidence that mindfulness-based interventions aiming to reduce stress can induce modest but significant reductions in markers of LGCI (hsCRP, IL-6, TNF, and NF- κB activation) [214]. Chronic stress is also believed to trigger 'inflammaging' (that is, the chronic LGCI that is frequently associated with aging), partly through increases in oxidative stress [215]. This might also be relevant for vaccine efficacy. Indeed, a meta-analysis concluded that psychological stress could decrease antibody response to influenza vaccination [216]. However, stress levels in the 10 days after influenza vaccination appeared to be more influential to the antibody response than stress in the 2 days prior, with stress-related loss of sleep being primarily responsible for reducing the humoral immune response post-vaccination [217]. Regardless, both short-term (e.g., an academic examination) and long-term stressors (e.g., caregiving) can impair vaccine responses [218–223]. A poorer virus-specific T-cell response following influenza vaccination was observed in caregivers of Alzheimer's disease patients compared to control individuals [224]. The aforementioned evidence suggests that psychological stress can contribute to LGCI and impair the normal response to infections and vaccines, which is relevant to the current pandemic situation.

Although we didn't find evidence directly linking COVID-19 infection with psychological disorders (such as depression), the stressful situations faced by the overall population during the pandemic are likely to impair immune function and, consequently, increase the risk of SARS-CoV-2 infection and perhaps even affect vaccination efficacy. Accordingly, stress management techniques (e.g., meditation, relaxation techniques and Yoga) that modulate the immune response through various mechanisms (e.g., reducing LGCI, as indicated by lowered levels of circulating IL-6 and TNF-α [214]) could be a potentially effective strategy to attenuate the virus effect on health [214,225–227]. There is also meta-analytic evidence linking regular PA with 45% and 28–48% lower odds of depression and anxiety symptoms, respectively [228]. In addition, a recent umbrella review including 16 meta-analyses and 152 RCT concluded that regular physical exercise can be an effective adjunctive treatment for improving symptoms across a broad range of mental disorders (such as anxiety, depression, and post-traumatic stress disorder) [229].

7. Sleep and Circadian Disruption

Numerous behaviors that are prevalent in westernised countries can result in sleep disorders, including shift work, long working hours, as well as 24-h access to artificial light (shops, telephone, television, or the Internet). In this context, sleep disturbances are emerging as another consequence of the COVID-19 pandemic. There is longitudinal evidence that the lockdown, imposed during the pandemic, had a negative impact on the sleep quality of a Spanish cohort [27]. Moreover, a study in over 5000 Canadian adults showed that the proportion of individuals with clinically meaningful sleep difficulties markedly increased from before (36%) to after the COVID-19 pandemic (50.5%) [230].

Lack of sleep and circadian disruption is associated with immune dysfunction and a pro-inflammatory status [13,231,232]. Sleep deprivation upregulates inflammatory cytokines such as TNF-α, IL-1, or IL-6 [233]. In older adults, ageing-related alterations in nocturnal wake time and daytime sleepiness are associated with elevations of both plasma IL-6 and cortisol concentrations [234]. In fact, Atienza et al. suggested that the combination of abnormal sleep, circadian disruption, and impaired immune response promotes inflammation [235]. In addition, sleep deprivation is associated with the decline in the number of myeloid dendritic cell precursors producing IL-12, a main inducer of Th1 responses [236]. These results support the importance of an optimal sleep for health maintenance, particularly in the context of the current COVID-19 pandemic. On the other hand, a recent meta-analysis found that long sleep duration, as well as sleep disturbances, was associated with higher levels of CRP and IL-6 [237]. A study with 1,310 individuals from Italy showed that, during home confinement, participants reported a lower sleep quality despite spending more time in bed [238]. This finding might be attributed to various factors such as stress and circadian disruption. The latter can be caused by exposure to light at night, which is associated with reduced melatonin synthesis [239,240]. Melatonin has important properties as an immunomodulator agent that exerts anti-inflammatory effects [241,242] while also stimulating the production of NK and CD4+ cells and inhibiting the release of CD8+ cells [243]. Yet the most documented function of melatonin is the regulation of circadian rhythms. In this regard, circadian disruption (independently of sleep loss), such as that suffered by night-shift workers, has been shown to increase hsCRP levels [244,245].

Since inadequate sleep along with circadian disruption can promote LGCI and contribute to inmunosenescence, it might also affect the immune response to infections and vaccines. In fact, each additional hour of sleep was shown to increase the secondary antibody levels after hepatitis B vaccination by 56% [246], whereas sleeping <6 h per night was associated with a lower likelihood of showing a clinically protective response to the vaccination vs. sleeping <7 h per night [246]. Compared to no sleep, sleep enhances immune memory, thereby generating benefits of antigen-specific T-helper cell response after hepatitis A vaccination that were maintained one year later [247]. On the other hand, more studies are needed to confirm whether acute sleep deprivation can affect the human antibody titer response to vaccination, since short-term studies have yielded conflicting results. For instance, sleep restriction before and after influenza vaccination, despite a prolonged period of sleep recovery following vaccine administration, decreased antibody titers 10 days after vaccination [248]. However, the short-term negative effects of sleep on the antibody response apparently disappeared from 3 to 4 weeks after vaccination, because antibody titers no longer differed among sleep-restricted individuals and those who maintained their usual bedtime prior to receiving the vaccine [248]. Likewise, sleep deprivation in the night after vaccination against influenza virus caused a lower antibody titer response 5 days after vaccination, although it did not affect antibody titers thereafter [249]. Notwithstanding, evidence consistently suggests a key a role for circadian rhythms and sleep on immune system homeostasis [250] and hence the timing of vaccination might also affect the immune response. Accordingly, men vaccinated in the morning vs. afternoon had a better peak antibody response to both hepatitis A and influenza vaccines [251].

Given the importance of sleep for immune health and the negative effect of the COVID-19 pandemic on sleep characteristics in most individuals, the promotion of 'chronic' interventions aimed at improving sleep quality such as regular exercise [252] and circadian synchronization [253] should be kept in mind in view of future pandemics.

8. Exposure to Environmental Pollution

Exposure to persistent organic pollutants—that is, chemical substances that have a long half-life in the environment and can be harmful to human health and/or the environment—could further aggravate the impact of pandemics. Air pollution has an adverse effect on global disease burden, and it has been identified as the fifth-largest mortality risk factor worldwide, representing 7.6% of all-cause mortality [254]. The use of pesticides and agricultural or industrial chemicals together with exposure to hazardous waste (e.g., electronic waste) is increasing, together with the spectrum of adverse effects on human health [255,256]. A special situation exists for the so-called *xenobiotics*. These are chemical substances found within an organism that are not naturally produced (or expected to be present) within the organism in question. An example is bisphenol A, a ubiquitous plasticizing agent found in food, beverage cans, and thermal receipt paper. Xenobiotics represent a stress factor for immune cells and can cause inflammation [257]. Tobacco smoking, which will be discussed in a later section, is another source of xenobiotics that has been associated with a variety of deleterious effects on human health [258].

Long-term exposure to air pollution leads to the overexpression of ACE2, thereby facilitating viral penetration and subsequent depletion of ACE2 and increasing the likelihood of poor outcomes of COVID-19 [259]. Exposure to air pollution may also influence the systemic inflammatory response [260], the alveolar macrophage-mediated inflammatory response to phagocytize the virus [261], and affect host immunity [262]. There is meta-analytical evidence suggesting that exposure to ambient pollutants is associated with an increased level of CRP. On the other hand, ambient pollutants can increase Th2 immune responses, which is a characteristic in the respiratory tract during severe virus-induced exacerbations [263], such as asthma and chronic obstructive pulmonary disease. The decreased immune response caused by air pollution could also affect vaccination efficacy. Exposure to metals such as mercury has been associated with a lower immune response to vaccination programs including hepatitis B, influenza, measles, pertussis, tetanus, and diphtheria in children [138]. However, further studies are needed to corroborate this association.

The bulk of evidence suggests that exposure to air pollution might increase the risk of respiratory infections and, consequently, contribute to a worse prognosis of COVID-19. While the COVID-19 pandemic has resulted in a large drop in pollution levels [264], exposure to air pollution may increase the odds of COVID-19 infection [259,265] as well as symptoms severity [259,266] and risk of death [259,267,268]. In terms of COVID-19 mortality, of the 4443 fatality cases recorded in 66 administrative regions from Italy, Spain, France, and Germany, a vast majority (83%) of COVID-19 fatalities occurred in the regions with the highest nitrogen dioxide levels [268]. Coronavirus is in the air [269], and ultraviolet reduction as a consequence of air pollution may promote viral persistence in the air [270]. Exposure to toxic metals such as arsenic, lead, cadmium, or mercury is associated with respiratory dysfunction and respiratory diseases (i.e., chronic obstructive pulmonary disease and bronchitis), and hence a link between metal exposure and COVID-19 risk and/or severity might exist [271].

Therefore, it seems therefore reasonable to promote interventions aimed at reducing pollution levels.

9. Smoking

Approximately 1.3 billion people smoke worldwide [272]. Despite the anti-smoking public health policies implemented over the last 50 years, tobacco smoking remains a leading global risk factor [258]. Smoking history decreases life expectancy by at least a decade compared to those who have never smoked [273]. In fact, the smoke we inhale from tobacco contains more than 60 carcinogens [274].

There is accumulating evidence that like SARS-CoV, SARS-CoV-2 utilizes the cell membrane receptor ACE2 [275] as the main entry point into target cells. One of the main constituents of cigarette smoke, nicotine, might be able to downregulate the expression or activity of ACE2 receptors [276]. It could be thus hypothesized that inhaled nicotine during smoking has a protective effect against COVID-19. A recently published report, however, found that pulmonary ACE2 receptors are more activated in smokers than in never smokers [277], indicating that smoking is potentially a risk factor for COVID-19 by modulating ACE2 expression.

Smoking is also a potential risk factor for COVID-19 because of its detrimental effects on lung function and the possible transmission of SARS-CoV-2 by finger–mouth contact during tobacco use. However, initially, there was controversy regarding the relationship between smoking and SARS-CoV-2 infection/disease severity [278–281], and there were conflicting hypotheses on the role of nicotine on immune function [12]. Some studies have suggested that nicotine has anti-inflammatory effects [282,283] that could be beneficial in attenuating the cytokine storm often produced in response to viral infection [281,284,285]. There is indeed some evidence supporting a therapeutic role for nicotine in patients with severe COVID-19 [284,285], which is consistent, at least partly, with the notion that, to some extent, COVID-19 might be a disease of the nicotinic cholinergic system [281]. However, meta-analytical evidence indicates that smoking worsens the prognosis of COVID-19 [286–289].

It should also be considered that cigarette smoking and vaping can weaken immune health and increase the risk of infection and outcomes [290–292], potentially making smokers more vulnerable to SARS-CoV-2 and future viruses. For instance, influenza risk is several-fold higher (and the clinical presentation of the disease is much more severe) in smokers than non-smokers [291]. On the other hand, the number and activity of NK cells are decreased in smokers [293–295]. In addition, higher production of the proinflammatory cytokines IL-1β, IL-6, and TNF-α together with an enhanced proliferative response to mitogens has been reported in smokers compared to non-smokers [295]. The molecular pathways by which tobacco exerts deleterious effects on the immune system would involve NFκB, mitogen-activated protein (commonly known as 'MAP') kinases signaling as well as histone modification [296]. Of note, the high level of toxic metals in tobacco smoke may also partly underlie the association between smoking and COVID-19 severity due to their role in the development of respiratory dysfunction, immunotoxicity, and severity of viral diseases [271].

There is meta-analytical evidence that smokers have a 1.53 higher risk of nonresponse to vaccines such as hepatitis B compared to non-smokers [71]. This impaired response to vaccination might be mediated by the proinflammatory status associated with smoking [297]. Another potential mechanism has been postulated in a study with a murine model showing that the impaired response to vaccines may be mediated by cigarette smoke-related inhibition of the pulmonary T-cell response to vaccination against influenza virus and *Mycobacterium tuberculosis* [298].

Further research is warranted when keeping in mind that there is also preclinical evidence suggesting that smoking could be protective against the infection and severity of COVID-19 [278–281]. However, in light of the multiple well-established adverse effects of smoking on human health and the lack of evidence on whether an eventual association between smoking and protection against COVID-19 reflects an actual causal effect, public health programs should continue to support smoking cessation.

10. Gut Microbiome

The gastrointestinal tract is inhabited by about 100 trillion microbes (or *microbiota*) [299], including mainly bacteria, collectively known as the *microbiome*, that regulate fundamental functions that preserve human health, including host nutrient metabolism, xenobiotic and drug metabolism, or maintenance of structural integrity of the gut mucosal barrier[2]. The gut microbiome also plays a pivotal role in immune tolerance, inflammation, and protection against pathogens [300]. In fact, the microbiome has an important effect on the training and development of major components of the host's innate and adaptive immune system [300]. Alterations of the gut microbiome (known as dysbiosis) might lead to dysregulated immune responses to commensal microbes and the stabilization of a proinflammatory community of microbes, hence contributing to LGCI [301]. Accordingly, dysbiosis is associated with a wide variety of conditions including obesity [302], type 2 diabetes [302], hypertension [303], colon cancer [304], autoimmune diseases (such as inflammatory bowel disease [305]), allergic asthma [306], and human immunodeficiency virus [307].

Although the gut microbiome is a part of the exposome, several of the aforementioned exposome factors can influence the status of the gut microbiome and lead to dysbiosis [108,308], reflecting the bidirectional and dynamic relationship between different components of the exposome, as well as the host. The inappropriate use of antibiotics and other medications (e.g., proton pump inhibitors, antipsychotics, opioids, and nonsteroidal anti-inflammatory drugs) has a notable impact on the overall architecture of the gut microbiome [309,310]. Other factors shown to influence the composition and function of the gut microbiome include physical exercise [311], psychosocial stress [312], tobacco and alcohol use [313,314], and, as mentioned before, diet [107,108]. For instance, a high-sodium intake can alter the composition of the gut microbiome [96], and this has been associated with increased and decreased pro- and anti-inflammatory activity, respectively, of CD4+ T cells and macrophages [96]. Likewise, a high-fat/low-fiber westernised diet is linked to a decrease in microbial diversity and species richness, with a low abundance of some beneficial species (such as *Bifidobacterium*, *Lactobacillium* or *Eubacterium*), whereas a Mediterranean diet has essentially the opposite effect [315]. On the other hand, probiotics, live microorganisms with purported health benefits for the host if consumed in adequate amounts, and microbiota-accessible carbohydrates (commonly abbreviated by 'MACs' and also known as prebiotics—carbohydrates that are resistant to digestion and are made available for gut microbiota to ferment or metabolize into beneficial compounds, such as short chain fatty acids) could favourably modulate the gut microbiota, thereby exerting immunomodulatory and anti-inflammatory effects [107,108,316,317]. Accordingly, low-fat yogurt, a fermented dairy product containing a variety of probiotic bacteria, is associated with a reduction in markers of chronic inflammation and abdominal obesity in interventional and observational studies [318–320]. On the other hand, paradoxically, the hygiene measures proposed to prevent COVID-19, such as hand washing, could alter the composition of the gut microbiome. According to the 'hygiene hypothesis', which proposes that exposure to germs and certain infections helps the development of the immune system, excessive hygiene measures could negatively affect the microbiome [321].

Therefore, based on the influence of the microbiome on immunity, and the existence of a crosstalk between the gut microbiota and the lungs, known as the gut–lung axis [322,323], it might be argued that a healthy gut microbiome could play an important role in preventing respiratory infections or at least attenuating their severity. Indeed, the microbiota has previously been shown to regulate immune defence against influenza virus infection in the respiratory tract [324]. More recently, some authors have suggested the existence of dysbiosis in COVID-19 patients [325,326]. Zuo et al. [325] found an inverse correlation between the abundance of the gut species *Faecalibacterium prausnitzii* (an anti-inflammatory bacterium) and disease severity. Yeoh et al. concluded that the gut microbiome is implicated in the magnitude of COVID-19 severity, possibly through the modulation of host immune responses [327]. These authors also found that even 30 days after disease resolution, gut microbiome composition was still altered, which could contribute to persistent symptoms [327]. In addition, there is evidence for an increased incidence of dysbiosis in critically ill patients, a phenomenon associated with sepsis, organ failure, and death [328,329].

A recent systematic network and meta-analysis analysed the potential antiviral mechanisms of probiotics [330]. The authors found that probiotics could affect ACE2-mediated virus entry and temper the pro-inflammatory status caused by activation of nucleotide-binding oligomerization domain (NOD), leucine-rich repeat (LRR)-containing proteins (NLR) P3 (NLRP3) inflammasome, with *NLRP3* inflammasome being a multimeric protein complex that initiates an inflammatory form of cell death and triggers the release of proinflammatory cytokines IL-1β and IL-18 [331]. Probiotics can also improve the systemic immune response to viral infection (thereby attenuating the resulting lung tissue damage and cardiovascular complications) and modulate glucose/lipid metabolic pathways affected by the infection [330]. These findings might suggest that probiotics could be considered a potential preventive and alternative treatment strategy for both mild and severe stages of COVID-19 [330], although the evidence is still limited.

The gut microbiome could also affect the immune response to vaccination [332,333]. There is reasonable evidence that the gut microbiome improves both B cell and T cell responses to vaccination [334]. Of note, vaccine responses can vary widely between people in a given region [335]. A possible explanation is the high variability in the types of gut microbiota between populations [334]. For example, a study conducted in Ghanaian children concluded that the gut microbiome composition, which correlates significantly with rotavirus vaccine immunogenicity, might contribute to the diminished efficacy of rotavirus vaccines reported in developing countries [336]. Another study analysed the influence of gut microbiome on mucosal IgA antibody response to the polio vaccine in a population of Chinese infants [337]. The authors found that the composition of the gut microbiome was significantly different, reporting a higher and lower abundance of *Firmicutes* and *Actinobacteria*, respectively, in IgA-negative children than in their IgA-positive peers [337]. On the other hand, antibiotic administration in individuals with low levels of pre-existing immunity impairs responses to a seasonal influenza vaccine [338]. Conversely, a recent systematic review on the role of probiotics on vaccine responses suggested that probiotics represent a relatively cheap intervention to improve vaccine efficacy and duration of protection [339].

Keeping a healthy gut microbiome represents an important first-line defence against pathogens such as SARS-CoV-2, regardless of their virulence. As for the potential impact of the gut microbiome in modulating vaccine immunogenicity, further work in different human populations is needed.

11. Limitations and Perspectives

This review has some methodological limitations that should be considered. First, its narrative nature is likely to induce some bias, as it lacks strict criteria for the inclusion/exclusion of studies. In addition, the overwhelming number of new studies published virtually every day on the COVID-19 pandemic implies that previous conclusions on a given area are frequently challenged and must be revisited, with new hypotheses frequently arising. In this regard, we finished writing the first draft of this review on 17 July 2021, and therefore, at the time this review is published, evidence might have been updated on certain topics. On the other hand, although exposome improvements seem to be a potentially effective strategy to deal with COVID-19, a vast amount of research still needs to be implemented not only to shed light on the effects of combining a healthy lifestyle with environmental exposure but also to disentangle potential pathophysiological underpinnings. After reviewing the current literature, we have provided practical, testable hypotheses for future research in the field.

12. Conclusions

Throughout the COVID-19 pandemic, a variety of lifestyle and environmental exposures, collectively referred to as the exposome, that are known to play a major role in immune health, have been worsened. Notably, these include an increased prevalence of physical inactivity and obesity, unhealthy dietary patterns, high levels of psychosocial stress, sleep deprivation and circadian disruption, as well as high exposure to air pollution, low sun exposure, and insufficient vitamin D levels (Figure 3). The need to implement 'traditional' measures aimed at avoiding viral transmission (e.g., home confinement, closure of parks and gyms) should not overshadow the deleterious effects that they can have on other health markers. As a society, we should be prepared for a potential recurrence of previous pandemias and the emergence of new ones, and this preparedness should start with the promotion of healthy lifestyles and environmental exposures.

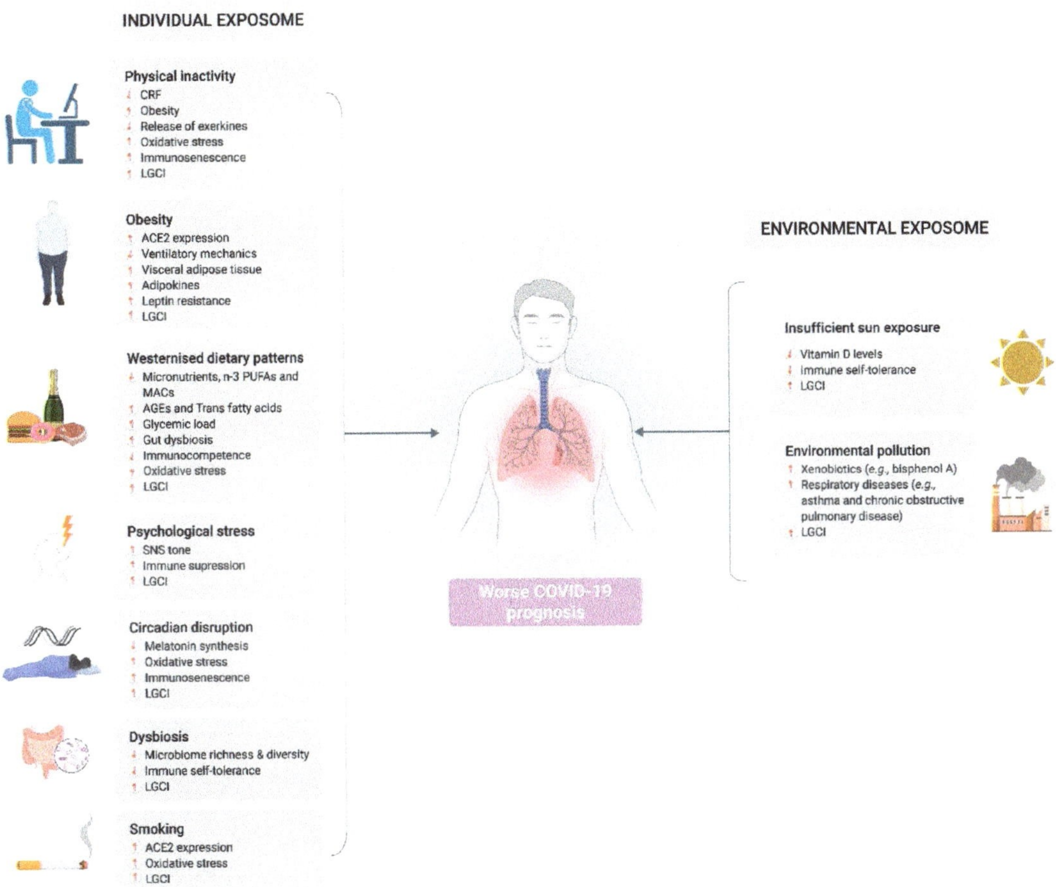

Figure 3. Summary of potential mechanisms underlying the negative effects of the different exposome components on the prognosis of COVID-19. Abbreviations: ACE2, angiotensin converting enzyme-2; AGEs, advanced glycation end products; CRF, cardiorespiratory fitness; LGCI, low-grade chronic inflammation; MACs, microbiota-accessible carbohydrates; PUFA, polyunsaturated fatty acids; SNS, sympathetic nervous system. Source: Self-elaboration based on the main results obtained in the scientific literature.

Author Contributions: Conceptualization: A.L., J.S.M., D.J.-P., P.C.-B. and P.L.V.; Drafting of the manuscript: J.S.M. and P.C.-B.; Visualization: A.C.-G. and J.B.; Critical revision for important intellectual content: All authors. All authors have read and agreed to the published version of the manuscript.

Funding: This work was supported by the Spanish Ministry of Economy and Competitiveness and Fondos Feder [PI18/00139 to A.L.]. Thanks to Biomedical Research Networking Center on Frailty and Healthy Aging (CIBERFES) and FEDER funds from the European Union (CB16/10/00477).

Institutional Review Board Statement: Not applicable.

Informed Consent Statement: Not applicable.

Acknowledgments: Figures were created in part with BioRender.com (accessed on 15 December 2021).

Conflicts of Interest: The authors declare no conflict of interest.

References

1. Cheng, V.C.C.; Lau, S.K.P.; Woo, P.C.Y.; Kwok, Y.Y. Severe acute respiratory syndrome coronavirus as an agent of emerging and reemerging infection. *Clin. Microbiol. Rev.* **2007**, *20*, 660–694. [CrossRef] [PubMed]
2. Dong, E.; Du, H.; Gardner, L. An interactive web-based dashboard to track COVID-19 in real time. *Lancet Infect. Dis.* **2020**, *20*, 533–534. [CrossRef]
3. Simpson, S.; Kaufmann, M.C.; Glozman, V.; Chakrabarti, A. Disease X: Accelerating the development of medical countermeasures for the next pandemic. *Lancet Infect. Dis.* **2020**, *20*, e108–e115. [CrossRef]
4. Chowdhury, M.A.; Hossain, N.; Kashem, M.A.; Shahid, M.A.; Alam, A. Immune response in COVID-19: A review. *J. Infect. Public Health* **2020**, *13*, 1619–1629. [CrossRef]
5. Calder, P.C.; Carr, A.C.; Gombart, A.F.; Eggersdorfer, M. Optimal Nutritional Status for a Well-Functioning Immune System Is an Important Factor to Protect against Viral Infections. *Nutrients* **2020**, *12*, 1181. [CrossRef]
6. Paludan, S.R.; Pradeu, T.; Masters, S.L.; Mogensen, T.H. Constitutive immune mechanisms: Mediators of host defence and immune regulation. *Nat. Rev. Immunol.* **2020**, *21*, 137–150. [CrossRef]
7. Martins, R.; Carlos, A.R.; Braza, F.; Thompson, J.A.; Bastos-Amador, P.; Ramos, S.; Soares, M.P. Disease Tolerance as an Inherent Component of Immunity. *Annu. Rev. Immunol.* **2019**, *37*, 405–437. [CrossRef]
8. Lange, K.W.; Nakamura, Y. Lifestyle factors in the prevention of COVID-19. *Glob. Health J.* **2020**, *4*, 146–152. [CrossRef] [PubMed]
9. Brodin, P.; Jojic, V.; Gao, T.; Bhattacharya, S.; Angel, C.J.L.; Furman, D.; Shen-Orr, S.; Dekker, C.L.; Swan, G.E.; Butte, A.J.; et al. Variation in the human immune system is largely driven by non-heritable influences. *Cell* **2015**, *160*, 37–47. [CrossRef]
10. Weyh, C.; Krüger, K.; Strasser, B. Physical activity and diet shape the immune system during aging. *Nutrients* **2020**, *12*, 622. [CrossRef]
11. De Heredia, F.P.; Gómez-Martínez, S.; Marcos, A. Chronic and degenerative diseases: Obesity, inflammation and the immune system. *Proc. Nutr. Soc.* **2012**, *71*, 332–338. [CrossRef]
12. Sopori, M. Effects of cigarette smoke on the immune system. *Nat. Rev. Immunol.* **2002**, *2*, 372–377. [CrossRef]
13. Besedovsky, L.; Lange, T.; Haack, M. The sleep-immune crosstalk in health and disease. *Physiol. Rev.* **2019**, *99*, 1325–1380. [CrossRef]
14. Zimmermann, P.; Curtis, N. Factors that influence the immune response to vaccination. *Clin. Microbiol. Rev.* **2019**, *32*, e00084-18. [CrossRef] [PubMed]
15. Lim, S.S.; Vos, T.; Flaxman, A.D.; Danaei, G.; Shibuya, K.; Adair-Rohani, H.; Amann, M.; Anderson, H.R.; Andrews, K.G.; Aryee, M.; et al. A comparative risk assessment of burden of disease and injury attributable to 67 risk factors and risk factor clusters in 21 regions, 1990-2010: A systematic analysis for the Global Burden of Disease Study 2010. *Lancet* **2012**, *380*, 2224–2260. [CrossRef]
16. López-Otín, C.; Kroemer, G. Hallmarks of Health. *Cell* **2021**, *184*, 33–63. [CrossRef] [PubMed]
17. Wild, C.P. Complementing the genome with an "exposome": The outstanding challenge of environmental exposure measurement in molecular epidemiology. *Cancer Epidemiol. Biomark. Prev.* **2005**, *14*, 1847–1850. [CrossRef] [PubMed]
18. Santos, S.; Maitre, L.; Warembourg, C.; Agier, L.; Richiardi, L.; Basagaña, X.; Vrijheid, M. Applying the exposome concept in birth cohort research: A review of statistical approaches. *Eur. J. Epidemiol.* **2020**, *35*, 193–204. [CrossRef] [PubMed]
19. Siroux, V.; Agier, L.; Slama, R. The exposome concept: A challenge and a potential driver for environmental health research. *Eur. Respir. Rev.* **2016**, *25*, 124–129. [CrossRef]
20. Nieuwenhuijsen, M.J. Urban and transport planning, environmental exposures and health-new concepts, methods and tools to improve health in cities. *Environ. Health* **2016**, *15* (Suppl. 1), 38. [CrossRef]
21. Vrijheid, M. The exposome: A new paradigm to study the impact of environment on health. *Thorax* **2014**, *69*, 876–878. [CrossRef] [PubMed]
22. Olvera Alvarez, H.A.; Kubzansky, L.D.; Campen, M.J.; Slavich, G.M. Early life stress, air pollution, inflammation, and disease: An integrative review and immunologic model of social-environmental adversity and lifespan health. *Neurosci. Biobehav. Rev.* **2018**, *92*, 226–242. [CrossRef] [PubMed]
23. Niedzwiecki, M.M.; Walker, D.I.; Vermeulen, R.; Chadeau-Hyam, M.; Jones, D.P.; Miller, G.W. The exposome: Molecules to populations. *Annu. Rev. Pharmacol. Toxicol.* **2019**, *59*, 107–127. [CrossRef]
24. Furman, D.; Campisi, J.; Verdin, E.; Carrera-Bastos, P.; Targ, S.; Franceschi, C.; Ferrucci, L.; Gilroy, D.W.; Fasano, A.; Miller, G.W.; et al. Chronic inflammation in the etiology of disease across the life span. *Nat. Med.* **2019**, *25*, 1822–1832. [CrossRef] [PubMed]
25. Guthold, R.; Stevens, G.A.; Riley, L.M.; Bull, F.C. Worldwide trends in insufficient physical activity from 2001 to 2016: A pooled analysis of 358 population-based surveys with 1·9 million participants. *Lancet Glob. Health* **2018**, *6*, e1077–e1086. [CrossRef]
26. Dunton, G.F.; Do, B.; Wang, S.D. Early effects of the COVID-19 pandemic on physical activity and sedentary behavior in children living in the U.S. *BMC Public Health* **2020**, *20*, 1351. [CrossRef]
27. Martínez-de-Quel, Ó.; Suárez-Iglesias, D.; López-Flores, M.; Pérez, C.A. Physical activity, dietary habits and sleep quality before and during COVID-19 lockdown: A longitudinal study. *Appetite* **2021**, *158*, 105019. [CrossRef]
28. Luciano, F.; Cenacchi, V.; Vegro, V.; Pavei, G. COVID-19 lockdown: Physical activity, sedentary behaviour and sleep in Italian medicine students. *Eur. J. Sport Sci.* **2020**, *21*, 1459–1468. [CrossRef]
29. Robinson, E.; Boyland, E.; Chisholm, A.; Harrold, J.; Maloney, N.G.; Marty, L.; Mead, B.R.; Noonan, R.; Hardman, C.A. Obesity, eating behavior and physical activity during COVID-19 lockdown: A study of UK adults. *Appetite* **2021**, *156*, 104853. [CrossRef]

30. Wilke, J.; Mohr, L.; Tenforde, A.S.; Edouard, P.; Fossati, C.; González-Gross, M.; Sánchez Ramírez, C.; Laiño, F.; Tan, B.; Pillay, J.D.; et al. A Pandemic within the Pandemic? Physical Activity Levels Substantially Decreased in Countries Affected by COVID-19. *Int. J. Environ. Res. Public Health* **2021**, *18*, 2235. [CrossRef]
31. Booth, F.W.; Roberts, C.K.; Thyfault, J.P.; Ruegsegger, G.N.; Toedebusch, R.G. Role of inactivity in chronic diseases: Evolutionary insight and pathophysiological mechanisms. *Physiol. Rev.* **2017**, *97*, 1351–1402. [CrossRef]
32. Chastin, S.F.M.; Abaraogu, U.; Bourgois, J.G.; Dall, P.M.; Darnborough, J.; Duncan, E.; Dumortier, J.; Pavón, D.J.; McParland, J.; Roberts, N.J.; et al. Effects of Regular Physical Activity on the Immune System, Vaccination and Risk of Community-Acquired Infectious Disease in the General Population: Systematic Review and Meta-Analysis. *Sports Med.* **2021**, *51*, 1673–1686. [CrossRef] [PubMed]
33. Llavero, F.; Alejo, L.; Fiuza-Luces, C.; López-Soto, A.; Valenzuela, P.; Castillo-García, A.; Morales, J.; Fernández-Moreno, D.; Pagola, I.; Ramírez, M.; et al. Exercise training effects on natural killer cells: A preliminary proteomics and systems biology approach. *Exerc. Immunol. Rev.* **2021**, *27*, 125–141. [PubMed]
34. Duggal, N.A.; Niemiro, G.; Harridge, S.D.R.; Simpson, R.J.; Lord, J.M. Can physical activity ameliorate immunosenescence and thereby reduce age-related multi-morbidity? *Nat. Rev. Immunol.* **2019**, *19*, 563–572. [CrossRef]
35. Nieman, D.C.; Wentz, L.M. The compelling link between physical activity and the body's defense system. *J. Sport Health Sci.* **2019**, *8*, 201–217. [CrossRef] [PubMed]
36. Steensberg, A.; Van Hall, G.; Osada, T.; Sacchetti, M.; Saltin, B.; Pedersen, B.K. Production of interleukin-6 in contracting human skeletal muscles can account for the exercise-induced increase in plasma interleukin-6. *J. Physiol.* **2000**, *529*, 237–242. [CrossRef]
37. Pedersen, B.K.; Febbraio, M.A. Muscle as an endocrine organ: Focus on muscle-derived interleukin-6. *Physiol. Rev.* **2008**, *88*, 1379–1406. [CrossRef]
38. Fiuza-Luces, C.; Santos-Lozano, A.; Joyner, M.; Carrera-Bastos, P.; Picazo, O.; Zugaza, J.L.; Izquierdo, M.; Ruilope, L.M.; Lucia, A. Exercise benefits in cardiovascular disease: Beyond attenuation of traditional risk factors. *Nat. Rev. Cardiol.* **2018**, *15*, 731–743. [CrossRef]
39. Nieman, D.C.; Henson, D.A.; Austin, M.D.; Sha, W. Upper respiratory tract infection is reduced in physically fit and active adults. *Br. J. Sports Med.* **2011**, *45*, 987–992. [CrossRef]
40. Zbinden-Foncea, H.; Francaux, M.; Deldicque, L.; Hawley, J.A. Does High Cardiorespiratory Fitness Confer Some Protection Against Proinflammatory Responses After Infection by SARS-CoV-2? *Obesity* **2020**, *28*, 1378–1381. [CrossRef]
41. Gao, Y.M.; Xu, G.; Wang, B.; Liu, B.C. Cytokine storm syndrome in coronavirus disease 2019: A narrative review. *J. Intern. Med.* **2021**, *289*, 147–161. [CrossRef]
42. Brawner, C.A.; Ehrman, J.K.; Bole, S.; Kerrigan, D.J.; Parikh, S.S.; Lewis, B.K.; Gindi, R.M.; Keteyian, C.; Abdul-Nour, K.; Keteyian, S.J. Maximal Exercise Capacity is Inversely Related to Hospitalization Secondary to Coronavirus Disease 2019. *Mayo Clin. Proc.* **2020**. [CrossRef]
43. Valenzuela, P.L.; Simpson, R.J.; Castillo-García, A.; Lucia, A. Physical activity: A coadjuvant treatment to COVID-19 vaccination? *Brain Behav. Immun.* **2021**. [CrossRef]
44. Pascoe, A.R.; Fiatarone Singh, M.A.; Edwards, K.M. The effects of exercise on vaccination responses: A review of chronic and acute exercise interventions in humans. *Brain Behav. Immun.* **2014**, *39*, 33–41. [CrossRef] [PubMed]
45. Grande, A.J.; Reid, H.; Thomas, E.E.; Nunan, D.; Foster, C. Exercise prior to influenza vaccination for limiting influenza incidence and its related complications in adults. *Cochrane Database Syst. Rev.* **2016**. [CrossRef]
46. Edwards, K.M.; Burns, V.E.; Allen, L.M.; McPhee, J.S.; Bosch, J.A.; Carroll, D.; Drayson, M.; Ring, C. Eccentric exercise as an adjuvant to influenza vaccination in humans. *Brain Behav. Immun.* **2007**, *21*, 209–217. [CrossRef] [PubMed]
47. Woods, J.A.; Keylock, K.T.; Lowder, T.; Vieira, V.J.; Zelkovich, W.; Dumich, S.; Colantuano, K.; Lyons, K.; Leifheit, K.; Cook, M.; et al. Cardiovascular Exercise Training Extends Influenza Vaccine Seroprotection in Sedentary Older Adults: The Immune Function Intervention Trial. *J. Am. Geriatr. Soc.* **2009**, *57*, 2183–2191. [CrossRef] [PubMed]
48. Wong, G.C.L.; Narang, V.; Lu, Y.; Camous, X.; Nyunt, M.S.; Carre, C.; Tan, C.; Xian, C.H.; Chong, J.; Chua, M.; et al. Hallmarks of improved immunological responses in the vaccination of more physically active elderly females. *Exerc. Immunol. Rev.* **2019**, *25*, 20–33. [PubMed]
49. World Health Organization. Obesity and Overweight. Available online: https://www.who.int/news-room/fact-sheets/detail/obesity-and-overweight (accessed on 15 December 2020).
50. González-Muniesa, P.; Mártinez-González, M.-A.; Hu, F.B.; Després, J.-P.; Matsuzawa, Y.; Loos, R.J.F.; Moreno, L.A.; Bray, G.A.; Martinez, J.A. Obesity. *Nat. Rev. Dis. Prim.* **2017**, *3*, 17034. [CrossRef] [PubMed]
51. Pérez, L.M.; Pareja-Galeano, H.; Sanchis-Gomar, F.; Emanuele, E.; Lucia, A.; Gálvez, B.G. 'Adipaging': Ageing and obesity share biological hallmarks related to a dysfunctional adipose tissue. *J. Physiol.* **2016**, *594*, 3187–3207. [CrossRef]
52. Popkin, B.M.; Du, S.; Green, W.D.; Beck, M.A.; Algaith, T.; Herbst, C.H.; Alsukait, R.F.; Alluhidan, M.; Alazemi, N.; Shekar, M. Individuals with obesity and COVID-19: A global perspective on the epidemiology and biological relationships. *Obes. Rev.* **2020**, *21*, e13128. [CrossRef]
53. Williamson, E.J.; Walker, A.J.; Bhaskaran, K.; Bacon, S.; Bates, C.; Morton, C.E.; Curtis, H.J.; Mehrkar, A.; Evans, D.; Inglesby, P.; et al. Factors associated with COVID-19-related death using OpenSAFELY. *Nature* **2020**, *584*, 430–436. [CrossRef] [PubMed]
54. Booth, A.; Reed, A.B.; Ponzo, S.; Yassaee, A.; Aral, M.; Plans, D.; Labrique, A.; Mohan, D. Population risk factors for severe disease and mortality in COVID-19: A global systematic review and meta-analysis. *PLoS ONE* **2021**, *16*, e0247461. [CrossRef]

55. Makki, K.; Froguel, P.; Wolowczuk, I. Adipose Tissue in Obesity-Related Inflammation and Insulin Resistance: Cells, Cytokines, and Chemokines. *ISRN Inflamm.* **2013**, *2013*, 139239. [CrossRef] [PubMed]
56. Kanneganti, T.D.; Dixit, V.D. Immunological complications of obesity. *Nat. Immunol.* **2012**, *13*, 707–712. [CrossRef] [PubMed]
57. Bähr, I.; Spielmann, J.; Quandt, D.; Kielstein, H. Obesity-Associated Alterations of Natural Killer Cells and Immunosurveillance of Cancer. *Front. Immunol.* **2020**, *11*, 245. [CrossRef] [PubMed]
58. Caci, G.; Albini, A.; Malerba, M.; Noonan, D.M.; Pochetti, P.; Polosa, R. COVID-19 and Obesity: Dangerous Liaisons. *J. Clin. Med.* **2020**, *9*, 2511. [CrossRef]
59. La Cava, A.; Matarese, G. The weight of leptin in immunity. *Nat. Rev. Immunol.* **2004**, *4*, 371–379. [CrossRef]
60. Maurya, R.; Bhattacharya, P.; Dey, R.; Nakhasi, H.L. Leptin functions in infectious diseases. *Front. Immunol.* **2018**, *9*, 2741. [CrossRef]
61. Gainsford, T.; Willson, T.A.; Metcalf, D.; Handman, E.; Mcfarlane, C.; Ng, A.; Nicola, N.A.; Alexander, W.S.; Hilton, D.J. Leptin can induce proliferation, differentiation, and functional activation of hemopoietic cells. *Proc. Natl. Acad. Sci. USA* **1996**, *93*, 14564–14568. [CrossRef] [PubMed]
62. Graßmann, S.; Wirsching, J.; Eichelmann, F.; Aleksandrova, K. Association between Peripheral Adipokines and Inflammation Markers: A Systematic Review and Meta-Analysis. *Obesity* **2017**, *25*, 1776–1785. [CrossRef]
63. Izquierdo, A.G.; Crujeiras, A.B.; Casanueva, F.F.; Carreira, M.C. Leptin, Obesity, and Leptin Resistance: Where are We 25 Years Later? *Nutrients* **2019**, *11*, 2704. [CrossRef]
64. Mclaughlin, T.; Ackerman, S.E.; Shen, L.; Engleman, E. Role of innate and adaptive immunity in obesity-associated metabolic disease. *J. Clin. Investig.* **2017**, *127*, 5–13. [CrossRef]
65. Al-Benna, S. Association of high level gene expression of ACE2 in adipose tissue with mortality of COVID-19 infection in obese patients. *Obes. Med.* **2020**, *19*, 100283. [CrossRef] [PubMed]
66. Cuervo, N.Z.; Grandvaux, N. Ace2: Evidence of role as entry receptor for sars-cov-2 and implications in comorbidities. *eLife* **2020**, *9*, e61390. [CrossRef] [PubMed]
67. Stefan, N.; Birkenfeld, A.L.; Schulze, M.B.; Ludwig, D.S. Obesity and impaired metabolic health in patients with COVID-19. *Nat. Rev. Endocrinol.* **2020**, *16*, 341–342. [CrossRef] [PubMed]
68. Grassi, L.; Kacmarek, R.; Berra, L. Ventilatory Mechanics in the Patient with Obesity. *Anesthesiology* **2020**, *132*, 1246–1256. [CrossRef] [PubMed]
69. Pellini, R.; Venuti, A.; Pimpinelli, F.; Abril, E.; Blandino, G.; Campo, F.; Conti, L.; De Virgilio, A.; de Marco, F.; Gino, E.; et al. Obesity may hamper SARS-CoV-2 vaccine immunogenicity. *medRxiv* **2021**, 1–10. [CrossRef]
70. Fan, W.; Chen, X.F.; Shen, C.; Guo, Z.R.; Dong, C. Hepatitis B vaccine response in obesity: A meta-analysis. *Vaccine* **2016**, *34*, 4835–4841. [CrossRef]
71. Yang, S.; Tian, G.; Cui, Y.; Ding, C.; Deng, M.; Yu, C.; Xu, K.; Ren, J.; Yao, J.; Li, Y.; et al. Factors influencing immunologic response to hepatitis B vaccine in adults. *Sci. Rep.* **2016**, *6*, 27251. [CrossRef]
72. Banga, N.; Guss, P.; Banga, A.; Rosenman, K.D. Incidence and variables associated with inadequate antibody titers after pre-exposure rabies vaccination among veterinary medical students. *Vaccine* **2014**, *32*, 979–983. [CrossRef]
73. Eliakim, A.; Swindt, C.; Zaldivar, F.; Casali, P.; Cooper, D.M. Reduced tetanus antibody titers in overweight children. *Autoimmunity* **2006**, *39*, 137–141. [CrossRef]
74. Sheridan, P.A.; Paich, H.A.; Handy, J.; Karlsson, E.A.; Hudgens, M.G.; Sammon, A.B.; Holland, L.A.; Weir, S.; Noah, T.L.; Beck, M.A. Obesity is associated with impaired immune response to influenza vaccination in humans. *Int. J. Obes.* **2012**, *36*, 1072–1077. [CrossRef] [PubMed]
75. Hotamisligil, G.S. Inflammation, metaflammation and immunometabolic disorders. *Nature* **2017**, *542*, 177–185. [CrossRef]
76. Hall, K.D.; Ayuketah, A.; Brychta, R.; Cai, H.; Cassimatis, T.; Chen, K.Y.; Chung, S.T.; Costa, E.; Courville, A.; Darcey, V.; et al. Ultra-Processed Diets Cause Excess Calorie Intake and Weight Gain: An Inpatient Randomized Controlled Trial of Ad Libitum Food Intake. *Cell Metab.* **2019**, *30*, 67–77.e3. [CrossRef]
77. Gill, S.; Panda, S. A Smartphone App Reveals Erratic Diurnal Eating Patterns in Humans that Can Be Modulated for Health Benefits. *Cell Metab.* **2015**, *22*, 789–798. [CrossRef] [PubMed]
78. Harris, L.; McGarty, A.; Hutchison, L.; Ells, L.; Hankey, C. Short-term intermittent energy restriction interventions for weight management: A systematic review and meta-analysis. *Obes. Rev.* **2018**, *19*, 1–13. [CrossRef] [PubMed]
79. Headland, M.; Clifton, P.M.; Carter, S.; Keogh, J.B. Weight-loss outcomes: A systematic review and meta-analysis of intermittent energy restriction trials lasting a minimum of 6 months. *Nutrients* **2016**, *8*, 354. [CrossRef] [PubMed]
80. Allaf, M.; Elghazaly, H.; Mohamed, O.G.; Fareen, M.F.K.; Zaman, S.; Salmasi, A.-M.; Tsilidis, K.; Dehghan, A. Intermittent fasting for the prevention of cardiovascular disease. *Cochrane Database Syst. Rev.* **2021**, *2021*, CD013496. [CrossRef]
81. Cioffi, I.; Evangelista, A.; Ponzo, V.; Ciccone, G.; Soldati, L.; Santarpia, L.; Contaldo, F.; Pasanisi, F.; Ghigo, E.; Bo, S. Intermittent versus continuous energy restriction on weight loss and cardiometabolic outcomes: A systematic review and meta-analysis of randomized controlled trials. *J. Transl. Med.* **2018**, *16*, 371. [CrossRef]
82. Sutton, E.F.; Beyl, R.; Early, K.S.; Cefalu, W.T.; Ravussin, E.; Peterson, C.M. Early Time-Restricted Feeding Improves Insulin Sensitivity, Blood Pressure, and Oxidative Stress Even without Weight Loss in Men with Prediabetes. *Cell Metab.* **2018**, *27*, 1212–1221.e3. [CrossRef] [PubMed]

83. Moro, T.; Tinsley, G.; Bianco, A.; Marcolin, G.; Pacelli, Q.F.; Battaglia, G.; Palma, A.; Gentil, P.; Neri, M.; Paoli, A. Effects of eight weeks of time-restricted feeding (16/8) on basal metabolism, maximal strength, body composition, inflammation, and cardiovascular risk factors in resistance-trained males. *J. Transl. Med.* **2016**, *14*, 290. [CrossRef] [PubMed]
84. McAllister, M.J.; Pigg, B.L.; Renteria, L.I.; Waldman, H.S. Time-restricted feeding improves markers of cardiometabolic health in physically active college-age men: A 4-week randomized pre-post pilot study. *Nutr. Res.* **2020**, *75*, 32–43. [CrossRef] [PubMed]
85. Trepanowski, J.F.; Kroeger, C.M.; Barnosky, A.; Klempel, M.; Bhutani, S.; Hoddy, K.K.; Rood, J.; Ravussin, E.; Varady, K.A. Effects of alternate-day fasting or daily calorie restriction on body composition, fat distribution, and circulating adipokines: Secondary analysis of a randomized controlled trial. *Clin. Nutr.* **2018**, *37*, 1871–1878. [CrossRef]
86. Cienfuegos, S.; Gabel, K.; Kalam, F.; Ezpeleta, M.; Wiseman, E.; Pavlou, V.; Lin, S.; Oliveira, M.L.; Varady, K.A. Effects of 4- and 6-h Time-Restricted Feeding on Weight and Cardiometabolic Health: A Randomized Controlled Trial in Adults with Obesity. *Cell Metab.* **2020**, *32*, 366–378.e3. [CrossRef]
87. Alam, I.; Gul, R.; Chong, J.; Tan, C.T.Y.; Chin, H.X.; Wong, G.; Doggui, R.; Larbi, A. Recurrent circadian fasting (RCF) improves blood pressure, biomarkers of cardiometabolic risk and regulates inflammation in men. *J. Transl. Med.* **2019**, *17*, 272. [CrossRef]
88. de Cabo, R.; Mattson, M.P. Effects of Intermittent Fasting on Health, Aging, and Disease. *N. Engl. J. Med.* **2019**, *381*, 2541–2551. [CrossRef]
89. Zhang, Q.; Wang, Y.; Fu, L. Dietary advanced glycation end-products: Perspectives linking food processing with health implications. *Compr. Rev. Food Sci. Food Saf.* **2020**, *19*, 2559–2587. [CrossRef]
90. Clarke, R.E.; Dordevic, A.L.; Tan, S.M.; Ryan, L.; Coughlan, M.T. Dietary advanced glycation end products and risk factors for chronic disease: A systematic review of randomised controlled trials. *Nutrients* **2016**, *8*, 125. [CrossRef] [PubMed]
91. Davis, K.E.; Prasad, C.; Vijayagopal, P.; Juma, S.; Imrhan, V. Advanced Glycation End Products, Inflammation, and Chronic Metabolic Diseases: Links in a Chain? *Crit. Rev. Food Sci. Nutr.* **2016**, *56*, 989–998. [CrossRef]
92. Sergi, D.; Boulestin, H.; Campbell, F.M.; Williams, L.M. The Role of Dietary Advanced Glycation End Products in Metabolic Dysfunction. *Mol. Nutr. Food Res.* **2021**, *65*, 1900934. [CrossRef] [PubMed]
93. Baye, E.; Kiriakova, V.; Uribarri, J.; Moran, L.J.; de Courten, B. Consumption of diets with low advanced glycation end products improves cardiometabolic parameters: Meta-analysis of randomised controlled trials. *Sci. Rep.* **2017**, *7*, 2266. [CrossRef]
94. Dickinson, S.; Hancock, D.P.; Petocz, P.; Ceriello, A.; Brand-Miller, J. High–glycemic index carbohydrate increases nuclear factor-κB activation in mononuclear cells of young, lean healthy subjects. *Am. J. Clin. Nutr.* **2008**, *87*, 1188–1193. [CrossRef]
95. Aljada, A.; Friedman, J.; Ghanim, H.; Mohanty, P.; Hofmeyer, D.; Chaudhuri, A.; Dandona, P. Glucose ingestion induces an increase in intranuclear nuclear factor κB, a fall in cellular inhibitor κB, and an increase in tumor necrosis factor α messenger RNA by mononuclear cells in healthy human subjects. *Metabolism* **2006**, *55*, 1177–1185. [CrossRef] [PubMed]
96. Müller, D.N.; Wilck, N.; Haase, S.; Kleinewietfeld, M.; Linker, R.A. Sodium in the microenvironment regulates immune responses and tissue homeostasis. *Nat. Rev. Immunol.* **2019**, *19*, 243–254. [CrossRef] [PubMed]
97. Oteng, A.-B.; Kersten, S. Mechanisms of Action of trans Fatty Acids. *Adv. Nutr.* **2020**, *11*, 697–708. [CrossRef] [PubMed]
98. Ruiz-Núñez, B.; Dijck-Brouwer, D.A.J.; Muskiet, F.A.J. The relation of saturated fatty acids with low-grade inflammation and cardiovascular disease. *J. Nutr. Biochem.* **2016**, *36*, 1–20. [CrossRef] [PubMed]
99. Huang, W.; Zhou, H.; Hodgkinson, C.; Montero, A.; Goldman, D.; Chang, S.L. Network Meta-Analysis on the Mechanisms Underlying Alcohol Augmentation of COVID-19 Pathologies. *Alcohol. Clin. Exp. Res.* **2021**, *45*, 675–688. [CrossRef]
100. Wen, W.; Wan, Z.; Ren, K.; Zhou, D.; Gao, Q.; Wu, Y.; Wang, L.; Yuan, Z.; Zhou, J. Potassium supplementation inhibits IL-17A production induced by salt loading in human T lymphocytes via p38/MAPK-SGK1 pathway. *Exp. Mol. Pathol.* **2016**, *100*, 370–377. [CrossRef]
101. Wen, W.; Wan, Z.; Zhou, D.; Zhou, J.; Yuan, Z. The Amelioration of Insulin Resistance in Salt Loading Subjects by Potassium Supplementation is Associated with a Reduction in Plasma IL-17A Levels. *Exp. Clin. Endocrinol. Diabetes* **2017**, *125*, 571–576. [CrossRef]
102. Emerson, S.R.; Kurti, S.P.; Harms, C.A.; Haub, M.D.; Melgarejo, T.; Logan, C.; Rosenkranz, S.K. Magnitude and Timing of the Postprandial Inflammatory Response to a High-Fat Meal in Healthy Adults: A Systematic Review. *Adv. Nutr.* **2017**, *8*, 213–225. [CrossRef] [PubMed]
103. Quintanilha, B.J.; Ferreira, L.R.P.; Ferreira, F.M.; Neto, E.C.; Sampaio, G.R.; Rogero, M.M. Circulating plasma microRNAs dysregulation and metabolic endotoxemia induced by a high-fat high-saturated diet. *Clin. Nutr.* **2020**, *39*, 554–562. [CrossRef]
104. Barbaresko, J.; Koch, M.; Schulze, M.B.; Nöthlings, U. Dietary pattern analysis and biomarkers of low-grade inflammation: A systematic literature review. *Nutr. Rev.* **2013**, *71*, 511–527. [CrossRef] [PubMed]
105. Afshin, A.; Sur, P.J.; Fay, K.A.; Cornaby, L.; Ferrara, G.; Salama, J.S.; Mullany, E.C.; Abate, K.H.; Abbafati, C.; Abebe, Z.; et al. Health effects of dietary risks in 195 countries, 1990–2017: A systematic analysis for the Global Burden of Disease Study 2017. *Lancet* **2019**, *393*, 1958–1972. [CrossRef]
106. Gakidou, E.; Afshin, A.; Abajobir, A.A.; Abate, K.H.; Abbafati, C.; Abbas, K.M.; Abd-Allah, F.; Abdulle, A.M.; Abera, S.F.; Aboyans, V.; et al. Global, regional, and national comparative risk assessment of 84 behavioural, environmental and occupational, and metabolic risks or clusters of risks, 1990–2016: A systematic analysis for the Global Burden of Disease Study 2016. *Lancet* **2017**, *390*, 1345–1422. [CrossRef]
107. Daïen, C.I.; Pinget, G.V.; Tan, J.K.; Macia, L. Detrimental Impact of Microbiota-Accessible Carbohydrate-Deprived Diet on Gut and Immune Homeostasis: An Overview. *Front. Immunol.* **2017**, *8*, 548. [CrossRef] [PubMed]

108. Sonnenburg, J.L.; Sonnenburg, E.D. Vulnerability of the industrialized microbiota. *Science* **2019**, *366*, eaaw9255. [CrossRef] [PubMed]
109. Hosseini, B.; Berthon, B.S.; Saedisomeolia, A.; Starkey, M.R.; Collison, A.; Wark, P.A.B.; Wood, L.G. Effects of fruit and vegetable consumption on inflammatory biomarkers and immune cell populations: A systematic literature review and meta-analysis. *Am. J. Clin. Nutr.* **2018**, *108*, 136–155. [CrossRef]
110. Ghanim, H.; Sia, C.L.; Upadhyay, M.; Korzeniewski, K.; Viswanathan, P.; Abuaysheh, S.; Mohanty, P.; Dandona, P. Orange juice neutralizes the proinflammatory effect of a high-fat, high-carbohydrate meal and prevents endotoxin increase and Toll-like receptor expression. *Am. J. Clin. Nutr.* **2010**, *91*, 940–949. [CrossRef]
111. Burton-Freeman, B.; Talbot, J.; Park, E.; Krishnankutty, S.; Edirisinghe, I. Protective activity of processed tomato products on postprandial oxidation and inflammation: A clinical trial in healthy weight men and women. *Mol. Nutr. Food Res.* **2012**, *56*, 622–631. [CrossRef]
112. Burton-Freeman, B.; Linares, A.; Hyson, D.; Kappagoda, T. Strawberry Modulates LDL Oxidation and Postprandial Lipemia in Response to High-Fat Meal in Overweight Hyperlipidemic Men and Women. *J. Am. Coll. Nutr.* **2013**, *29*, 46–54. [CrossRef] [PubMed]
113. Chaves, D.F.S.; Carvalho, P.C.; Brasili, E.; Rogero, M.M.; Hassimotto, N.A.; Diedrich, J.K.; Moresco, J.J.; John, R.; Yates, I.; Lajolo, F.M. Proteomic Analysis of Peripheral Blood Mononuclear Cells after a High-Fat, High-Carbohydrate Meal with Orange Juice. *J. Proteome Res.* **2017**, *16*, 4086–4092. [CrossRef]
114. Iddir, M.; Brito, A.; Dingeo, G.; del Campo, S.S.F.; Samouda, H.; La Frano, M.R.; Bohn, T. Strengthening the Immune System and Reducing Inflammation and Oxidative Stress through Diet and Nutrition: Considerations during the COVID-19 Crisis. *Nutrients* **2020**, *12*, 1562. [CrossRef]
115. Zhu, F.; Du, B.; Xu, B. Anti-inflammatory effects of phytochemicals from fruits, vegetables, and food legumes: A review. *Crit. Rev. Food Sci. Nutr.* **2018**, *58*, 1260–1270. [CrossRef]
116. Dibaba, D.T.; Xun, P.; He, K. Dietary magnesium intake is inversely associated with serum C-reactive protein levels: Meta-analysis and systematic review. *Eur. J. Clin. Nutr.* **2014**, *68*, 510–516. [CrossRef]
117. Simental-Mendía, L.E.; Sahebkar, A.; Rodríguez-Morán, M.; Zambrano-Galván, G.; Guerrero-Romero, F. Effect of magnesium supplementation on plasma C-reactive protein concentrations: A systematic review and meta-analysis of randomized controlled trials. *Curr. Pharm. Des.* **2017**, *23*, 4678–4686. [CrossRef]
118. Fatahi, S.; Pezeshki, M.; Mousavi, S.M.; Teymouri, A.; Rahmani, J.; Varkaneh, H.K.; Ghaedi, E. Effects of folic acid supplementation on C-reactive protein: A systematic review and meta-analysis of randomized controlled trials. *Nutr. Metab. Cardiovasc. Dis.* **2019**, *29*, 432–439. [CrossRef]
119. Asbaghi, O.; Ghanavati, M.; Ashtary-Larky, D.; Bagheri, R.; Kelishadi, M.R.; Nazarian, B.; Nordvall, M.; Wong, A.; Dutheil, F.; Suzuki, K.; et al. Effects of Folic Acid Supplementation on Oxidative Stress Markers: A Systematic Review and Meta-Analysis of Randomized Controlled Trials. *Antioxidants* **2021**, *10*, 871. [CrossRef] [PubMed]
120. Gombart, A.F.; Pierre, A.; Maggini, S. A Review of Micronutrients and the Immune System–Working in Harmony to Reduce the Risk of Infection. *Nutrients* **2020**, *12*, 236. [CrossRef] [PubMed]
121. Jafarnejad, S.; Boccardi, V.; Hosseini, B.; Taghizadeh, M.; Hamedifard, Z. A Meta-analysis of Randomized Control Trials: The Impact of Vitamin C Supplementation on Serum CRP and Serum hs-CRP Concentrations. *Curr. Pharm. Des.* **2018**, *24*, 3520–3528. [CrossRef] [PubMed]
122. Corrao, S.; Bocchio, R.M.; Monaco, M.L.; Natoli, G.; Cavezzi, A.; Troiani, E.; Argano, C. Does Evidence Exist to Blunt Inflammatory Response by Nutraceutical Supplementation during COVID-19 Pandemic? An Overview of Systematic Reviews of Vitamin D, Vitamin C, Melatonin, and Zinc. *Nutrients* **2021**, *13*, 1261. [CrossRef] [PubMed]
123. Saboori, S.; Shab-Bidar, S.; Speakman, J.R.; Yousefi Rad, E.; Djafarian, K. Effect of vitamin E supplementation on serum C-reactive protein level: A meta-analysis of randomized controlled trials. *Eur. J. Clin. Nutr.* **2015**, *69*, 867–873. [CrossRef]
124. Rayman, M.P.; Calder, P.C. Optimising COVID-19 vaccine efficacy by ensuring nutritional adequacy. *Br. J. Nutr.* **2021**, *126*, 1919–1920. [CrossRef]
125. Pecora, F.; Persico, F.; Argentiero, A.; Neglia, C.; Esposito, S. The Role of Micronutrients in Support of the Immune Response against Viral Infections. *Nutrients* **2020**, *12*, 3198. [CrossRef] [PubMed]
126. Heller, R.A.; Sun, Q.; Hackler, J.; Seelig, J.; Seibert, L.; Cherkezov, A.; Minich, W.B.; Seemann, P.; Diegmann, J.; Pilz, M.; et al. Prediction of survival odds in COVID-19 by zinc, age and selenoprotein P as composite biomarker. *Redox Biol.* **2021**, *38*, 101764. [CrossRef]
127. Hackler, J.; Heller, R.A.; Sun, Q.; Schwarzer, M.; Diegmann, J.; Bachmann, M.; Moghaddam, A.; Schomburg, L. Relation of Serum Copper Status to Survival in COVID-19. *Nutrients* **2021**, *13*, 1898. [CrossRef] [PubMed]
128. Moghaddam, A.; Heller, R.A.; Sun, Q.; Seelig, J.; Cherkezov, A.; Seibert, L.; Hackler, J.; Seemann, P.; Diegmann, J.; Pilz, M.; et al. Selenium Deficiency Is Associated with Mortality Risk from COVID-19. *Nutrients* **2020**, *12*, 2098. [CrossRef] [PubMed]
129. Carlucci, P.M.; Ahuja, T.; Petrilli, C.; Rajagopalan, H.; Jones, S.; Rahimian, J. Zinc sulfate in combination with a zinc ionophore may improve outcomes in hospitalized COVID-19 patients. *J. Med. Microbiol.* **2020**, *69*, 1228–1234. [CrossRef] [PubMed]
130. Frontera, J.A.; Rahimian, J.O.; Yaghi, S.; Liu, M.; Lewis, A.; de Havenon, A.; Mainali, S.; Huang, J.; Scher, E.; Wisniewski, T.; et al. Treatment with Zinc is Associated with Reduced In-Hospital Mortality Among COVID-19 Patients: A Multi-Center Cohort Study. *Res. Sq.* **2020**, rs-3. [CrossRef]

131. Thomas, S.; Patel, D.; Bittel, B.; Wolski, K.; Wang, Q.; Kumar, A.; Il'Giovine, Z.J.; Mehra, R.; McWilliams, C.; Nissen, S.E.; et al. Effect of High-Dose Zinc and Ascorbic Acid Supplementation vs Usual Care on Symptom Length and Reduction Among Ambulatory Patients With SARS-CoV-2 Infection: The COVID A to Z Randomized Clinical Trial. *JAMA Netw. Open* **2021**, *4*, e210369. [CrossRef]
132. Fromonot, J.; Gette, M.; Lassoued, A.B.; Guéant, J.-L.; Guéant-Rodriguez, R.-M.; Guieu, R. Hypozincemia in the early stage of COVID-19 is associated with an increased risk of severe COVID-19. *Clin. Nutr.* **2021**. [CrossRef] [PubMed]
133. Leisman, D.E.; Ronner, L.; Pinotti, R.; Taylor, M.D.; Sinha, P.; Calfee, C.S.; Hirayama, A.V.; Mastroiani, F.; Turtle, C.J.; Harhay, M.O.; et al. Cytokine elevation in severe and critical COVID-19: A rapid systematic review, meta-analysis, and comparison with other inflammatory syndromes. *Lancet Respir. Med.* **2020**, *8*, 1233–1244. [CrossRef]
134. Mburu, A.S.W.; Thurnham, D.I.; Mwaniki, D.L.; Muniu, E.M.; Alumasa, F.M. The influence of inflammation on plasma zinc concentration in apparently healthy, HIV+ Kenyan adults and zinc responses after a multi-micronutrient supplement. *Eur. J. Clin. Nutr.* **2010**, *64*, 510–517. [CrossRef]
135. Rifai, N.; Horvath, A.R.; Wittwer, C. *Tietz Textbook of Clinical Chemistry and Molecular Diagnostics*, 6th ed.; Elsevier: Amsterdam, The Netherlands, 2017; ISBN 9780323548489.
136. Gasmi, A.; Chirumbolo, S.; Peana, M.; Noor, S.; Menzel, A.; Dadar, M.; Bjørklund, G. The Role of Diet and Supplementation of Natural Products in COVID-19 Prevention. *Biol. Trace Elem. Res.* **2021**, *200*, 27–30. [CrossRef]
137. El-Gamal, Y.; Aly, R.H.; Hossny, E.; Afify, E.; El-Taliawy, D. Response of Egyptian infants with protein calorie malnutrition to hepatitis B vaccination. *J. Trop. Pediatr.* **1996**, *42*, 144–145. [CrossRef]
138. Wyatt, L.; Permar, S.R.; Ortiz, E.; Berky, A.; Woods, C.W.; Amouou, G.F.; Itell, H.; Hsu-Kim, H.; Pan, W. Mercury exposure and poor nutritional status reduce response to six expanded program on immunization vaccines in children: An observational cohort study of communities affected by gold mining in the peruvian amazon. *Int. J. Environ. Res. Public Health* **2019**, *16*, 638. [CrossRef] [PubMed]
139. Mohammed, I.; Damisah, M.M. The immunological response to polyvalent meningococcal vaccine in Bauchi State, Nigeria. *Trans. R. Soc. Trop. Med. Hyg.* **1982**, *76*, 351–353. [CrossRef]
140. Suskind, R.; Sirishinha, S.; Vithayasai, V.; Edelman, R.; Damrongsak, D.; Charupatana, C.; Olson, R.E. Immunoglobulins and antibody response in children with protein calorie malnutrition. *Am. J. Clin. Nutr.* **1976**, *29*, 836–841. [CrossRef]
141. Brüssow, H.; Sidoti, J.; Dirren, H.; Freire, W.B. Effect of malnutrition in Ecuadorian children on titers of serum antibodies to various microbial antigens—PubMed. *Clin. Diagn. Lab. Immunol.* **1995**, *2*, 62–68. [CrossRef]
142. Park, H.L.; Shim, S.H.; Lee, E.Y.; Cho, W.; Park, S.; Jeon, H.J.; Ahn, S.Y.; Kim, H.; Nam, J.H. Obesity-induced chronic inflammation is associated with the reduced efficacy of influenza vaccine. *Hum. Vaccines Immunother.* **2014**, *10*, 1181–1186. [CrossRef]
143. Painter, S.D.; Ovsyannikova, I.G.; Poland, G.A. The weight of obesity on the human immune response to vaccination. *Vaccine* **2015**, *33*, 4422–4429. [CrossRef]
144. Damms-Machado, A.; Weser, G.; Bischoff, S.C. Micronutrient deficiency in obese subjects undergoing low calorie diet. *Nutr. J.* **2012**, *11*, 34. [CrossRef] [PubMed]
145. Kimmons, J.E.; Blanck, H.M.; Tohill, B.C.; Zhang, J.; Khan, L.K. Associations between Body Mass Index and the Prevalence of Low Micronutrient Levels among US Adults. *Medscape Gen. Med.* **2006**, *8*, 59.
146. Poli, V.F.S.; Sanches, R.B.; dos Santos Moraes, A.; Fidalgo, J.P.N.; Nascimento, M.A.; Bresciani, P.; Andrade-Silva, S.G.; Cipullo, M.A.T.; Clemente, J.C.; Caranti, D.A. The excessive caloric intake and micronutrient deficiencies related to obesity after a long-term interdisciplinary therapy. *Nutrition* **2017**, *38*, 113–119. [CrossRef]
147. Gibson, A.; Edgar, J.D.; Neville, C.E.; Gilchrist, S.E.C.M.; McKinley, M.C.; Patterson, C.C.; Young, I.S.; Woodside, J.V. Effect of fruit and vegetable consumption on immune function in older people: A randomized controlled trial. *Am. J. Clin. Nutr.* **2012**, *96*, 1429–1436. [CrossRef] [PubMed]
148. D'Alessandro, A.; De Pergola, G. The Mediterranean Diet: Its definition and evaluation of a priori dietary indexes in primary cardiovascular prevention. *Int. J. Food Sci. Nutr.* **2018**, *69*, 647–659. [CrossRef] [PubMed]
149. Chrysohoou, C.; Panagiotakos, D.B.; Pitsavos, C.; Das, U.N.; Stefanadis, C. Adherence to the Mediterranean diet attenuates inflammation and coagulation process in healthy adults: The ATTICA study. *J. Am. Coll. Cardiol.* **2004**, *44*, 152–158. [CrossRef]
150. Ghosh, T.S.; Rampelli, S.; Jeffery, I.B.; Santoro, A.; Neto, M.; Capri, M.; Giampieri, E.; Jennings, A.; Candela, M.; Turroni, S.; et al. Mediterranean diet intervention alters the gut microbiome in older people reducing frailty and improving health status: The NU-AGE 1-year dietary intervention across five European countries. *Gut* **2020**, *69*, 1218–1228. [CrossRef]
151. Bonaccio, M.; Di Castelnuovo, A.; De Curtis, A.; Costanzo, S.; Persichillo, M.; Donati, M.B.; Cerletti, C.; Iacoviello, L.; De Gaetano, G. Adherence to the Mediterranean diet is associated with lower platelet and leukocyte counts: Results from the Moli-sani study. *Blood* **2014**, *123*, 3037–3044. [CrossRef]
152. Schwingshackl, L.; Hoffmann, G. Mediterranean dietary pattern, inflammation and endothelial function: A systematic review and meta-analysis of intervention trials. *Nutr. Metab. Cardiovasc. Dis.* **2014**, *24*, 929–939. [CrossRef]
153. Sofi, F.; Abbate, R.; Gensini, G.F.; Casini, A. Accruing evidence on benefits of adherence to the Mediterranean diet on health: An updated systematic review and meta-analysis. *Am. J. Clin. Nutr.* **2010**, *92*, 1189–1196. [CrossRef] [PubMed]
154. Estruch, R.; Ros, E.; Salas-Salvadó, J.; Covas, M.-I.; Corella, D.; Arós, F.; Gómez-Gracia, E.; Ruiz-Gutiérrez, V.; Fiol, M.; Lapetra, J.; et al. Primary Prevention of Cardiovascular Disease with a Mediterranean Diet Supplemented with Extra-Virgin Olive Oil or Nuts. *N. Engl. J. Med.* **2018**, *378*, e34. [CrossRef]

155. Serino, A.; Salazar, G. Protective role of polyphenols against vascular inflammation, aging and cardiovascular disease. *Nutrients* **2019**, *11*, 53. [CrossRef] [PubMed]
156. Pandey, K.B.; Rizvi, S.I. Plant polyphenols as dietary antioxidants in human health and disease. *Oxidative Med. Cell. Longev.* **2009**, *2*, 270–278. [CrossRef] [PubMed]
157. Chiang, N.; Serhan, C.N. Specialized pro-resolving mediator network: An update on production and actions. *Essays Biochem.* **2020**, *64*, 443–462. [CrossRef] [PubMed]
158. Angelidi, A.M.; Kokkinos, A.; Katechaki, E.; Ros, E.; Mantzoros, C.S. Mediterranean diet as a nutritional approach for COVID-19. *Metabolism* **2021**, *114*, 154407. [CrossRef] [PubMed]
159. Maiorino, M.I.; Bellastella, G.; Longo, M.; Caruso, P.; Esposito, K. Mediterranean Diet and COVID-19: Hypothesizing Potential Benefits in People with Diabetes. *Front. Endocrinol.* **2020**, *11*, 574315. [CrossRef]
160. Green, M.W.; Roberts, A.P.; Frugé, A.D. Negative Association between Mediterranean Diet Adherence and COVID-19 Cases and Related Deaths in Spain and 23 OECD Countries: An Ecological Study. *Front. Nutr.* **2021**, *8*, 591964. [CrossRef]
161. Holick, M.F. Sunlight, uv radiation, vitamin d, and skin cancer: How much sunlight do we need? *Adv. Exp. Med. Biol.* **2020**, *1268*, 19–36. [CrossRef]
162. Bishop, L.E.; Ismailova, A.; Dimeloe, S.; Hewison, M.; White, J.H. Vitamin D and Immune Regulation: Antibacterial, Antiviral, Anti-Inflammatory. *JBMR Plus* **2021**, *5*, e10405. [CrossRef]
163. Vanherwegen, A.S.; Gysemans, C.; Mathieu, C. Regulation of Immune Function by Vitamin D and Its Use in Diseases of Immunity. *Endocrinol. Metab. Clin. N. Am.* **2017**, *46*, 1061–1094. [CrossRef]
164. Beard, J.A.; Bearden, A.; Striker, R. Vitamin D and the anti-viral state. *J. Clin. Virol.* **2011**, *50*, 194–200. [CrossRef] [PubMed]
165. Çolak, Y.; Nordestgaard, B.G.; Afzal, S. Low vitamin D and risk of bacterial pneumonias: Mendelian randomisation studies in two population-based cohorts. *Thorax* **2020**, *76*, 468–478. [CrossRef] [PubMed]
166. Peterson, C.A.; Heffernan, M.E. Serum tumor necrosis factor-alpha concentrations are negatively correlated with serum 25(OH)D concentrations in healthy women. *J. Inflamm.* **2008**, *5*, 10. [CrossRef]
167. Beilfuss, J.; Berg, V.; Sneve, M.; Jorde, R.; Kamycheva, E. Effects of a 1-year supplementation with cholecalciferol on interleukin-6, tumor necrosis factor-alpha and insulin resistance in overweight and obese subjects. *Cytokine* **2012**, *60*, 870–874. [CrossRef] [PubMed]
168. Zhang, Y.; Leung, D.Y.M.; Richers, B.N.; Liu, Y.; Remigio, L.K.; Riches, D.W.; Goleva, E. Vitamin D Inhibits Monocyte/Macrophage Proinflammatory Cytokine Production by Targeting MAPK Phosphatase-1. *J. Immunol.* **2012**, *188*, 2127–2135. [CrossRef]
169. Liang, S.; Cai, J.; Li, Y.; Yang, R. 1,25-Dihydroxy-Vitamin D3 induces macrophage polarization to M2 by upregulating T-cell Ig-mucin-3 expression. *Mol. Med. Rep.* **2019**, *49*, 3707–3713. [CrossRef]
170. Pham, H.; Rahman, A.; Majidi, A.; Waterhouse, M.; Neale, R.E. Acute Respiratory Tract Infection and 25-Hydroxyvitamin D Concentration: A Systematic Review and Meta-Analysis. *Int. J. Environ. Res. Public Health* **2019**, *16*, 3020. [CrossRef]
171. Martineau, A.R.; Jolliffe, D.A.; Hooper, R.L.; Greenberg, L.; Aloia, J.F.; Bergman, P.; Dubnov-Raz, G.; Esposito, S.; Ganmaa, D.; Ginde, A.A.; et al. Vitamin D supplementation to prevent acute respiratory tract infections: Systematic review and meta-analysis of individual participant data. *BMJ* **2017**, *356*, i6583. [CrossRef]
172. Autier, P.; Mullie, P.; Macacu, A.; Dragomir, M.; Boniol, M.; Coppens, K.; Pizot, C.; Boniol, M. Effect of vitamin D supplementation on non-skeletal disorders: A systematic review of meta-analyses and randomised trials. *Lancet Diabetes Endocrinol.* **2017**, *5*, 986–1004. [CrossRef]
173. Ilie, P.C.; Stefanescu, S.; Smith, L. The role of vitamin D in the prevention of coronavirus disease 2019 infection and mortality. *Aging Clin. Exp. Res.* **2020**, *32*, 1195–1198. [CrossRef]
174. Laird, E.; Rhodes, J.; Kenny, R. Vitamin D and Inflammation: Potential Implications for Severity of Covid-19. *Ir. Med. J.* **2020**, *113*, 81.
175. D'avolio, A.; Avataneo, V.; Manca, A.; Cusato, J.; De Nicolò, A.; Lucchini, R.; Keller, F.; Cantù, M. 25-hydroxyvitamin D concentrations are lower in patients with positive PCR for SARS-CoV-2. *Nutrients* **2020**, *12*, 1359. [CrossRef] [PubMed]
176. Kaufman, H.W.; Niles, J.K.; Kroll, M.H.; Bi, C.; Holick, M.F. SARS-CoV-2 positivity rates associated with circulating 25-hydroxyvitamin D levels. *PLoS ONE* **2020**, *15*, e0239252. [CrossRef] [PubMed]
177. Panagiotou, G.; Tee, S.A.; Ihsan, Y.; Athar, W.; Marchitelli, G.; Kelly, D.; Boot, C.S.; Stock, N.; Macfarlane, J.; Martineau, A.R.; et al. Low serum 25-hydroxyvitamin D (25[OH]D) levels in patients hospitalized with COVID-19 are associated with greater disease severity. *Clin. Endocrinol.* **2020**, *93*, 508–511. [CrossRef]
178. Crafa, A.; Cannarella, R.; Condorelli, R.A.; Mongioì, L.M.; Barbagallo, F.; Aversa, A.; La Vignera, S.; Calogero, A.E. Influence of 25-hydroxy-cholecalciferol levels on SARS-CoV-2 infection and COVID-19 severity: A systematic review and meta-analysis. *EClinicalMedicine* **2021**, *37*, 100967. [CrossRef] [PubMed]
179. Wang, Z.; Joshi, A.; Leopold, K.; Jackson, S.; Christensen, S.; Nayfeh, T.; Mohammed, K.; Creo, A.; Tebben, P.; Kumar, S. Association of Vitamin D Deficiency with COVID-19 Infection Severity: Systematic Review and Meta-analysis. *Clin. Endocrinol.* **2021**, cen.14540. [CrossRef]
180. Sabico, S.; Enani, M.A.; Sheshah, E.; Aljohani, N.J.; Aldisi, D.A.; Alotaibi, N.H.; Alshingetti, N.; Alomar, S.Y.; Alnaami, A.M.; Amer, O.E.; et al. Effects of a 2-Week 5000 IU versus 1000 IU Vitamin D3 Supplementation on Recovery of Symptoms in Patients with Mild to Moderate COVID-19: A Randomized Clinical Trial. *Nutrients* **2021**, *13*, 2170. [CrossRef]

181. Pal, R.; Banerjee, M.; Bhadada, S.K.; Shetty, A.J.; Singh, B.; Vyas, A. Vitamin D supplementation and clinical outcomes in COVID-19: A systematic review and meta-analysis. *J. Endocrinol. Investig.* **2021**. [CrossRef]
182. Gilani, S.J.; Bin-Jumah, M.; Nadeem, M.S.; Kazmi, I. Vitamin D attenuates COVID-19 complications via modulation of proinflammatory cytokines, antiviral proteins, and autophagy. *Expert Rev. Anti-Infect. Ther.* **2021**. [CrossRef]
183. Al-Jarallah, M.; Rajan, R.; Dashti, R.; Al Saber, A.; Pan, J.; Zhanna, K.D.; Abdelnaby, H.; Aboelhassan, W.; Almutairi, F.; Abdullah, M.; et al. In-hospital mortality in SARS-CoV-2 stratified by serum 25-hydroxy-vitamin D levels: A retrospective study. *J. Med. Virol.* **2021**, *93*, 5880–5885. [CrossRef]
184. Rawat, D.; Roy, A.; Maitra, S.; Shankar, V.; Khanna, P.; Baidya, D.K. Vitamin D supplementation and COVID-19 treatment: A systematic review and meta-analysis. *Diabetes Metab. Syndr.* **2021**, *15*, 102189. [CrossRef] [PubMed]
185. Griffin, G.; Hewison, M.; Hopkin, J.; Kenny, R.A.; Quinton, R.; Rhodes, J.; Subramanian, S.; Thickett, D. Perspective: Vitamin D supplementation prevents rickets and acute respiratory infections when given as daily maintenance but not as intermittent bolus: Implications for COVID-19. *Clin. Med.* **2021**, *21*, e144–e149. [CrossRef]
186. Martineau, A.R.; Jolliffe, D.A.; Greenberg, L.; Aloia, J.F.; Bergman, P.; Dubnov-Raz, G.; Esposito, S.; Ganmaa, D.; Ginde, A.A.; Goodall, E.C.; et al. Vitamin D supplementation to prevent acute respiratory infections: Individual participant data meta-analysis. *Health Technol. Assess.* **2019**, *23*, 1–44. [CrossRef]
187. Sadarangani, S.P.; Whitaker, J.A.; Poland, G.A. "let there be light": The role of Vitamin D in the immune response to vaccines. *Expert Rev. Vaccines* **2015**, *14*, 1427–1440. [CrossRef] [PubMed]
188. Zimmerman, R.K.; Lin, C.J.; Raviotta, J.M.; Nowalk, M.P. Do vitamin D levels affect antibody titers produced in response to HPV vaccine? *Hum. Vaccines Immunother.* **2015**, *11*, 2345–2349. [CrossRef]
189. Lee, M.D.; Lin, C.H.; Lei, W.T.; Chang, H.Y.; Lee, H.C.; Yeung, C.Y.; Chiu, N.C.; Chi, H.; Liu, J.M.; Hsu, R.J.; et al. Does vitamin D deficiency affect the immunogenic responses to influenza vaccination? A systematic review and meta-analysis. *Nutrients* **2018**, *10*, 409. [CrossRef] [PubMed]
190. Goncalves-Mendes, N.; Talvas, J.; Dualé, C.; Guttmann, A.; Corbin, V.; Marceau, G.; Sapin, V.; Brachet, P.; Evrard, B.; Laurichesse, H.; et al. Impact of Vitamin D supplementation on influenza vaccine response and immune functions in deficient elderly persons: A randomized placebo-controlled trial. *Front. Immunol.* **2019**, *10*, 65. [CrossRef]
191. Kriesel, J.D.; Spruance, J. Calcitriol (1,25-dihydroxy-vitamin D3) coadministered with influenza vaccine does not enhance humoral immunity in human volunteers. *Vaccine* **1999**, *17*, 1883–1888. [CrossRef]
192. Kashi, D.S.; Oliver, S.J.; Wentz, L.M.; Roberts, R.; Carswell, A.T.; Tang, J.C.Y.; Jackson, S.; Izard, R.M.; Allan, D.; Rhodes, L.E.; et al. Vitamin D and the hepatitis B vaccine response: A prospective cohort study and a randomized, placebo-controlled oral vitamin D3 and simulated sunlight supplementation trial in healthy adults. *Eur. J. Nutr.* **2021**, *60*, 475. [CrossRef]
193. Wise, J. Covid-19: Evidence is lacking to support vitamin D's role in treatment and prevention. *BMJ* **2020**, *371*, m4912. [CrossRef]
194. Martineau, A.R.; Forouhi, N.G. Vitamin D for COVID-19: A case to answer? *Lancet Diabetes Endocrinol.* **2020**, *8*, 735–736. [CrossRef]
195. Hart, P.H.; Norval, M. More Than Effects in Skin: Ultraviolet Radiation-Induced Changes in Immune Cells in Human Blood. *Front. Immunol.* **2021**, *12*, 2250. [CrossRef]
196. Hart, P.H.; Norval, M. Ultraviolet radiation-induced immunosuppression and its relevance for skin carcinogenesis. *Photochem. Photobiol. Sci.* **2018**, *17*, 1872–1884. [CrossRef]
197. Hart, P.H.; Gorman, S.; Finlay-Jones, J.J. Modulation of the immune system by UV radiation: More than just the effects of vitamin D? *Nat. Rev. Immunol.* **2011**, *11*, 584–596. [CrossRef]
198. Hart, P.H.; Norval, M. Are there differences in immune responses following delivery of vaccines through acutely or chronically sun-exposed compared with sun-unexposed skin? *Immunology* **2020**, *159*, 133. [CrossRef] [PubMed]
199. Linder, N.; Abudi, Y.; Abdalla, W.; Badir, M.; Amitai, Y.; Samuels, J.; Mendelson, E.; Levy, I. Effect of season of inoculation on immune response to rubella vaccine in children. *J. Trop. Pediatr.* **2011**, *57*, 299–302. [CrossRef] [PubMed]
200. Schuit, M.; Gardner, S.; Wood, S.; Bower, K.; Williams, G.; Freeburger, D.; Dabisch, P. The influence of simulated sunlight on the inactivation of influenza virus in aerosols. *J. Infect. Dis.* **2021**, *221*, 372–378. [CrossRef]
201. Moriyama, M.; Hugentobler, W.J.; Iwasaki, A. Annual review of virology seasonality of respiratory viral infections. *Annu. Rev. Virol.* **2020**, *7*, 83–101. [CrossRef]
202. Ma, Y.; Pei, S.; Shaman, J.; Dubrow, R.; Chen, K. Role of meteorological factors in the transmission of SARS-CoV-2 in the United States. *Nat. Commun.* **2021**, *12*, 3602. [CrossRef]
203. Daly, M.; Sutin, A.; Robinson, E. Longitudinal changes in mental health and the COVID-19 pandemic: Evidence from the UK Household Longitudinal Study. *Psychol. Med.* **2020**. [CrossRef] [PubMed]
204. Pierce, M.; Hope, H.; Ford, T.; Hatch, S.; Hotopf, M.; John, A.; Kontopantelis, E.; Webb, R.; Wessely, S.; McManus, S.; et al. Mental health before and during the COVID-19 pandemic: A longitudinal probability sample survey of the UK population. *Lancet Psychiatry* **2020**, *7*, 883–892. [CrossRef]
205. Salari, N.; Hosseinian-Far, A.; Jalali, R.; Vaisi-Raygani, A.; Rasoulpoor, S.; Mohammadi, M.; Rasoulpoor, S.; Khaledi-Paveh, B. Prevalence of stress, anxiety, depression among the general population during the COVID-19 pandemic: A systematic review and meta-analysis. *Glob. Health* **2020**, *16*, 57. [CrossRef] [PubMed]
206. Glaser, R.; Kiecolt-Glaser, J.K. Stress-induced immune dysfunction: Implications for health. *Nat. Rev. Immunol.* **2005**, *5*, 243–251. [CrossRef] [PubMed]

207. Segerstrom, S.C.; Miller, G.E. Psychological stress and the human immune system: A meta-analytic study of 30 years of inquiry. *Psychol. Bull.* **2004**, *130*, 601–630. [CrossRef] [PubMed]
208. Cohen, S.; Tyrrell, D.A.J.; Smith, A.P. Psychological Stress and Susceptibility to the Common Cold. *N. Engl. J. Med.* **1991**, *325*, 606–612. [CrossRef]
209. Cohen, S.; Janicki-Deverts, D.; Miller, G.E. Psychological stress and disease. *J. Am. Med. Assoc.* **2007**, *298*, 1685–1687. [CrossRef]
210. Marsland, A.L.; Walsh, C.; Lockwood, K.; John-Henderson, N.A. The effects of acute psychological stress on circulating and stimulated inflammatory markers: A systematic review and meta-analysis. *Brain Behav. Immun.* **2017**, *64*, 208–219. [CrossRef]
211. Xu, W.; Chen, B.; Guo, L.; Li, Z.; Zhao, Y.; Zeng, H. High-sensitivity CRP: Possible link between job stress and atherosclerosis. *Am. J. Ind. Med.* **2015**, *58*, 773–779. [CrossRef]
212. Alley, D.E.; Seeman, T.E.; Ki Kim, J.; Karlamangla, A.; Hu, P.; Crimmins, E.M. Socioeconomic status and C-reactive protein levels in the US population: NHANES IV. *Brain Behav. Immun.* **2006**, *20*, 498–504. [CrossRef]
213. Nazmi, A.; Victora, C.G. Socioeconomic and racial/ethnic differentials of C-reactive protein levels: A systematic review of population-based studies. *BMC Public Health* **2007**, *7*, 212. [CrossRef] [PubMed]
214. Sanada, K.; Montero-Marin, J.; Barceló-Soler, A.; Ikuse, D.; Ota, M.; Hirata, A.; Yoshizawa, A.; Hatanaka, R.; Valero, M.S.; Demarzo, M.; et al. Effects of mindfulness-based interventions on biomarkers and low-grade inflammation in patients with psychiatric disorders: A meta-analytic review. *Int. J. Mol. Sci.* **2020**, *21*, 2484. [CrossRef] [PubMed]
215. Yegorov, Y.E.; Poznyak, A.V.; Nikiforov, N.G.; Sobenin, I.A.; Orekhov, A.N. The link between chronic stress and accelerated aging. *Biomedicines* **2020**, *8*, 198. [CrossRef] [PubMed]
216. Pedersen, A.F.; Zachariae, R.; Bovbjerg, D.H. Psychological stress and antibody response to influenza vaccination: A meta-analysis. *Brain. Behav. Immun.* **2009**, *23*, 427–433. [CrossRef]
217. Miller, G.E.; Cohen, S.; Pressman, S.; Barkin, A.; Rabin, B.S.; Treanor, J.J. Psychological Stress and Antibody Response to Influenza Vaccination: When Is the Critical Period for Stress, and How Does It Get Inside the Body? *Psychosom. Med.* **2004**, *66*, 215–223. [CrossRef]
218. Vedhara, K. Chronic stress in elderly carers of dementia patients and antibody response to influenza vaccination. *Lancet* **1999**, *353*, 627–631. [CrossRef]
219. Kiecolt-Glaser, J.K.; Glaser, R.; Gravenstein, S.; Malarkey, W.B.; Sheridan, J. Chronic stress alters the immune response to influenza virus vaccine in older adults. *Proc. Natl. Acad. Sci. USA* **1996**, *93*, 3043–3047. [CrossRef]
220. Glaser, R.; Sheridan, J.; Malarkey, W.B.; MacCallum, R.C.; Kiecolt-Glaser, J.K. Chronic stress modulates the immune response to a pneumococcal pneumoaia vaccine. *Psychosom. Med.* **2000**, *62*, 804–807. [CrossRef] [PubMed]
221. Glaser, R.; Kiecolt-Glaser, J.K.; Bonneau, R.H.; Malarkey, W.; Kennedy, S.; Hughes, J. Stress-induced modulation of the immune response to recombinant hepatitis B vaccine. *Psychosom. Med.* **1992**, *54*, 22–29. [CrossRef]
222. Gallagher, S.; Phillips, A.C.; Drayson, M.T.; Carroll, D. Parental caregivers of children with developmental disabilities mount a poor antibody response to pneumococcal vaccination. *Brain Behav. Immun.* **2009**, *23*, 338–346. [CrossRef]
223. Gallagher, S.; Phillips, A.C.; Drayson, M.T.; Carroll, D. Caregiving for children with developmental disabilities is associated with a poor antibody response to influenza vaccination. *Psychosom. Med.* **2009**, *71*, 341–344. [CrossRef]
224. Glaser, R.; Kiecolt-Glaser, J.K.; Malarkey, W.B.; Sheridan, J.F. The influence of psychological stress on the immune response to vaccines. *Ann. N. Y. Acad. Sci.* **1998**, *840*, 649–655. [CrossRef] [PubMed]
225. Black, D.S.; Slavich, G.M. Mindfulness meditation and the immune system: A systematic review of randomized controlled trials. *Ann. N. Y. Acad. Sci.* **2016**, *1373*, 13–24. [CrossRef] [PubMed]
226. Morgan, N.; Irwin, M.R.; Chung, M.; Wang, C. The effects of mind-body therapies on the immune system: Meta-analysis. *PLoS ONE* **2014**, *9*, e100903. [CrossRef]
227. Djalilova, D.M.; Schulz, P.S.; Berger, A.M.; Case, A.J.; Kupzyk, K.A.; Ross, A.C. Impact of Yoga on Inflammatory Biomarkers: A Systematic Review. *Biol. Res. Nurs.* **2019**, *21*, 198–209. [CrossRef] [PubMed]
228. Rebar, A.L.; Stanton, R.; Geard, D.; Short, C.; Duncan, M.J.; Vandelanotte, C. A meta-meta-analysis of the effect of physical activity on depression and anxiety in non-clinical adult populations. *Health Psychol. Rev.* **2015**, *9*, 366–378. [CrossRef]
229. Ashdown-Franks, G.; Firth, J.; Carney, R.; Carvalho, A.F.; Hallgren, M.; Koyanagi, A.; Rosenbaum, S.; Schuch, F.B.; Smith, L.; Solmi, M.; et al. Exercise as Medicine for Mental and Substance Use Disorders: A Meta-review of the Benefits for Neuropsychiatric and Cognitive Outcomes. *Sports Med.* **2020**, *50*, 151–170. [CrossRef]
230. Robillard, R.; Dion, K.; Pennestri, M.H.; Solomonova, E.; Lee, E.; Saad, M.; Murkar, A.; Godbout, R.; Edwards, J.D.; Quilty, L.; et al. Profiles of sleep changes during the COVID-19 pandemic: Demographic, behavioural and psychological factors. *J. Sleep Res.* **2020**, *30*, e13231. [CrossRef]
231. Medic, G.; Wille, M.; Hemels, M.E.H. Short- and long-term health consequences of sleep disruption. *Nat. Sci. Sleep* **2017**, *9*, 151–161. [CrossRef]
232. Lange, T.; Dimitrov, S.; Born, J. Effects of sleep and circadian rhythm on the human immune system. *Ann. N. Y. Acad. Sci.* **2010**, *1193*, 48–59. [CrossRef] [PubMed]
233. Ali, T.; Choe, J.; Awab, A.; Wagener, T.L.; Orr, W.C. Sleep, immunity and inflammation in gastrointestinal disorders. *World J. Gastroenterol.* **2013**, *19*, 9231–9239. [CrossRef] [PubMed]

234. Vgontzas, A.N.; Zoumakis, M.; Bixler, E.O.; Lin, H.M.; Prolo, P.; Vela-Bueno, A.; Kales, A.; Chrousos, G.P. Impaired nighttime sleep in healthy old versus young adults is associated with elevated plasma interleukin-6 and cortisol levels: Physiologic and therapeutic implications. *J. Clin. Endocrinol. Metab.* **2003**, *88*, 2087–2095. [CrossRef]
235. Atienza, M.; Ziontz, J.; Cantero, J.L. Low-grade inflammation in the relationship between sleep disruption, dysfunctional adiposity, and cognitive decline in aging. *Sleep Med. Rev.* **2018**, *42*, 171–183. [CrossRef] [PubMed]
236. Dimitrov, S.; Lange, T.; Nohroudi, K.; Born, J. Number and function of circulating human antigen presenting cells regulated by sleep. *Sleep* **2007**, *30*, 401–411. [CrossRef]
237. Irwin, M.R.; Olmstead, R.; Carroll, J.E. Sleep disturbance, sleep duration, and inflammation: A systematic review and meta-analysis of cohort studies and experimental sleep deprivation. *Biol. Psychiatry* **2016**, *80*, 40–52. [CrossRef]
238. Cellini, N.; Canale, N.; Mioni, G.; Costa, S. Changes in sleep pattern, sense of time and digital media use during COVID-19 lockdown in Italy. *J. Sleep Res.* **2020**, *29*, e13074. [CrossRef] [PubMed]
239. Touitou, Y.; Reinberg, A.; Touitou, D. Association between light at night, melatonin secretion, sleep deprivation, and the internal clock: Health impacts and mechanisms of circadian disruption. *Life Sci.* **2017**, *173*, 94–106. [CrossRef] [PubMed]
240. Stebelova, K.; Roska, J.; Zeman, M. Impact of dim light at night on urinary 6-sulphatoxymelatonin concentrations and sleep in healthy humans. *Int. J. Mol. Sci.* **2020**, *21*, 7736. [CrossRef]
241. Mauriz, J.L.; Collado, P.S.; Veneroso, C.; Reiter, R.J.; González-Gallego, J. A review of the molecular aspects of melatonin's anti-inflammatory actions: Recent insights and new perspectives. *J. Pineal Res.* **2013**, *54*, 1–14. [CrossRef] [PubMed]
242. Tarocco, A.; Caroccia, N.; Morciano, G.; Wieckowski, M.R.; Ancora, G.; Garani, G.; Pinton, P. Melatonin as a master regulator of cell death and inflammation: Molecular mechanisms and clinical implications for newborn care. *Cell Death Dis.* **2019**, *10*, 1–12. [CrossRef]
243. Srinivasan, V.; Maestroni, G.J.M.; Cardinali, D.P.; Esquifino, A.I.; Pandi Perumal, S.R.; Miller, S.C. Melatonin, immune function and aging. *Immun. Ageing* **2005**, *2*, 17. [CrossRef]
244. Leproult, R.; Holmbäck, U.; Van Cauter, E. Circadian misalignment augments markers of insulin resistance and inflammation, independently of sleep loss. *Diabetes* **2014**, *63*, 1860–1869. [CrossRef]
245. Morris, C.J.; Purvis, T.E.; Mistretta, J.; Hu, K.; Scheer, F.A.J.L. Circadian Misalignment Increases C-Reactive Protein and Blood Pressure in Chronic Shift Workers. *J. Biol. Rhythms* **2017**, *32*, 154–164. [CrossRef] [PubMed]
246. Prather, A.A.; Hall, M.; Fury, J.M.; Ross, D.C.; Muldoon, M.F.; Cohen, S.; Marsland, A.L. Sleep and antibody response to hepatitis B vaccination. *Sleep* **2012**, *35*, 1063–1069. [CrossRef] [PubMed]
247. Lange, T.; Dimitrov, S.; Bollinger, T.; Diekelmann, S.; Born, J. Sleep after Vaccination Boosts Immunological Memory. *J. Immunol.* **2011**, *187*, 283–290. [CrossRef] [PubMed]
248. Spiegel, K. Effect of Sleep Deprivation on Response to Immunizaton. *JAMA J. Am. Med. Assoc.* **2002**, *288*, 1471–1472. [CrossRef]
249. Benedict, C.; Brytting, M.; Markström, A.; Broman, J.E.; Schiöth, H.B. Acute sleep deprivation has no lasting effects on the human antibody titer response following a novel influenza A H1N1 virus vaccination. *BMC Immunol.* **2012**, *13*, 1. [CrossRef]
250. Haspel, J.A.; Anafi, R.; Brown, M.K.; Cermakian, N.; Depner, C.; Desplats, P.; Gelman, A.E.; Haack, M.; Jelic, S.; Kim, B.S.; et al. Perfect timing: Circadian rhythms, sleep, and immunity—An NIH workshop summary. *JCI Insight* **2020**, *5*, e131487. [CrossRef]
251. Phillips, A.C.; Gallagher, S.; Carroll, D.; Drayson, M. Preliminary evidence that morning vaccination is associated with an enhanced antibody response in men. *Psychophysiology* **2008**, *45*, 663–666. [CrossRef] [PubMed]
252. Wu, K.; Wei, X. Analysis of Psychological and Sleep Status and Exercise Rehabilitation of Front-Line Clinical Staff in the Fight against COVID-19 in China. *Med. Sci. Monit. Basic Res.* **2020**, *26*, e924085. [CrossRef]
253. Xie, Y.; Tang, Q.; Chen, G.; Xie, M.; Yu, S.; Zhao, J.; Chen, L. New insights into the circadian rhythm and its related diseases. *Front. Physiol.* **2019**, *10*, 682. [CrossRef] [PubMed]
254. Cohen, A.J.; Brauer, M.; Burnett, R.; Anderson, H.R.; Frostad, J.; Estep, K.; Balakrishnan, K.; Brunekreef, B.; Dandona, L.; Dandona, R.; et al. Estimates and 25-year trends of the global burden of disease attributable to ambient air pollution: An analysis of data from the Global Burden of Diseases Study 2015. *Lancet* **2017**, *389*, 1907–1918. [CrossRef]
255. Chen, A.; Dietrich, K.N.; Huo, X.; Ho, S.M. Developmental neurotoxicants in e-waste: An emerging health concern. *Environ. Health Perspect.* **2011**, *119*, 431–438. [CrossRef]
256. Udeigwe, T.K.; Teboh, J.M.; Eze, P.N.; Hashem Stietiya, M.; Kumar, V.; Hendrix, J.; Mascagni, H.J.; Ying, T.; Kandakji, T. Implications of leading crop production practices on environmental quality and human health. *J. Environ. Manag.* **2015**, *151*, 267–279. [CrossRef] [PubMed]
257. Pollard, K.M.; Christy, J.M.; Cauvi, D.M.; Kono, D.H. Environmental xenobiotic exposure and autoimmunity. *Curr. Opin. Toxicol.* **2018**, *10*, 15–22. [CrossRef]
258. Reitsma, M.B.; Fullman, N.; Ng, M.; Salama, J.S.; Abajobir, A.; Abate, K.H.; Abbafati, C.; Abera, S.F.; Abraham, B.; Abyu, G.Y.; et al. Smoking prevalence and attributable disease burden in 195 countries and territories, 1990-2015: A systematic analysis from the global burden of disease study 2015. *Lancet* **2017**, *389*, 1885–1906. [CrossRef]
259. Frontera, A.; Cianfanelli, L.; Vlachos, K.; Landoni, G.; Cremona, G. Severe air pollution links to higher mortality in COVID-19 patients: The "double-hit" hypothesis. *J. Infect.* **2020**, *81*, 255–259. [CrossRef]
260. Van Eeden, S.F.; Tan, W.C.; Suwa, T.; Mukae, H.; Terashima, T.; Fujii, T.; Qui, D.; Vincent, R.; Hogg, J.C. Cytokines involved in the systemic inflammatory response induced by exposure to particulate matter air pollutants (PM10). *Am. J. Respir. Crit. Care Med.* **2001**, *164*, 826–830. [CrossRef]

261. Becker, S.; Soukup, J.M. Exposure to urban air particulates alters the macrophage-mediated inflammatory response to respiratory viral infection. *J. Toxicol. Environ. Health Part A* **1999**, *57*, 445–457. [CrossRef]
262. Ciencewicki, J.; Jaspers, I. Air pollution and respiratory viral infection. *Inhal. Toxicol.* **2007**, *19*, 1135–1146. [CrossRef]
263. Glencross, D.A.; Ho, T.R.; Camiña, N.; Hawrylowicz, C.M.; Pfeffer, P.E. Air pollution and its effects on the immune system. *Free Radic. Biol. Med.* **2020**, *151*, 56–68. [CrossRef] [PubMed]
264. Berman, J.D.; Ebisu, K. Changes in U.S. air pollution during the COVID-19 pandemic. *Sci. Total Environ.* **2020**, *739*, 139864. [CrossRef]
265. Zhu, Y.; Xie, J.; Huang, F.; Cao, L. Association between short-term exposure to air pollution and COVID-19 infection: Evidence from China. *Sci. Total Environ.* **2020**, *727*, 138704. [CrossRef] [PubMed]
266. Benmarhnia, T. Linkages between air pollution and the health burden from covid-19: Methodological challenges and opportunities. *Am. J. Epidemiol.* **2020**, *189*, 1238–1243. [CrossRef]
267. Wu, X.; Nethery, R.C.; Sabath, M.B.; Braun, D.; Dominici, F. Air pollution and COVID-19 mortality in the United States: Strengths and limitations of an ecological regression analysis. *Sci. Adv.* **2020**, *6*, eabd4049. [CrossRef] [PubMed]
268. Ogen, Y. Assessing nitrogen dioxide (NO_2) levels as a contributing factor to coronavirus (COVID-19) fatality. *Sci. Total Environ.* **2020**, *726*, 138605. [CrossRef]
269. Coronavirus is in the air—there's too much focus on surfaces. *Nature* **2021**, *590*, 7. [CrossRef] [PubMed]
270. Bourdrel, T.; Annesi-Maesano, I.; Alahmad, B.; Maesano, C.N.; Bind, M.-A. The impact of outdoor air pollution on COVID-19: A review of evidence from in vitro, animal, and human studies. *Eur. Respir. Rev.* **2021**, *30*, 200242. [CrossRef]
271. Skalny, A.V.; Lima, T.R.R.; Ke, T.; Zhou, J.C.; Bornhorst, J.; Alekseenko, S.I.; Aaseth, J.; Anesti, O.; Sarigiannis, D.A.; Tsatsakis, A.; et al. Toxic metal exposure as a possible risk factor for COVID-19 and other respiratory infectious diseases. *Food Chem. Toxicol.* **2020**, *146*, 111809. [CrossRef] [PubMed]
272. World Health Organization. Tobacco. Available online: https://www.who.int/news-room/fact-sheets/detail/tobacco (accessed on 15 December 2020).
273. Jha, P.; Ramasundarahettige, C.; Landsman, V.; Rostron, B.; Thun, M.; Anderson, R.N.; McAfee, T.; Peto, R. 21st-Century Hazards of Smoking and Benefits of Cessation in the United States. *N. Engl. J. Med.* **2013**, *368*, 341–350. [CrossRef]
274. Hecht, S.S. Tobacco carcinogens, their biomarkers and tobacco-induced cancer. *Nat. Rev. Cancer* **2003**, *3*, 733–744. [CrossRef]
275. Zhou, P.; Yang, X.L.; Wang, X.G.; Hu, B.; Zhang, L.; Zhang, W.; Si, H.R.; Zhu, Y.; Li, B.; Huang, C.L.; et al. A pneumonia outbreak associated with a new coronavirus of probable bat origin. *Nature* **2020**, *579*, 270–273. [CrossRef] [PubMed]
276. Oakes, J.M.; Fuchs, R.M.; Gardner, J.D.; Lazartigues, E.; Yue, X. Nicotine and the renin-angiotensin system. *Am. J. Physiol. Regul. Integr. Comp. Physiol.* **2018**, *315*, R895–R906. [CrossRef]
277. Cai, G.; Bossé, Y.; Xiao, F.; Kheradmand, F.; Amos, C.I. Tobacco smoking increases the lung gene expression of ACE2, the Receptor of SARS-CoV-2. *Am. J. Respir. Crit. Care Med.* **2020**, *201*, 1557–1559. [CrossRef]
278. Lippi, G.; Henry, B.M. Active smoking is not associated with severity of coronavirus disease 2019 (COVID-19). *Eur. J. Intern. Med.* **2020**, *75*, 107–108. [CrossRef]
279. Simons, D.; Shahab, L.; Brown, J.; Perski, O. The association of smoking status with SARS-CoV-2 infection, hospitalization and mortality from COVID-19: A living rapid evidence review with Bayesian meta-analyses (version 7). *Addiction* **2020**, *116*, 1319–1368. [CrossRef] [PubMed]
280. Silverio, A.; Di Maio, M.; Citro, R.; Esposito, L.; Iuliano, G.; Bellino, M.; Baldi, C.; De Luca, G.; Ciccarelli, M.; Vecchione, C.; et al. Cardiovascular risk factors and mortality in hospitalized patients with COVID-19: Systematic review and meta-analysis of 45 studies and 18,300 patients. *BMC Cardiovasc. Disord.* **2021**, *21*, 23. [CrossRef] [PubMed]
281. Farsalinos, K.; Barbouni, A.; Niaura, R. Systematic review of the prevalence of current smoking among hospitalized COVID-19 patients in China: Could nicotine be a therapeutic option? *Intern. Emerg. Med.* **2020**, *15*, 845–852. [CrossRef]
282. Wang, H.; Yu, M.; Ochani, M.; Amelia, C.A.; Tanovic, M.; Susarla, S.; Li, J.H.; Wang, H.; Yang, N.; Ulloa, L.; et al. Nicotinic acetylcholine receptor α7 subunit is an essential regulator of inflammation. *Nature* **2003**, *421*, 384–388. [CrossRef]
283. Pavlov, V.A.; Tracey, K.J. The cholinergic anti-inflammatory pathway. *Brain. Behav. Immun.* **2005**, *19*, 493–499. [CrossRef] [PubMed]
284. Tizabi, Y.; Getachew, B.; Copeland, R.L.; Aschner, M. Nicotine and the nicotinic cholinergic system in COVID-19. *FEBS J.* **2020**, *287*, 3656–3663. [CrossRef] [PubMed]
285. Gonzalez-Rubio, J.; Navarro-Lopez, C.; Lopez-Najera, E.; Lopez-Najera, A.; Jimenez-Diaz, L.; Navarro-Lopez, J.D.; Najera, A. Cytokine Release Syndrome (CRS) and Nicotine in COVID-19 Patients: Trying to Calm the Storm. *Front. Immunol.* **2020**, *11*, 1359. [CrossRef]
286. Dorjee, K.; Kim, H.; Bonomo, E.; Dolma, R. Prevalence and predictors of death and severe disease in patients hospitalized due to COVID-19: A comprehensive systematic review and meta-analysis of 77 studies and 38,000 patients. *PLoS ONE* **2020**, *15*, e0243191. [CrossRef]
287. Mesas, A.E.; Cavero-Redondo, I.; Álvarez-Bueno, C.; Cabrera, M.A.S.; de Andrade, S.M.; Sequí-Dominguez, I.; Martínez-Vizcaíno, V. Predictors of in-hospital COVID-19 mortality: A comprehensive systematic review and meta-analysis exploring differences by age, sex and health conditions. *PLoS ONE* **2020**, *15*, e0241742. [CrossRef] [PubMed]
288. Patanavanich, R.; Glantz, S.A. Smoking is Associated with COVID-19 Progression: A Meta-analysis. *Nicotine Tob. Res.* **2020**, *22*, 1653–1656. [CrossRef]

289. Umnuaypornlert, A.; Kanchanasurakit, S.; Lucero-Prisno, D.E.; Saokaew, S. Smoking and risk of negative outcomes among COVID-19 patients: A systematic review and meta-analysis. *Tob. Induc. Dis.* **2021**, *19*, 9. [CrossRef]
290. Bauer, C.M.T.; Morissette, M.C.; Stämpfli, M.R. The influence of cigarette smoking on viral infections: Translating bench science to impact COPD pathogenesis and acute exacerbations of COPD clinically. *Chest* **2013**, *143*, 196–206. [CrossRef] [PubMed]
291. Arcavi, L.; Benowitz, N.L. Cigarette smoking and infection. *Arch. Intern. Med.* **2004**, *164*, 2206–2216. [CrossRef]
292. Gotts, J.E.; Jordt, S.E.; McConnell, R.; Tarran, R. What are the respiratory effects of e-cigarettes? *BMJ* **2019**, *366*, l5275. [CrossRef] [PubMed]
293. Tollerud, D.J.; Clark, J.W.; Brown, L.M.; Neuland, C.Y.; Mann, D.L.; Pankiw-Trost, L.K.; Blattner, W.A.; Hoover, R.N. Association of cigarette smoking with decreased numbers of circulating natural killer cells. *Am. Rev. Respir. Dis.* **1989**, *139*, 194–198. [CrossRef]
294. Phillips, B.; Marshall, M.E.; Brown, S.; Thompson, J.S. Effect of smoking on human natural killer cell activity. *Cancer* **1985**, *56*, 2789–2792. [CrossRef]
295. Zeidel, A.; Beilin, B.; Yardeni, I.; Mayburd, E.; Smirnov, G.; Bessler, H. Immune response in asymptomatic smokers. *Acta Anaesthesiol. Scand.* **2002**, *46*, 959–964. [CrossRef] [PubMed]
296. Qiu, F.; Liang, C.L.; Liu, H.; Zeng, Y.Q.; Hou, S.; Huang, S.; Lai, X.; Dai, Z. Impacts of cigarette smoking on immune responsiveness: Up and down or upside down? *Oncotarget* **2017**, *8*, 268–284. [CrossRef]
297. Younas, M.; Carrat, F.; Desaint, C.; Launay, O.; Corbeau, P. Immune activation, smoking, and vaccine response. *AIDS* **2017**, *31*, 171–173. [CrossRef]
298. Feng, Y.; Kong, Y.; Barnes, P.F.; Huang, F.F.; Klucar, P.; Wang, X.; Samten, B.; Sengupta, M.; MacHona, B.; Donis, R.; et al. Exposure to cigarette smoke inhibits the pulmonary T-cell response to influenza virus and mycobacterium tuberculosis. *Infect. Immun.* **2011**, *79*, 229–237. [CrossRef]
299. Rosenbaum, M.; Knight, R.; Leibel, R.L. The gut microbiota in human energy homeostasis and obesity. *Trends Endocrinol. Metab.* **2015**, *26*, 493–501. [CrossRef]
300. Zheng, D.; Liwinski, T.; Elinav, E. Interaction between microbiota and immunity in health and disease. *Cell Res.* **2020**, *30*, 492–506. [CrossRef]
301. Honda, K.; Littman, D.R. The microbiota in adaptive immune homeostasis and disease. *Nature* **2016**, *535*, 75–84. [CrossRef] [PubMed]
302. Fan, Y.; Pedersen, O. Gut microbiota in human metabolic health and disease. *Nat. Rev. Microbiol.* **2020**, *19*, 55–71. [CrossRef]
303. Ge, X.; Zheng, L.; Zhuang, R.; Yu, P.; Xu, Z.; Liu, G.; Xi, X.; Zhou, X.; Fan, H. The Gut Microbial Metabolite Trimethylamine N-Oxide and Hypertension Risk: A Systematic Review and Dose-Response Meta-analysis. *Adv. Nutr.* **2020**, *11*, 66–76. [CrossRef] [PubMed]
304. Ahn, J.; Sinha, R.; Pei, Z.; Dominianni, C.; Wu, J.; Shi, J.; Goedert, J.J.; Hayes, R.B.; Yang, L. Human gut microbiome and risk for colorectal cancer. *J. Natl. Cancer Inst.* **2013**, *105*, 1907–1911. [CrossRef]
305. Nishida, A.; Inoue, R.; Inatomi, O.; Bamba, S.; Naito, Y.; Andoh, A. Gut microbiota in the pathogenesis of inflammatory bowel disease. *Clin. J. Gastroenterol.* **2018**, *11*, 1–10. [CrossRef] [PubMed]
306. Russell, S.L.; Gold, M.J.; Hartmann, M.; Willing, B.P.; Thorson, L.; Wlodarska, M.; Gill, N.; Blanchet, M.R.; Mohn, W.W.; McNagny, K.M.; et al. Early life antibiotic-driven changes in microbiota enhance susceptibility to allergic asthma. *EMBO Rep.* **2012**, *13*, 440–447. [CrossRef] [PubMed]
307. Shukla, S.; Kumari, S.; Bal, S.K.; Monaco, D.C.; Ribeiro, S.P.; Sekaly, R.P.; Sharma, A.A. "Go", "No Go," or "Where to Go"; does microbiota dictate T cell exhaustion, programming, and HIV persistence? *Curr. Opin. HIV AIDS* **2021**, *16*, 215–222. [CrossRef]
308. O'Toole, P.W.; Shiels, P.G. The role of the microbiota in sedentary lifestyle disorders and ageing: Lessons from the animal kingdom. *J. Intern. Med.* **2020**, *287*, 271–282. [CrossRef]
309. Sonnenburg, E.D.; Sonnenburg, J.L. The ancestral and industrialized gut microbiota and implications for human health. *Nat. Rev. Microbiol.* **2019**, *17*, 383–390. [CrossRef]
310. Le Bastard, Q.; Al-Ghalith, G.A.; Grégoire, M.; Chapelet, G.; Javaudin, F.; Dailly, E.; Batard, E.; Knights, D.; Montassier, E. Systematic review: Human gut dysbiosis induced by non-antibiotic prescription medications. *Aliment. Pharmacol. Ther.* **2018**, *47*, 332–345. [CrossRef]
311. Ortiz-Alvarez, L.; Xu, H.; Martinez-Tellez, B. Influence of Exercise on the Human Gut Microbiota of Healthy Adults: A Systematic Review. *Clin. Transl. Gastroenterol.* **2020**, *11*, e00126. [CrossRef] [PubMed]
312. Reber, S.O.; Peters, S.; Slattery, D.A.; Hofmann, C.; Schölmerich, J.; Neumann, I.D.; Obermeier, F. Mucosal immunosuppression and epithelial barrier defects are key events in murine psychosocial stress-induced colitis. *Brain. Behav. Immun.* **2011**, *25*, 1153–1161. [CrossRef]
313. Savin, Z.; Kivity, S.; Yonath, H.; Yehuda, S. Smoking and the intestinal microbiome. *Arch. Microbiol.* **2018**, *200*, 677–684. [CrossRef]
314. Mutlu, E.A.; Gillevet, P.M.; Rangwala, H.; Sikaroodi, M.; Naqvi, A.; Engen, P.A.; Kwasny, M.; Lau, C.K.; Keshavarzian, A. Colonic microbiome is altered in alcoholism. *Am. J. Physiol.-Gastrointest. Liver Physiol.* **2012**, *302*, G966–G978. [CrossRef]
315. Dong, T.S.; Gupta, A. Influence of Early Life, Diet, and the Environment on the Microbiome. *Clin. Gastroenterol. Hepatol.* **2019**, *17*, 231–242. [CrossRef] [PubMed]
316. West, C.E.; Renz, H.; Jenmalm, M.C.; Kozyrskyj, A.L.; Allen, K.J.; Vuillermin, P.; Prescott, S.L. The gut microbiota and inflammatory noncommunicable diseases: Associations and potentials for gut microbiota therapies. *J. Allergy Clin. Immunol.* **2015**, *135*, 3–13. [CrossRef]

317. Custodero, C.; Mankowski, R.T.; Lee, S.A.; Chen, Z.; Wu, S.; Manini, T.M.; Hincapie Echeverri, J.; Sabbà, C.; Beavers, D.P.; Cauley, J.A.; et al. Evidence-based nutritional and pharmacological interventions targeting chronic low-grade inflammation in middle-age and older adults: A systematic review and meta-analysis. *Ageing Res. Rev.* **2018**, *46*, 42–59. [CrossRef] [PubMed]
318. Pei, R.; Dimarco, D.M.; Putt, K.K.; Martin, D.A.; Gu, Q.; Chitchumroonchokchai, C.; White, H.M.; Scarlett, C.O.; Bruno, R.S.; Bolling, B.W. Low-fat yogurt consumption reduces biomarkers of chronic inflammation and inhibits markers of endotoxin exposure in healthy premenopausal women: A randomised controlled trial. *Br. J. Nutr.* **2017**, *118*, 1043–1051. [CrossRef]
319. Pei, R.; DiMarco, D.; Putt, K.; Martin, D.; Bruno, R.; Bolling, B. Low-fat Yogurt Consumption Reduces Markers of Chronic Inflammation in Apparently Healthy Lean and Obese Women. *FASEB J.* **2016**, *30*, 905–909. [CrossRef]
320. Santiago, S.; Sayón-Orea, C.; Babio, N.; Ruiz-Canela, M.; Martí, A.; Corella, D.; Estruch, R.; Fitó, M.; Aros, F.; Ros, E.; et al. Yogurt consumption and abdominal obesity reversion in the PREDIMED study. *Nutr. Metab. Cardiovasc. Dis.* **2016**, *26*, 468–475. [CrossRef]
321. Brett Finlay, B.; Amato, K.R.; Azad, M.; Blaser, M.J.; Bosch, T.C.G.; Chu, H.; Dominguez-Bello, M.G.; Ehrlich, S.D.; Elinav, E.; Geva-Zatorsky, N.; et al. The hygiene hypothesis, the COVID pandemic, and consequences for the human microbiome. *Proc. Natl. Acad. Sci. USA* **2021**, *118*, 2021. [CrossRef]
322. He, Y.; Wen, Q.; Yao, F.; Xu, D.; Huang, Y.; Wang, J. Gut–lung axis: The microbial contributions and clinical implications. *Crit. Rev. Microbiol.* **2017**, *43*, 81–95. [CrossRef]
323. de Oliveira, G.L.V.; Oliveira, C.N.S.; Pinzan, C.F.; de Salis, L.V.V.; de Cardoso, C.R.B. Microbiota Modulation of the Gut-Lung Axis in COVID-19. *Front. Immunol.* **2021**, *12*, 214. [CrossRef]
324. Ichinohe, T.; Pang, I.K.; Kumamoto, Y.; Peaper, D.R.; Ho, J.H.; Murray, T.S.; Iwasaki, A. Microbiota regulates immune defense against respiratory tract influenza a virus infection. *Proc. Natl. Acad. Sci. USA* **2011**, *108*, 5354–5359. [CrossRef]
325. Zuo, T.; Zhang, F.; Lui, G.C.Y.; Yeoh, Y.K.; Li, A.Y.L.; Zhan, H.; Wan, Y.; Chung, A.C.K.; Cheung, C.P.; Chen, N.; et al. Alterations in Gut Microbiota of Patients With COVID-19 During Time of Hospitalization. *Gastroenterology* **2020**, *159*, 944–955.e8. [CrossRef] [PubMed]
326. Gu, S.; Chen, Y.; Wu, Z.; Chen, Y.; Gao, H.; Lv, L.; Guo, F.; Zhang, X.; Luo, R.; Huang, C.; et al. Alterations of the gut microbiota in patients with coronavirus disease 2019 or H1N1 influenza. *Clin. Infect. Dis.* **2020**, *71*, 2669–2678. [CrossRef]
327. Yeoh, Y.K.; Zuo, T.; Lui, G.C.Y.; Zhang, F.; Liu, Q.; Li, A.Y.L.; Chung, A.C.K.; Cheung, C.P.; Tso, E.Y.K.; Fung, K.S.C.; et al. Gut microbiota composition reflects disease severity and dysfunctional immune responses in patients with COVID-19. *Gut* **2021**, *70*, 698–706. [CrossRef] [PubMed]
328. McDonald, D.; Ackermann, G.; Khailova, L.; Baird, C.; Heyland, D.; Kozar, R.; Lemieux, M.; Derenski, K.; King, J.; Vis-Kampen, C.; et al. Extreme Dysbiosis of the Microbiome in Critical Illness. *mSphere* **2016**, *1*, e00199-16. [CrossRef]
329. Shimizu, K.; Ogura, H.; Hamasaki, T.; Goto, M.; Tasaki, O.; Asahara, T.; Nomoto, K.; Morotomi, M.; Matsushima, A.; Kuwagata, Y.; et al. Altered gut flora are associated with septic complications and death in critically ill patients with systemic inflammatory response syndrome. *Dig. Dis. Sci.* **2011**, *56*, 1171–1177. [CrossRef] [PubMed]
330. Patra, S.; Saxena, S.; Sahu, N.; Pradhan, B.; Roychowdhury, A. Systematic Network and Meta-analysis on the Antiviral Mechanisms of Probiotics: A Preventive and Treatment Strategy to Mitigate SARS-CoV-2 Infection. *Probiotics Antimicrob. Proteins* **2021**, *13*, 1138–1156. [CrossRef]
331. Swanson, K.V.; Deng, M.; Ting, J.P.-Y. The NLRP3 inflammasome: Molecular activation and regulation to therapeutics. *Nat. Rev. Immunol.* **2019**, *19*, 477–489. [CrossRef] [PubMed]
332. Lynn, D.J.; Pulendran, B. The potential of the microbiota to influence vaccine responses. *J. Leukoc. Biol.* **2017**, *103*, 225–231. [CrossRef]
333. de Jong, S.E.; Olin, A.; Pulendran, B. The Impact of the Microbiome on Immunity to Vaccination in Humans. *Cell Host Microbe* **2020**, *28*, 169–179. [CrossRef]
334. Lynn, D.J.; Benson, S.C.; Lynn, M.A.; Pulendran, B. Modulation of immune responses to vaccination by the microbiota: Implications and potential mechanisms. *Nat. Rev. Immunol.* **2021**, 1–14. [CrossRef]
335. Praharaj, I.; John, S.M.; Bandyopadhyay, R.; Kang, G. Probiotics, antibiotics and the immune responses to vaccines. *Philos. Trans. R. Soc. B Biol. Sci.* **2015**, *370*, 20140144. [CrossRef] [PubMed]
336. Harris, V.C.; Armah, G.; Fuentes, S.; Korpela, K.E.; Parashar, U.; Victor, J.C.; Tate, J.; De Weerth, C.; Giaquinto, C.; Wiersinga, W.J.; et al. Significant Correlation between the Infant Gut Microbiome and Rotavirus Vaccine Response in Rural Ghana. *J. Infect. Dis.* **2017**, *215*, 34–41. [CrossRef] [PubMed]
337. Zhao, T.; Li, J.; Fu, Y.; Ye, H.; Liu, X.; Li, G.; Yang, X.; Yang, J. Influence of gut microbiota on mucosal IgA antibody response to the polio vaccine. *NPJ Vaccines* **2020**, *5*, 47. [CrossRef] [PubMed]
338. Hagan, T.; Cortese, M.; Rouphael, N.; Boudreau, C.; Linde, C.; Maddur, M.S.; Das, J.; Wang, H.; Guthmiller, J.; Zheng, N.Y.; et al. Antibiotics-Driven Gut Microbiome Perturbation Alters Immunity to Vaccines in Humans. *Cell* **2019**, *178*, 1313–1328.e13. [CrossRef]
339. Zimmermann, P.; Curtis, N. The influence of probiotics on vaccine responses—A systematic review. *Vaccine* **2018**, *36*, 207–213. [CrossRef]

nutrients

Article

Anthropometric Dimensions and Bone Quality in International Male Beach Handball Players: Junior vs. Senior Comparison

Alejandro Martínez-Rodríguez [1,2,*], Javier Sánchez-Sánchez [3,*], Manuel Vicente-Martínez [4], María Martínez-Olcina [1], Laura Miralles-Amorós [1] and Juan Antonio Sánchez-Sáez [5]

1 Department of Analytical Chemistry, Nutrition and Food Science, Faculty of Sciences, Alicante University, 03690 Alicante, Spain; maria.martinezolcina@ua.es (M.M.-O.); lma52@alu.ua.es (L.M.-A.)
2 Alicante Institute for Health and Biomedical Research (ISABIAL Foundation), 03010 Alicante, Spain
3 School of Sport Sciences, Universidad Europea de Madrid, 28670 Madrid, Spain
4 Faculty of Health Science, Miguel de Cervantes European University, 47012 Valladolid, Spain; mvmartinez11006@alumnos.uemc.es
5 GDOT Research Group, Faculty of Sport, Universidad Católica de Murcia, 30107 Murcia, Spain; jasanchez419@ucam.edu
* Correspondence: amartinezrodriguez@ua.es (A.M.-R.); javier.sanchez2@universidadeuropea.es (J.S.-S.)

Abstract: Background: Beach handball is a recent team sport characterized by defensive and offensive actions on a sand surface. Scientific evidence has shown that body composition is fundamental in sports performance. The main objective of this study was to know the body composition, anthropometric characteristics, and bone mineral density of elite beach handball players. Furthermore, another purpose was to analyze the differences between categories (junior and senior) and playing position. *Methods:* A descriptive, cross-sectional study of 36 male players (18 juniors and 18 seniors) of the Spanish National Beach Handball Team was conducted. Full profile anthropometry and calcaneal ultrasound measurements were used. *Results*: Significant differences between categories ($p < 0.05$) were found in: height, body mass, arm span, BMI, muscle mass, fat mass, bone mass, skinfolds, and body perimeters. The somatotype changes depending on the playing position. Bone mineral density of the players was adequate. No significant differences were found by playing position. *Conclusions*: Senior players had a better body composition due to the presence of less fat mass than junior players. This study provides reference values of elite junior and senior beach handball players and by playing positions. This data is useful for the identification of talents and players who should be trained to improve their body composition.

Keywords: body composition; team sports; exercise; athletes; bone mineral density; muscle mass; phantom; proportionality

Citation: Martínez-Rodríguez, A.; Sánchez-Sánchez, J.; Vicente-Martínez, M.; Martínez-Olcina, M.; Miralles-Amorós, L.; Sánchez-Sáez, J.A. Anthropometric Dimensions and Bone Quality in International Male Beach Handball Players: Junior vs. Senior Comparison. *Nutrients* **2021**, *13*, 1817. https://doi.org/10.3390/nu13061817

Academic Editor: Pedro L. Valenzuela

Received: 25 April 2021
Accepted: 26 May 2021
Published: 27 May 2021

1. Introduction

Beach handball (BH) is a sport that derives from indoor handball. This specialty became popular in Italy in the 1990s, however, it was not until the last ten years that it became a global sport [1]. BH players play on an unstable surface such as sand, which means an increase in energy expenditure and neuromuscular needs compared to indoor handball [2]. In beach handball there are various actions such as throwing, passing, jumping, blocking, running, etc. that make it an intermittent high intensity contact sport [3,4]. The different playing positions are goalkeepers, wings, specialist, pivots, and defenders [5,6].

In recent years, research has begun on this sport, finding that the main variables affecting performance are morphology, body composition and, physical and physiological characteristics [2,5,7–12]. This is because BH is a sport with defensive and offensive actions of great speed to achieve the ultimate objective of scoring a goal [13].

The specific characteristics of beach handball are frequent changes in intensity, specific skills and social factors. These aspects define the determinants of coordination, endurance, strength and cognition in this sport [14,15]. To achieve optimal performance, actions must be performed with maximum intensity [16,17]. In BH players, groupings are made by date of birth, dividing them into juniors and seniors [16]. Therefore, depending on the age category, body composition and technical abilities differ, influencing success and development as a player [16,18].

As mentioned above, numerous studies have shown that body composition and anthropometric measurements are determinant in youth and senior handball players, both in indoor and beach handball [16,18–20]. Many research studies have shown that optimal body composition in athletes is associated with improvements in physical performance (aerobic and anaerobic) and muscle strength [21–26]. For optimal performance of BH players, it is necessary that their weight and fat percentage are within the recommended parameters for their age group, position, and sex [6,9].

Anthropometric characteristics have been shown to be decisive in indoor handball in junior and senior teams [16,18,20,27]. In addition, a direct influence between body composition and performance tests has been observed [6,28]. Milanese et al. [29] evaluated body composition as a function of playing position and found some significant differences between players. Body mass index (BMI) and indirect estimates of fat mass were commonly used to analyze body composition [16]. However, these methods have been discarded due to their limitations, as BMI is not only related to fat mass, but also to lean mass [30]. Therefore, in recent years, higher-quality investigations use methods such as dual X-ray densitometry (DXA) and full anthropometry [30].

Whole body composition as a whole includes body size and the proportion of body compartments. Body composition is usually analyzed through anthropometric measurement of weight, skinfolds, circumferences, diameters, heights and BMI [31]. Body size is of great importance for throwing in attack or blocking in defense, achieving higher ball velocity in jump throwing also having a strong positive effect on throwing performance and isometric strength [14,32]. The presence of a high percentage of fat is associated with multiple diseases and inflammation, so it has negative health consequences [6]. The optimal composition of athletes is framed by small amounts of fat mass and high amounts of muscle mass [33,34]. The specific percentage for adequate performance depends on the sporting position [33,35,36].

Forward players have displayed more favorable body composition results than other playing positions in indoor handball [37]. The morphology and composition of the upper limbs are fundamental aspects in beach handball. The best elite indoor handball players have shown higher values for humerus amplitude and hand length and width, these traits are found in the upper extremities and cannot be modified by training [38].

Therefore, it can be seen how the assessment of body composition is a fundamental aspect in sport due to its relation with performance and injury prevention, highlighting the importance of fat and muscle mass content [39,40]. It has been shown that fat mass, as opposed to muscle mass, is dead weight for jumping and sprinting, actions frequently performed in BH [39,41].

Bone mass is another relevant component to consider. The assessment of bone mineral density (BMD) is a measure that informs us about bone condition and strength. BMD is inversely related to the occurrence of fractures [42]. Skeletal injuries are rare in athletes, but their occurrence can have serious consequences for the athlete's health and professional life [43]. Physical exercise plays an important role in bone mass during growth. Beach handball is a sport that involves high mechanical stress on the lower limbs due to high intensity running, jumping and landing, causes osteogenic reactions [42,44].

Despite the increase of research in this sport in recent years, data about physical characteristics and bone mineral density in elite BH players are scarce [9]. Knowledge of the anthropometric profiles of these players is necessary to be able to identify the most important aspects which will have to be improved in order to achieve optimal sport performance.

The main objective of this research was to describe the body composition of elite male junior and senior BH players. The specific objectives were: (a) to know the body composition and bone mineral density of elite BH players by categories and playing position (b) to analyze the differences in body composition according to categories. The initial hypothesis was that body composition would be different between youth and senior players; and that the players with the best body composition would be the forwards.

2. Materials and Methods

2.1. *Study Design*

A descriptive, cross-sectional study was used to analyze the body composition and bone mineral density of male beach handball players, measured by anthropometry and calcaneal ultrasound, respectively. The research was conducted in accordance with the ethical standards recognized by the Declaration of Helsinki. The study was approved by the Ethical Committee of Alicante University (UA-2019-04-09).

2.2. *Subjects*

The study sample consisted of 36 male beach handball players (18 junior; 16.7 ± 0.46 years and 18 seniors; 25.0 ± 5.19 years). All of them were professional players of the National Beach Handball Team of the Royal Spanish Handball Federation, therefore, they represent the elite of BH players. The sample is divided into goalkeepers, wings, specialists, pivots, and defenders. All players received information about the objectives of the research, the experimental protocol, and the study procedures. Each of the participants signed the informed consent document. In the case of underage players, parents or legal tutors gave permission. Anonymity was preserved for all participants.

2.3. *Anthropometric Data*

Anthropometric variables were measured for each subject. For this purpose, full profile was developed, following the standard protocol of the International Society for the Advancement of Kinanthropometry (ISAK) [45].

All measurements were performed by the same investigator, an ISAK level 2 anthropometrist. The mean technical error was less than 1% for perimeters, circumferences, lengths, and heights and less than 5% for skinfolds. All measurements were performed on the first day of the concentration, under basal conditions, in the same location and at room temperature (22 ± 1 °C).

The following anthropometric material was used as approved and previously calibrated: wall measuring rod (accuracy, 1 mm); digital scale (BC545N, Tanita, Tokyo, Japan; accuracy, 100 g); metallic, narrow, and an inextensible measuring tape (Lufkin, TX, USA; accuracy, 1 mm); small bone diameter pachymeter (Smartmet, Jalisco, Mexico; accuracy, 1 mm); skinfold caliper (Harpenden, UK; accuracy, 0.2 mm), complementary material (demographic pencil to mark the players) and anthropometric bench measuring 40 × 50 × 30 cm.

Height and seated height were determined using a mobile anthropometer (Seca 213, SECA Deutschland, Hamburg, Germany) to the nearest millimeter, with the participant's head maintained in the Frankfort Horizontal Plane position. The length of wingspan was measured with an arm span meter (Smartmec, Zapopan Jalisco, México), made with a steel tape 5 m long and 18 mm wide, with an accuracy of 1 mm. Eight skinfolds were collected (subscapular, tricipital, bicipital, iliac crest, supraspinal, abdominal, anterior thigh and medial calf); 13 perimeters (head, neck, thorax, relaxed arm, contracted arm, forearm, wrist, waist, hip, thigh 1 cm from the glute, medial thigh, maximum leg and minimum ankle); 9 bone diameters (biacromial, anteroposterior abdominal, biliocrestal, transverse thorax, anteroposterior thorax, biepicondylar humerus, bi-styloid and bicondylar femur, bimalleolar); 8 lengths and heights (foot length, acromiale-radiale, radiale- stylion, midstylion-dactylion, iliospinale height, trochanterion height, trochanterion-tibiale laterale, tibiale laterale height, tibiale medial-sphyrion tibiale). The sum of 6 skinfolds was also computed (subscapular, triceps, supraspinale, abdominal, front thigh and medial calf).

Body composition was calculated using the following models: fat mass was estimated using the methods of Withers et al. [46] and Faulkner [47]. Muscle and bone masses were determined using the methods of Lee et al. [48] and Rocha [49], respectively. According to the Spanish Committee of Kinanthropometry, these methods are the most suitable for high performance players [49].

2.4. Somatotype

The mean somatotype and classification were determined using the anthropometric method of Heath and Carter [50] and its classification [51]. The somatotype is defined as the quantification of the shape and composition of the human body. It is represented by three components: (1) endomorphy (2) mesomorphy and (3) ectomorphy. Each component was calculated with its corresponding formulas [52].

2.5. Anthropometric Dimensions—Proportionality

Proportionality analysis were performed using the Phantom stratagem; a bilaterally symmetrical, bilaterally symmetrical, conceptually modeled, reference human derived from male and female reference data, proposed and revised by Ross and Ward [53]. Each variable was adjusted to the Phantom size using z-score = $(1/s) \times v \times [(170.18/h)^{d} - p]$; where z = proportionality value, v = size of any given variable, 170.18 = Phantom stature constant, h = subject's stature, d = dimensional exponent, P = Phantom value for variable v, and s = Phantom standard deviation value for variable based on an hypothetical universal human population. The z-values have a mean of 0, so a z-value of 0.0 indicates that the variable v is proportionally equal to that of the Phantom; a z-value greater than 0.0 means that the subject is proportionally greater than the Phantom for the variable v; otherwise, a z-value less than 0.0 shows that the subject is proportionally less than the Phantom for that variable [53].

2.6. Bone Quality

A heel ultrasound densitometer (Achilles EXP II, GE Healthcare, Chicago, IL, USA) was used to measure the bilateral calcaneus of each subject. Quality assurance was performed before the first measurement, by calibrating the device on a dedicated phantom supplied by the manufacturer. In addition, to ensure good contact, an ultrasound gel was applied. Broadband ultrasound attenuation (BUA) and speed of sound (SOS) were directly measured during each ultrasonographic evaluation. The calcaneal stiffness index was calculated using the following formula, previously used in other studies [54]:

$$\text{Calcaneal stiffness (A.U.)} = (0.67 - \text{BUA} + 0.28 - \text{SOS}) - 420$$

The elastic resistance of the bone is measured by the variable SOS, while the loss of ultrasound energy that occurs by absorption or scattering (and correlates with bone density) is evaluated by the variable BUA. By a combination of SOS and BUA, stiffness is achieved.

2.7. Statistical Analyses

To show the characteristics of the participants, descriptive statistics were made for all variables (Mean $\pm$ SD). To test the normality of the sample Kolmogorov-Smirnov, Shapiro-Wilk and Levene's test were applied. Analysis of variance (ANOVA), with Bonferroni post hoc comparisons to identify differences in basic anthropometric and demographic characteristics between players. Analysis of covariance (ANCOVA) with the correction of Bonferroni was used to compare differences between age groups (junior vs. senior), only the variables related to body composition were adjusted by BMI. The Somatotype Attitudinal Distance (SAD) was used to compare somatotype group means of junior and senior players. Statistical significance was set at $p < 0.05$. Cohen's d was used as a measure of the effect size (ES) of the differences between junior and senior players. The thresholds stipulated by Cohen [55] were considered; small (d = 0.2), moderate (d = 0.6), large (d = 1.2), very large (d = 2.0) and extremely large (d = 4.0). Mean differences in the chosen anthropometric characteristics, body composition and somatotype components of the players between playing positions were tested using a general linear model with a Tukey's post hoc test ($p < 0.05$) and using BMI as a covariate. All statistical analysis were performed using the Jamovi 1.1.3.0 software (The jamovi project, Sydney, Australia). The z-phantom scores were obtained from Excel and were represented in graphic form.

3. Results

A total of 32 male beach handball players participated in this study: 50% juniors and 50% seniors. Table 1 shows the basic anthropometric measurements. Mean weight is 78.1 ± 12.2 kg and 90.1 ± 13.4 kg for juniors and seniors, respectively. Height is 181 ± 5.90 cm for juniors and 188 ± 7.73 cm for seniors. Senior players show higher values, presenting significant differences ($p < 0.05$) in all variables, including arm span, which is 184 ± 7.45 cm for junior and 193 ± 9.35 cm for senior. In addition, generally the effect sizes were moderate to high. Due to these differences, BMI will be used as a covariate to analyze all the differences in the rest of the variables analyzed.

Table 1. Basic anthropometric and demographic characteristics of the sample.

Variable	Junior (n = 18)	Senior (n = 18)	ANOVA			
	Mean ± SD	Mean ± SD	Mean Difference	t	p	Cohen's d
Age (years)	16.7 ± 0.46	25.0 ± 5.19	−8.28	−6.75	<0.001	2.25
Body height (cm)	181 ± 5.90	188 ± 7.73	−7.65	−3.34	0.002	1.11
Body mass (kg)	78.1 ± 12.2	90.1 ± 13.4	−12.0	−2.82	0.008	0.94
Arm span (cm)	184 ± 7.45	193 ± 9.35	−8.84	−3.14	0.004	1.05
BMI (kg/m^2)	23.9 ± 2.82	25.4 ± 2.50	−1.47	−1.65	0.107	0.55

SD: Standard Deviation; BMI: Body Mass Index; Cohen's d (Effect Size); Mean differences were significant at $p < 0.05$.

Table 2 shows the body composition values (fat mass, muscle mass, bone mass, residual mass) and Table 3 the SOS, BUA and Stiffness values measured by ultrasound of all players, separated by age group: senior vs. junior. Statistically significant differences were observed in muscle mass ($p < 0.01$), fat mass measured by the Withers equation and bone mass ($p < 0.05$). In all variables, the results were higher in seniors, except in the percentage of fat calculated with the Withers formula.

Table 2. Descriptive data on body composition and differences between senior and junior.

Variable	Junior	Senior	Ancova (Adjusting by BMI)			
	Mean ± SD	Mean ± SD	Mean Difference	t	p	Cohen's d
Muscular mass (kg)	32.9 ± 3.38	38.2 ± 3.87	−3.88	−4.22	<0.001	1.460
Muscular mass (%)	42.5 ± 3.45	42.8 ± 4.03	−1.71	−1.86	0.072	0.644
BFM Withers (kg)	11.4 ± 7.17	12.2 ± 6.23	3.32	2.66	0.012	0.920
BFM Withers (%)	13.8 ± 6.73	13.1 ± 5.03	2.31	1.88	0.070	0.650
BFM Faulkner (kg)	10.4 ± 4.23	12.1 ± 4.19	1.06	1.52	0.137	0.528
BFM Faulkner (%)	12.9 ± 3.39	13.2 ± 3.01	0.260	0.36	0.722	0.124
Bone mass (kg)	12.0 ± 1.28	13.3 ± 1.58	−0.845	−2.12	0.041	0.736
Bone mass (%)	15.5 ± 1.34	14.9 ± 1.07	0.0923	0.35	0.727	0.122
Residual mass (kg)	22.9 ± 4.49	26.5 ± 5.68	−1.30	−1.33	0.191	0.462
Residual mass (%)	29.1 ± 2.02	29.2 ± 2.30	0.553	0.85	0.399	0.296

SD: Standard Deviation; BFM: Body Fat Mass; t: t student; Mean differences were significant at $p < 0.05$.

Table 3. Descriptive data on bone quality and differences between senior and junior.

Variable	Junior	Senior	Ancova (Adjusting by BMI)			
	Mean ± SD	Mean ± SD	Mean Difference	t	*p*	Cohen's d
BUA (dB/MHz)	131 ± 10.3	131 ± 9.24	1.43	0.43	0.672	0.148
SOS (m/s)	1640 ± 33.0	1657 ± 33.1	−11.9	−1.07	0.293	0.370
Stiffness (A.U)	127 ± 14.5	133 ± 11.9	−2.39	−0.54	0.537	0.188

SD: Standard Deviation; BUA: Broadband ultrasound attenuation; SOS: Speed of sound; t: t student; Mean differences were significant at $p < 0.05$.

The differences in somatotype, ponderal index and Somatotype Attitudinal Distance (SAD) between juniors and seniors are shown in Table 4. Significant differences were observed in the endomorphic ($p < 0.05$), ectoomorphic ($p < 0.05$) and ponderal index ($p < 0.05$) components. In all 3 variables the values are higher in junior players. As shown in Figures 1 and 2, the mean somatotype for junior and senior male players can be defined as balanced mesomorph (2.6-3.7-2.7) and (2.8-3.4-2.9), respectively.

Table 4. Somatotype components and difference between male and female players.

Variable	Junior	Senior	Ancova (Adjusting by BMI)			
	Mean ± SD	Mean ± SD	Mean Difference	t	*p*	Cohen ´s d
Endomorphy	2.79 ± 1.32	2.69 ± 1.16	0.104	0.251	0.033	0.770
Mesomorphy	3.40 ± 0.97	3.73 ± 1.00	−0.021	−0.07	0.941	0.026
Ectomorphy	2.91 ± 1.18	2.70 ± 0.96	−0.340	−2.39	0.023	0.826
Ponderal index	43.0 ± 1.61	42.7 ± 1.30	−0.464	−2.39	0.023	0.826
SAD	3.30 ± 3.01	2.77 ± 1.76	0.317	0.369	0.715	0.128

SAD: Somatotype Attitudinal Distance; SD: Standard Deviation; t: t student; Mean differences were significant at $p < 0.05$.

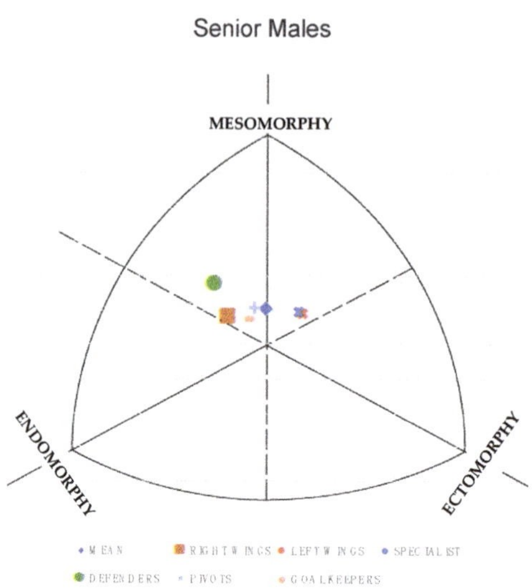

Figure 1. Somatotype distribution of elite male junior handball players.

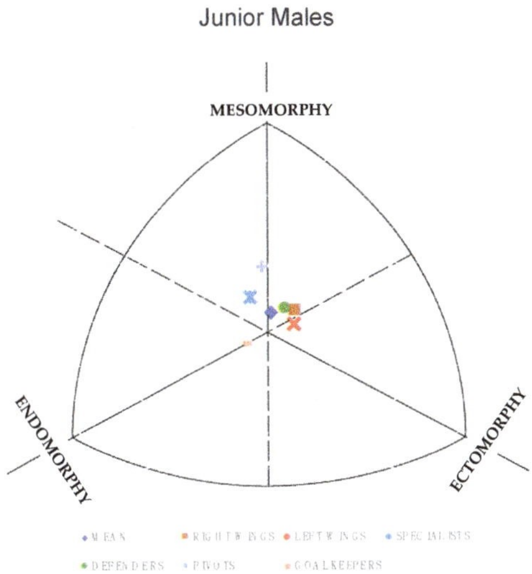

Figure 2. Somatotype distribution of elite male senior beach handball players.

However, if somatotype is analyzed as a function of playing position, as shown in the figure, the trends are different. For juniors, goalkeepers present a balanced endomorph somatotype, while right and left wings and defenders are mesomorph-ectomorph. In the senior category, defenders and right wings have a mesomorphic-endomorphic somatotype, while specialists and left wings tend to have a mesomorphic-ectomorphic somatotype.

Table 5 There are significant differences in some skinfolds such as triceps ($p < 0.01$), biceps ($p < 0.05$), front thigh ($p < 0.05$) and medial calf ($p < 0.01$), as well as in the sum of 6 skinfolds ($p < 0.05$). There was a general tendency for senior players to have lower skinfold values. Overall effect sizes were moderate to large.

Table 5. Descriptive data on skinfolds, circumferences, diameters, and the differences between junior and senior are presented in Table 4.

		Junior	Senior	Ancova (Adjusting by BMI)			
	Variable	**Mean ± SD**	**Mean ± SD**	**Mean Difference**	**t**	***p***	**Cohen's d**
Skinfolds	Triceps (mm)	10.7 ± 4.96	9.09 ± 3.65	3.52	3.75	<0.001	1.300
	Subscapular (mm)	9.87 ± 3.83	10.8 ± 3.98	0.416	0.392	0.697	0.136
	Biceps (mm)	6.08 ± 4.21	5.11 ± 1.84	2.01	2.16	0.038	0.748
	Iliac crest (mm)	17.0 ± 9.01	17.0 ± 7.97	3.61	1.89	0.067	0.655
	Supraspinale (mm)	9.53 ± 5.36	10.2 ± 5.72	1.58	1.22	0.230	0.423
	Abdominal (mm)	16.1 ± 8.73	18.1 ± 8.04	1.45	0.750	0.458	0.260
	Front thigh (mm)	15.4 ± 8.50	13.5 ± 6.67	4.99	2.72	0.010	0.944
	Medial calf (mm)	10.3 ± 5.41	7.31 ± 3.50	4.82	4.38	<0.001	1.520
	6 skinfolds (mm)	71.9 ± 34.8	69.1 ± 27.3	16.8	2.59	0.014	0.898
Girths	Relaxed arm (cm)	30.6 ± 3.12	33.7 ± 2.50	−1.75	−3.17	0.003	1.100
	Flexed arm (cm)	32.6 ± 2.37	35.9 ± 2.38	−2.28	−4.15	<0.001	1.440
	Thigh (cm)	54.1 ± 6.27	56.2 ± 3.83	0.523	0.616	0.542	0.214
	Calf (cm)	37.8 ± 2.77	39.1 ± 2.76	−0.077	−0.139	0.890	0.048
	Waist (cm)	79.5 ± 5.72	87.1 ± 6.57	−4.71	−4.20	<0.001	1.460
	Hip (cm)	99.7 ± 8.85	104 ± 6.32	−0.335	−0.289	0.775	0.100
Breadths	Humerus (cm)	7.13 ± 0.33	7.33 ± 0.31	−0.0902	−1.06	0.297	0.367
	Stylion (cm)	5.54 ± 0.37	5.79 ± 0.34	−0.154	−1.39	0.173	0.483
	Femur (cm)	9.56 ± 0.55	9.76 ± 0.53	0.0366	0.322	0.750	0.111

SD: Standard Deviation; t: t student; Mean differences were significant at $p < 0.05$.

The results in Table 6 show the descriptive statistics and the differences of the selected variables between players according to their playing position. Significant differences ($p < 0.05$) were only observed between goalkeepers and wings in the variable SOS.

Table 6. Position-related differences in selected anthropometric characteristics, body composition and somatotype components of male and female players.

Variable	Goalkeepers (n = 6)	Wings (n = 12)	Specialists (n = 6)	Pivots (n = 5)	Defenders (n = 7)	ANOVA		
	Mean ± SD	Mean ± SD	Mean ± SD	Mean ± SD	Mean ± SD	F	p	$\eta p2$
Body height (cm)	187 ± 3.11	180 ± 7.27	185 ± 12.2	188 ± 6.05	186 ± 6.50	0.643	0.636	0.079
Body mass (kg)	88.9 ± 10.9	75.1 ± 10.7	84.9 ± 15.6	92.9 ± 13.9	88.6 ± 15.3	0.540	0.708	0.067
Arm span (cm)	190 ± 6.22	184 ± 7.88	193 ± 16.7	193 ± 6.82	189 ± 6.00	0.709	0.592	0.086
BMI (kg/m^2)	25.4 ± 3.14	23.1 ± 2.22	24.6 ± 2.51	26.1 ± 2.51	25.5 ± 2.93			
6 skinfolds (mm)	81.6 ± 40.1	61.2 ± 24.9	69.9 ± 28.0	75.0 ± 30.2	74.3 ± 38.7	0.526	0.718	0.065
Endomorphy	3.37 ± 1.77	2.45 ± 0.992	2.54 ± 1.05	2.67 ± 0.796	2.92 ± 1.52	1.23	0.321	0.140
Mesomorphy	3.19 ± 1.28	3.39 ± 0.975	3.68 ± 1.14	3.93 ± 0.589	3.85 ± 0.920	0.799	0.535	0.096
Ectomorphy	2.69 ± 1.46	3.20 ± 0.992	2.82 ± 1.13	2.38 ± 0.759	2.51 ± 0.978	0.682	0.610	0.083
MM (%)	40.6 ± 3.12	44.0 ± 3.91	43.2 ± 4.54	42.1 ± 3.68	41.9 ± 2.89	0.507	0.731	0.063
BFM Withers (%)	15.9 ± 8.08	11.7 ± 4.57	13.0 ± 5.09	14.1 ± 5.59	14.0 ± 7.23	0.622	0.650	0.077
BFM Faulkner (%)	14.7 ± 4.13	12.1 ± 2.59	12.5 ± 2.53	13.3 ± 2.55	13.3 ± 4.14	1.17	0.346	0.135
SOS (m/s)	1616 ± 24.1 #	1651 ± 33.5 #	1658 ± 27.6	1669 ± 37.9	1649 ± 31.5	3.11	0.030	0.293
BUA (dB/MHz)	129 ± 8.23	127 ± 10.6	139 ± 8.57	132 ± 6.31	132 ± 9.97	1.370	0.268	0.154
Stiffness (A.U)	119 ± 11.2	128 ± 13.0	137 ± 12.2	135 ± 11.4	130 ± 14.3	2.25	0.087	0.231

SD: Standard Deviation; BFM: Body Fat Mass; MM: Muscular mass; BUA: Broadband ultrasound attenuation; SOS: Speed of sound; t: t student; Mean differences were significant at $p < 0.05$; #: statistical significance between goalkeepers and wings.

Results shows that there has been a slight difference in some of the variables analyzed between juniors and seniors. The comparison between goalkeepers and specialists gave values of $p = 0.076$ and ES = 1.57, between goalkeepers and pivots of $p = 0.067$ and ES = 1.68; therefore, the ES in both cases were high. For the Stiffness variable, between the goalkeepers and the wings the values were, $p = 0.057$ and ES = 1.64, so there were also differences.

Figure 3 shows the anthropometric dimensions, as proportionality profiles of the junior and senior players. Goalkeepers have been excluded due to the particularity of their playing position. After analysis, significant differences were observed in some variables such as Z skinfold calf ($p = 0.032$; ES = 0.744; MD = 0.661), Z relaxed arm ($p = 0.041$; ES = −0.704; MD = −0.691), Z Flexed arm ($p = 0.005$; ES = −0.990; MD = −0.726); Z forearm ($p = 0.049$; ES = −2.94; MD = −0.543); Z Chest (mesosternale) ($p = 0.030$; ES = −0.756; MD = −0.591) and waist circumference ($p = 0.019$; ES = −0.825; MD = −0.851). In all the variables described, the results are lower for junior players.

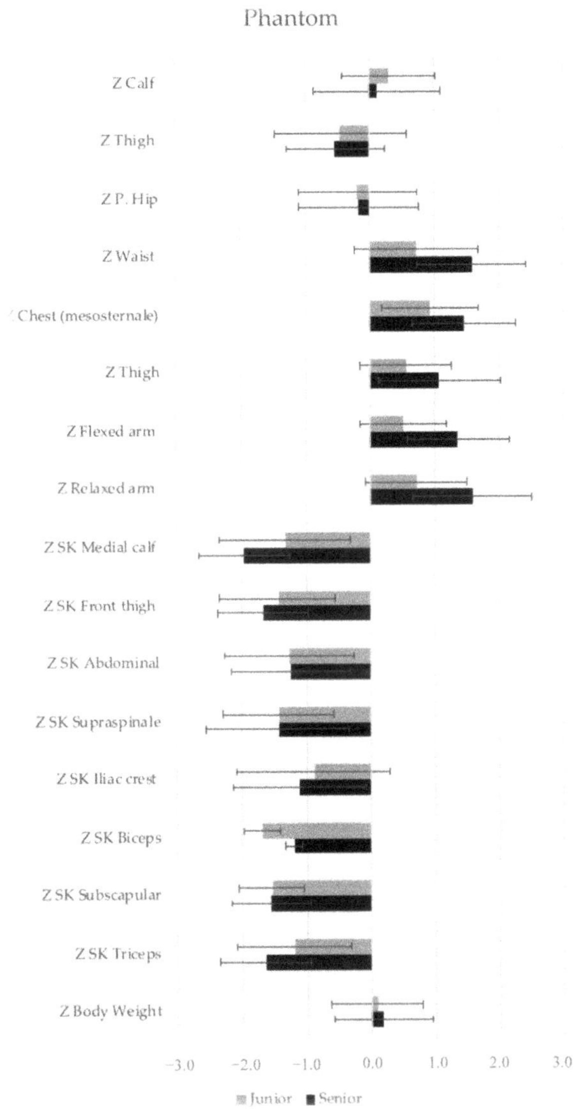

Figure 3. Representation of the proportionality with respect to the phantom. SK = Skinfolds. Data are presented as mean and standard deviation.

4. Discussion

The aim of this research was to analyse the anthropometric profile, body composition and somatotype of elite BH players according to category (junior vs. senior) and playing positions. The results showed significant differences between junior and senior categories in several components such as kg of muscle mass, kg of fat mass and kg of bone mass, as well as skinfolds (triceps, biceps, thigh, calf and sum of six skinfolds) and perimeters (arm, contracted arm and waist). However, no differences in body composition and anthropometric profile by playing position have been found. Other studies have investigated body composition in Spanish senior elite BH players [9,12]. However, the study by Zapardiel et al. [12] only analysed weight, height and BMI. On the other hand,

Pueo et al. [9] did study the anthropometric profile and somatotype, but the study was of doubtful reliability due to the small sample size used. Another of identified weaknesses in this study is the grouping of players according to playing position: goalkeepers, front players and back players; categorising wings-specialists and pivots-defenders as the same, an aspect that undermines the principle of specificity in training. In the present research, each specific position has been studied individually: goalkeepers, wings, specialists, pivots, and defenders. So far, no studies have been conducted to examine the anthropometric, BMD and somatotype characteristics of elite junior BH players. One strength of this scientific paper is that it provides a frame of reference for junior elite BH players.

The junior elite BH players showed a mean height of 181 ± 5.90 cm and a body mass of 78.1 ± 12.2 kg, while the seniors had a height of 188 ± 7.73 cm and weight of 90.1 ± 13.4 kg. The differences found are due to the different stages of development of the junior vs. senior players. These results are slightly higher than the ones obtained in similar studies for senior players where the mean height results were: 187.4 ± 8.2 cm [9] and 187.5 ± 7.5 cm [12]; and mean weights of: 85.2 ± 11.3 kg [9] and 87.0 ± 9.5 kg [12]. Thus, according to the results of the present study, senior BH players are moderately taller and heavier than the players analysed in other studies. Consequently, the BMI presented in the senior players of the study (25.4 ± 2.50 kg/m^2), is higher than those presented in the studies of Pueo et al. [9] and Zapardiel et al. [12] being 24.2 ± 2.5 kg/m^2 and 24.9 kg/m^2, respectively.

The body composition of the players studied showed significant differences in muscle mass (kg), fat mass, measured with Wither's formula (kg), and bone mass (kg). This distinction can be explained by the significant difference between juniors and seniors in total body mass. The juniors showed a muscle mass of 42.5 ± 3.45%, while the seniors had a percentage of 42.8 ± 4.03%. The data was similar to the one obtained from the research carried out by Pueo et al. [9] in which the muscle mass results were 42.7 ± 2.6%.

Regarding fat mass, both studies used the Withers formula for its calculation and for this reason, they are comparable. The present study obtained a fat mass in juniors of 13.8 ± 6.73% and in seniors of 13.1 ± 5.03%. The senior players who participated in the study by Pueo et al. showed a fat percentage of 11.7 ± 3.9% [9]. These results were lower than those presented by the players in our study, possibly due to the fact that the players were in better physical shape, also because the data collection could take place at a different time of the season. Comparing these results with the indoor modality [56], players playing on court have lower values of fat mass (11.3 ± 2.4%) than those of the present study and other BH studies [9].

Significant differences were found between juniors and seniors in skinfolds. The sum of 6 skinfolds presented by the juniors was 71.9 ± 34.8 mm, while for seniors was 69.1 ± 27.3 mm. These results coincided with the data obtained for fat mass and were similar to the results of other studies such as Pueo et al. [9]; 62.9 ± 24.1 mm. The present data was lower than those found in elite indoor handball players (77.2 ± 27.5 mm) [57]. Therefore, it can be concluded that skinfold measurements in indoor handball are higher, i.e., with more subcutaneous fat, than in BH [9].

Regarding bone mass and BMD, the junior players had 15.5 ± 1.34% bone mass and BUA, SOS and Stiffness values of 131 ± 10.3 dB/MHz, 1640 ± 33 m/s and 127 ± 14.5 (A.U), respectively. On the other hand, senior players obtained a bone mass of 14.9 ± 1.07% and BUA, SOS and Stiffness of 131 ± 9.24 dB/MHz, 1657 ± 33.1 m/s and 133 ± 11.9 (A.U). Pueo et al. [9] obtained similar results in senior BH players 15.7 ± 1.6%, however, they did not analyse BMD, so BUA, SOS and Stiffness results cannot be compared with other BH players due to the lack of studies. Studies conducted in Spanish senior population yield lower results in BUA than those presented in the current research (93.42 ± 18.38 dB/MHz) [58] and (84.5 ± 18.4 dB/MHz) [59]. The results found for SOS were also lower than the ones showed on the paper (1567.5 ± 33.3 m/s) [59]. In regard to BMD assessment in juniors, other populations have obtained a BUA of 89.46 ± 14.41 dB/MHz and an SOS of 1503.54 ± 13.45 m/s [60]. These differences from the results of the present investigation are due to the fact that exercise is associated with an increase in bone mineral density [61].

The junior and senior elite BH players presented a balanced mesomorphic somatotype (2.79-3.40-2.91 and 2.69-3.73-2.70, respectively). These results were similar to those presented in the study by Pueo et al. [9], although the mesomorphy value was lower (2.6-4.4-2.7).

In respect of variations in anthropometric profile and body composition between playing positions, the present study found no significant differences except in SOS. However, Pueo et al. [9] found variations to be considered in height, weight and wingspan, but not in the rest of the components. These differences can be explained by the small sample size analysed in the Pueo et al. [9] research.

The body proportionality profiles of the BH players were similar to each other, although the junior players showed lower results. Significant differences were found in calf skinfold, flexed arm, forearm, thorax and waist circumferences. To the authors' knowledge, this is the first study to assess proportionality in beach handball players, so comparisons with other similar studies cannot be made. This research will be useful to confirm the proportionality values through further studies.

The present study was not exempt from limitations, one of the limitations may be that both body composition and BMD values were studied with full anthropometry and calcaneal ultrasound due to the feasibility of the research. Another limitation that should make the results between playing positions to be interpreted with caution, is that there were not the same number of players in the different categories. Future investigations should be carried out on a sufficient and equal number of players per playing position and with gold standard instruments such as DXA. Furthermore, these data refer to Caucasian players, so for other populations these data should be interpreted with caution.

However, considering the above limitations, the results of this research are of great relevance since they incorporate junior category data, so far not studied in BH, and also provide more complete information and a larger number of samples than previous research carried out in BH players [9,12]. These data should be useful for the recruitment and selection of players with the optimum profile for performance in beach handball and the detection of talent in young players.

5. Conclusions

The anthropometric profile, as well as body composition and somatotype, play a fundamental role in the optimal performance of elite BH players. This research examined the differences in male BH players by categories (junior vs. senior) and by playing positions (goalkeepers, wings, specialists, pivots, and defenders).

Differences between age groups were found in height, body mass, arm span, BMI, muscle mass, fat mass, bone mass, skinfolds, and body perimeters. Body composition was more optimal in senior players due to the presence of less fat mass. The mean somatotype of both categories was mesomorph balanced. No significant differences were found in anthropometric and body characteristics according to playing position.

The data provided by this study is considered of great interest to compare and obtain a reference for elite BH players. Future research should focus on analyzing these parameters on a larger number of players per playing position and to achieve decisive references using more precise body estimation methods such as DXA.

Author Contributions: Conceptualization, A.M.-R., J.S.-S. and J.A.S.-S.; data curation, M.M.-O., L.M.-A. and M.V.-M.; formal analysis, A.M.-R., M.V.-M. and M.M.-O.; investigation, A.M.-R., J.S.-S., M.V.-M. and J.A.S.-S.; methodology, A.M.-R., J.S.-S. and J.A.S.-S.; resources, A.M.-R., J.S.-S., M.V.-M. and J.A.S.-S.; software, M.M.-O., M.V.-M. and A.M.-R.; validation, A.M.-R., J.S.-S. and J.A.S.-S.; writing—original draft, A.M.-R., M.V.-M., M.M.-O. and L.M.-A.; writing—review and editing, A.M.-R., J.S.-S. and J.A.S.-S. All authors have read and agreed to the published version of the manuscript.

Funding: This research received no external funding.

Institutional Review Board Statement: The study was conducted according to the guidelines of the Declaration of Helsinki and approved by the Institutional Ethics Committee of the Alicante University.

Informed Consent Statement: Informed consent was obtained from all subjects involved in the study.

Data Availability Statement: The data presented in this study is available on request from the corresponding author. The data are not publicly available due to is personal health information.

Acknowledgments: To the players and coaches of the Spanish Beach Handball National Team, to the Royal Spanish Handball Federation and to the European Institute of Exercise and Health (EIEH) of Alicante University for their selfless collaboration in this research.

Conflicts of Interest: The authors declare no conflict of interest.

References

1. Morillo, J.P.; Reigal, R.E.; Hernández-Mendo, A. *Balonmano Playa;* Editorial Wanceulen, S.L.: Sevilla, Spain, 2009.
2. Lemos, L.F.; Oliveira, V.C.; Duncan, M.J.; Ortega, J.P.; Martins, C.M.; Ramirez-Campillo, R.; Sanchez, J.S.; Nevill, A.M.; Nakamura, F.Y. Physical Fitness Profile in Elite Beach Handball Players of Different Age Categories. *J. Sports Med. Phys. Fit.* **2020**, *60*, 1536–1543. [CrossRef] [PubMed]
3. Reigal, R.E.; Vázquez-Diz, J.A.; Morillo-Baro, J.P.; Hernández-Mendo, A.; Morales-Sánchez, V. Psychological Profile, Competitive Anxiety, Moods and Self-Efficacy in Beach Handball Players. *Int. J. Environ. Res. Public Health* **2020**, *17*, 241. [CrossRef] [PubMed]
4. Achenbach, L.; Loose, O.; Laver, L.; Zeman, F.; Nerlich, M.; Angele, P.; Krutsch, W. Beach Handball Is Safer than Indoor Team Handball: Injury Rates during the 2017 European Beach Handball Championships. *Knee Surg. Sports Traumatol. Arthrosc. Off. J. ESSKA* **2018**, *26*, 1909–1915. [CrossRef]
5. Pueo, B.; Jimenez-Olmedo, J.M.; Penichet-Tomas, A.; Ortega Becerra, M.; Espina Agullo, J.J. Analysis of Time-Motion and Heart Rate in Elite Male and Female Beach Handball. *J. Sports Sci. Med.* **2017**, *16*, 450–458. [PubMed]
6. Martínez-Rodríguez, A.; Martínez-Olcina, M.; Hernández-García, M.; Rubio-Arias, J.Á.; Sánchez-Sánchez, J.; Lara-Cobos, D.; Vicente-Martínez, M.; Carvalho, M.J.; Sánchez-Sáez, J.A. Mediterranean Diet Adherence, Body Composition and Performance in Beach Handball Players: A Cross Sectional Study. *Int. J. Environ. Res. Public Health* **2021**, *18*, 2837. [CrossRef] [PubMed]
7. Gutiérrez-Vargas, R.; Gutiérrez-Vargas, J.C.; Ugalde-Ramírez, J.A.; Rojas-Valverde, D. Kinematics and Thermal Sex-Related Responses during an Official Beach Handball Game in Costa Rica: A Pilot Study. *Arch. Med. Del. Deport* **2019**, *36*, 13–18.
8. Lara Cobos, D. Analysis of Heart Rate in Female Beach Handball Players. *Apunt. Sports Med.* **2011**, *46*, 131–136.
9. Pueo, B.; Espina-Agullo, J.J.; Selles-Perez, S.; Penichet-Tomas, A. Optimal Body Composition and Anthropometric Profile of World-Class Beach Handball Players by Playing Positions. *Sustainability* **2020**, *12*, 6789. [CrossRef]
10. Massuça, L.M.; Fragoso, I.; Teles, J. Attributes of top elite team-handball players. *J. Strength Cond. Res.* **2014**, *28*, 178–186. [CrossRef]
11. Sánchez-Sáez, J.A.; Sánchez-Sánchez, J.; Martínez-Rodríguez, A.; Felipe, J.L.; García-Unanue, J.; Lara-Cobos, D. Global Positioning System Analysis of Physical Demands in Elite Women's Beach Handball Players in an Official Spanish Championship. *Sensors* **2021**, *21*, 850. [CrossRef]
12. Zapardiel, J.C.; Asín-Izquierdo, I. Conditional Analysis of Elite Beach Handball According to Specific Playing Position through Assessment with GPS. *Int. J. Perform. Anal. Sport* **2020**, *20*, 118–132. [CrossRef]
13. Saavedra, J.M. Handball Research: State of the Art. *J. Hum. Kinet.* **2018**, *63*, 5–8. [CrossRef] [PubMed]
14. Wagner, H.; Finkenzeller, T.; Würth, S.; von Duvillard, S.P. Individual and Team Performance in Team-Handball: A Review. *J. Sports Sci. Med.* **2014**, *13*, 808–816.
15. Aasheim, C.; Stavenes, H.; Andersson, S.H.; Engbretsen, L.; Clarsen, B. Prevalence and Burden of Overuse Injuries in Elite Junior Handball. *BMJ Open Sport Exerc. Med.* **2018**, *4*, e000391. [CrossRef]
16. Molina-López, J.; Barea Zarzuela, I.; Sáez-Padilla, J.; Tornero-Quiñones, I.; Planells, E. Mediation Effect of Age Category on the Relationship between Body Composition and the Physical Fitness Profile in Youth Handball Players. *Int. J. Environ. Res. Public Health* **2020**, *17*, 2350. [CrossRef]
17. Ronglan, L.T.; Raastad, T.; Børgesen, A. Neuromuscular Fatigue and Recovery in Elite Female Handball Players. *Scand. J. Med. Sci. Sports* **2006**, *16*, 267–273. [CrossRef]
18. Hammami, M.; Hermassi, S.; Gaamouri, N.; Aloui, G.; Comfort, P.; Shephard, R.J.; Chelly, M.S. Field Tests of Performance and Their Relationship to Age and Anthropometric Parameters in Adolescent Handball Players. *Front. Physiol.* **2019**, *10*, 1124. [CrossRef] [PubMed]
19. Rousanoglou, E.N.; Noutsos, K.S.; Bayios, I.A. Playing Level and Playing Position Differences of Anthropometric and Physical Fitness Characteristics in Elite Junior Handball Players. *J. Sports Med. Phys. Fit.* **2014**, *54*, 611–621.
20. Ziv, G.; Lidor, R. Physical Attributes, Physiological Characteristics, on-Court Performances and Nutritional Strategies of Female and Male Basketball Players. *Sports Med.* **2009**, *39*, 547–568. [CrossRef]
21. Karaba Jakovljevic, D.; Jovanovic, G.; Eric, M.; Klasnja, A.; Slavic, D.; Lukac, D. Anthropometric Characteristics and Functional Capacity of Elite Rowers and Handball Players. *Med. Pregl.* **2016**, *69*, 267–273. [CrossRef]

22. Högström, G.M.; Pietilä, T.; Nordström, P.; Nordström, A. Body Composition and Performance: Influence of Sport and Gender among Adolescents. *J. Strength Cond. Res.* **2012**, *26*, 1799–1804. [CrossRef] [PubMed]
23. Brun, J.-F.; Varlet-Marie, E.; Cassan, D.; Raynaud de Mauverger, E. Blood Rheology and Body Composition as Determinants of Exercise Performance in Female Rugby Players. *Clin. Hemorheol. Microcirc.* **2011**, *49*, 207–214. [CrossRef] [PubMed]
24. Silva, A.M.; Fields, D.A.; Heymsfield, S.B.; Sardinha, L.B. Body Composition and Power Changes in Elite Judo Athletes. *Int. J. Sports Med.* **2010**, *31*, 737–741. [CrossRef]
25. Silva, A.M.; Fields, D.A.; Heymsfield, S.B.; Sardinha, L.B. Relationship between Changes in Total-Body Water and Fluid Distribution with Maximal Forearm Strength in Elite Judo Athletes. *J. Strength Cond. Res.* **2011**, *25*, 2488–2495. [CrossRef] [PubMed]
26. Granados, C.; Izquierdo, M.; Ibáñez, J.; Ruesta, M.; Gorostiaga, E.M. Effects of an Entire Season on Physical Fitness in Elite Female Handball Players. *Med. Sci. Sports Exerc.* **2008**, *40*, 351–361. [CrossRef]
27. Hermassi, S.; Van Den Tillaar, R.; Khlifa, R.; Chelly, M.S.; Chamari, K. Comparison of In-Season-Specific Resistance vs. A Regular Throwing Training Program on Throwing Velocity, Anthropometry, and Power Performance in Elite Handball Players. *J. Strength Cond. Res.* **2015**, *29*, 2105–2114. [CrossRef]
28. Santos, D.A.; Dawson, J.A.; Matias, C.N.; Rocha, P.M.; Minderico, C.S.; Allison, D.B.; Sardinha, L.B.; Silva, A.M. Reference Values for Body Composition and Anthropometric Measurements in Athletes. *PLoS ONE* **2014**, *9*, e97846. [CrossRef]
29. Milanese, C.; Piscitelli, F.; Lampis, C.; Zancanaro, C. Anthropometry and Body Composition of Female Handball Players According to Competitive Level or the Playing Position. *J. Sports Sci.* **2011**, *29*, 1301–1309. [CrossRef]
30. Tovar-Galvez, M.I.; González-Jiménez, E.; Martí-García, C.; Schmidt-RioValle, J. Body Composition in a Population of School Adolescents: A Comparison of Simple Anthropometric Methods and Bioelectrical Impedance. *Endocrinol. Diabetes Nutr.* **2017**, *64*, 424–431. [CrossRef]
31. Wang, Z.; Heymsfield, S.B.; Pi-Sunyer, F.X.; Gallagher, D.; Pierson, R.N.J. Body Composition Analysis: Cellular Level Modeling of Body Component Ratios. *Int. J. Body Compos. Res.* **2008**, *6*, 173–184.
32. Cichy, I.; Dudkowski, A.; Kociuba, M.; Ignasiak, Z.; Sebastjan, A.; Kochan, K.; Koziel, S.; Rokita, A.; Malina, R.M. Sex Differences in Body Composition Changes after Preseason Training in Elite Handball Players. *Int. J. Environ. Res. Public Health* **2020**, *17*, 3880. [CrossRef]
33. Stanforth, P.R.; Crim, B.N.; Stanforth, D.; Stults-Kolehmainen, M.A. Body Composition Changes among Female NCAA Division 1 Athletes across the Competitive Season and over a Multiyear Time Frame. *J. Strength Cond. Res.* **2014**, *28*, 300–307. [CrossRef] [PubMed]
34. Turnagöl, H.H. Body Composition and Bone Mineral Density of Collegiate American Football Players. *J. Human Kinet.* **2016**, *51*, 103–112. [CrossRef] [PubMed]
35. Cárdenas-Fernández, V.; Chinchilla-Minguet, J.L.; Castillo-Rodríguez, A. Somatotype and Body Composition in Young Soccer Players According to the Playing Position and Sport Success. *J. Strength Cond. Res.* **2019**, *33*, 1904–1911. [CrossRef] [PubMed]
36. Fields, J.B.; Merrigan, J.J.; White, J.B.; Jones, M.T. Body Composition Variables by Sport and Sport-Position in Elite Collegiate Athletes. *J. Strength Cond. Res.* **2018**, *32*, 3153–3159. [CrossRef] [PubMed]
37. Ilic, V.; Ranisavljev, I.; Stefanovic, D.; Ivanovic, V.; Mrdakovic, V. Impact of Body Composition and Vo2 Max on the Competitive Success in Top-Level Handball Players. *Coll. Antropol.* **2015**, *39*, 535–540.
38. Ferragut, C.; Vila, H.; Abraldes, J.A.; Manchado, C. Influence of Physical Aspects and Throwing Velocity in Opposition Situations in Top-Elite and Elite Female Handball Players. *J. Human Kinet.* **2018**, *63*, 23–32. [CrossRef]
39. Cavedon, V.; Zancanaro, C.; Milanese, C. Anthropometric Prediction of DXA-Measured Body Composition in Female Team Handball Players. *PeerJ* **2018**, *6*, e5913. [CrossRef] [PubMed]
40. Hermassi, S.; Laudner, K.; Schwesig, R. Playing Level and Position Differences in Body Characteristics and Physical Fitness Performance Among Male Team Handball Players. *Front. Bioeng. Biotechnol.* **2019**, *7*, 149. [CrossRef]
41. Reilly, T. *Science and Soccer*; Routledge: London, UK, 2003; ISBN 1134504810.
42. Krahenbühl, T.; Barros-Filho, A.D.A.; Barbeta, C.J.D.O.; Guerra-Júnior, G.; Gonçalves, E.M. Geometric Indices of Femur Bone Strength in Female Handball Players. *Women Health* **2020**, *60*, 1118–1128. [CrossRef]
43. Laabes, E.P.; Vanderjagt, D.J.; Obadofin, M.O.; Sendeht, A.J.; Glew, R.H. Assessment of the Bone Quality of Black Male Athletes Using Calcaneal Ultrasound: A Cross-Sectional Study. *Nutr. Metab.* **2008**, *5*, 13. [CrossRef]
44. Mrabet Bahri, D.; Selmi, A.; Abdelkéfi, M.; Mbarek, M.; Sahli, H.; Sellami, S. Study of bone mineral density in adolescent handball players: A study of 20 cases. *La Tunis. Med.* **2013**, *91*, 633–637.
45. Esparza-Ros, F.; Vaquero-Cristóbal, R.; Marfell-Jones, M. Protocolo Internacional Para La Valoración Antropométrica. *Perf. Completo Murcia Int. Soc. Adv. Kinanthropometry ISAK* **2019**. [CrossRef]
46. Withers, R.T.; Craig, N.P.; Bourdon, P.C.; Norton, K.I. Relative Body Fat and Anthropometric Prediction of Body Density of Male Athletes. *Eur. J. Appl. Physiol. Occup. Physiol.* **1987**, *56*, 191–200. [CrossRef]
47. Pires-Neto, C.; Glaner, M. The "Faulkner Equation" for Predicting Body Fat: The End of a Myth. *Rev. Bras. Cineantropometria Desempenho Hum.* **2007**, *9*, 208–213.
48. Lee, R.C.; Wang, Z.; Heo, M.; Ross, R.; Janssen, I.; Heymsfield, S.B. Total-Body Skeletal Muscle Mass: Development and Cross-Validation of Anthropometric Prediction Models. *Am. J. Clin. Nutr.* **2000**, *72*, 796–803. [CrossRef]

49. Alvero Cruz, J.R.; Cabañas Armesilla, M.D.; Herrero de Lucas, Á.; Martínez Riaza, L.; Moreno Pascual, C.; Porta Manzañido, J.; Sillero Quintana, M.; Sirvent Belando, J.E. Protocolo de Valoración de La Composición Corporal Para El Reconocimiento Médico-Deportivo. Documento de Consenso Del Grupo Español de Cineantropometría (GREC) de La Federación Española de Medicina Del Deporte (FEMEDE). *Arch. Med. Deporte* **2010**, *26*, 330–343.
50. Heath, B.H.; Carter, J.E.L. A Modified Somatotype Method. *Am. J. Phys. Anthropol.* **1967**, *27*, 57–74. [CrossRef]
51. Malina, R.M. Ratios and Derived Indicators in the Assessment of Nutritional Status. In *Anthropometric Assessment of Nutritional Status*; Wiley-Liss: New York, NY, USA, 1991; pp. 151–171.
52. Carter, J.E.L. *The Heath-Carter Anthropometric Somatotype-Instruction Manual-Somatotype Instruction Manual 2 Part 1: The Heath-Carter Anthropometric Somatotype-Instruction Manual*; San Diego State University: San Diego, CA, USA, 2002.
53. Ross, W.; Ward, R. Human Proportionality and Sexual Dimorphism. In *Sexual Dimorphism in Homo Sapiens: A Question of Size*; Praeger: New York, NY, USA, 1982; pp. 317–361; ISBN 003056963X.
54. Lara, B.; Salinero, J.J.; Gutiérrez, J.; Areces, F.; Abián-Vicén, J.; Ruiz-Vicente, D.; Gallo-Salazar, C.; Jiménez, F.; del Coso, J. Influence of Endurance Running on Calcaneal Bone Stiffness in Male and Female Runners. *Eur. J. Appl. Physiol.* **2016**, *116*, 327–333. [CrossRef]
55. Cohen, J. *Statistical Power Analysis for the Behavioral Sciences*, 2nd ed.; Lawrence Erlbaum Associates: Mahwah, NJ, USA, 1969.
56. Šibila, M.; Pori, P. Position-Related Differences in Selected Morphological Body Characteristics of Top-Level Handball Players. *Coll. Antropol.* **2009**, *33*, 1079–1086.
57. Garrido-Chamorro, R.; Sirvent-Belando, J.E.; González-Lorenzo, M.; Blasco-Lafarga, C.; Roche, E. Skinfold Sum: Reference Values for Top Athletes. *Int. J. Morphol.* **2012**, *30*, 803–809. [CrossRef]
58. Correa-Rodríguez, M.; Rio-Valle, J.S.; González-Jiménez, E.; Rueda-Medina, B. The Effects of Body Composition, Dietary Intake, and Physical Activity on Calcaneus Quantitative Ultrasound in Spanish Young Adults. *Biol. Res. Nurs.* **2016**, *18*, 439–444. [CrossRef]
59. Sosa, M.; Saavedra, P.; Muñoz-Torres, M.; Alegre, J.; Gómez, C.; González-Macías, J.; Guañabens, N.; Hawkins, F.; Lozano, C.; Martínez, M.; et al. Quantitative Ultrasound Calcaneus Measurements: Normative Data and Precision in the Spanish Population. *Osteoporos. Int.* **2002**, *13*, 487–492. [CrossRef]
60. Szmodis, M.; Zsákai, A.; Bosnyák, E.; Protzner, A.; Trájer, E.; Farkas, A.; Szőts, G.; Tóth, M. Reference Data for Ultrasound Bone Characteristics in Hungarian Children Aged 7–19 Years. *Ann. Hum. Biol.* **2017**, *44*, 704–714. [CrossRef] [PubMed]
61. Karlsson, M.K.; Magnusson, H.; Karlsson, C.; Seeman, E. The Duration of Exercise as a Regulator of Bone Mass. *Bone* **2001**, *28*, 128–132. [CrossRef]

nutrients
MDPI

Review

Does Acute Caffeine Supplementation Improve Physical Performance in Female Team-Sport Athletes? Evidence from a Systematic Review and Meta-Analysis

Alejandro Gomez-Bruton [1,2,3,*], Jorge Marin-Puyalto [1,4], Borja Muñiz-Pardos [1,2], Angel Matute-Llorente [1,2,3], Juan Del Coso [5], Alba Gomez-Cabello [1,6], German Vicente-Rodriguez [1,2,3,7], Jose A. Casajus [1,3,7,8] and Gabriel Lozano-Berges [1,2,3,7]

1 GENUD (Growth, Exercise, Nutrition and Development) Research Group, FIMS Collaborating Center of Sports Medicine, 50012 Zaragoza, Spain; jmarinp@unizar.es (J.M.-P.); bmuniz@unizar.es (B.M.-P.); amatute@unizar.es (A.M.-L.); agomez@unizar.es (A.G.-C.); gervicen@unizar.es (G.V.-R.); joseant@unizar.es (J.A.C.); glozano@unizar.es (G.L.-B.)
2 Department of Physiatry and Nursing, Faculty of Health and Sport Sciences (FCSD), University of Zaragoza, 22001 Huesca, Spain
3 Physiopathology of Obesity and Nutrition Networking Biomedical Research Center (CIBERObn), 28029 Madrid, Spain
4 Department of Physiatry and Nursing, Faculty of Health Sciences, University of Zaragoza, 50012 Zaragoza, Spain
5 Centre for Sports Studies, Rey Juan Carlos University, 28943 Fuenlabrada, Spain; juan.delcoso@urjc.es
6 Centro Universitario de la Defensa, University of Zaragoza, 50090 Zaragoza, Spain
7 Instituto Agroalimentario de Aragon IA2 (CITA-Universidad de Zaragoza), 50009 Zaragoza, Spain
8 Department of Physiatry and Nursing, Faculty of Medicine, University of Zaragoza, 50012 Zaragoza, Spain
* Correspondence: bruton@unizar.es; Tel.: +34-876553755

Citation: Gomez-Bruton, A.; Marin-Puyalto, J.; Muñiz-Pardos, B.; Matute-Llorente, A.; Del Coso, J.; Gomez-Cabello, A.; Vicente-Rodriguez, G.; Casajus, J.A.; Lozano-Berges, G. Does Acute Caffeine Supplementation Improve Physical Performance in Female Team-Sport Athletes? Evidence from a Systematic Review and Meta-Analysis. *Nutrients* **2021**, *13*, 3663. https://doi.org/10.3390/nu13103663

Academic Editor: Ajmol Ali

Received: 7 September 2021
Accepted: 18 October 2021
Published: 19 October 2021

Abstract: Introduction: Recent original research and meta-analyses suggest that acute caffeine supplementation improves exercise performance in team-sport athletes (TSA). Nonetheless, most of the studies testing the effects of caffeine on TSA included samples of male athletes, and there is no meta-analysis of the performance-enhancing effects of caffeine on female TSA. The aim of the present study was to synthesize the existing literature regarding the effect of caffeine supplementation on physical performance in adult female TSA. Methods: A search was performed in Pubmed/Medline, SPORTDiscus and Scopus. The search was performed from the inception of indexing until 1 September 2021. Crossover randomized controlled trials (RCT) assessing the effects of oral caffeine intake on several aspects of performance in female TSA were selected. The methodological quality and risk of bias were assessed for individual studies using the Physiotherapy Evidence Database scale (PEDro) and the RoB 2 tool. A random-effects meta-analysis of standardized mean differences (SMD) was performed for several performance variables. Results: The search retrieved 18 articles that fulfilled the inclusion/exclusion criteria. Overall, most of the studies were of excellent quality with a low risk of bias. The meta-analysis results showed that caffeine increased performance in specific team-sport skills (SMD: 0.384, 95% confidence interval (CI): 0.077–0.691), countermovement jump (SMD: 0.208, CI: 0.079–0.337), total body impacts (SMD: 0.488; 95% CI: 0.050, 0.927) and handgrip strength (SMD: 0.395, CI: 0.126–0.665). No effects were found on the ratings of perceived exertion, squat jumps, agility, repeated sprint ability or agility tests performed after fatigue. Conclusions: The results of the meta-analysis revealed that acute caffeine intake was effective in increasing some aspects of team-sports performance in women athletes. Hence, caffeine could be considered as a supplementation strategy for female athletes competing in team sports.

Keywords: soccer; volleyball; basketball; ergogenic aid; elite athletes; sports performance

1. Introduction

The use of caffeine in sporting events was controlled until 1 January 2004, since a post-competition urinary concentration above 12 micrograms per milliliter was considered an adverse analytical finding by the World Anti-Doping Agency [1]. However, at that date, caffeine was removed from the list of prohibited substances in the monitoring program of the World Anti-Doping Agency [2]. The removal of caffeine from the list of prohibited substances, in addition to increasing scientific knowledge about the potential ergogenic effects of caffeine, has caused an increase in caffeine intake in both men and women athletes over recent years [3].

The widespread use of this supplement in sport is based on scientific evidence, as it has been classified by the International Society of Sports Nutrition (ISSN) as a "*Strong evidence to support efficacy and apparently safe*" supplement [4], with recommended doses ranging from 3 to 6 mg per kg of body mass with a timing of ingestion of 1 h before exercise. A vast amount of research indicates that caffeine intake can have a positive effect on several forms of athletic performance [5,6]. Grgic and colleagues performed an umbrella review in 2019 including 21 published meta-analyses, revealing that caffeine supplementation elicited an ergogenic effect on muscle endurance and strength, anaerobic power and aerobic endurance, which are critical variables for team-sports performance [5].

In team-sport athletes (TSA), the efficacy of caffeine supplementation in enhancing performance is less clear than in other sport disciplines, because success is explained by a combination of physical, technical and tactical skills. Brown et al. suggested via a meta-analysis that caffeine had no effect on repeated sprint ability (RSA) in TSA [7]. These results were contradicted by a review performed by Chia et al. [8], who found improvements in sprint performance (in 8 out of 10 studies) and vertical jump (in 7 out of 8 studies) in ball game athletes. These findings were reaffirmed by a later meta-analysis developed by Salinero et al. [9] evaluating TSA and also by a systematic review developed by Mielgo-Ayuso et al. [10] focusing on soccer players. Both studies concluded that acute caffeine ingestion improved jump height and RSA [9,10] in addition to agility performance, total running distance and number of performed sprints during a match [9]. Nonetheless, Ferreira and colleagues [11] recently performed a meta-analysis focusing on the effects of caffeine on soccer, finding no significant improvements in soccer-related performance following caffeine supplementation. Therefore, although the positive effects that caffeine supplementation may have on athletic performance in certain individual sports (e.g., running, cycling, etc.) are evident, it seems that more research is needed to determine the ergogenic effect of acute caffeine intake in team sports.

Moreover, most of the studies included in the above-mentioned systematic reviews and meta-analyses only included male athletes, as stated in a recent letter to the editor by Salinero et al. entitled "*More research is necessary to establish the ergogenic effect of caffeine in female athletes*" [12]. In this letter, the authors analyzed the percentage of females in studies evaluating the ergogenic effects of caffeine, reporting that only 13% of the participants were female. Moreover, although some studies included both male and female participants (contributing to the aforementioned 13%), most of them drew conclusions for the whole sample, irrespective of potential sex differences [13,14].

Despite the lack of research specifically analyzing female athletes, current guidelines for caffeine supplementation are identically applied for both males and females [15]. However, these guidelines were established primarily from studies developed in males, which is a clear limitation and raises concerns about their practicality. Although recent evidence suggests that the pharmacokinetics of acute caffeine intake seems to be similar in all phases of the menstrual cycle and that women athletes benefit from caffeine intake across all phases of the menstrual cycle [16], it is still possible that women obtain lower ergogenic effects of oral caffeine intake due to the interaction of caffeine and female sex hormones [17]. Along these lines, Temple and Ziegler [18] found sex differences in subjective and physiological responses to caffeine that were mediated by changes in circulating steroid hormones. In fact, inconsistent results have been found when comparing the ergogenic effects of caffeine in both sexes, with some studies finding some differences [19] while others found none [20,21]. Moreover, some researchers have concluded that the ergogenic effect of oral caffeine intake is present in both sexes but differs in its magnitude [22]. Along these lines, Mielgo-Ayuso et al. [10] recently developed a systematic review including 10 studies that evaluated the ergogenic effect of caffeine on both males and females. These authors concluded that caffeine supplementation produced a similar ergogenic benefit regarding aerobic performance and fatigue index in men and women, finding larger effects of caffeine intake in men when anaerobic performance was evaluated, which could be critical for team sports. However, the above-mentioned review only focused on the sex comparison; consequently, many studies that only recruited females were excluded, and due to the low number of included studies the authors chose not to perform a meta-analysis.

Thus, the aim of the present study is to perform a qualitative and quantitative analysis of the existing literature regarding the effect of caffeine supplementation on physical performance in adult female TSA.

2. Methods

2.1. Search Strategy

This systematic review and meta-analysis was carried out following the Preferred Reporting Items for Systematic reviews and Meta-Analyses (PRISMA) 2020 guidelines [23] and was pre-registered in PROSPERO (CRD42021223046). A systematic search was performed in the Pubmed/Medline, SPORTDiscus and Scopus databases. The search was performed from the inception of indexing until 1 September 2021, using the same search syntax as Salinero et al. [9] for Pubmed. An analogous search was performed for SPORTDiscus and Scopus (Supplementary Material: Table S1). All articles were downloaded to a CSV document to identify duplicates, and the whole process (i.e., identification, screening and selection of studies) was independently performed by two authors, with any disagreements resolved through discussion.

2.2. Inclusion and Exclusion Criteria

The following inclusion criteria were applied to selected studies: (1) studies evaluating the effect of an acute dose of isolated caffeine (e.g., not mixed with other supplements) on physical performance in female TSA (if studies included both sexes we only selected data for females, and if these data were not available we contacted the corresponding author and requested them); (2) studies including adults (18 years of age or over); (3) crossover studies that compared the intake of caffeine and a placebo; (4) studies using a blinded and randomized design; (5) studies in English or Spanish. Studies that supplied doses below 1 mg/kg or above 9 mg/kg, that did not present a true placebo condition (thus not allowing for blinding) or that did not evaluate performance-related variables (e.g., only evaluated oxidative stress markers) were excluded. Note that performance-related variables are explained in detail in the "Data Extraction" section.

2.3. Quality Assessment and Risk of Bias

The Physiotherapy Evidence Database scale (PEDro) was used to evaluate the individual quality of each study, with studies being classified as excellent (score 9–10), good (score 6–8), fair (score 4–5) or poor (score < 4). The PEDro scale has been shown to be valid and reliable for assessing the internal validity of randomized controlled trials [24].

Following the Cochrane Collaboration guidelines, the RoB 2 tool for randomized crossover designs was applied to assess the risk of bias of each study included [25]. RoB 2 includes the following domains for crossover trials: (1) bias arising from the randomization process; (2) bias due to deviations from the intended intervention; (3) bias due to missing outcome data; (4) bias in the measurement of the outcome; (5) bias in the selection of the reported results. Due to the characteristics of the crossover design, another domain related to bias arising from the period effect and the carryover effect should be considered (domain

S). Finally, each study was classified as having a high risk of bias, some concerns or a low risk of bias.

Both the PEDro and RoB2 tools were applied by two independent researchers, with any disagreement resolved through consensus.

2.4. Data Extraction

Data from each individual study were collected for every variable presented in Table 1, including: (1) the first author, year and country; (2) the number and characteristics of participants and the sports modality; (3) the participants' daily caffeine intake; (4) the menstrual cycle phase and the presence of women using oral contraceptives; (5) the caffeine administration form, timing and dosage; (6) the state of fatigue when the athletes were tested (rest/fatigue condition); (7) the main performance outcomes.

For item 5, if the experiment involved different conditions besides isolated caffeine (e.g., mixing sodium phosphate with caffeine [26]), we only included the results of the isolated caffeine condition [26,27]. Regarding item 6, we identified three possible conditions: (a) fatigue: tests developed after a fatigue-inducing protocol, match or strenuous effort that would cause fatigue to the participant; (b) match or simulated match: efforts developed during a regular match situation with official rules (in some cases the match duration was modified); (c) rest: tests developed without previous fatigue. These conditions were analyzed separately, given that the effects of caffeine might be different in rested and fatigued states. In a rested condition, the aim of evaluating caffeine intake would be to assess its effect on the performance of a specific task (e.g., jump performance). However, in the fatigued condition, the main aim would be to evaluate the effect of caffeine intake in minimizing the performance decline associated with fatigue by modulating the fatigue itself or its perception (e.g., jump performance after a soccer match or at half-time). Finally, for the match variables, the main aim would be to evaluate the effects of caffeine ingestion during real match situations (accelerations, decelerations, etc.) that are influenced by both physical and cognitive factors. For item 7, the main outcomes selected were team-sport performance variables such as: jump performance; single sprint and RSA performance; agility tests; maximal voluntary isometric-, concentric- and eccentric-force tests; muscular endurance; anaerobic power (Wingate test); specific task performance (e.g., throwing a ball of the specific sport); specific match variables (body impacts, sprint speed, total sprint distance, accelerations and decelerations). We also considered the rating of perceived exertion (RPE) and fatigue indexes, as they are reliable proxies for physical performance despite not being direct outcomes of athletic performance.

2.5. Meta-Analyses

For the meta-analyses, we collected mean and error measures or effect sizes with confidence intervals. When these were not provided or when mean and error measures were only presented in figures, we contacted the corresponding authors [27–34] to obtain specific information (all authors replied).

Five studies included both males and females and analyzed them together, presenting pooled data. We collected mean and error values only for the female group after contacting the corresponding authors of two of the studies [14,35]. We did not include two studies [36,37] that presented both sexes because the corresponding authors confirmed that they involved the same participants and tests that were presented in the following two studies that were included in the meta-analysis [32,38]. We did not contact the authors of one study that analyzed males and females together [13] because the measured main outcomes of the study were not of interest for the present review and meta-analysis.

Table 1. Characteristics of studies included in the systematic review.

Authors, Year, (Country) and PEDro Score	Sample Level +	Caffeine Consumption or Restrictions	Menstrual Cycle and Oral Contraceptives	Timing + Intervention + Washout	Sample State	Outcomes	R
Astorino et al. 2011 (USA) PEDro: 8/10	15 NAIA soccer players (19.5 ± 1.1 years) Level: semi-professional	12/15 were caffeine consumers (dose not reported) Instructed not to ingest any caffeine 48 h before each trial	Not controlled	60 min pre-test CAF: Red bull (80 mg: 1.3 mg/kg) PLA: Canada dry ginger ale Washout: 72–96 h	Rest	Agility *t*-test: Set 1/3 of 8 reps.	⇄
					Fatigue	Agility *t*-test: Sets 2 and 3/3 of 8 reps	⇄
						RPE	⇄
Del Coso et al. 2013 (Spain) PEDro: 10/10	16 rugby sevens National Team (23 ± 2 years)Level: elite	Light caffeine consumers: <60 mg/day Encouraged to abstain from all dietary sources of caffeine for 48 h before	Not controlled	60 min pre-test CAF: Powder caffeine-energy drink 3 mg/kg (Fure®) PLA: Powder drink 0 mg/kg Washout: 72 h	Rest	6 × 30 m sprint test	⇄
					Match	Distance covered walking	⇄
						Distance covered jogging	⇄
						Distance covered cruising	↑
						Distance covered striding	↑
						Distance covered high intensity running	↑
						Distance covered sprinting	↑
						Match: RPE	⇄
					Fatigue	15 s maximal CMJs: total power	↑
Lee et al. 2014 (Taiwan) PEDro: 10/10	11 Division I collegiate team-sport athletes (Basketball or Volleyball) (21.3 ± 1.2 years) Level: semi-professional	Light caffeine consumers: 50–100 mg/day	Not controlled	60 min pre-test CAF: 6 mg/kg capsulesPLA: Cellulose capsules Washout: at least 1 week	Rest	Agility *t*-test	⇄
					Fatigue	Cycle-ergometer repeated sprint peak power	⇄
						Cycle-ergometer repeated sprint mean power	⇄
						Cycle-ergometer repeated sprint total work	⇄
						Cycle-ergometer repeated sprint decrement	⇄
						Agility *t*-test	⇄
						Blood lactate	↓
						RPE	⇄

Table 1. *Cont.*

Authors, Year, (Country) and PEDro Score	Sample Level +	Caffeine Consumption or Restrictions	Menstrual Cycle and Oral Contraceptives	Timing + Intervention + Washout	Sample State	Outcomes	R
Lara et al. 2014 (Spain) PEDro: 10/10	18 soccer players (21 ± 2 years) Level: not reported	Light caffeine consumers: not more than one cup of coffee or energy drink per day Encouraged to abstain from all dietary sources of caffeine for 48 h before	Not controlled	60 min pre-test CAF: Powder caffeine-energy drink 3 mg/kg (Fure®) PLA: Powder drink 0 mg/kg Washout: 1 week	Rest	7 × 30 m sprint average speed	↑
						7 × 30 m sprint maximal speed	↑
						CMJ height	↑
						CMJ Power	⇄
					Match	Total distance covered	↑
						Time standing	↑
						Time walking	⇄
						Time running (3.1–8 km/h)	↑
						Time running (8.1–13 km/h)	↑
						Time running (13.1–18 km/h)	⇄
						Time running (>18 km/h)	↑
						Number of sprint bouts	↑
						Maximal speed	⇄
						RPE	⇄
Buck et al. 2015 (Australia) PEDro: 10/10	12 amateur team-sports (netball, basketball and soccer) (25.5 ± 1.9 years) Level: amateur	Caffeine consumption not reported Participants were advised to abstain from consuming CAF for 48 h prior to each trial	3 days post (follicular phase) menstruation 9 were taking Levlen ED for birth control 3 took no oral contraceptives	60 min pre-test CAF: Capsule (6 mg/kg BM) PLA: Capsule (1 g glucose) Washout: ≈21 days	Rest	6 × 20 m sprint before PSM	⇄
						Best 6 × 20 m sprint before PSM	⇄
						Total 6 × 20 m sprint time before PSM	⇄
					Fatigue	6 × 20 m sprint half-time PSM	⇄
						6 × 20 m sprint after PSM	⇄
						Best 6 × 20 m sprint half-time PSM	⇄
						Best 6 × 20 m sprint after PSM	⇄
						Total 6 × 20 m sprint time half-time PSM	⇄
						Total 6 × 20 m sprint time after PSM	⇄
						RPE during and after PSM	⇄
						Blood lactate during and after PSM	⇄

Table 1. *Cont.*

Authors, Year, (Country) and PEDro Score	Sample Level +	Caffeine Consumption or Restrictions	Menstrual Cycle and Oral Contraceptives	Timing + Intervention + Washout	Sample State	Outcomes	R
Chen et al. 2015 (Taiwan) PEDro: 10/10	10 elite collegiate athletes (tennis, soccer, basketball) (19.9 ± 0.9 years) Level: semi-professional	No regular caffeine consumption < 200 mg/week	Instructed to participate during their early follicular phase and avoid taking contraception	60 min pre-test CAF: Capsule 6 mg/kg PLA: Diet flour in capsule Washout: 1 week	Rest	MVIC	↑
						Isometric fatigue protocol	↑
					Fatigue	Fatigued MVIC	↑
						Fatigue index	↑
						Blood lactate	↓
Mahdavi et al. 2015 (Iran) PEDro: 10/10	24 basketball players (24.2 ± 2.6 years) Level: not reported	116.8 ± 26.7 mg/day	Not controlled	70 min pre-test CAF: Capsules 5 mg/kg PLA: Capsules with dextrose Washout: 1 week	Rest	30 s WT: Peak power	⇄
						30 s WT: Mean power	⇄
						30 s WT: End power	⇄
						30 s WT: Power drop	⇄
						30 s WT: Fatigue index	⇄
						30 s WT: Lactate	↑
Fernandez-Campos et al. 2015 (Costa Rica) PEDro: 9/10	19 volleyball players from the elite league of Costa Rica (22.3 ± 4.9 years) Level: elite	Not reported	Not controlled	30 min pre-test CAF: Energy drink 6 ml/kg with 73 mg of CAF in 273 mL. (1.7 mg/kg) PLA: flavored drink Washout: 1 week	Rest	Right handgrip strength	↑
						Left handgrip strength	⇄
						CMJ height	⇄
						SJ height	⇄
						WT peak power	⇄
						WT mean power	⇄
						WT fatigue index	⇄

Table 1. *Cont.*

Authors, Year, (Country) and PEDro Score	Sample Level +	Caffeine Consumption or Restrictions	Menstrual Cycle and Oral Contraceptives	Timing + Intervention + Washout	Sample State	Outcomes	R
Perez-Lopez et al. 2015 (Spain) PEDro: 10/10	13 volleyball players from the second division of the Spanish league (25.2 ± 4.8) Level: semi-professional	On the day of the trial participants were encouraged to refrain from all dietary sources of caffeine	4 during follicular phase9 during luteal phase	60 min pre-test CAF: Powder energy drink (Fure®) 3 mg/kg PLA: Powder with 0 mg/kg of CAF Washout: 1 week	Rest	Handgrip	↑
						Spike jump height and peak power	↑
						Block jump height and peak power	↑
						Squat jump height and peak power	↑
						CMJ height and peak power	↑
						Agility t-test	↑
						Standing spike ball velocity	↑
						Jumping spike ball velocity	↑
					Match	Body accelerations	↑
						Positive game actions	↑
						Neutral game actions	⇄
						Negative game actions	↑
						Body impacts 0–1 g	↑
						Body impacts 1.1–2 g	↑
						Body impacts 2.1–3 g	↑
						Body impacts 3.1–4 g	⇄
						Body impacts 4.1–5 g	↑
						Body impacts 5.1–6 g	↑

Table 1. *Cont.*

Authors, Year, (Country) and PEDro Score	Sample Level +	Caffeine Consumption or Restrictions	Menstrual Cycle and Oral Contraceptives	Timing + Intervention + Washout	Sample State	Outcomes	R
Ali et al. 2016a (New Zealand) PEDro: 10/10	10 healthy team sport players (soccer, hockey and netball) (24 ± 4 years) Level: amateur and elite	Self-reported daily caffeine intake varied from 0 to 300 mg/day	All participants were taking a monophasic oral contraceptive (Monofeme, Microgynon, Levlen ED or Nordette)	60 min pre-test CAF: Capsules 6 mg/kg PLA: Capsules with artificial sweetener Washout: 13–17 days	Rest	Knee flexor ecc. PT pre-PSM	⇄
						Knee extensor ecc. PT pre-PSM	⇄
						Knee flexor ecc. Power pre-PSM	⇄
						Knee extensor ecc. Power pre-PSM	⇄
						Isometric knee flexor pre-PSM	⇄
						Isometric knee extensor pre-PSM	⇄
						CMJ height and power pre-PSM	⇄
					Fatigue	Knee flexor ecc. PT mid-PSM	↑
						Knee flexor ecc. PT post-PSM	⇄
						Knee flexor ecc. PT 12 h-post-PSM	↑
						Knee extensor ecc. PT mid-PSM	⇄
						Knee extensor ecc. PT post-PSM	⇄
						Knee extensor ecc. PT 12 h-post-PSM	⇄
						Knee flexor ecc. Power mid-PSM	↑
						Knee flexor ecc. Power post-PSM	⇄
						Knee flexor ecc. Power 12 h-post-PSM	↑
						Knee extensor ecc. Power mid-PSM	↑
						Knee extensor ecc. Power post-PSM	⇄
						Knee extensor ecc. Power 12 h-post-PSM	⇄
						Isometric knee flexor mid-PSM	⇄
						Isometric knee flexor post-PSM	⇄
						Isometric knee flexor 12 h post-PSM	⇄
						Isometric knee extensor mid-PSM	⇄
						Isometric knee extensor post-PSM	⇄
						Isometric knee extensor 12 h post-PSM	⇄
						CMJ height and power post-PSM	⇄
						CMJ height and power 12 h post-PSM	⇄

Table 1. *Cont.*

Authors, Year, (Country) and PEDro Score	Sample Level +	Caffeine Consumption or Restrictions	Menstrual Cycle and Oral Contraceptives	Timing + Intervention + Washout	Sample State	Outcomes	R
Ali et al. 2016b (New Zealand) PEDro: 10/10	10 healthy team sport players (soccer, hockey and netball) (24 ± 4 years) Level: amateur and elite	Self-reported daily caffeine intake varied from 0 to 300 mg/day	All participants were taking a monophasic oralcontraceptive	60 min pre-test CAF: Capsules 6 mg/kg PLA: Capsules with artificial sweetener Washout: 13–17 days	Fatigue	RPE	⇄
Portillo et al. 2017 (Spain) PEDro: 10/10	16 rugby sevens national team players (23 ± 2 years) Level: elite	Light caffeine consumers: <60 mg/day	Not controlled	60 min pre-test CAF: Powder 3 mg/kg PLA: Powder with 0 mg/kg of CAF Washout: 72 h	Match	Body impacts 0–6 g	↑
						Body impacts 6.01–6.5 g	↑
						Body impacts 6.51–7 g	↑
						Body impacts 7.01–8 g	⇄
						Body impacts 8.01–10 g	↑
						Body impacts > 10 g	⇄
						Frequency of technical action	⇄
						Ratings of skill performance	⇄
Puente et al. 2017 (Spain) PEDro: 10/10	10 professional basketaball players (27.9 ± 6.1 years) Level: semi-professional and elite	Light caffeine consumers < 100 mg/day Encouraged to abstain from CAF ingestion during the study	All participants were tested during their luteal phase	60 min pre-test CAF: Capsule 3 mg/kgPLA: Capsule 0 mg/kg of CAF Washout: 1 week	Rest	Abalakov jump	NA
						CODAT	
						Free throws	
						CODAT with ball	
					Match	Body impacts 0–0.99 g	
						Body impacts 1–1.99 g	
						Body impacts 2–2.99 g	
						Body impacts 3–3.99 g	
						Body impacts 4–4.99 g	
						Body impacts >5 g	
						RPE	

Table 1. *Cont.*

Authors, Year, (Country) and PEDro Score	Sample Level +	Caffeine Consumption or Restrictions	Menstrual Cycle and Oral Contraceptives	Timing + Intervention + Washout	Sample State	Outcomes	R
Pfeifer et al. 2017 (USA) PEDro: 8/10	8 volleyball NAIA volleyball (18–22 years)Level: semi-professional	CAF consumption was not restricted	Not controlled	Prior to and during the competition CAF: PowerBar® PowerGel® 50 mg of caffeine. Averaged 1.39 mg/kg PLA: Non-nutritive gel Washout: ≈1 week	Fatigue	Vertical jump with a two-step approach	⇄
						Three cone drill agility	⇄
						6 × 30 m sprint	⇄
Stojanovic et al. 2019 (Serbia) PEDro: 10/10	10 professional basketball players (20.2 ± 3.9 years) Level: elite	Light caffeine consumers: <100 mg/day	Completed testing in the luteal phase of their menstrual cycle Use of oral contraceptives not reported by authors	60 min pre-test CAF: Capsule (3 mg/kg BM) PLA: Capsule (Dextrose) Washout: 1 week	Rest	CMJ height	⇄
						SJ height	⇄
						ABA height	⇄
						Lane agility	⇄
						5 m sprint	⇄
						10 m sprint	↑
						20 m sprint	↑
						5 m sprint-dibbling 10 m sprint-dibbling	⇄ ⇄
						20 m sprint-dibbling	⇄
						RSP: Suicide run	⇄
						RPE	↑
Tan et al. 2020 (Singapore) PEDro: 8/10	6 basketball players Level: semi-professional	Less than 200 mg caffeine per day	Not controlled	60 min pre-test CAF: Powders (6 mg/kg BM) PLA: Powders (Maltodextrine) Washout: 72 h	Fatigue	Free throws	NA
						RPE	

Table 1. *Cont.*

Authors, Year, (Country) and PEDro Score	Sample Level +	Caffeine Consumption or Restrictions	Menstrual Cycle and Oral Contraceptives	Timing + Intervention + Washout	Sample State	Outcomes	R
Muñoz et al. 2020 (Spain) PEDro: 10/10	15 elite handball players (22.6 ± 3.6 years) Level: elite	Light caffeine consumers: 50 ± 30 mg/day	10 during follicular phase 5 during luteal phase Use of oral contraceptives not reported by authors	60 min pre-test CAF: Capsule (3 mg/kg BM) PLA: Capsule (Cellulose) Washout: 1 week	Rest	7m ball throws	↑
						9m ball throws	↑
						7m ball throws goalk.	↑
						9m ball throws goalk.	↑
						CMJ height	↑
						Handgrip	↑
						Agility: MATT	⇄
						30m sprint	↑
					Match	Accelerations frequency	↑
						Decelerations frequency	↑
						Body impacts	↑
						Total distance	⇄
						Sprint distance	⇄
						Maximal speed	⇄
						RPE	⇄
Karayigit et al. 2021 (Turkey) PEDro: 10/10	17 female team sports (rugby, handball and soccer) 23 ± 2 years) Level: elite and semi-professional	Light caffeine consumers: <25 mg/day	All sessions were performed during the luteal phase of the menstrual cycle All subjects stopped oral contraceptive consumpletion 3 months before the commencement of the study	60 min pre-test CAF: Coffee (3 mg/kg BM) (6 mg/kg BM) PLA: Decaffeinated coffee Washout: 48–72 h	Rest	3 set of repetitions to failure 40% 1 RM bench press	↑
						3 set of repetitions to failure 40% 1 RM squat	⇄

↑: caffeine supplementation improved performance (for variables like lactate levels, standing time or sprint times this would entail a lower lactate increase or a lower sprint and standing time); ⇄: no differences between placebo and caffeine groups; ↓: caffeine supplementation decreased performance (for variables like lactate levels, standing time or sprint times this would entail a higher lactate increase or a higher sprint and standing time). + If the participant's category was described as recreational or amateur, the sport level was classified as amateur. If the player's category in each study was described as collegiate or second division, the sport level was classified as semi-professional. If the player's category in each study was elite (national team) or professional, the sport level was classified as elite. ABA: Abalakov jump; BM: body mass; CAF: caffeine group; CMJ: countermovement jump; CODAT: change-of-direction and acceleration test; Ecc.: eccentric; Goalk.: drill performed with a goalkeeper; ISOfatig: submaximal voluntary isometric fatigue protocol; Lane agility: lane agility drill; Match: match following official rules; MATT: modified version of the agility *t* test; MVIC: maximal volumetric isometric contractions; MVICpost: voluntary isometric contraction after fatigue protocol; NA: not applicable because the statistical analyses presented in the studies were performed for males and females without an individual comparison for females; NAIA: National Association of Intercollegiate athletics; Perc. Performance: perceived performance; PLA: placebo; PSM: protocol simulating the fatigue generated during a match; PT: peak torque; R: results; RPE: rate of perceived exertion; RSP: repeated sprint performance; SF: sodium phosphate; SJ: squat jump; SM: simulated match; SP: self-perceived; WT: Wingate test.

2.6. Statistical Analyses

After calculating the standardized mean difference as the individual effect size of each study for each relevant variable, the results were pooled using the DerSimonian–Laird method in a random-effects meta-analysis [39]. A minimum of three studies was required in order to perform the meta-analyses. When calculating the standardized mean difference between conditions within each meta-analysis, the data were set to indicate that a positive value always represented a difference in performance favoring the caffeine condition.

A sensitivity analysis was performed excluding those studies that administered less than 2 mg of caffeine per kg of body mass [33,40,41] as this has been suggested to be the minimum effective ergogenic dose [17].

We tested the heterogeneity using the I^2 statistic [42]. This statistic describes the variance between studies as a proportion of the total variance. A value of 25–50% indicates low heterogeneity, between 50–75% indicates moderate heterogeneity and >75% indicates high heterogeneity.

3. Results

3.1. Main Search

The literature search provided a total of 588 studies, with 4 additional studies found through cross-referencing. A total of 54 full-text articles were read, and 18 met the inclusion criteria and were included in the systematic review. Figure 1 presents the PRISMA flow chart and the reasons for excluding articles from the final sample of selected studies.

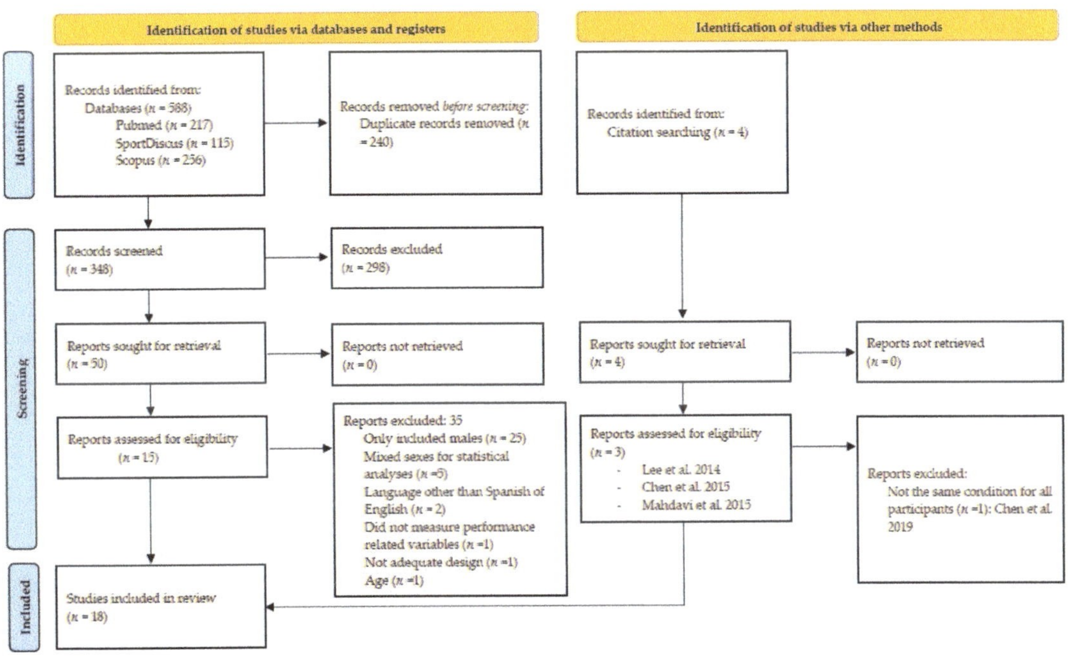

Figure 1. PRISMA flow-chart diagram.

3.2. Quality Assessment and Risk of Bias

The individual PEDro quality scores ranged from 8 to 10, being excellent in 15 studies and good in 3 studies (Supplementary Material: Table S2). Three crossover trials did not meet the requirements related to therapist and assessor blinding [33,35,40], and the study performed by Fernandez-Campos et al. [41] did not include drop-outs in the analysis.

Regarding the RoB 2 tool results, 14 studies showed a low risk of bias in all domains, 4 studies demonstrated some concerns for domain 2 "bias due to deviations from intended interventions" and 3 studies showed some concerns for domain 4 "bias in measurement of the outcome" (Supplementary Material: Table S3). Additionally, all studies had a low risk of bias in the specific domain for crossover designs "bias arising from the period effect and carryover effect" (domain S). Thus, the overall biases were low for 14 studies, with some concern in the other studies.

3.3. Description of Participants and Studies

Six studies were performed in Spain. Two studies were developed in the United States of America, New Zealand and Taiwan. Australia, Iran, Costa Rica, Serbia, Turkey and Singapore each provided one study. The origin of each individual study is presented in the first column of Table 1.

The main characteristics of each study are presented in Table 1. The 18 studies included provided a total of 240 young adult female TSA (the mean age for all studies was in the range of 18 to 26 years). Of this sample, 50 participants were basketball players [14,35,38,43], 40 were volleyball players [30,33,41], 37 were soccer players [29,40], 32 were rugby players [28,31] and 15 were handball players [32]. The rest of the studies used a sample of mixed TSA including basketball, volleyball, handball, soccer, rugby, softball, hockey and netball players [26,27,34,44–46].

3.4. Caffeine Supplementation and Doses

Caffeine doses ranged from 1.3 mg/kg to 6 mg/kg, mainly ingested through: capsules: nine studies [14,26,27,32,34,38,43–45], powders: five studies [28–31,35], energy drinks: two studies [40,41], power bars: one study [33] or coffee [46].

All studies supplied the caffeine 60 min before the experiments, except for Mahdavi et al. [43], who provided the caffeine supplementation 70 min before, Fernandez-Campos et al. [41] who provided it 30 min before and Pfeifer et al. [33] who specified that the dose "was administered immediately prior to and during the competition".

Regarding caffeine withdrawal as part of the standardization procedures, although different instructions to volunteers were found among the studies (Specified in Table 1), most studies required participants to abstain from all dietary sources of caffeine for 48 h before the trials.

Finally, regarding the days that passed between the placebo and caffeine conditions, five studies performed washout periods of 48 to 96 h, with most studies performing one-week washout periods (10 studies). Three studies performed even longer washouts (13 to 21 days). Individual information for each study is provided in Table 1.

3.5. Menstrual Cycle

In the first four studies that were published between 2011 and 2014 [27–29,40], the phase of the menstrual cycle and the use of oral contraceptives was not reported. From 2015, some studies reported the menstrual cycle phase while others were even more strict and performed the evaluations when participants were in a specific phase. For example, Buck et al. [26] standardized the assessments with the protocol of starting in the first three days after the last menstruation (follicular phase), Chen et al. [34] instructed athletes to participate during their early follicular phase and Puente et al. [14], Stojanovic et al. [38] and Karayigit et al. [46] completed their assessments during the luteal phase. Specific phases and the use of oral contraceptives are specified in Table 1.

3.6. Rested, Match and Fatigued Conditions

For the rested and match conditions, enough studies were included to perform a meta-analysis, as presented below. For the fatigued condition, meta-analyses of RPE, agility, RSA and maximal voluntary isometric contraction (MVIC) were performed. We could not perform a meta-analysis for the other fitness tests in a fatigued condition due to the heterogeneity of the performed tests. Nonetheless, the last column of Table 1 presents three different symbols reflecting the effectiveness of caffeine supplementation in each individual study, with an up-arrow representing a positive effect. Of the 18 included studies, 10 performed tests including a fatigued state. Of these 10 studies, a total of 46 variables were analyzed after participants were already fatigued, finding a positive effect of caffeine for only 8 variables, as specified in the last column of Table 1.

3.7. Meta-Analysis Results

3.7.1. Simulated Match Body Impacts

Four studies evaluated body impacts during a match, including studies of volleyball [30], basketball [14], handball [32] and rugby players [31]. The meta-analysis including total body impacts is presented in Figure 2A and shows that caffeine did improve intensity during a match (standardized mean difference (SMD): 0.488; 95% CI: 0.050, 0.927). Heterogeneity among the studies was low (I^2 49%, $p = 0.117$).

3.7.2. Specific Sport Drills

Four studies analyzed a specific sport movement (Figure 2B). On the one hand, Perez-Lopez et al. [30] analyzed the speed of a volleyball ball in a jumping spike, while Muñoz et al. analyzed the speed of a 9 m handball throw against a goalkeeper. On the other hand, Puente et al. [14] and Tan et al. [35] measured basketball throw performance. Caffeine improved performance on overall specific sport drills (SMD: 0.384; 95% CI: 0.077, 0.691). Heterogeneity among the studies was low (I^2 0, $p = 0.699$). A subgroup meta-analysis was performed, showing that caffeine improved ball speed (SMD: 0.440; 95% CI: 0.098; I^2 0% $p = 0.903$) but did not improve effectiveness during basketball free throws (SMD: 0.150, 95% CI: −0.549, 0.849; I^2 0% $p = 0.347$).

3.7.3. Jump Performance

Seven studies evaluated jump performance using either countermovement jumps (CMJ), Abalakov jumps (ABA) or squat jumps (SJ). One study did not describe the jump performed, calling it a vertical jump [33]. As shown in Figure 2C, caffeine showed a positive effect on CMJ performance (SMD: 0.208, 95% CI: 0.079, 0.338; I^2 0% $p = 0.989$). The sensitivity analysis excluding the Fernandez-Campos study due to the supplied dosage of caffeine (<2 mg/kg) revealed similar results (SMD: 0.217, 95% CI: 0.085, 0.348) with a low heterogeneity (I^2 0% $p = 0.994$).

Another meta-analysis was performed including three studies that measured SJ with the intake of caffeine showing no improvement in SJ performance (Figure 2D: SMD: 0.241, 95% CI: −0.189, 0.671; I^2 0% $p = 0.870$). The sensitivity analysis excluding the Fernandez-Campos study revealed similar results (SMD: 0.345, 95% CI: −0.237, 0.928; I^2 0% $p = 0.926$).

3.7.4. Agility

From the six studies that evaluated agility in a rested state, three used the *t*-test [27,30,40], while one study used a modified version of the t-test [32], one study used the change-of-direction and acceleration test (CODAT) [14] and one study used the lane agility drill [38]. Figure 3A presents the performed meta-analysis including all the agility tests, showing that caffeine did not improve agility (SMD: 0.144, 95% CI: −0.127, 0.416; I^2 0% $p = 0.939$).

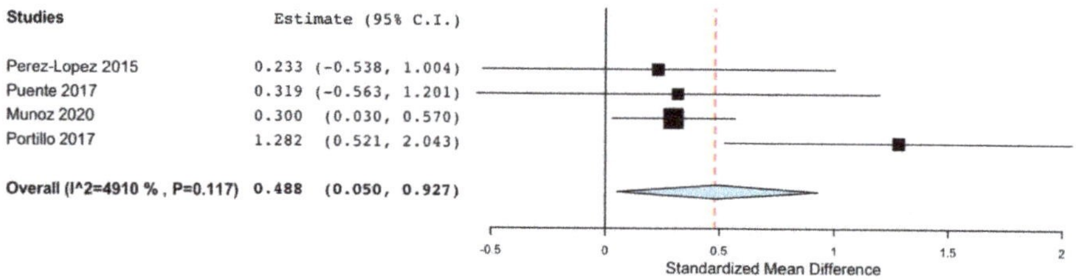

(A)

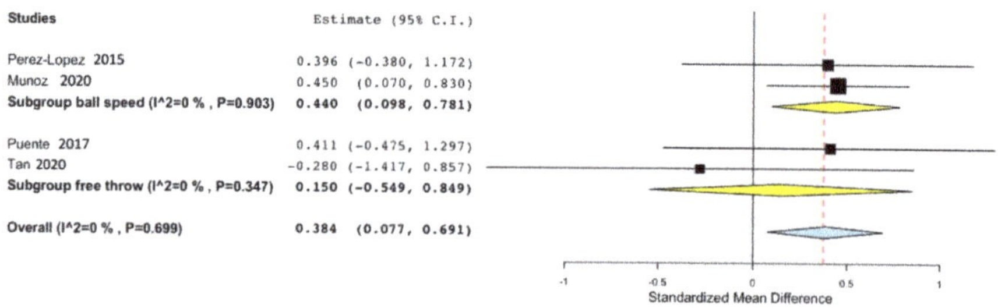

(B)

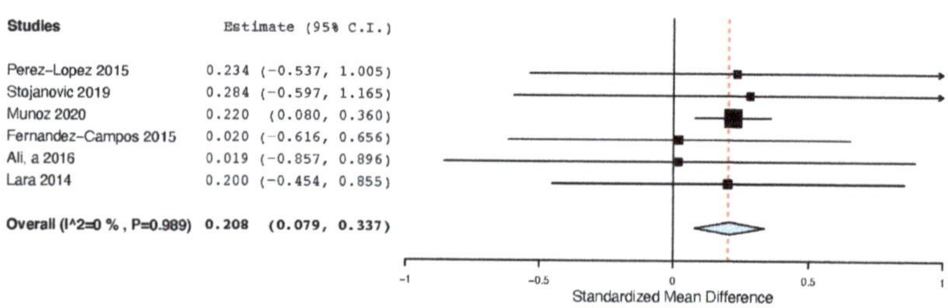

(C)

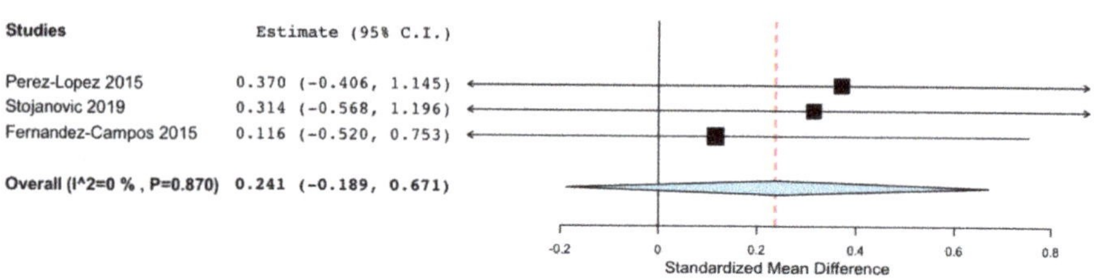

(D)

Figure 2. (**A**): Effects of caffeine on body impacts during a simulated match. (**B**): Effects of caffeine on specific skills. (**C**): Effects of caffeine on countermovement jump. (**D**): Effects of caffeine on squat jump.

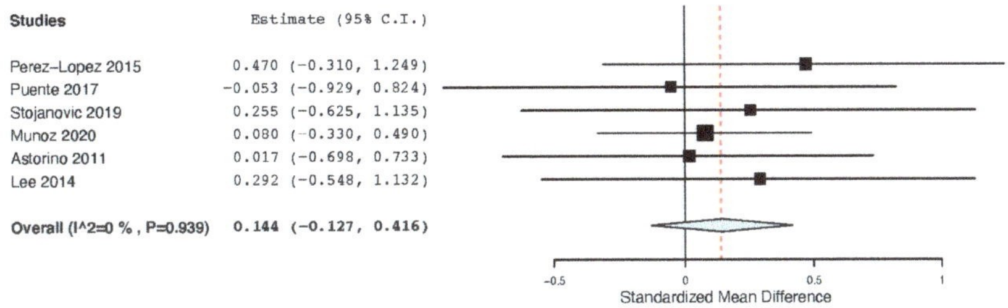

(**A**)

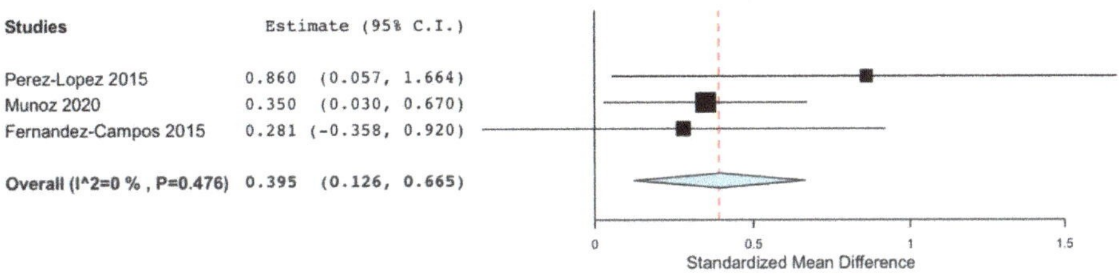

(**B**)

Figure 3. (**A**): Effects of caffeine on agility. (**B**): Effects of caffeine on handgrip strength.

The sensitivity analysis excluding the Astorino et al. study showed similar results (SMD: 0.166, 95% CI: −0.128, 0.459; I^2 0% p = 0.892).

3.7.5. Handgrip

Figure 3B shows the effects of caffeine on handgrip strength, which was measured in three studies, with Muñoz [32] reporting the mean strength of both hands in handball players, while Perez-Lopez [30] and Fernandez-Campos [41] reported separated values for the left and right hands of volleyball players (the right hand was selected for the present meta-analysis as it is usually the dominant hand). The meta-analysis showed that caffeine had a positive effect on handgrip performance (SMD: 0.395, 95% CI: 0.126, 0.665). A low heterogeneity was found (I^2 0% p = 0.476). A sensitivity analysis excluding the Fernandez-Campos study did not change the main effect of caffeine (SMD: 0.467, 95% CI: 0.047, 0.887) or the low heterogeneity (I^2 25% p = 0.238).

3.7.6. Single Sprint Performance

Single sprint performance was evaluated in five studies, from which two performed a single sprint [32,38] and three performed an RSA test, with the first sprint selected for the present meta-analysis [26,28,29]. A subgroup meta-analysis was performed for studies that used a single sprint on the one hand and for studies that used the first sprint of an RSA test on the other hand. All the studies performed a 30 m sprint except for that of Stojanović and colleagues [38] who used a 20 m sprint. As presented in Figure 4A, caffeine showed no effect on single sprint performance (SMD: 0.225, 95% CI: −0.022, 0.472; I^2 0% p = 0.685). Nonetheless, when dividing studies into two groups according to the type of measurement performed (single sprint or first sprint of an RSA test), we found that those studies that performed a single sprint reported a performance improvement (SMD: 0.347, 95% CI: 0.038, 0.656; I^2 0% p = 0.903), while in those studies that performed a RSA test, caffeine did not improve the performance of the first sprint (SMD: 0.011, 95% CI: −0.399, 0.420; I^2 0% p = 0.737).

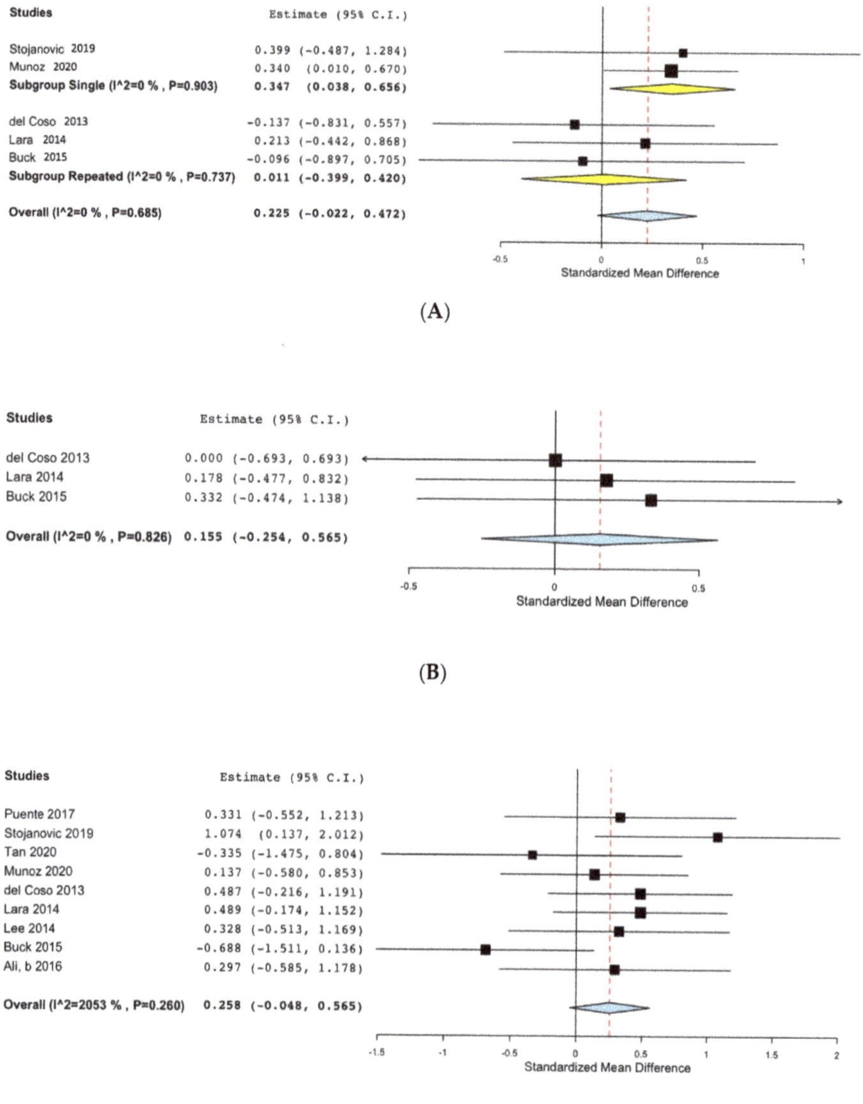

(C)

Figure 4. (**A**): Effects of caffeine on single sprint performance. (**B**): Effects of caffeine on repeated sprint ability performance. (**C**): Effects of caffeine on rate of perceived exertion.

3.7.7. RSA

Three studies included an RSA test, with Del Coso et al. [28] using a 6 × 30 m RSA test, Lara et al. [29] using a 7 × 30 m RSA test and Buck et al. [26] using a 6 × 20 m RSA test. As shown in Figure 4B, caffeine showed no effect on RSA (SMD: 0.155, 95% CI: −0.254, 0.565; I^2 0% $p = 0.826$).

3.7.8. RPE

As shown in Figure 4C, nine studies evaluated RPE after performing an exercise protocol after caffeine supplementation, finding no effect of this supplement on RPE (SMD: 0.258, 95% CI: −0.048, 0.565; I^2 0.26% p = 0.260).

3.7.9. Fatigued State

Six studies performed the assessments after applying a specific fatigue protocol or after a match. A meta-analysis could only be performed for the agility tests, as three studies evaluated agility after performing several all-out sprint tests [27,40] or after a match [33], with the pooled results showing no positive effects on agility after fatiguing the participants, as shown in Figure 5 (SMD: 0.069, 95% CI: −0.400, 0.538; I^2 0% p = 0.858). It should be highlighted that the caffeine doses for two of the aforementioned studies were below 2 mg/kg [33,40].

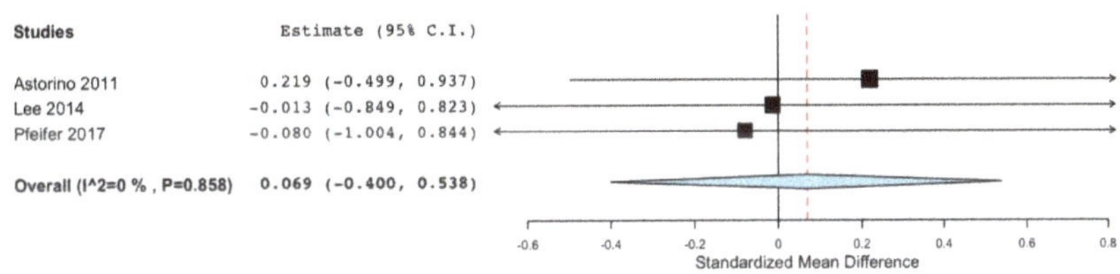

Figure 5. Effects of caffeine on agility after a fatigue protocol.

4. Discussion

The main findings of the present systematic review and meta-analysis suggest that oral caffeine administration before exercise has an ergogenic effect on specific team-sport skills, CMJ height, handgrip strength and total body impacts in female TSA. Nonetheless, caffeine did not show an ergogenic effect on RPE, SJ, agility, RSA or tests performed in a fatigued state.

The positive effects of caffeine supplementation on CMJ are in accordance with most of the previous systematic reviews and meta-analyses developed for team sports [8–10], although Ferreira and colleagues [11] did not find a positive effect of caffeine in their meta-analysis including male soccer players. Nonetheless, we also found that caffeine had no effect on SJ performance. This could partially be explained by the low number of studies (n = 3) evaluating the effect of caffeine on SJ performance. When considering Figure 2D, it appears that caffeine had a positive effect in the three studies, although the overall effect was not significant probably due to the low number of studies.

Muscle force and consequently CMJ could both determine specific athletic skills performance, which is of critical importance for TSA and was found to be improved by caffeine supplementation. Nonetheless, we only found a positive effect for the subgroup meta-analysis that included ball speed, which might be influenced by technique and upper-body strength/power. This would suggest that caffeine could be useful for those team sports in which upper-body strength/power is a determinant (e.g., volleyball, basketball or handball). Nevertheless, these results should be interpreted with caution, as only two studies measured ball speed, and the two studies that evaluated accuracy (through basketball free throws) found no ergogenic effects [14,35].

The improvement in CMJ performance was accompanied by an improvement in single sprint performance (when studies that only performed one sprint were included). This is in line with previous systematic reviews and meta-analyses, which found positive results in single sprints developed with TSA [8,9]. When we included the first sprint of studies that performed an RSA test the ergogenic effect of caffeine disappeared. We could therefore hypothesize that those participants who were going to complete an RSA test might not have performed the first sprint at their maximal capacity, and that caffeine supplementation does indeed have a positive effect on single sprint performance when participants are performing a single maximal-effort sprint.

Although single sprint performance is important, most team-sport athletes will need to perform several sprints during a match with short low-intensity periods between them. Consequently, several studies performed RSA tests in order to evaluate the ability of athletes to maintain sprint intensity. We found that caffeine supplementation had no effect on RSA in our meta-analysis, which disagrees with some previous systematic reviews and meta-analyses carried out with samples of men and women involved in team sports [9,10] but is in line with others [7,11]. Again, a small number of studies were included in our meta-analysis (n = 3), and therefore the results should be interpreted with caution, as more studies including female TSA are necessary.

The positive findings in upper-limbs isometric muscle force are in line with a recent meta-analysis developed by Grgic and Del Coso [47] focusing on the effects of caffeine on strength and power, finding that caffeine improved upper-body performance in women. This could be critical for female TSA, as an improvement in muscular endurance and strength could enable TSA to develop improved performance during a match. Along these lines, we did find improvements in total body impacts (a proxy for the players' match intensity), which would imply higher intensities during competition. Consequently, although athletes might not be able to improve RSA under laboratory conditions, they might be more motivated during a match and be capable of improving intensity due to the ergogenic effect of caffeine. These positive findings are in line with previous meta-analyses that found improvements in the performed number of sprints during a real or simulated match after acute caffeine ingestion [9].

The lack of effect of caffeine ingestion on agility tests was surprising and contradicted results from a previous meta-analysis which included mainly male participants (two studies evaluated females out of eight studies included) [9]. These contrasting results highlight the importance of performing more research with female athletes, as the scientific community may be assuming that what works with males will work in exactly the same way with females, while we have found some differences in the current meta-analysis.

Regarding RPE, our findings are similar to those of previous meta-analyses developed for team sports [9,11] which found no effects of caffeine on RPE. These studies and ours, which are all focused on team sports, show opposite results to those found in a larger meta-analysis developed in 2005 [48] which found a 6% reduction in RPE after the ingestion of caffeine in endurance tests. In the 21 included studies (where 7 measured females), there were 13 cycling tests, 5 running tests, 2 rowing tests and 1 swimming test. It is important to notice that the aforementioned meta-analysis showed a reduction in RPE only when constant loads were applied. Team sports are characterized by numerous high-intensity efforts followed by rest periods and do not follow a constant load pattern, which could explain the lack of effect of caffeine on RPE found in the present meta-analysis. Nonetheless, this may only be partially true, as a previous study [48] also found that, although no differences were found at the end of a test to exhaustion, caffeine attenuated RPE during exercise, which could partially explain the performance improvements found in some athletes. Most of the studies included in our meta-analysis only included an RPE assessment at the end of the tests or matches, but it would be interesting for future studies to consider RPE throughout exercise. This would allow researchers to test if a reduced RPE, and therefore an increased physical performance for the same intensity, is found during a match or a laboratory test.

Along the same lines, it would be interesting to evaluate the effects of caffeine in fatigued conditions, as many of the presented studies in the current meta-analysis were developed in laboratory settings and included participants in a rested state who performed the test (agility, jumps, etc.) 60 min after the ingestion of caffeine. Nonetheless, given that TSA are usually exposed to fatiguing efforts, it would be interesting to develop more studies in fatigued conditions, as caffeine presents the ability to cross the blood–brain barrier and block the adenosine receptors in the brain, mitigating the negative effects of fatigue. Very few studies have evaluated the effects of caffeine after applying a fatigue protocol (n = 3, 2 and 2 for agility, RSA and MVIC, respectively). The only meta-analysis performed showed a lack of effect of caffeine on agility performance when participants were fatigued. Nonetheless, caffeine doses for two [33,40] of the three studies included were below 2 mg/kg, and therefore further studies are required to evaluate the effects of higher doses in fatigued female TSA. Although we could not perform a further meta-analysis including the fatigued state, the results from Table 1 suggest a lack of effect as the last column shows that out of the 46 variables that were registered in fatigued conditions, only 8 improved after caffeine ingestion.

In order to improve research in this topic, we would encourage future studies to report the menstrual cycle phase of participants when performing the experiments and to perform both placebo and supplementation trials during the same menstrual cycle phase, in order to reduce the possible effect of the menstrual cycle phase. The use of oral contraceptives should also be registered. Experiments should test both rested and fatigued conditions, register individual responses to caffeine which were not reported in most of the studies included in the present meta-analysis and evaluate if in "responders" lower dosages have the same effect or if increasing the dose in "non-responders" has a positive effect. This is because previous articles have identified substantial inter-individual variations following caffeine ingestion in sport [49]. These differences seem to be mediated by genetic variations, and the characterization of the athlete's genetic profile could potentially help in individualizing the caffeine dose accurately to optimize its effect on physical performance [49].

Finally, it is worth mentioning that five of the included studies used energy drinks that, in addition to caffeine, contained other substances that could also have an ergogenic effect, such as sugar, glucuronolactone and taurine. Nonetheless, three [28–30] of these studies specified that the placebo drink and the energy drink were exactly the same drinks with the only difference being the caffeine content (the placebo had 0 mg/kg). The two remaining studies were those developed by Astorino et al. [40] and by Fernandez-Campos et al. [41]. Astorino et al. [40] used an energy drink containing both taurine and glucuronolactone. The taurine content was 1 g, which is far from the 6 g suggested to have an ergogenic effect [50,51]. In the case of glucuronolactone, as stated by Campos-Perez in the book *Sports and Energy drinks*: "because of the few investigations on the isolate glucuronolactone in humans, there is no evidence to support the idea of adding this compound to energy drinks to improve physical and sport performance, not even as a complement to the action of taurine and/or caffeine" [52]. Therefore, the only added ingredient that could make a difference in the included studies and influence performance was sugar, with the Astorino et al. [40] study showing a difference of 7 g (energy drink 27 g vs. placebo 20 g of sugar) and the Fernandez-Campos et al. [41] study showing a difference of 31 g (energy drink 31 g vs. placebo 0 g of sugar). Nonetheless, both studies were included in the sensitivity analyses, and we consequently repeated the meta-analyses without including them, finding similar results. Therefore, the possible effect that other ergogenic substances might have that could enhance the findings attributed to caffeine were controlled for in the present meta-analysis.

Although the present meta-analysis presents several strengths, such as the focus on an athlete population with limited previous scientific evidence (female TSA), the effort to contact the corresponding authors to obtain specific data for this group and the inclusion of the updated 2021 PRISMA guidelines, it is not without limitations, the main one being the low number of studies included in some of the meta-analyses (n = 3).

5. Conclusions

Although caffeine is generally considered as one of the most useful supplements used to increase athletic performance, the results of the present meta-analysis suggest that more research is needed in female TSA. Female TSA obtained benefits from caffein supplementation as it was shown to improve upper-body strength and sport-specific tasks related to upper-body strength (ball speed), in addition to CMJ, single sprint performance and body impacts during a match (match intensity).

Supplementary Materials: The following are available online at https://www.mdpi.com/article/10.3390/nu13103663/s1, Table S1: Search strategy; Table S2: Quality Assessment of included randomized controlled trials (PEDro scores); Table S3: Quality Assessment of included randomized controlled trials (RoB 2 tool).

Author Contributions: Conceptualization: A.G.-B. and G.L.-B.; methodology, A.G.-B., G.L.-B., J.M.-P., B.M.-P.; formal analysis, A.G.-B. and J.M.-P.; resources, A.G.-C.; writing—original draft preparation, A.G.-B. and G.L.-B.; writing—review and editing, J.D.C., J.A.C., A.M.-L., G.V.-R., A.G.-C., J.M.-P. and B.M.-P.; funding acquisition, A.G.-B. and A.G.-C. All authors have read and agreed to the published version of the manuscript.

Funding: The APC was funded by "Proyectos Unizar CUD, 2020": UZCUD2020-BIO-02.

Institutional Review Board Statement: Not applicable.

Informed Consent Statement: Not applicable.

Data Availability Statement: Not applicable.

Acknowledgments: The present research has been possible thanks to the funding obtained from "Proyectos Unizar CUD, 2020": UZCUD2020-BIO-02.

Conflicts of Interest: The authors declare no conflict of interest.

References

1. Del Coso, J.; Muñoz, G.; Muñoz-Guerra, J. Prevalence of caffeine use in elite athletes following its removal from the World Anti-Doping Agency list of banned substances. *Appl. Physiol. Nutr. Metab.* **2011**, *36*, 555–561. [CrossRef] [PubMed]
2. WADA. *Monitoring Program*; World Anti-Doping Agency: Montreal, QC, Canada, 2020.
3. Aguilar-Navarro, M.; Muñoz, G.; Salinero, J.J.; Muñoz-Guerra, J.; Fernández-Álvarez, M.; Plata, M.D.M.; Del Coso, J. Urine Caffeine Concentration in Doping Control Samples from 2004 to 2015. *Nutrients* **2019**, *11*, 286. [CrossRef] [PubMed]
4. Kerksick, C.M.; Wilborn, C.D.; Roberts, M.D.; Smith-Ryan, A.; Kleiner, S.M.; Jäger, R.; Collins, R.; Cooke, M.; Davis, J.N.; Galvan, E.; et al. ISSN exercise & sports nutrition review update: Research & recommendations. *J. Int. Soc. Sports Nutr.* **2018**, *15*, 38. [CrossRef] [PubMed]
5. Grgic, J.; Grgic, I.; Pickering, C.; Schoenfeld, B.J.; Bishop, D.J.; Pedisic, Z. Wake up and smell the coffee: Caffeine supplementation and exercise performance—An umbrella review of 21 published meta-analyses. *Br. J. Sports Med.* **2019**, *54*, 681–688. [CrossRef]
6. Southward, K.; Rutherfurd-Markwick, K.J.; Ali, A. The Effect of Acute Caffeine Ingestion on Endurance Performance: A Systematic Review and Meta–Analysis. *Sports Med.* **2018**, *48*, 1913–1928. [CrossRef]
7. Brown, S.J.; Brown, J.; Foskett, A. The Effects of Caffeine on Repeated Sprint Performance in Team Sport Athletes—A Meta-Analysis. *Sport Sci. Rev.* **2013**, *22*, 25–32. [CrossRef]
8. Chia, J.S.; Barrett, L.A.; Chow, J.Y.; Burns, S.F. Effects of Caffeine Supplementation on Performance in Ball Games. *Sports Med.* **2017**, *47*, 2453–2471. [CrossRef]
9. Salinero, J.J.; Lara, B.; Del Coso, J. Effects of acute ingestion of caffeine on team sports performance: A systematic review and meta-analysis. *Res. Sports Med.* **2019**, *27*, 238–256. [CrossRef]
10. Mielgo-Ayuso, J.; Calleja-Gonzalez, J.; Del Coso, J.; Urdampilleta, A.; León-Guereño, P.; Fernández-Lázaro, D. Caffeine Supplementation and Physical Performance, Muscle Damage and Perception of Fatigue in Soccer Players: A Systematic Review. *Nutrients* **2019**, *11*, 440. [CrossRef]
11. Ferreira, R.E.S.; Pacheco, R.L.; de Oliveira Cruz Latorraca, C.; Riera, R.; Eid, R.G.; Martimbianco, A.L.C. Effects of Caffeine Supplementation on Physical Performance of Soccer Players: Systematic Review and Meta-Analysis. *Sports Health* **2021**, *13*, 347–358. [CrossRef]
12. Salinero, J.J.; Lara, B.; Jim´énez-Ormeño, E.; Romero-Moraleda, B.; Giráldez-Costas, V.; Baltazar-Martins, G.; Del Coso, J. More Research Is Necessary to Establish the Ergogenic Effect of Caffeine in Female Athletes. *Nutrients* **2019**, *11*, 1600. [CrossRef]
13. Bello, M.L.; Walker, A.J.; McFadden, B.A.; Sanders, D.J.; Arent, S.M. The effects of TeaCrine® and caffeine on endurance and cognitive performance during a simulated match in high-level soccer players. *J. Int. Soc. Sports Nutr.* **2019**, *16*, 20. [CrossRef]
14. Puente, C.; Abián-Vicén, J.; Salinero, J.J.; Lara, B.; Areces, F.; Del Coso, J. Caffeine Improves Basketball Performance in Experienced Basketball Players. *Nutrients* **2017**, *9*, 1033. [CrossRef]
15. Maughan, R.J.; Burke, L.M.; Dvorak, J.; Larson-Meyer, D.E.; Peeling, P.; Phillips, S.M.; Rawson, E.S.; Walsh, N.P.; Garthe, I.; Geyer, H.; et al. IOC consensus statement: Dietary supplements and the high-performance athlete. *Br. J. Sports Med.* **2018**, *52*, 439–455. [CrossRef]

16. Lara, B.; Hellín, J.G.; Ruiz-Mereno, C.; Romero-Moraleda, B.; Del Coso, J. Acute caffeine intake increases performance in the 15-s Wingate test during the menstrual cycle. *Br. J. Clin. Pharmacol.* **2020**, *86*, 745–752. [CrossRef]
17. Guest, N.S.; VanDusseldorp, T.A.; Nelson, M.T.; Grgic, J.; Schoenfeld, B.J.; Jenkins, N.D.M.; Arent, S.M.; Antonio, J.; Stout, J.R.; Trexler, E.T.; et al. International society of sports nutrition position stand: Caffeine and exercise performance. *J. Int. Soc. Sports Nutr.* **2021**, *18*, 1. [CrossRef]
18. Temple, J.L.; Ziegler, A.M. Gender Differences in Subjective and Physiological Responses to Caffeine and the Role of Steroid Hormones. *J. Caffeine Res.* **2011**, *1*, 41–48. [CrossRef]
19. Sabblah, S.; Dixon, D.; Bottoms, L. Sex differences on the acute effects of caffeine on maximal strength and muscular endurance. *Comp. Exerc. Physiol.* **2015**, *11*, 89–94. [CrossRef]
20. Skinner, T.; Desbrow, B.; Arapova, J.; Schaumberg, M.A.; Osborne, J.; Grant, G.D.; Anoopkumar-Dukie, S.; Leveritt, M.D. Women Experience the Same Ergogenic Response to Caffeine as Men. *Med. Sci. Sports Exerc.* **2019**, *51*, 1195–1202. [CrossRef]
21. Lara, B.; Salinero, J.J.; Giráldez-Costas, V.; Del Coso, J. Similar ergogenic effect of caffeine on anaerobic performance in men and women athletes. *Eur. J. Nutr.* **2021**, *60*, 4107–4114. [CrossRef]
22. Chen, H.-Y.; Chen, Y.-C.; Tung, K.; Chao, H.-H.; Wang, H.-S. Effects of caffeine and sex on muscle performance and delayed-onset muscle soreness after exercise-induced muscle damage: A double-blind randomized trial. *J. Appl. Physiol.* **2019**, *127*, 798–805. [CrossRef]
23. Page, M.J.; McKenzie, J.E.; Bossuyt, P.M.; Boutron, I.; Hoffmann, T.C.; Mulrow, C.D.; Shamseer, L.; Tetzlaff, J.M.; Akl, E.A.; Brennan, S.E.; et al. The PRISMA 2020 statement: An updated guideline for reporting systematic reviews. *BMJ* **2021**, *372*, n71. [CrossRef]
24. Maher, C.G.; Sherrington, C.; Herbert, R.D.; Moseley, A.M.; Elkins, M. Reliability of the PEDro Scale for Rating Quality of Randomized Controlled Trials. *Phys. Ther.* **2003**, *83*, 713–721. [CrossRef]
25. Sterne, J.A.C.; Savović, J.; Page, M.; Elbers, R.G.; Blencowe, N.; Boutron, I.; Cates, C.; Cheng, H.-Y.; Corbett, M.S.; Eldridge, S.M.; et al. RoB 2: A revised tool for assessing risk of bias in randomised trials. *BMJ* **2019**, *366*, l4898. [CrossRef]
26. Kopec, B.J.; Dawson, B.T.; Buck, C.; Wallman, K.E. Effects of sodium phosphate and caffeine ingestion on repeated-sprint ability in male athletes. *J. Sci. Med. Sport* **2016**, *19*, 272–276. [CrossRef]
27. Lee, C.-L.; Cheng, C.-F.; Astorino, T.A.; Lee, C.J.; Huang, H.-W.; Chang, W.-D. Effects of carbohydrate combined with caffeine on repeated sprint cycling and agility performance in female athletes. *J. Int. Soc. Sports Nutr.* **2014**, *11*, 17. [CrossRef]
28. Del Coso, J.; Portillo, J.; Muñoz, G.; Abián-Vicén, J.; Gonzalez-Millán, C.; Muñoz-Guerra, J. Caffeine-containing energy drink improves sprint performance during an international rugby sevens competition. *Amino Acids* **2013**, *44*, 1511–1519. [CrossRef]
29. Lara, B.; González-Millán, C.; Salinero, J.J.; Abián-Vicén, J.; Areces, F.; Barbero-Alvarez, J.C.; Muñoz, V.; Portillo, L.J.; Gonzalez-Rave, J.M.; Del Coso, J. Caffeine-containing energy drink improves physical performance in female soccer players. *Amino Acids* **2014**, *46*, 1385–1392. [CrossRef]
30. Pérez-López, A.; Salinero, J.J.; Abián-Vicén, J.; Valadés, D.; Lara, B.; Hernandez, C.; Areces, F.; González, C.; Del Coso, J. Caffeinated Energy Drinks Improve Volleyball Performance in Elite Female Players. *Med. Sci. Sports Exerc.* **2015**, *47*, 850–856. [CrossRef]
31. Portillo, J.; Del Coso, J.; Abián-Vicén, J. Effects of Caffeine Ingestion on Skill Performance During an International Female Rugby Sevens Competition. *J. Strength Cond. Res.* **2017**, *31*, 3351–3357. [CrossRef]
32. Muñoz, A.; López-Samanes, A.; Pérez-López, A.; Aguilar-Navarro, M.; Moreno-Heredero, B.; Rivilla-García, J.; González-Frutos, P.; Pino-Ortega, J.; Morencos, E.; Del Coso, J. Effects of Caffeine Ingestion on Physical Performance in Elite Women Handball Players: A Randomized, Controlled Study. *Int. J. Sports Physiol. Perform.* **2020**, *15*, 1406–1413. [CrossRef] [PubMed]
33. Pfeifer, D.R.; Arvin, K.M.; Herschberger, C.N.; Haynes, N.J.; Renfrow, M.S. A Low Dose Caffeine and Carbohydrate Supplement does not Improve Athletic Performance during Volleyball Competition. *Int. J. Exerc. Sci.* **2017**, *10*, 340–353. [PubMed]
34. Chen, H.-Y.; Wang, H.-S.; Tung, K.; Chao, H.-H. Effects of Gender Difference and Caffeine Supplementation on Anaerobic Muscle Performance. *Int. J. Sports Med.* **2015**, *36*, 974–978. [CrossRef] [PubMed]
35. Tan, Z.S.; Burns, S.F.; Pan, J.W.; Kong, P.W. Effect of caffeine ingestion on free-throw performance in college basketball players. *J. Exerc. Sci. Fit.* **2020**, *18*, 62–67. [CrossRef]
36. Scanlan, A.T.; Dalbo, V.J.; Conte, D.; Stojanović, E.; Stojiljković, N.; Stanković, R.; Antić, V.; Milanović, Z. No Effect of Caffeine Supplementation on Dribbling Speed in Elite Basketball Players. *Int. J. Sports Physiol. Perform.* **2019**, *14*, 997–1000. [CrossRef]
37. Muñoz, A.; López-Samanes, A.; Aguilar-Navarro, M.; Varillas-Delgado, D.; Rivilla-García, J.; Moreno-Pérez, V.; Del Coso, J. Effects of *CYP1A2* and *ADORA2A* Genotypes on the Ergogenic Response to Caffeine in Professional Handball Players. *Genes* **2020**, *11*, 933. [CrossRef]
38. Stojanovic, E.; Stojiljkovic, N.; Scanlan, A.T.; Dalbo, V.J.; Stankovic, R.; Antic, V.; Milanovic, Z. Acute caffeine supplementation promotes small to moderate improvements in performance tests indicative of in-game success in professional female basketball players. *Appl. Physiol. Nutr. Metab.* **2019**, *44*, 849–856. [CrossRef]
39. Higgins, J.P.T.; Thomas, J.; Chandler, J.; Cumpston, M.; Li, T.; Page, M.J.; Welch, V.A. *Cochrane Handbook for Systematic Reviews of Interventions*; Higgins, J.P.T., Thomas, J., Chandler, J., Cumpston, M., Li, T., Page, M.J., Welch, V.A., Eds.; Wiley: Hoboken, NJ, USA, 2019; ISBN 9781119536628.
40. Astorino, T.A.; Matera, A.J.; Basinger, J.; Evans, M.; Schurman, T.; Marquez, R. Effects of red bull energy drink on repeated sprint performance in women athletes. *Amino Acids* **2012**, *42*, 1803–1808. [CrossRef]

41. Fernández-Campos, C.; Dengo, A.L.; Moncada-Jiménez, J. Acute Consumption of an Energy Drink Does Not Improve Physical Performance of Female Volleyball Players. *Int. J. Sport Nutr. Exerc. Metab.* **2015**, *25*, 271–277. [CrossRef]
42. Higgins, J.P.T.; Thompson, S.G.; Deeks, J.; Altman, D.G. Measuring inconsistency in meta-analyses. *BMJ* **2003**, *327*, 557–560. [CrossRef]
43. Mahdavi, R.; Daneghian, S.; Jafari, A.; Homayouni, A. Effect of Acute Caffeine Supplementation on Anaerobic Power and Blood Lactate Levels in Female Athletes. *J. Caffeine Res.* **2015**, *5*, 83–87. [CrossRef]
44. Ali, A.; O'Donnell, J.; Foskett, A.; Rutherfurd-Markwick, K. The influence of caffeine ingestion on strength and power performance in female team-sport players. *J. Int. Soc. Sports Nutr.* **2016**, *13*, 46. [CrossRef]
45. Ali, A.; O'Donnell, J.; Von Hurst, P.; Foskett, A.; Holland, S.; Starck, C.; Rutherfurd-Markwick, K. Caffeine ingestion enhances perceptual responses during intermittent exercise in female team-game players. *J. Sports Sci.* **2016**, *34*, 330–341. [CrossRef]
46. Karayigit, R.; Naderi, A.; Akca, F.; Da Cruz, C.J.G.; Sarshin, A.; Yasli, B.C.; Ersoz, G.; Kaviani, M. Effects of Different Doses of Caffeinated Coffee on Muscular Endurance, Cognitive Performance, and Cardiac Autonomic Modulation in Caffeine Naive Female Athletes. *Nutrients* **2020**, *13*, 2. [CrossRef]
47. Grgic, J.; Del Coso, J. Ergogenic Effects of Acute Caffeine Intake on Muscular Endurance and Muscular Strength in Women: A Meta-Analysis. *Int. J. Environ. Res. Public Health* **2021**, *18*, 5773. [CrossRef]
48. Doherty, M.; Smith, P.M. Effects of caffeine ingestion on rating of perceived exertion during and after exercise: A meta-analysis. *Scand. J. Med. Sci. Sports* **2005**, *15*, 69–78. [CrossRef]
49. Pickering, C.; Kiely, J. Are the Current Guidelines on Caffeine Use in Sport Optimal for Everyone? Inter-individual Variation in Caffeine Ergogenicity, and a Move Towards Personalised Sports Nutrition. *Sports Med* **2018**, *48*, 7–16. [CrossRef]
50. Zhang, M.; Izumi, I.; Kagamimori, S.; Sokejima, S.; Yamagami, T.; Liu, Z.; Qi, B. Role of taurine supplementation to prevent exercise-induced oxidative stress in healthy young men. *Amino Acids* **2004**, *26*, 203–207. [CrossRef]
51. Ward, R.; Bridge, C.A.; McNaughton, L.R.; Sparks, S.A. The effect of acute taurine ingestion on 4-km time trial performance in trained cyclists. *Amino Acids* **2016**, *48*, 2581–2587. [CrossRef]
52. Campos-Perez, J.; Camara-Martos, F. Influence of substances present in energy and sports drinks in improving athletic performance. *Sports Energy Drinks* **2019**, *10*, 297–337.

nutrients

Article

Effects of Resveratrol on Muscle Inflammation, Energy Utilisation, and Exercise Performance in an Eccentric Contraction Exercise Mouse Model

Liang-Yu Su [1], Wen-Ching Huang [2], Nai-Wen Kan [3,4], Te-Hsuan Tung [4], Linh Ba Phuong Huynh [4,5] and Shih-Yi Huang [1,4,6,7,*]

1 Graduate Institute of Metabolism and Obesity Sciences, Taipei Medical University, Taipei 110301, Taiwan
2 Department of Exercise and Health Science, National Taipei University of Nursing and Health Sciences, Taipei 112303, Taiwan
3 Office of Physical Education Affairs, Taipei Medical University Hospital, Taipei 110301, Taiwan
4 School of Nutrition and Health Sciences, Taipei Medical University, Taipei 110301, Taiwan
5 Department of Public Health, Nutrition and Food Safety, Lien Chieu Hospital, Danang 551000, Vietnam
6 Nutrition Research Center, Taipei Medical University Hospital, Taipei 110301, Taiwan
7 TMU Research Center for Digestive Medicine, Taipei Medical University, Taipei 110301, Taiwan
* Correspondence: sihuang@tmu.edu.tw; Tel.: +886-2-27361661-6543

Abstract: Eccentric contraction can easily cause muscle damage and an inflammatory response, which reduces the efficiency of muscle contraction. Resveratrol causes anti-inflammatory effects in muscles, accelerates muscle repair, and promotes exercise performance after contusion recovery. However, whether resveratrol provides the same benefits for sports injuries caused by eccentric contraction is unknown. Thus, we explored the effects of resveratrol on inflammation and energy metabolism. In this study, mice were divided into four groups: a control group, an exercise group (EX), an exercise with low-dose resveratrol group (EX + RES25), and an exercise with high-dose resveratrol group (EX + RES150). The results of an exhaustion test showed that the time before exhaustion of the EX + RES150 group was greater than that of the EX group. Tumour necrosis factor-α (*Tnfα*) mRNA expression was lower in the EX + RES150 group than in the EX group. The energy utilisation of the EX + RES150 group was greater than that of the EX + RES25 group in different muscles. High-dose resveratrol intervention decreased *Tnfα* mRNA expression and enhanced the mRNA expressions of sirtuin 1, glucose transporter 4, AMP-activated protein kinase α1, and AMP-activated protein kinase α2 in muscles. These results revealed that high-dose resveratrol supplementation can reduce inflammation and oxidation and improve energy utilisation during short-duration high-intensity exercise.

Keywords: resveratrol; eccentric contraction; downhill running; anti-inflammation; energy utilization

Citation: Su, L.-Y.; Huang, W.-C.; Kan, N.-W.; Tung, T.-H.; Huynh, L.B.P.; Huang, S.-Y. Effects of Resveratrol on Muscle Inflammation, Energy Utilisation, and Exercise Performance in an Eccentric Contraction Exercise Mouse Model. *Nutrients* **2023**, *15*, 249. https://doi.org/10.3390/nu15010249

Academic Editor: Juha Hulmi

Received: 7 December 2022
Revised: 29 December 2022
Accepted: 30 December 2022
Published: 3 January 2023

1. Introduction

A habit of exercise contributes to effective metabolism, strong muscles, and low fatigue [1] and protects against metabolic disorders and even cognitive impairment in older adults [2,3]. However, poor exercise habits can cause muscle damage. Mice were made to execute eccentric contraction that caused the overextension of muscle fibres [4]. When such muscle damage occurs, macrophages are polarised as M1 macrophages by tumour necrosis factor-α (TNF-α) and interleukin 6 (IL-6) to prevent damage to the muscle cells [4,5]. During a rest period, these M1 macrophages are converted to M2 macrophages by anti-inflammatory factors (i.e., insulin-like growth factor 1 and interleukin 10) for muscle reconstruction [5,6]. Increased levels of IL-6 and TNF-α in adipose tissue have been observed in individuals with obesity during long-duration eccentric contraction exercise [7]; however, the related cytokine mechanism is not understood.

For improved sports performance, 500 mg/d of resveratrol has been combined with physical exercise to improve mitochondrial volume density and muscle function and increase total myonuclei in older adults [8]. Resveratrol use has been reported to prevent muscle stiffness and soreness resulting from damage to sarcomeres in muscle fibre [9] and the excitation–contraction coupling system [10]; damage which further causes delayed onset muscle soreness. Studies have also supported that resveratrol is involved in the activation of AMP-activated protein kinase (AMPK) during muscle contraction over a longer exercise period [11]. Active AMPK is attributed to the translocation and activation of glucose transporter 4 (GLUT4) to improve glucose utilisation and the proliferation of mitochondria in muscles [12].

Most resting muscles present as contracted. However, in the early stages of muscle excitement, fewer reactive oxidative species (ROS), which promote more muscle contraction to balance energy utilisation, are produced [13]. The more intensive the exercise is, the more ROS are produced by muscle excitement [14]. During high-intensity short-duration exercise, greater muscle contraction causes more ROS production, resulting in injury and reduced muscle contraction as well as overtraining syndrome (OTS) [13]. Cheng et al. reported that selected antioxidant treatments did not improve force recovery after fatiguing stimulation of skeletal muscle fibres in a mouse model [15]. However, some studies have shown that intervention targeting selected antioxidants altered oxidative stress in athletes with OTS by reducing plasma malondialdehyde levels [16] and resulted in improved muscle function in individuals with adjuvant-induced arthritis [17]. The effects of antioxidant intervention in various exercise types remain disputed and unclear.

Resveratrol use has been reported to benefit health and has therapeutic effects in humans [18]. Many studies have shown that resveratrol possesses antiaging [19], anti-cancer, anti-atherosclerosis, and anti-inflammatory effects; increases insulin sensitivity; and contributes to the reduction in ROS levels [20]. Resveratrol presents as a *trans*-form polyphenolic compound in nature, commonly found in grape skin, cherries, and peanuts. When consumed orally, trans-resveratrol is rapidly converted to the more biologically active form of dihydroresveratrol [21]. This resveratrol form has been reported to regulate sirtuin 1 (SIRT 1), peroxisome proliferator-activated receptor gamma coactivator 1-α (PGC-1α), AMPK, and TNF-α, which enforces cell mitochondrial function, increases insulin sensitivity, and inhibits inflammation and low-density lipoprotein oxidation in individuals with diabetes [20,22,23].

This study used a downhill running exercise to mimic eccentric contraction injury and assess the efficacy of resveratrol in mice models. We hypothesised that giving mice different doses of resveratrol would protect against the damage caused by short-duration high-intensity eccentric exercise. The mechanisms of resveratrol involved in muscle inflammation, energy utilisation, and exercise performance were also evaluated.

2. Materials and Methods

2.1. Materials

Trans-resveratrol was provided by Tokyo Chemistry Industry. All chemicals used in this study were obtained from Sigma-Aldrich (St. Louis, MO, USA).

2.2. Animals

C57BL/6J mice (aged 6 weeks) were purchased from the National Laboratory Animal Center (Taipei, Taiwan). All animals were fed on a chow diet (Rodent Laboratory Chow 5001, LabDiet, St. Louis, MO, USA) and distilled water *ad libitum*. Mice were housed in a regular cycle (12 h light/dark) at room temperature (23 $\pm$ 2 °C) and 60–70% humidity in the Taipei Medical University Laboratory Animal Center. All animal experimental protocols were reviewed and approved by the Institutional Animal Care and Use Committee of Taipei Medical University (LAC-2021-0310).

2.3. Experiment Design

C57BL/6J mice were housed in the animal facility for 1 week for them to adapt to the environment before the study. Twenty-four mice were randomly assigned into four equal groups: control (NC), exercise (EX), exercise with low-dose resveratrol (25 mg/kg body weight; EX + RES25), and exercise with high-dose resveratrol (150 mg/kg body weight; EX + RES150). The mice in the EX, EX + RES25, and EX + RES150 groups underwent 3 days of acclimation running before undertaking the incremental load test (ILT). Acclimation involved running 10 m/min for 15 min with an incline of 0° each day for 3 days. All the mice underwent an exhaustion test the day after the ILT, and the downhill running section of the study started the following week. Resveratrol was dissolved in distilled water. EX-treated mice were gavaged with various amounts (25 mg/kg/d [RES25] and 150 mg/kg/d [RES150] in 0.5 mL of normal saline) of resveratrol or the vehicle (0.5 mL of normal saline) for C and EX groups for 4 weeks (Figure 1).

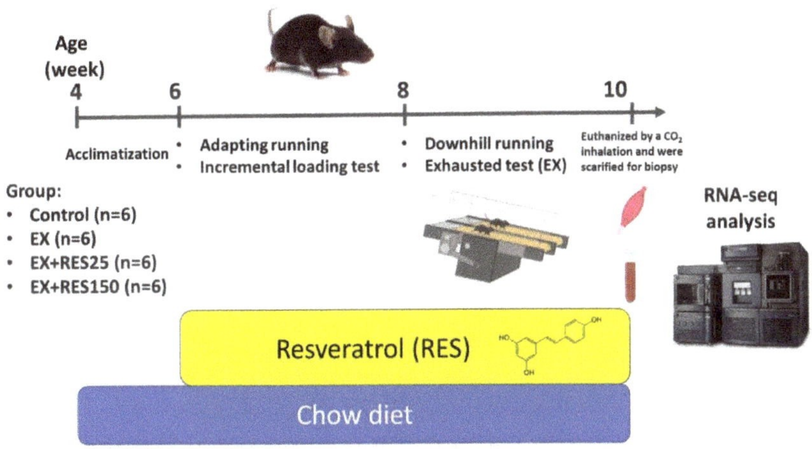

Figure 1. Experimental design of short-term downhill training. NC: control (n = 6); EX: exercise (n = 6); EX + RES25: exercise with resveratrol 25 mg/kg (n = 6); EX + RES150: exercise with resveratrol 150 mg/kg (n = 6).

2.4. ILT, Exhaustion Test, and Downhill Running

Mice undertook the ILT on a motorised treadmill (Rodent Treadmill 47300, Ugo Basile, Italy). The intensity of exercise was programmed to increase by 3 m/min (initial speed: 12 m/min) in the first 3 min and mice ran on a 0% gradient until exhaustion [24]. Individual exhaustion velocity (EV) was determined from the results. The same exercise protocol was used in the exhaustion test. After a 3-day acclimation to running and the ILT, the mice of groups EX, EX + RES25 and EX + RES150 ran on a motorised treadmill (−15° slope) at 22 m/min (60% EV), 2 h/day, 5 days/week for 2 weeks [25]. Training interventions were conducted between 10 am and 6 pm.

2.5. Sample Collection

After the downhill running test, mice were euthanized by a CO_2 inhalation overdose and were sacrificed for biopsy, including biopsies of the liver, epididymal adipose tissue (eWAT), gastrocnemius muscle, soleus muscle, and tibialis anterior muscle, which were collected and stored at −80 °C for biochemical analyses. Skin irritation was also evaluated in all animals at the end of the study.

2.6. Quantitative Reverse Transcription Polymerase Chain Reaction (RT-qPCR)

RNA was extracted using RNAzol RT (Molecular Research Center, Cincinnati, OH, USA) according to manufacturer guidelines. 1 μg of RNA was reverse transcribed using a TOOLSQuant II fast RT kit (BIOTOOLS, Taiwan). Genes were quantified using specific primers with SYBR green using the Applied Biosystems QuantStudio 1 Real-Time PCR System. The final quantification was executed using the $2-\Delta\Delta CT$ method with glyceraldehyde 3-phosphate dehydrogenase (GAPDH) primer as a control. The sequences of primers are shown in Table 1.

Table 1. Primers list for qPCR.

Genes	Direction	Primer Sequence (5′to 3′)
Gapdh	Forward	TGGTGAAGGTCGGTGTGAAC
	Reverse	AATGAAGGGGTCGTTGATGG
Tnfα	Forward	CCACCACGCTCTTCTGTCTAC
	Reverse	AGGGTCTGGGCCATAGAACT
Il6	Forward	GCTTAATTACACATGTTCTCTGGGAAA
	Reverse	CAAGTGCATCATCGTTGTTCATAC
Il1β	Forward	TGGACCTTCCAGGATGAGGACA
	Reverse	GTTCATCTCGGAGCCTGTAGTG
Sirt1	Forward	CAGACCCTCAAGCCATGTTT
	Reverse	ACACAGAGACGGCTGGAACT
Glut4	Forward	GTAACTTCATTGTCGGCATGG
	Reverse	AGCTGAGATCTGGTCAAACG
Ampkα1	Forward	CTCAGTTCCTGGAGAAAGATGG
	Reverse	CTGCCGGTTGAGTATCTTCAC
Ampkα2	Forward	CAGGCCATAAAGTGGCAGTTA
	Reverse	AAAAGTCTGTCGGAGTGCTGA
Pgc1α	Forward	TGATGTGAATGACTTGGATACAGACA
	Reverse	GCTCATTGTTGTACTGGTTGGATATG

2.7. Next Generation Sequencing Analysis

First, cDNA libraries were collected from four independent samples in each group. The cDNA libraries were assessed using the Agilent 2100 Bioanalyzer system and the Real-Time PCR system. β-Actin served as an internal control to verify the quality and quantity of cDNA in the PCR system. The sequenced libraries underwent fragment size detection using the Agilent Bioanalyzer 2100 system and library concentration determination using the Real-Time PCR system; the quality-confirmed libraries underwent 150-bp paired-end sequencing on the Illumina NovaSeq 6000 sequencer (Genomics, BioSci & Tech Company, New Taipei City, Taiwan). Raw sequencing reads were filtered using Trimmomatic (version 0.36) [26]. Reads were aligned using Bowtie2 (version 2.3.5) [27]. Raw gene counts were extracted using RSEM (version 1.3.3) [28]. The R package edgeR (v3.16.5) was used for the differential gene expression analysis of two sample groups. Furthermore, the $\log_2$ fold change was calculated as $\log_2$(sample count 1/sample count 2). The *t*-test was used to identify significant differences between samples from the two groups ($p < 0.05$). Gene ontology (GO) enrichment analysis was conducted on the differential genes obtained through screening. When $p < 0.05$, GO terms were significantly enriched [29]. The Kyoto Encyclopedia of Genes and Genomes was used for the gene enrichment of differentially expressed genes.

2.8. Statistical Analysis

All results are expressed in terms of the mean ± SEM. The significance of the difference was examined using GraphPad Prism version 9.0 (GraphPad Software; San Diego, CA, USA). All data were normally distributed. Significant differences were analyzed using a student's t-test or one-way analysis of variance with Tukey's test and Bonferroni's test for multiple comparisons. A *p*-value less than 0.05 was considered statistically significant.

3. Results

3.1. Average Body Weight, Food Intake, and Tissue Relative Weight

Average body weight, food intake, and tissue relative weight are shown in Table 2. No significant differences in the body weight, food and water intake, and selected biopsy results were found. However, the relative weights of the eWAT in the EX, EX + RES25, and EX + RES150 groups were significantly lower than that of the NC group ($p < 0.05$).

Table 2. Body weight, food and water intake and tissue relative weight in mice.

Parameters	NC	EX	EX + RES25	EX + RES150
Body weight (g)	23.2 ± 0.5	23.5 ± 0.5	23.3 ± 0.4	23.3 ± 0.5
Food intake (g/mice/day)	6.10 ± 0.71	6.60 ± 0.59	6.60 ± 0.61	6.50 ± 0.81
Water intake (mL/mice/day)	3.80 ± 0.06	4.00 ± 0.03	4.00 ± 0.03	4.00 ± 0.09
Liver (% of BW)	3.80 ± 0.05	3.80 ± 0.22	3.50 ± 0.07	3.50 ± 0.08
Gastrocnemius muscle (% of BW)	1.10 ± 0.03	1.10 ± 0.03	1.10 ± 0.02	1.10 ± 0.02
Tibialis anterior muscle (% of BW)	0.36 ± 0.03	0.36 ± 0.03	0.34 ± 0.02	0.37 ± 0.03
eWAT (% of BW)	1.00 ± 0.05 ^{a}	0.61 ± 0.05 ^{b}	0.60 ± 0.03 ^{b}	0.68 ± 0.04 ^{b}

Data displayed as mean ± S.E.M. Data were analysed using one-way analysis of variance and a *t*-test followed by the Bonferroni multiple comparison test. Different superscripts (a and b) in each row indicate significant differences among groups ($p < 0.05$).

3.2. Exercise Performance in Exhaustion Test

The time before exhaustion in the EX group was shorter than in the NC group ($p < 0.05$); however, the time before exhaustion of the EX and EX + RES25 groups showed no difference. A significant difference was found between the results of the EX and EX + RES150 groups ($p < 0.05$; Figure 2).

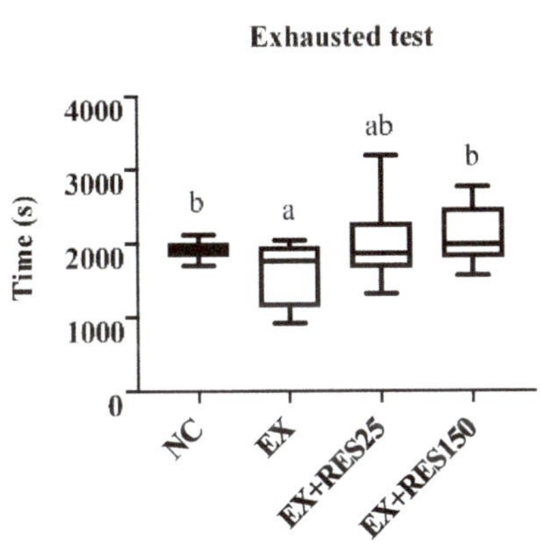

Figure 2. Exhaustion test in different groups. NC: control ($n = 6$); EX: exercise ($n = 6$); EX + RES25: exercise with resveratrol 25 mg/kg ($n = 6$); EX + RES150: exercise with resveratrol 150 mg/kg ($n = 6$). Data are presented as mean ± SEM. Data were analysed using one-way analysis of variance and a *t*-test followed by the Bonferroni multiple comparison test. Superscript letters (a and b) in columns denote a significant difference ($p < 0.05$).

3.3. Lactate Dehydrogenase (LDH) and Creatine Kinase (CK)

The blood biochemical values of the mice after the exhaustion test showed that the levels of LDH and CK in the EX group were significantly higher than those in the NC group ($p < 0.05$). Compared with the NC group, LDH and CK in the EX + RES25 and EX + RES150 groups were also significantly increased ($p < 0.05$ for both), but LDH and CK in the EX + RES150 group were significantly lower than those in the EX group ($p < 0.05$; Figure 3).

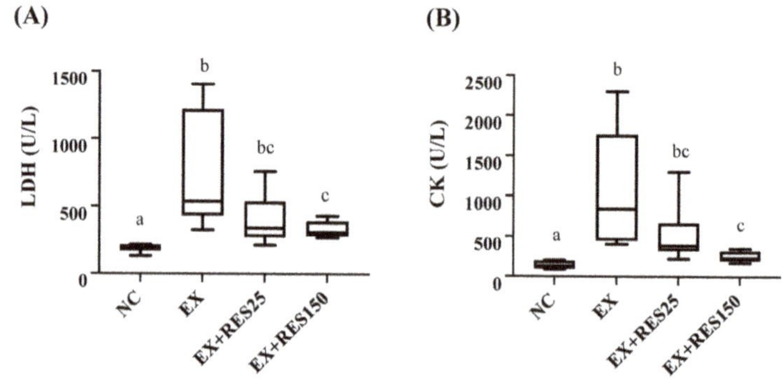

Figure 3. Effects of resveratrol on (**A**) lactate dehydrogenase and (**B**) creatine kinase with eccentric exercise–induced muscle damage. NC: control (n = 6); EX: exercise (n = 6); EX + RES25: exercise with resveratrol 25 mg/kg (n = 6); EX + RES150: exercise with resveratrol 150 mg/kg (n = 6). Data are presented as mean ± SEM. Data were analysed using one-way analysis of variance and a t-test followed by the Bonferroni multiple comparison test. Superscript letters (a, b and c) in columns denote a significant difference ($p < 0.05$).

3.4. Gene Expression of Inflammatory Factors in Muscles

3.4.1. Gastrocnemius Muscle

Compared with that of the NC group and the EX + RES150 group, the mRNA expression of TNF-α in the gastrocnemius muscle was increased higher in the EX group ($p < 0.05$; Figure 4A-1). *Il6* mRNA expression was significantly lower in the EX group than in the other groups ($p < 0.05$; Figure 4B-1).

3.4.2. Tibialis Anterior Muscle

Compared with the NC group, the mRNA expression of TNF-α and IL-6 in the tibialis anterior muscle were significantly higher in the EX, EX + RES25, and EX + RES150 groups ($p < 0.05$; Figure 4A-2,B-2). *Tnfα* mRNA expression in the EX + RES25 and EX + RES150 groups was significantly higher than that in the NC group ($p < 0.05$; Figure 4A-2). The mRNA expression of TNF-α in the EX + RES25 and EX + RES150 groups was significantly lower than that in the EX group (Figure 4A-2). No difference in *Il6* mRNA expression among the four groups was found (Figure 4B-2).

3.4.3. Soleus Muscle

Compared with that of the NC group, the mRNA expression of TNF-α in the soleus muscle was significantly higher in the EX group. After resveratrol was administered, soleus-muscle *Tnfα* mRNA expression in the EX + RES25 and EX + RES150 groups was significantly lower than that in the EX group ($p < 0.05$; Figure 4A-3). No difference in soleus muscle *Il6* mRNA expression between the groups was found (Figure 4B-3).

3.5. Gene Expression of Energy Metabolism and Antioxidant Factors in Muscles

3.5.1. Gastrocnemius Muscle

The results showed that the mRNA expression of SIRT1, AMPK α1, and AMPK α2 in the gastrocnemius muscle in the EX + RES25 group was significantly higher than that in the EX group ($p < 0.05$; Figure 5A,C,D). The mRNA expression levels of GLUT4, AMPK α1, and PGC-1α in the gastrocnemius muscle in the EX + RES150 group were significantly higher than those in the EX group ($p < 0.05$; Figure 5B,C,E). The mRNA expression of SIRT1 and PGC-1α significantly differed between the EX + RES25 and EX + RES150 groups ($p < 0.05$; Figure 5A,E).

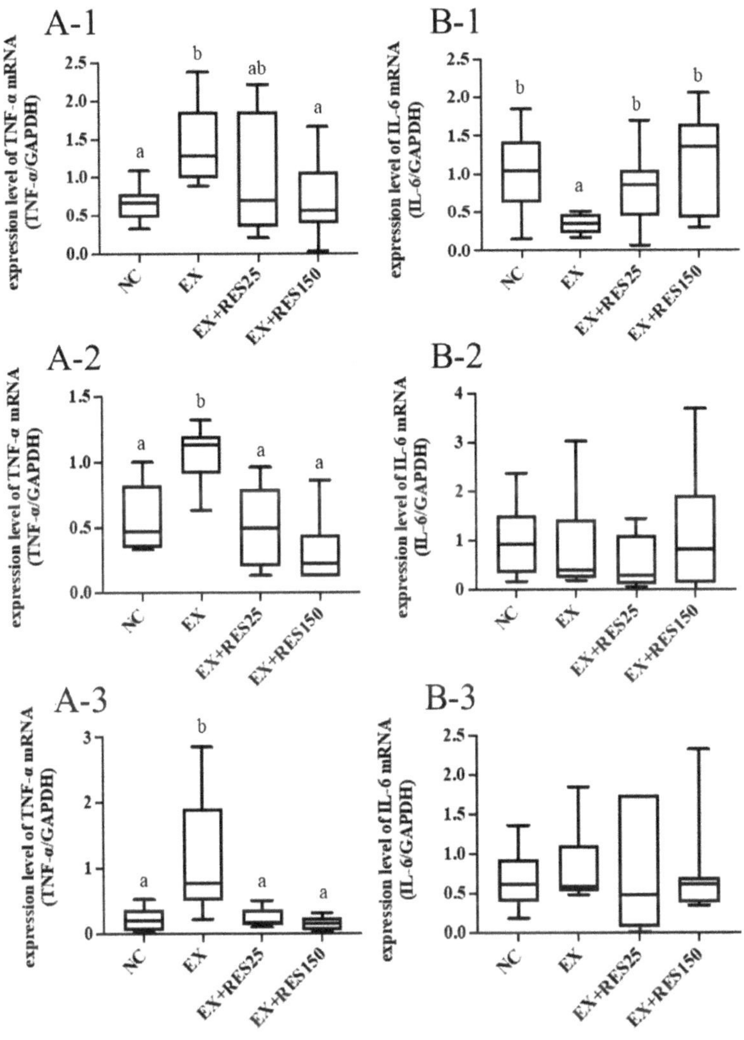

Figure 4. Effects of resveratrol on inflammatory cytokines (**A**) *Tnfα* and (**B**) IL-6 mRNA expression in (1) gastrocnemius muscle, (2) tibialis anterior muscle, and (3) soleus muscle during short-duration downhill running. mRNA expression was normalized to GAPDH and expressed as fold change relative to the control group. NC: control ($n = 6$); EX: exercise ($n = 6$); EX + RES25: exercise with resveratrol 25 mg/kg ($n = 6$); EX + RES150: exercise with resveratrol 150 mg/kg ($n = 6$). Data are presented as mean ± SEM. Data were analysed using one-way analysis of variance and a t-test followed by the Bonferroni multiple comparison test. Superscript letters (a and b) in columns denote a significant difference ($p < 0.05$).

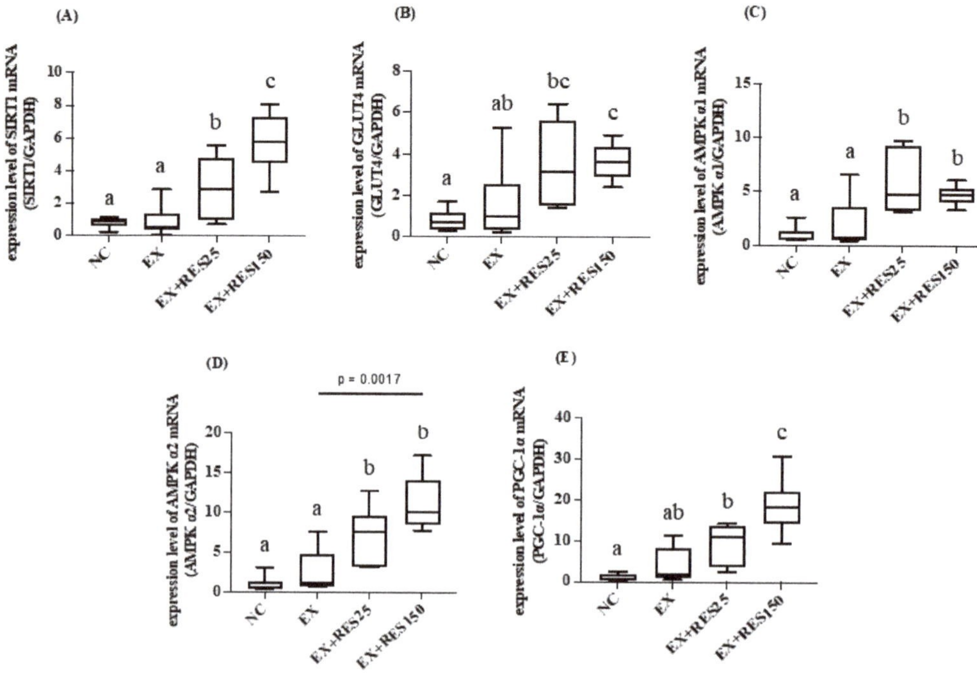

Figure 5. Effects of resveratrol on energy utilization and antioxidative mRNA expression in gastrocnemius muscle during short-duration downhill running. (**A**) *Sirt1* mRNA (**B**) *Ampkα1* mRNA (**C**) *Ampkα2* mRNA (**D**) *Glut4* mRNA (**E**) *Pgc1α* mRNA. mRNA expression was normalized to GAPDH and is expressed in terms of fold change relative to the control group. NC: control ($n = 6$); EX: exercise ($n = 6$); EX + RES25: exercise with resveratrol 25 mg/kg ($n = 6$); EX + RES150: exercise with resveratrol 150 mg/kg ($n = 6$). Data are presented as mean ± SEM. Data were analysed using one-way analysis of variance and a t-test followed by the Bonferroni multiple comparison test. Superscript letters (a, b and c) in columns denote a significant difference ($p < 0.05$).

3.5.2. Tibialis Anterior Muscle

The mRNA expression levels of SIRT1 and AMPK α1 in the tibialis anterior muscle in the EX + RES150 group were significantly higher compared with those in the NC and EX groups ($p < 0.05$; Figure 6A,C). The mRNA expression of AMPK α1 increased significantly with resveratrol dosage, exhibiting a dose-dependent effect in the two RES groups ($p < 0.05$; Figure 6C). The mRNA expression of PGC-1α was significantly higher in the EX, EX + RES25, and EX + RES150 groups than in the NC group ($p < 0.05$; Figure 6E). No difference between the groups in the expression of GLUT4 and AMPK α2 was found (Figure 6B,D).

3.5.3. Soleus Muscle

The soleus muscle mRNA expression levels of SIRT1, GLUT4, AMPK α1, AMPK α2, and PGC-1α in the EX + RES150 group were significantly higher than in the NC group ($p < 0.05$; Figure 6). *Sirt1*, *Glut4*, *Ampkα2*, and *Pgc1α* mRNA expression increased with resveratrol dosage significantly ($p < 0.05$; Figure 7A,B,D,E). The mRNA expression level of GLUT4 in the EX group was significantly lower than in the NC group (Figure 7B).

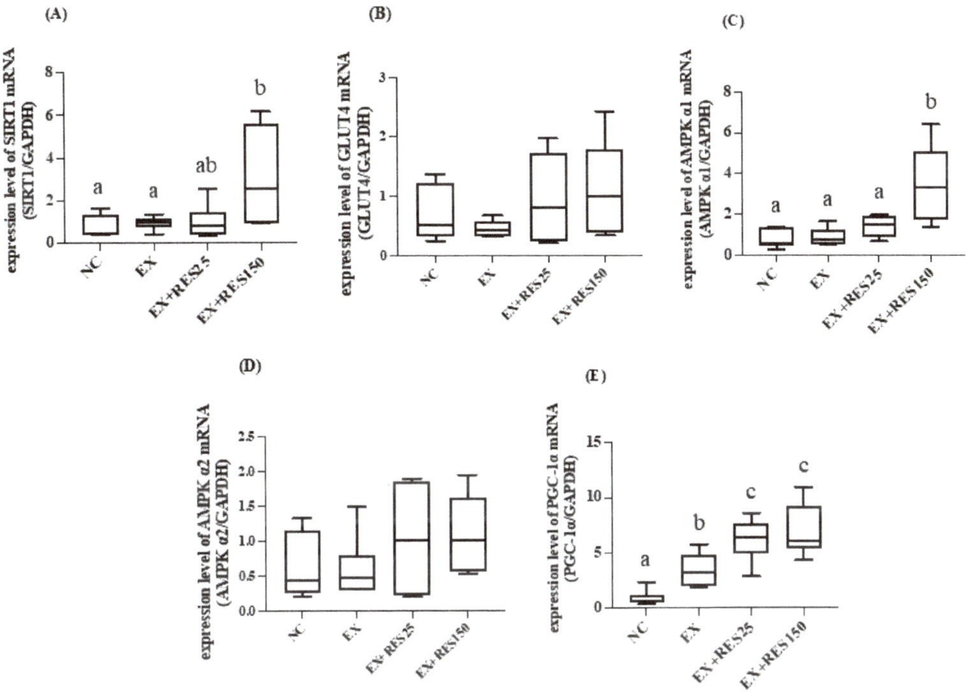

Figure 6. Effects of resveratrol on energy utilization and antioxidative mRNA expression in tibialis anterior muscle during short-duration downhill running training. (**A**) *Sirt1* mRNA (**B**) *Ampkα1* mRNA (**C**) *Ampkα2* mRNA (**D**) *Glut4* mRNA (**E**) *Pgc1α* mRNA. mRNA expression was normalized to GAPDH and is expressed in terms of fold change relative to the control group. NC: control ($n = 6$); EX: exercise ($n = 6$); EX + RES25: exercise with resveratrol 25 mg/kg ($n = 6$); EX + RES150: exercise with resveratrol 150 mg/kg ($n = 6$). Data are presented as mean ± SEM. Data were analysed using one-way analysis of variance and a t-test followed by the Bonferroni multiple comparison test. Superscript letters (a, b and c) in columns denote a significant difference ($p < 0.05$).

3.6. MA Plot, Volcano Plot, and Bar Charts for EX vs. EX + RES150 Groups

In the EX and EX + RES150 groups, 37 genes were more significantly upregulated, and 77 genes were more significantly downregulated in the high-dose group than in the EX group (Figure 8).

As shown in the biological process plot, pathway regulation occurred due to the intervention of high-dose resveratrol, such as the positive regulation of cytokine production (Figure 9A). Analysis of molecular function showed that the regulation of pathways related to energy hydrolysis enzymes also occurred, indicated, for example, by nucleoside-triphosphatase regulator activity and GTPase regulator activity (Figure 9B). In addition, as shown by the cellular component bar chart, most regulated pathways were found to be related to immunity, such as MHC class II proteins or lysosomal membrane proteins (Figure 9C). Higher doses of resveratrol have a greater effect on facial features during exercise and may have greater anti-inflammatory, energy utilisation-related, and immune-boosting effects.

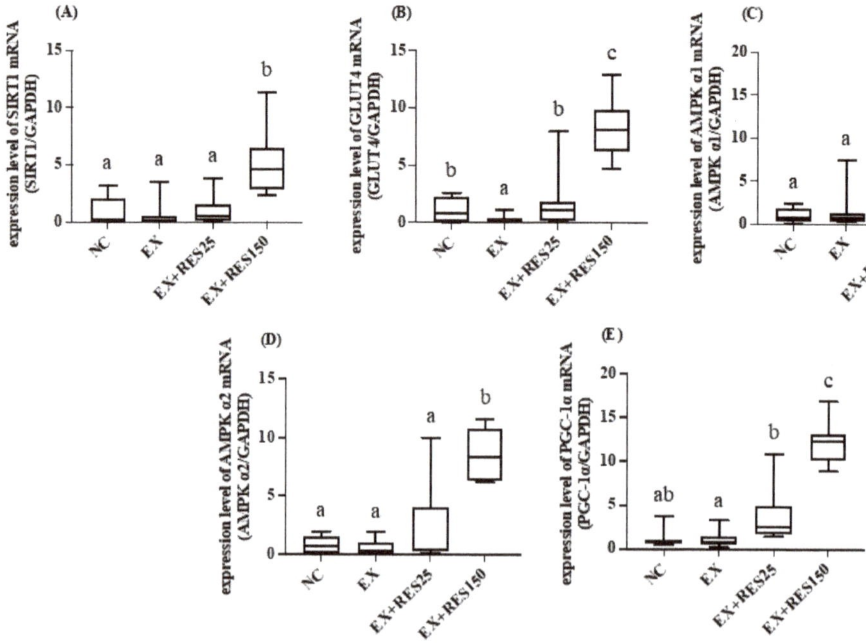

Figure 7. Effects of resveratrol on energy utilization and antioxidative mRNA expression in soleus muscle during short-duration downhill running training. (**A**) *Sirt1* mRNA (**B**) *Ampkα1* mRNA (**C**) *Ampα2* mRNA (**D**) *Glut4* mRNA (**E**) *Pgc1α* mRNA. mRNA expression was normalized to GAPDH and is expressed in terms of fold change relative to the control group. NC: control (n = 6); EX: exercise (n = 6); EX + RES25: exercise with resveratrol 25 mg/kg (n = 6); EX + RES150: exercise with resveratrol 150 mg/kg (n = 6). Data are presented as mean ± SEM. Data were analysed using one-way analysis of variance and a t-test followed by the Bonferroni multiple comparison test. Superscript letters (a, b and c) in columns denote a significant difference ($p < 0.05$).

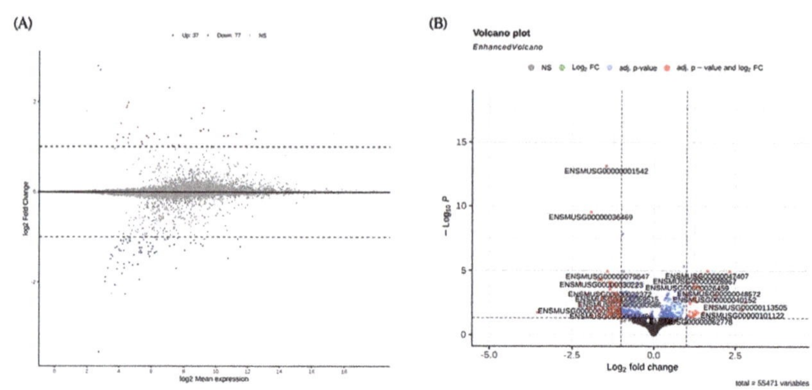

Figure 8. Different gene expression in EX + RES150 and EX groups. (**A**) MA plot illustrating the distribution of upregulated and downregulated genes (coloured dots) for EX + RES150 group vs. EX group; (**B**) volcano plot illustrating significance and fold change of the up and downregulated genes (coloured dots) for EX + RES150 group vs. EX group.

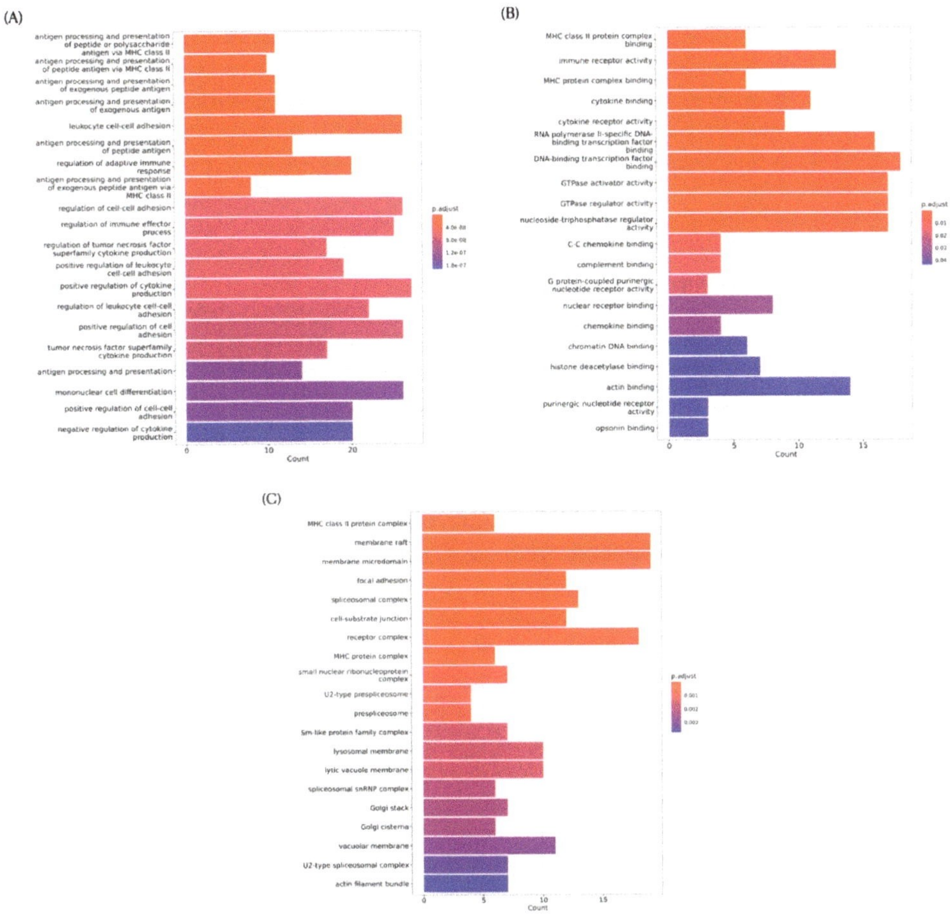

Figure 9. Gene ontology (GO) analysis of EX + RES150 group vs. NC group. (**A**) GO analysis of biological process pathways for EX + RES150 group vs. EX group; (**B**) GO analysis of molecular function pathways for EX + RES150 group vs. EX group; (**C**) GO analysis of cellular component pathways for EX + RES150 group vs. EX group.

4. Discussion

In this experiment, we used short-duration downhill running and different dosages of resveratrol to evaluate inflammation and energy utilisation in the different muscles of mice. The main findings were: (1) the time before exhaustion decreased due to exercise injury; this was counteracted by the intervention of resveratrol; (2) inflammation in the muscles was reduced by the intervention of resveratrol; (3) the expression of genes related to energy utilisation in the EX + RES150 group was significantly higher than in the EX group, indicating that the intervention of resveratrol increases muscle energy utilisation.

The time to exhaustion in the EX group was significantly lower than that in the NC, EX + RES25, and EX + RES150 groups. The results of this experiment demonstrate that resveratrol supplementation is beneficial for endurance exercise. Our study found no difference in endurance performance between the low-dose group and the high-dose group. This difference between this study and ours may have been due to differences in exercise mode (weight-loaded swimming in the previous study).

TNF-α and IL-6 levels are often used to indicate inflammation. When an inflammatory response occurs, the production of cytokines in injured tissues increases significantly. *Tnfα* mRNA expression in the EX group was significantly higher than that in the NC group, confirming that exercise injury elevated the production of TNF-α [30]. Resveratrol effectively reduced inflammation; high doses of resveratrol exerted anti-inflammatory effects in different muscles. In long-duration exercises, reaching exhaustion always results in high levels of oxidative stress. A high-intensity cycling-based clinical trial demonstrated that resveratrol supplementation attenuated exercise-induced serum interleukin-6 levels but not oxidative stress [31]. Such physical phenomena imply that resveratrol affects anti-inflammation and antioxidation processes independently. IL-6 production is positively correlated with glucose uptake by GLUT4 in muscles [32–34]. In our study, the mRNA expression of IL-6 did not differ between different muscle tissues, but the repression of *Glut4* mRNA was observed in the gastrocnemius and soleus muscles. This suggests that increased mRNA levels of IL-6 and GLUT4 occur synchronously; thus, IL-6 may trigger GLUT4-induced glucose utilisation in muscle.

Many studies have found that during endurance exercise, due to the reduction in available glycogen in the body, more AMPK is activated to facilitate the production of downstream products, providing the body with energy [35]. During exercise, the intervention of resveratrol resulted in the activation not only of AMPK but also SIRT1 and its downstream proteins GLUT4 and PGC-1α and in miR-22-3p in a muscle cell model [36]. Resveratrol also exhibited dual bioactive effects in our study; however, the effects of resveratrol remain unclear.

Type I muscle fibres support long-duration exercise, type II fibres support explosive short-duration exercise, and type IIx fibres transform into different types of fibres in relation to the intensity of the physical activity at hand [37]. The mRNA expression of AMPK α1 in the gastrocnemius and tibialis anterior muscles in the EX group did not differ from that in the NC group. We hypothesise that the type IIx muscle fibres in these muscles were not converted into type I muscle fibres because the exercise period was not long enough for the fibres to adapt to endurance exercise. The effect of resveratrol on AMPK activation in the gastrocnemius and tibialis anterior muscles was greater than that caused by exercise. However, no differences in *Ampkα1* and *Ampkα2* mRNA expression in the soleus muscle between the EX and the NC groups were found. These apparently conflicting results were also observed in a 12-week study [38], and we speculate that the two-week duration of this experiment was insufficient for a long-term exercise study. However, the soleus muscle has a high proportion of red muscle, which supports aerobic exercise. Thus, the significant differences between the NC and EX groups can be attributed to resveratrol intervention.

The mRNA expression of GLUT4 in the gastrocnemius muscle and soleus muscle in the EX + RES150 group was significantly higher than that in the EX group. This result is consistent with the findings of a previous study that the intervention of resveratrol in muscle cells effectively increases the amount of GLUT4 translocated to the plasma membrane [39]. The tibialis anterior muscle does not exhibit similar effects; the ratio of red to white muscle in the tibialis anterior muscle may contribute to this [38]. Studies have demonstrated that white muscle fibres can activate GLUT4 translocation during exercise [40]; the gastrocnemius muscle has a higher proportion of white muscle and exhibits higher *Glut4* mRNA expression. Pereira BC et al. reported that excessive eccentric contraction training impairs insulin signal transduction in mice's skeletal muscles and reduces the rate of GLUT4 translocation [41]. Thus, muscle injury may have caused the mRNA expression of GLUT4 in the soleus muscle in the EX group to be significantly lower than in the other groups.

As an oxidoreductase, SIRT1 regulates various cellular events, including apoptosis, cell survival, endocrine signalling, and gene transcription [42]. SIRT1 activates the downstream product PGC-1α, and PGC-1α regulates mitochondrial biosynthesis to facilitate the regulation of oxidative metabolism [43]. The mRNA expression of SIRT1 and PGC-1α in the gastrocnemius muscle, tibialis anterior muscle, and soleus muscle increased significantly with the intervention of high-dose resveratrol compared with the NC group, which is consistent with the results of previous studies [44], indicating resveratrol intervention for short-duration exercise can effectively increase energy utilisation and cause an antioxidising effect.

In this study, we assessed genome expression under resveratrol intervention in short-duration eccentric contraction exercises. We focused on muscle inflammation and energy utilisation–related gene expression. One gene that was intensively activated after high-dose resveratrol intervention was myosin light chain kinase 2 (ENSMUSG00000027470), which is intensively expressed in cardiac and skeletal muscle [45] and regulates the interaction of myosin and actin through the concentration of calcium ions protein cross bridge [46]. In this experiment, high-dose resveratrol intensively activated this gene, thus we hypothesise that resveratrol increases muscle contraction ability during exercise. NADH dehydrogenase subunit 5 (ENSMUSG00000064367) is part of mitochondrial complex I, a large enzyme complex that is active in mitochondria [47]. We found that this gene was upregulated in the presence of intervening resveratrol. Therefore, we hypothesise that due to the increase in the expression of this gene, oxidative phosphorylation on the inner mitochondrial membrane and the production of ATP increased, providing the cell with more energy and thereby increasing the utilisation of energy during exercise. Gene ontology enrichment table of EX vs. EX + RES150 included biological process, molec-ular function and cellular component is shown in Supplementary Table S1.

5. Conclusions

High-dose resveratrol intervention prolonged the time before exhaustion for short-duration downhill running. High-dose resveratrol intervention decreased *Tnfα* mRNA expression and enhanced the mRNA expressions of SIRT1, GLUT4, AMPK α1, and AMPK α2 in some muscles. These results indicate that high-dose resveratrol supplementation can reduce inflammation and oxidation and improve the utilisation of energy during short-duration high-intensity exercise.

Supplementary Materials: The following supporting information can be downloaded at: https://www.mdpi.com/article/10.3390/nu15010249/s1, Table S1: Gene ontology enrichment table of EX vs. EX+RES150— biological process, molecular function & cellular component.

Author Contributions: The authors' responsibilities were as follows: Data curation, L.-Y.S.; formal analysis, L.-Y.S.; funding acquisition, S.-Y.H.; investigation, L.-Y.S., T.-H.T. and L.B.P.H.; methodology, L.-Y.S., T.-H.T., W.-C.H., N.-W.K., and S.-Y.H.; project administration, L.-Y.S.; resources, W.-C.H., N.-W.K., and S.-Y.H.; software, L.-Y.S.; supervision, S.-Y.H.; validation, L.-Y.S.; visualisation, L.-Y.S.; writing-original draft, L.-Y.S. and S.-Y.H.; writing-review and editing, S.-Y.H. All authors participated in the analytical discussion of the results. All authors will be informed about each step of the manuscript's processing by the journal, including calls for submission and revision, by email. All authors have read and agreed to the published version of the manuscript.

Funding: This study was supported by grants from the Taiwan National Science and Technology Council (109-2314-B-038-007, 109-2320-B-038-057-MY3, and 110-2314-B-038-154).

Institutional Review Board Statement: All animal experimental protocols were reviewed and approved by the Institutional Animal Care and Use Committee of Taipei Medical University (LAC-2021-0310).

Informed Consent Statement: Not applicable.

Data Availability Statement: Not applicable.

Acknowledgments: Authors appreciated the technical assistances from Core Facility Center of Taipei Medical University.

Conflicts of Interest: The authors declare no conflict of interest. The funders had no role in the design of the study; in the collection, analyses, or interpretation of data; in the writing of the manuscript, or in the decision to publish the results.

Abbreviations

AMPK: AMP activated protein kinase; CK, creatine kinase; COX-2, cyclooxygenase-2; DOMS, delayed onset muscle soreness; EC, excitation-contraction; EV, exhaustion velocity; FOXO1, forkhead box O1; GSH, glutathione; GSH-PX, glutathione peroxidase; GSSG, oxidized glutathione; HIIT, high intensity interval training; IGF-1, insulin-like growth factor-1; IL-1, interleukin-1; IL-6, interleukin-6; IL-10, interleukin-10, LDH, lactate dehydrogenase; MDA, malondialdehyde, NFAT, nuclear factor of activated T cells; NF-κB, nuclear factor kappa-light-chain-enhancer of activated B cells; PGC-1α, peroxisome proliferator-activated receptor gamma coactivator 1-alpha; ROS, reactive oxygen species; TBARS, 2-thiobarbituric acid reacting substances test; TNF-α, tumor necrosis factor- α; SIRT 1, sirtuin 1.

References

1. Mujika, I.; Rønnestad, B.R.; Martin, D.T. Effects of Increased Muscle Strength and Muscle Mass on Endurance-Cycling Performance. *Int. J. Sports Physiol. Perform.* **2016**, *11*, 283–289. [CrossRef] [PubMed]
2. Stricker, P.R.; Faigenbaum, A.D.; McCambridge, T.M.; LaBella, C.R.; Brooks, M.A.; Canty, G.; Diamond, A.B.; Hennrikus, W.; Logan, K.; Moffatt, K.; et al. Resistance Training for Children and Adolescents. *Pediatrics* **2020**, *145*, e20201011. [CrossRef] [PubMed]
3. Kirwan, J.P.; Sacks, J.; Nieuwoudt, S. The essential role of exercise in the management of type 2 diabetes. *Clevel. Clin. J. Med.* **2017**, *84*, S15–S21. [CrossRef] [PubMed]
4. Peake, J.M.; Neubauer, O.; Della Gatta, P.A.; Nosaka, K. Muscle damage and inflammation during recovery from exercise. *J. Appl. Physiol.* **2017**, *122*, 559–570. [CrossRef] [PubMed]
5. Mills, C.D.; Kincaid, K.; Alt, J.M.; Heilman, M.J.; Hill, A.M. M-1/M-2 Macrophages and the Th1/Th2 Paradigm. *J. Immunol.* **2000**, *164*, 6166–6173. [CrossRef]
6. Dumont, N.A.; Bentzinger, C.F.; Sincennes, M.C.; Rudnicki, M.A. Satellite Cells and Skeletal Muscle Regeneration. *Compr. Physiol.* **2015**, *5*, 1027–1059. [CrossRef]
7. Saltiel, A.R.; Olefsky, J.M. Inflammatory mechanisms linking obesity and metabolic disease. *J. Clin. Investig.* **2017**, *127*, 1–4. [CrossRef]
8. Alway, S.E.; McCrory, J.L.; Kearcher, K.; Vickers, A.; Frear, B.; Gilleland, D.L.; Bonner, D.E.; Thomas, J.M.; Donley, D.A.; Lively, M.W.; et al. Resveratrol Enhances Exercise-Induced Cellular and Functional Adaptations of Skeletal Muscle in Older Men and Women. *J. Gerontol. Ser. A* **2017**, *72*, 1595–1606. [CrossRef]
9. Morgan, D.L.; Allen, D.G. Early events in stretch-induced muscle damage. *J. Appl. Physiol.* **1999**, *87*, 2007–2015. [CrossRef]
10. Warren, G.L.; Ingalls, C.P.; Lowe, D.A.; Armstrong, R.B. Excitation-Contraction Uncoupling: Major Role in Contraction-Induced Muscle Injury. *Exerc. Sport Sci. Rev.* **2001**, *29*, 82–87. [CrossRef]
11. Thomson, D. The Role of AMPK in the Regulation of Skeletal Muscle Size, Hypertrophy, and Regeneration. *Int. J. Mol. Sci.* **2018**, *19*, 3125. [CrossRef] [PubMed]
12. Huang, C.-C.; Liu, C.-C.; Tsao, J.-P.; Hsu, C.-L.; Cheng, I.-S. Effects of Oral Resveratrol Supplementation on Glycogen Replenishment and Mitochondria Biogenesis in Exercised Human Skeletal Muscle. *Nutrients* **2020**, *12*, 3721. [CrossRef] [PubMed]
13. Andrade, F.H.; Reid, M.B.; Allen, D.G.; Westerblad, H. Effect of hydrogen peroxide and dithiothreitol on contractile function of single skeletal muscle fibres from the mouse. *J. Physiol.* **1998**, *509*, 565–575. [CrossRef]
14. Sakellariou, G.K.; Vasilaki, A.; Palomero, J.; Kayani, A.; Zibrik, L.; McArdle, A.; Jackson, M. Studies of Mitochondrial and Nonmitochondrial Sources Implicate Nicotinamide Adenine Dinucleotide Phosphate Oxidase(s) in the Increased Skeletal Muscle Superoxide Generation That Occurs During Contractile Activity. *Antioxid. Redox Signal.* **2013**, *18*, 603–621. [CrossRef]
15. Cheng, A.J.; Bruton, J.D.; Lanner, J.T.; Westerblad, H. Antioxidant treatments do not improve force recovery after fatiguing stimulation of mouse skeletal muscle fibres. *J. Physiol.* **2015**, *593*, 457–472. [CrossRef]
16. Tanskanen, M.; Atalay, M.; Uusitalo, A. Altered oxidative stress in overtrained athletes. *J. Sports Sci.* **2010**, *28*, 309–317. [CrossRef]
17. Yamada, T.; Abe, M.; Lee, J.; Tatebayashi, D.; Himori, K.; Kanzaki, K.; Wada, M.; Bruton, J.D.; Westerblad, H.; Lanner, J.T. Muscle dysfunction associated with adjuvant-induced arthritis is prevented by antioxidant treatment. *Skelet. Muscle* **2015**, *5*, 20. [CrossRef]
18. Berman, A.Y.; Motechin, R.A.; Wiesenfeld, M.Y.; Holz, M.K. The therapeutic potential of resveratrol: A review of clinical trials. *NPJ Precis. Oncol.* **2017**, *1*, 35. [CrossRef]
19. Zhou, D.-D.; Luo, M.; Huang, S.-Y.; Saimaiti, A.; Shang, A.; Gan, R.-Y.; Li, H.-B. Effects and Mechanisms of Resveratrol on Aging and Age-Related Diseases. *Oxidative Med. Cell. Longev.* **2021**, *2021*, 9932218. [CrossRef] [PubMed]
20. Meng, T.; Xiao, D.; Muhammed, A.; Deng, J.; Chen, L.; He, J. Anti-Inflammatory Action and Mechanisms of Resveratrol. *Molecules* **2021**, *26*, 229. [CrossRef]
21. Williams, L.D.; Burdock, G.A.; Edwards, J.A.; Beck, M.; Bausch, J. Safety studies conducted on high-purity trans-resveratrol in experimental animals. *Food Chem. Toxicol.* **2009**, *47*, 2170–2182. [CrossRef] [PubMed]
22. Novelle, M.G.; Wahl, D.; Diéguez, C.; Bernier, M.; De Cabo, R. Resveratrol supplementation: Where are we now and where should we go? *Ageing Res. Rev.* **2015**, *21*, 1–15. [CrossRef]

23. Springer, M.; Moco, S. Resveratrol and Its Human Metabolites—Effects on Metabolic Health and Obesity. *Nutrients* **2019**, *11*, 143. [CrossRef] [PubMed]
24. Ferreira, J.C.B.; Rolim, N.P.L.; Bartholomeu, J.B.; Gobatto, C.; Kokubun, E.; Brum, P.C. Maximal Lactate Steady State in Running Mice: Effect of Exercise Training. *Clin. Exp. Pharmacol. Physiol.* **2007**, *34*, 760–765. [CrossRef] [PubMed]
25. Pinto, A.P.; da Rocha, A.L.; Cabrera, E.M.; Marafon, B.B.; Kohama, E.B.; Rovina, R.L.; Simabuco, F.M.; Junior, C.R.B.; de Moura, L.P.; Pauli, J.R.; et al. Role of interleukin-6 in inhibiting hepatic autophagy markers in exercised mice. *Cytokine* **2020**, *130*, 155085. [CrossRef] [PubMed]
26. Bolger, A.M.; Lohse, M.; Usadel, B. Trimmomatic: A flexible trimmer for Illumina sequence data. *Bioinformatics* **2014**, *30*, 2114–2120. [CrossRef]
27. Langmead, B.; Salzberg, S.L. Fast gapped-read alignment with Bowtie 2. *Nat. Methods* **2012**, *9*, 357–359. [CrossRef]
28. Li, B.; Dewey, C.N. RSEM: Accurate transcript quantification from RNA-Seq data with or without a reference genome. *BMC Bioinform.* **2011**, *12*, 323. [CrossRef]
29. Ashburner, M.; Ball, C.A.; Blake, J.A.; Botstein, D.; Butler, H.; Cherry, J.M.; Davis, A.P.; Dolinski, K.; Dwight, S.S.; Eppig, J.T.; et al. Gene ontology: Tool for the unification of biology. *Nat. Genet.* **2000**, *25*, 25–29. [CrossRef]
30. Tomazoni, S.S.; Machado, C.D.S.M.; De Marchi, T.; Casalechi, H.L.; Bjordal, J.M.; Carvalho, P.D.T.C.D.; Leal-Junior, E.C.P. Infrared Low-Level Laser Therapy (Photobiomodulation Therapy) before Intense Progressive Running Test of High-Level Soccer Players: Effects on Functional, Muscle Damage, Inflammatory, and Oxidative Stress Markers—A Randomized Controlled Trial. *Oxidative Med. Cell. Longev.* **2019**, *2019*, 6239058. [CrossRef]
31. Tsao, J.-P.; Liu, C.-C.; Wang, H.-F.; Bernard, J.R.; Huang, C.-C.; Cheng, I.-S. Oral Resveratrol supplementation attenuates exercise-induced Interleukin-6 but not Oxidative Stress after a high intensity cycling challenge in adults. *Int. J. Med. Sci.* **2021**, *18*, 2137–2145. [CrossRef] [PubMed]
32. Helge, J.W.; Stallknecht, B.; Pedersen, B.K.; Galbo, H.; Kiens, B.; Richter, E.A. The effect of graded exercise on IL-6 release and glucose uptake in human skeletal muscle. *J. Physiol.* **2003**, *546*, 299–305. [CrossRef] [PubMed]
33. Marko, D.M.; Foran, G.; Vlavcheski, F.; Baron, D.C.; Hayward, G.C.; Baranowski, B.J.; Necakov, A.; Tsiani, E.; MacPherson, R.E.K. Interleukin-6 Treatment Results in GLUT4 Translocation and AMPK Phosphorylation in Neuronal SH-SY5Y Cells. *Cells* **2020**, *9*, 1114. [CrossRef]
34. Ikeda, S.-I.; Tamura, Y.; Kakehi, S.; Sanada, H.; Kawamori, R.; Watada, H. Exercise-induced increase in IL-6 level enhances GLUT4 expression and insulin sensitivity in mouse skeletal muscle. *Biochem. Biophys. Res. Commun.* **2016**, *473*, 947–952. [CrossRef] [PubMed]
35. Hawley, J.A.; Lundby, C.; Cotter, J.D.; Burke, L.M. Maximizing Cellular Adaptation to Endurance Exercise in Skeletal Muscle. *Cell Metab.* **2018**, *27*, 962–976. [CrossRef] [PubMed]
36. Wen, W.; Chen, X.; Huang, Z.; Chen, D.; Chen, H.; Luo, Y.; He, J.; Zheng, P.; Yu, J.; Yu, B. Resveratrol regulates muscle fiber type conversion via miR-22-3p and AMPK/SIRT1/PGC-1α pathway. *J. Nutr. Biochem.* **2020**, *77*, 108297. [CrossRef] [PubMed]
37. Ruple, B.A.; Godwin, J.S.; Mesquita, P.H.C.; Osburn, S.C.; Sexton, C.L.; Smith, M.A.; Ogletree, J.C.; Goodlett, M.D.; Edison, J.L.; Ferrando, A.A.; et al. Myofibril and Mitochondrial Area Changes in Type I and II Fibers Following 10 Weeks of Resistance Training in Previously Untrained Men. *Front. Physiol.* **2021**, *12*, 728683. [CrossRef]
38. Tarini, V.A.F.; Carnevali, L.C.; Arida, R.M.; Cunha, C.A.; Alves, E.S.; Seeleander, M.C.L.; Schmidt, B.; Faloppa, F. Effect of exhaustive ultra-endurance exercise in muscular glycogen and both Alpha1 and Alpha2 Ampk protein expression in trained rats. *J. Physiol. Biochem.* **2013**, *69*, 429–440. [CrossRef]
39. Vlavcheski, F.; Hartogh, D.J.D.; Giacca, A.; Tsiani, E. Amelioration of High-Insulin-Induced Skeletal Muscle Cell Insulin Resistance by Resveratrol Is Linked to Activation of AMPK and Restoration of GLUT4 Translocation. *Nutrients* **2020**, *12*, 914. [CrossRef]
40. Stuart, C.A.; Howell, M.E.A.; Baker, J.D.; Dykes, R.J.; Duffourc, M.M.; Ramsey, M.W.; Stone, M.H. Cycle Training Increased GLUT4 and Activation of Mammalian Target of Rapamycin in Fast Twitch Muscle Fibers. *Med. Sci. Sports Exerc.* **2010**, *42*, 96–106. [CrossRef]
41. Pereira, B.C.; da Rocha, A.L.; Pinto, A.P.; Pauli, J.R.; Moura, L.P.; Mekary, R.A.; de Freitas, E.C.; da Silva, A.S.R. Excessive training impairs the insulin signal transduction in mice skeletal muscles. *J. Endocrinol.* **2016**, *230*, 93–104. [CrossRef] [PubMed]
42. Sakamoto, J.; Miura, T.; Shimamoto, K.; Horio, Y. Predominant expression of Sir2α, an NAD-dependent histone deacetylase, in the embryonic mouse heart and brain. *FEBS Lett.* **2004**, *556*, 281–286. [CrossRef]
43. Waldman, M.; Cohen, K.; Yadin, D.; Nudelman, V.; Gorfil, D.; Laniado-Schwartzman, M.; Kornwoski, R.; Aravot, D.; Abraham, N.G.; Arad, M.; et al. Regulation of diabetic cardiomyopathy by caloric restriction is mediated by intracellular signaling pathways involving 'SIRT1 and PGC-1α'. *Cardiovasc. Diabetol.* **2018**, *17*, 111. [CrossRef]
44. Nishigaki, A.; Kido, T.; Kida, N.; Kakita-Kobayashi, M.; Tsubokura, H.; Hisamatsu, Y.; Okada, H. Resveratrol protects mitochondrial quantity by activating SIRT1/PGC-1α expression during ovarian hypoxia. *Reprod. Med. Biol.* **2020**, *19*, 189–197. [CrossRef] [PubMed]
45. Soung, Y.H.; Lee, J.W.; Kim, S.Y.; Nam, S.W.; Park, W.S.; Lee, J.Y.; Yoo, N.J.; Lee, S.H. Mutational analysis of the kinase domain of MYLK2 gene in common human cancers. *Pathol. Res. Pract.* **2006**, *202*, 137–140. [CrossRef] [PubMed]

46. Hu, Z.; Cao, J.; Zhang, J.; Ge, L.; Zhang, H.; Liu, X. Skeletal Muscle Transcriptome Analysis of Hanzhong Ma Duck at Different Growth Stages Using RNA-Seq. *Biomolecules* **2021**, *11*, 315. [CrossRef] [PubMed]
47. Bourges, I.; Ramus, C.; de Camaret, B.M.; Beugnot, R.; Remacle, C.; Cardol, P.; Hofhaus, G.; Issartel, J.-P. Structural organization of mitochondrial human complex I: Role of the ND4 and ND5 mitochondria-encoded subunits and interaction with prohibitin. *Biochem. J.* **2004**, *383*, 491–499. [CrossRef] [PubMed]

nutrients MDPI

Review

Dietary Supplementation for Attenuating Exercise-Induced Muscle Damage and Delayed-Onset Muscle Soreness in Humans

Yoko Tanabe [1,2,*], **Naoto Fujii** [1,2] **and Katsuhiko Suzuki** [3,*]

[1] Faculty of Health and Sport Sciences, University of Tsukuba, Ibaraki 305-8574, Japan; fujii.naoto.gb@u.tsukuba.ac.jp
[2] Advanced Research Initiative for Human High Performance (ARIHHP), University of Tsukuba, Ibaraki 305-8574, Japan
[3] Faculty of Sport Sciences, Waseda University, Saitama 359-1192, Japan
* Correspondence: tanabe.yoko.gt@u.tsukuba.ac.jp (Y.T.); katsu.suzu@waseda.jp (K.S.); Tel.: +81-4-2947-6898 (K.S.)

Abstract: Dietary supplements are widely used as a nutritional strategy to improve and maintain performance and achieve faster recovery in sports and exercise. Exercise-induced muscle damage (EIMD) is caused by mechanical stress and subsequent inflammatory responses including reactive oxygen species and cytokine production. Therefore, dietary supplements with anti-inflammatory and antioxidant properties have the potential to prevent and reduce muscle damage and symptoms characterized by loss of muscle strength and delayed-onset muscle soreness (DOMS). However, only a few supplements are considered to be effective at present. This review focuses on the effects of dietary supplements derived from phytochemicals and listed in the International Olympic Committee consensus statement on muscle damage evaluated by blood myofiber damage markers, muscle soreness, performance, and inflammatory and oxidative stress markers. In this review, the effects of dietary supplements are also discussed in terms of study design (i.e., parallel and crossover studies), exercise model, and such subject characteristics as physical fitness level. Future perspectives and considerations for the use of dietary supplements to alleviate EIMD and DOMS are also discussed.

Keywords: curcumin; tart cherry juice; beetroot juice; quercetin; isothiocyanate; oxidative stress; cytokines; inflammation; supplementation strategies; nutritional intervention; athletes

Citation: Tanabe, Y.; Fujii, N.; Suzuki, K. Dietary Supplementation for Attenuating Exercise-Induced Muscle Damage and Delayed-Onset Muscle Soreness in Humans. *Nutrients* **2022**, *14*, 70. https://doi.org/10.3390/nu14010070

Academic Editor: David C. Nieman

Received: 26 November 2021
Accepted: 20 December 2021
Published: 24 December 2021

1. Introduction

Unaccustomed, strenuous high-intensity, or long-duration exercise can induce muscle damage, so-called exercise-induced muscle damage (EIMD). EIMD is characterized by a primary response as a result of mechanical stress that occurs during exercise and a secondary inflammatory response [1,2]. Mechanical force, especially that induced by eccentric contraction, leads to the primary response. More specifically, the overstretching and disruption of sarcomeres, followed by increased Ca^{2+} influx into the muscle cells, result in muscle passive tension and myofibrillar disruption [3]. These responses subsequently trigger secondary inflammatory responses, including the production of reactive oxygen species (ROS) and cytokines, by promoting the activation of transcription factors [e.g., nuclear factor-kappa B (NF-κB), mitogen-activated protein kinase (MAPK), and nuclear factor erythroid 2-related factor 2 (Nrf2)]. In addition, ROS and cytokines can be released from neutrophils and phagocytic macrophages [4,5]. ROS and exercise-induced inflammatory responses are essential for muscle repair, regeneration, and adaptation of redox signaling pathways; however, if left uncontrolled, they can result in cell infiltration into the damaged tissues, accelerating secondary muscle damage. Consequently, EIMD appears to cause several symptoms, such as loss of muscle function (e.g., force loss and reduced range of motion), delayed-onset muscle soreness (DOMS), and increased leakage of muscle proteins, such as creatine kinase (CK), myoglobin (Mb), and aspartate transaminase (AST), into the circulation. These symptoms can attenuate exercise performance. Therefore, it is important to minimize these symptoms to optimize athletic performance and conditioning as well.

Several nutritional strategies have been proposed to restore muscle function, relieve DOMS, and reduce inflammation after exercise. Based on the International Olympic Committee (IOC) consensus statement on dietary supplements and high-performance athletes, several dietary supplements, including creatine monohydrate, beta-hydroxybeta-methylbutyrate (HMB), omega 3-fatty acids, vitamin D, gelatin, vitamin C/collagen, and anti-inflammatory supplements, such as curcumin and tart cherry juice, may be effective in improving training capacity, recovery, muscle soreness, and injury management [6,7]. Among these supplements, anti-inflammatory supplements may attenuate DOMS [8,9]. Reduced DOMS may be important in sports activities, wherein soreness may impair performance in a subsequent bout of exercise [10]. Furthermore, it has been suggested that both inflammatory responses and ROS and free radicals produced during and following exercise may be involved in DOMS [11]. Thus, nutrition-based interventions targeting post-exercise inflammation and/or oxidative stress responses have received much attention. However, few supplements are considered effective [12].

When interpreting research outcomes, the study design needs to be carefully considered. The aforementioned IOC consensus statement notes that:

> *"the gold standard for investigating the effects of supplements on sports performance is the prospective, randomized, controlled scientific trial, in which subjects are randomly allocated to receive either an experimental or placebo treatment (ideally in a double-blind manner) or crossed over to receive both treatments in counterbalanced order, under standardized conditions"* [6].

The effects of supplements can be minimal, and it is therefore necessary to select a proper study design. In particular, since EIMD markers, including DOMS and CK exhibit large inter-individual differences [13,14], the study design needs to be carefully considered to detect small effects of supplements. In a parallel design, an appropriately large sample size should be selected. Furthermore, individual characteristics, especially fitness level and training history, should be carefully considered. On the other hand, the influence of inter-individual differences can be eliminated by employing a crossover design, though care should be taken to eliminate or minimize the repeated bout effect, which is the adaptation whereby a single bout of eccentric exercise protects against muscle damage from subsequent eccentric bouts. For example, after testing one limb for the first assessment, testing the contralateral limb for the second assessment would minimize the repeated bout effect. It should also be noted that when employing a contralateral exercise model, a longer washout period between the first and second measurements is required to minimize the contralateral repeated bout effect, which exerts a protective effect on the contralateral limb [15]. Moreover, testing trained individuals would be effective in minimizing repeated bout effect after exercise with submaximal intensity or sport-specific exercises [16,17].

In addition to study designs (i.e., parallel and crossover designs), the exercise model and physical fitness level should also be considered when interpreting supplement effects on EIMD. Regarding the exercise model, CK activity, which is an index of muscle fiber damage, was remarkably increased with a local muscle contraction model that accompanies eccentric exercises, such as drop jump, calf-raise, leg press, and arm curl. In addition, a greater degree of damage is associated with upper-limb exercise than with lower-limb exercise when matching the relative exercise intensity. However, elevations in inflammatory markers, such as cytokines (e.g., IL-1, IL-6, IL-10) and ROS, in response to local muscle contraction are relatively small, whereas whole-body exercises, such as endurance running and cycling, can greatly elevate these markers [18,19]. As for fitness level, trained individuals have less muscle damage than untrained individuals, despite both groups performing total-work matched exercise [20].

This review summarizes the supplementation strategies used to prevent and attenuate EIMD and DOMS in humans, with a focus on dietary supplements that are introduced in the IOC consensus statement and that have anti-inflammatory and/or antioxidant effects: (1) curcumin; (2) tart cherry juice; (3) beetroot juice, and (4) quercetin. Moreover, as an emerging new supplement, (5) isothiocyanate is also discussed. The potential effects of study design, exercise model, and physical fitness level are discussed. Additionally, future perspectives and considerations for the use of dietary supplements to alleviate EIMD and DOMS are also discussed.

2. Curcumin

Curcumin (*Curcuma longa* L.) is a natural polyphenolic substance extracted from turmeric. Curcumin has various physiological effects, and its underlying mechanisms have long been assessed in the field of clinical medicine. The major physiological effects of curcumin are anti-inflammatory and antioxidant effects [9], and responses occur through a decrease in the expression of pro-inflammatory genes. Therefore, curcumin has been shown to cure various diseases, including cancer, heart failure, and Alzheimer's dementia [21–23]. In addition, curcumin exerts analgesic effects on acute and chronic pain by de-sensitizing the transient receptor potential vanilloid 1, an ion channel responsible for pain sensation, thereby reducing pain sensitivity [24,25]. Curcumin also regulates inflammatory cascades, such as NF-κB and Nrf2 pathways [26], and therefore possibly limits post-exercise inflammation, which subsequently reduces pain sensitivity and DOMS. As curcumin can act as a strong free radical scavenger [27], it may reduce secondary muscle damage. Therefore, in the IOC consensus statement, curcumin is classified as a nutritional supplement that may improve training capacity, recovery, muscle soreness, and injury management [6]. Regarding the antioxidant effect of curcumin after exercise, Takahashi et al. (2014) reported that curcumin ingestion lowers derivatives of reactive oxygen metabolites (d-ROMs), thioredoxin-1 (TRX-1), and glutathione (GSH), whereas it increases biological antioxidant potential (BAP) after treadmill walking or running at 65% VO_{2max} [28]. Chilelli et al. (2016) reported that the reduction of endogenous advanced glycation end products (AGEs) and malondialdehyde (MDA) was observed with curcumin ingestion in trained cyclists [29]. Notably, the bioavailability of curcumin was very low. Piperine, the active component of black pepper, can increase the bioavailability of curcumin when piperine and curcumin are co-ingested [30]. Microparticulation and surface treatment techniques have also been shown to enhance the bioavailability of curcumin [31,32]. Previous paralleled and crossover design studies that examined the effect of curcumin on EIMD and DOMS markers are summarized below (Table 1).

2.1. Paralleled Design Studies

Drobnic et al. (2014) reported that moderately active individuals who ingested curcumin (4 days, 200 mg/day) exhibited lower IL-8 and DOMS in the lower limbs 2 h after a downhill running compared to the control condition, without differences in serum CK activity and oxidative stress markers [33]. Tanabe et al. (2019) reported that 7-day pre-exercise curcumin intake (180 mg/day) did not modulate maximum voluntary isometric contraction (MVIC) torque or range of motion (ROM) following eccentric contractions of the elbow flexors relative to the placebo intake. However, they reported that 3-day post-exercise curcumin intake (180 mg/day) improved the recovery of ROM and muscle soreness compared with the placebo intake [34]. This indicates that post-exercise curcumin intake may provide more beneficial effects in terms of reducing ROM and muscle soreness. More recently, Faria et al. (2020) demonstrated that long-term curcumin ingestion (29 days, 1500 mg/day) resulted in a lower Mb concentration and a greater increase in IL-10 following the half-marathon race compared with the placebo ingestion [35], suggesting that some anti-inflammatory mechanisms were induced by curcumin in EIMD.

Table 1. Effect of curcumin on EIMD and DOMS markers.

Reference (Year)	Population	Supplementation		Exercise	Outcome				
		Dose	Duration		Blood Damage Maker	Functional Performance Marker	DOMS, Pain	Inflammatory Marker	Oxidative Stress Marker
Paralleled design studies									
Drobnic et al. (2014) [33]	Healthy, moderately active males	200 mg of curcumin or placebo, twice/day	4 d (2 d pre- and 2 d post-Ex)	Downhill run	CK: ×		VAS: ○	IL-8: ○ CRP, MCP-1: ×	FRAT, CAT, GPx: ×
Tanabe et al. (2019) [34]	Healthy young males	PRE, POST: 90 mg of curcumin, twice/day PLA: 90 mg of placebo, twice/day	PRE: 7 d pre-Ex POST: 4 d post-Ex CON: 4 d post-Ex	Eccentric Ex (elbow flexors)	CK: ×	ROM: ○ (POST) ROM: ×(PRE) MVIC: ×	VAS: ○ (POST) VAS: ×(PRE)		
Faria et al. (2020) [35]	Healthy normal-weight males	500 mg of curcumin or placebo, three times/day	29 d	Half-marathon	Mb: ○ CK, LDH, AST: ×			IL-10: ○ IL-6: ×	
Crossover design studies									
Tanabe et al. (2015) [31]	Untrained young males	150 mg of curcumin or placebo	1 h pre- and 12 h post-Ex	Eccentric Ex (elbow flexors)	CK: ○	MVIC: ○ ROM, swelling: ×	VAS: ×	IL-6, TNF-α: ×	
Nicol et al. (2015) [36]	Physically active males	2.5 g/day of curcumin or placebo, twice/day	5 d (2.5 d pre- and 2.5 d post-Ex)	Eccentric Ex (single-leg press)	CK: ○	Jump performance: ○ Swelling: ×	VAS: ○	IL-6: ○ TNF-α: ×	
Delecroix et al. (2017) [30]	Male elite rugby players	2 g of curcumin + 20 mg of piperine, or placebo, three times/day	4 d (2 d pre- and 2 d post-Ex)	Single leg jumps on an 8% downhill slope	CK: ×	Sprint: ○	VAS: ×		
Tanabe et al. (2019) [37] Experiment 1	Healthy males	90 mg of curcumin or placebo, twice/day	7 d pre-Ex	Eccentric Ex (elbow flexors)	CK: ×	MVIC, ROM: × Swelling: ×	VAS: ×	IL-8: ○ TNF-α: ×	d-ROMs, BAP: ×
Tanabe et al. (2019) [37] Experiment 2	Healthy males	90 mg of curcumin or placebo, twice/day	7 d post-Ex	Eccentric Ex (elbow flexors)	CK: ○	MVIC, ROM: ○ Swelling: ×	VAS: ○	IL-8: × TNF-α: ×	d-ROMs, BAP: ×

○, effective; ×, ineffective; DOMS, delayed-onset muscle soreness; IL-6, interleukin-6; IL-8, interleukin-8; IL-10, interleukin-10; TNF-α, tumor necrosis factor-α; CRP, C-reactive protein; MCP-1, monocyte chemoattractant protein 1; CK, creatine kinase; Mb, myoglobin; LDH, lactate dehydrogenase; AST, aspartate aminotransferase; MVIC, maximal voluntary isometric contraction; ROM, range of motion; VAS, visual analogue scale; FRAP, ferric reducing ability plasma; CAT, catalase; GPx, glutathione peroxidase; d-ROMs, diacron-reactive oxygen metabolites; BAP, biological antioxidant power; PLA, placebo; PRE, pre-exercise supplementation; POST, post-exercise supplementation; Ex, exercise.

2.2. Crossover Design Studies

Nicol et al. (2015) reported that curcumin ingestion (5 days, 5 g/day) decreased CK and IL-6 concentrations after leg press resistance exercise relative to the placebo ingested condition [36]. In this study, curcumin ingestion resulted in reductions in pain and an improvement in muscle performance, as assessed by an increase in jump height during single-leg squats 24 and 48 h after eccentric single-leg press exercise in physically active individuals. Tanabe et al. (2015) demonstrated that curcumin intake 1 h before and 12 h after eccentric exercise of the elbow flexors (each 150 mg) attenuated the reduction in MVIC torque and an increase in serum CK activity in untrained men, without modulating IL-6, tumor necrosis factor-α (TNF-α), and other markers (DOMS, ROM, and upper-arm circumference) [31]. Delecroix et al. (2017) assessed responses in elite rugby players, demonstrating that 4-day (2 days before and 2 days after exercise) curcumin ingestion (6 g curcumin and 60 mg piperin) attenuated reductions in power output during repetitive sprint in comparison to the placebo condition, with no effect on DOMS and CK [30]. Tanabe et al. (2019) reported that pre-exercise curcumin ingestion (7 days, 180 mg/day) attenuated increases in IL-8 after elbow flexor exercise, but this response was not observed when curcumin was administered post-exercise (7 days, 180 mg/day) compared to the placebo ingestion condition. However, post-exercise curcumin ingestion attenuated elevations in CK, muscle soreness, and reductions in MVIC torque of the elbow flexors and ROM of the elbow joint [37]. Markers of oxidative stress (i.e., d-ROMs) and oxidative elimination ability (i.e., BAP) did not change over the course of the experiment.

2.3. Summary

Irrespective of paralleled [33–35] or crossover [30,31,36,37] design, previous studies demonstrated that curcumin ingestion attenuates some inflammatory responses, as assessed by IL-6, IL-8, TNF-α, and/or IL-10, regardless of exercise modalities (e.g., aerobic or resistance exercise) [33,35–37]. Based on previous studies (Table 1), starting curcumin intake at least 2 days prior to exercise appears to be necessary for reducing inflammatory responses, regardless of the type of exercise. Regarding the antioxidant effect on responses associated with muscle-damaging exercise, only two studies are available (one for parallel study design [33] and the other for crossover design [37]), suggesting that no measurable antioxidant effect of curcumin is detected after downhill running [33] and upper arm eccentric exercise [37]. Regarding DOMS, due to the analgesic effects of curcumin [38], positive effects were observed in the parallel design [33,34], whereas the results were equivocal for the crossover design, such that two studies reported positive effects [36,37] while the other two reported no effects [30,31]. Given that a previous study reported no effects in elite rugby players [30], the effect of curcumin on attenuating DOMS might be diminished in elite or highly trained athletes. Moreover, DOMS was alleviated only when curcumin was administered consecutively after exercise [34,37]. Thus, continuous ingestion of curcumin during the post-exercise period might be necessary to attenuate DOMS. Regarding the performance markers, positive effects were observed in parallel design [34] and all crossover design [30,31,36,37] studies, including MVIC [31,37], jump height [36], and sprint [30]. However, the effect of curcumin on ROM is ambiguous [31,34,37], and no effect has been reported on swelling [31,36,37].

3. Tart Cherry or Tart Cherry Juice

Tart cherry juice, made from tart Montmorency cherries, contains numerous phytochemicals, including anthocyanins and flavonoids [39]. Anthocyanins with high antioxidant content are thought to scavenge ROS and limit ROS production [40]. Tart cherry juice has been shown to lower the risk of diabetes and cardiovascular diseases [41]. Anthocyanins and flavonoids in the tart cherry juice can inhibit enzyme activities, such as cycrooxigenage-2 (COX-2) and phospholipase A2, and may ultimately exhibit anti-inflammatory effects [42,43]. Therefore, tart cherry juice may better maintain the inflammatory response and redox balance, thereby improving recovery following strenuous exercise [44]. The IOC consensus statement mentions that the anti-inflammatory effects of tart cherry juice may be beneficial in promoting recovery, although benefits may be sport/training-specific. The dose of tart cherry juice needed to promote recovery appears to be 250–350 mL (30 mL if concentrated) twice daily for 4–5 days before an athletic event or for 2–3 days afterwards. Moreover, the amount of tart cherry juice intake, especially total phenolic content, is a key factor that determines its effects. A recent review article concluded that enhancing recovery following muscle damage via antioxidant and anti-inflammatory mechanisms may require >1000 mg polyphenols per day for 3 or more days prior to and following exercise [45]. Review articles concluded that tart cherry juice may attenuate inflammatory and oxidative responses to EIMD, ultimately accelerating faster recovery after bouts of muscle-damaging exercise [46,47]. Previous paralleled and crossover design studies that examined the effect of tart cherry juice on EIMD and DOMS markers are summarized below (Table 2).

3.1. Paralleled Design Studies

Howatson et al. (2010) reported that 236 mL of tart cherry juice ingested twice per day for 8 days attenuated decreased MVIC and inflammatory markers [IL-6, C-reactive protein (CRP)] after marathon running in recreational runners [39]. Moreover, total antioxidant status (TAS) was greater and oxidative stress, as assessed by thiobarbituric acid reactive species (TBARS), was lower in the tart cherry juice group than in the placebo group. Bell et al. (2016) reported that individuals who ingested tart cherry juice (8 days, 30 mL twice/day) exhibited lower IL-6 and DOMS in the lower limbs and a faster recovery of knee extensor MVIC, CMJ, and agility after the Loughborough intermittent shuttle test (LIST) compared to the control group, without differences in serum CK activity and oxidative stress marker (LOOH) in semi-professional male soccer players [48]. Recently, Quinlan et al. (2019) reported that tart cherry juice (8 days, 30 mL twice/day) accelerated the recovery of CMJ, 20-m sprint, and MVIC of knee extensors following LIST compared to the placebo conditions in team sports players (football, hockey, or netball sports) [49]. In contrast, Lamb et al. (2019) demonstrated that 9-day tart cherry juice ingestion (30 mL twice/day) had no effects on MVIC, DOMS, CK, or ROM after the elbow flexors of the non-dominant arm exercise relative to the placebo drink ingestion group in non-resistant trained men [50].

3.2. Crossover Design Studies

Connolly et al. (2006) reported that 355 mL of tart cherry juice twice/day (for 8 days) ingestion attenuated decreased MVIC and DOMS after eccentric exercise of the elbow flexors in college students [51]. On the other hand, in well-trained male, Bowtell et al. (2011) reported that 30 mL twice/day (for 10 days) ingestion attenuated reductions in MVIC and increases in protein carbonyls without affecting CK, CRP, DOMS, and other antioxidant status markers (nitrotyrosine and TAS) after knee extensions [52]. Meanwhile, in professional athletes, Morehen et al. (2020) reported that 8-day tart cherry juice consumption (30 mL twice/day) had no effect on cytokine responses (IL-6, IL-8, and IL-10), DOMS, or jump performance (CMJ and drop jump) after professional league matches in rugby players compared with the placebo [53]. Similarly, Abbott et al. (2020) reported no effects of tart cherry juice ingestion (2 shots × 30 mL, before and after the match, 12 and 36 h after the match) on muscle function (CMJ and reactive strength index), self-reported well-being, and muscle soreness after a 90-min soccer match in male professional soccer players in comparison to the control group [54].

Table 2. Effect of tart cherry juice on EIMD and DOMS markers.

Reference (Year)	Population	Supplementation		Exercise	Outcome				
		Dose	Duration		Blood Damage Maker	Functional Performance Marker	DOMS, Pain	Inflammatory Marker	Oxidative Stress Marker
Paralleled design studies									
Howatson et al. (2010) [39]	Recreational marathon runners, males and females	236 mL TCJ or placebo, twice/day	8 d (5 d pre-Ex, Ex-d, and 2 d post-Ex)	Marathon	CK, LDH: ×	MVIC: ○	VAS: ×	IL-6, CRP, Uric Acid: ○	TAS, TBARS: ○ PC: ×
Bell et al. (2016) [48]	Semi-professional male soccer players	30 mL TCJ or placebo, twice/day	8 d (4 d pre-Ex, Ex-d, and 3 d post-Ex)	LIST	CK: ×	MVIC, CMJ, agility: ○ Sprint: ×	VAS: ○	IL-6: ○ IL-8, IL-1-β CRP, TNF-α: ×	LOOH: ×
Quinlan et al. (2019) [49]	Team-sport players, males and females	30 mL TCJ or placebo, twice/day	8 d (5 d pre- Ex, Ex-d, and 2 d post-Ex).	LIST	CK: ×	MVIC, CMJ, sprint: ○	VAS: ×	CRP: ×	
Lamb et al. (2019) [50]	Non-resistance trained males	TCJ: 30 mL TCJ, twice/day POM: 250 mL of pomegranate juice, twice/day PLA: placebo drink, twice/day	9 d (4 d pre-Ex, Ex-d, and 4 d post-Ex)	Eccentric Ex (elbow flexors)	CK: ×	MVIC, ROM: ×	VAS: ×		
Crossover design studies									
Connolly et al. (2006) [51]	Male college students	355 mL TCJ or placebo, twice/day	8 d (4 d pre-Ex, Ex-d, and 3 d post-Ex)	Eccentric Ex (elbow flexors)		MVIC: ○ ROM: ×	VAS: ○		
Bowtell et al. (2011) [52]	Well-trained males	30 mL TCJ or placebo, twice/day	10 d (7 d pre-Ex, and 2 d post-Ex)	Single-leg knee extensions at 80% 1RM	CK: ×	MVIC: ○	PPT: ×	CRP: ×	Nitrotyrosine, TAS: × PC: ○
Morehen et al. (2020) [53]	Professional male rugby players	30 mL TCJ or placebo, twice/day	8 d (5 d pre-Ex, Ex-d and 2 d post-Ex)	Rugby match		CMJ, drop jump: ×	VAS: ×	IL-6, IL-8, IL-10: ×	
Abbott et al. (2020) [54]	Professional male soccer players	30 mL TCJ or placebo, twice/day	3 d (pre- and post-Ex and 12 and 36 h post- Ex)	90-min soccer match		CMJ, reactive strength: ×	VAS: ×		

○, effective; ×, ineffective; DOMS, delayed-onset muscle soreness; IL-1-β, interleukin-1-beta; IL-6, interleukin-6; IL-8, interleukin-8; IL-10, interleukin-10; TNF-α, tumor necrosis factor-α; CRP, C-reactive protein; CK, creatine kinase; LDH, lactate dehydrogenase; MVIC, maximal voluntary isometric contraction; ROM, range of motion; CMJ, counter movement jump; VAS, visual analogue scale; PPT, pressure pain threshold; TAS, total antioxidant status; TBARS, thiobarbituric acid reactive substances; PC, protein carbonyls; CAT, catalase; GPx, glutathione peroxidase; LOOH, lipid hydroperoxides; PLA, placebo; TCJ, tart cherry juice; POM, pomegranate juice; Ex, exercise; 1RM; 1-repetition maximum; LIST, Loughborough intermittent shuttle test.

3.3. Summary

Irrespective of the study design, mixed results have been reported regarding the effects on exercise performance. Among these, positive effects were reported for the types of markers assessed in MVIC [39,48,49,51,52], CMJ [48,49], and sprint [49]. As for DOMS, most studies reported no effects in both parallel [39,49,50] and crossover [52–54] studies; however, some studies also reported positive effects [48,51], regardless of the study design. The effects of tart cherry on inflammatory (IL-6, IL-8, IL-10, and CRP) and oxidative stress (TAS, TBARS, LOOH, nitrotyrosine, and protein carbonyls) markers are not universal in parallel studies [39,48,49]. However, in crossover studies, no effect was detected on inflammatory markers [52,53], but protein carbonyls, an oxidative stress marker, were reduced [52]. No effect of tart cherry juice was consistently observed on muscle damage markers in blood (CK and LDH), regardless of a parallel [39,48–50] or crossover [52] study design. Notably, two crossover studies reported no effect on professional soccer [54] or rugby [53] players. Thus, the effect of tart cherry on indices associated with EIMD and DOMS may be diminished in elite or highly trained individuals. In addition, the aforementioned crossover studies assessed responses before and after match play, which would mediate less muscle damage relative to laboratory-based exercise loads, such as eccentric exercise. Therefore, the effect of tart cherry juice might be hardly detectable under conditions where sport-specific exercises, such as soccer and rugby match, are employed. In the future, studies will be needed to delineate the optimal amount and duration of tart cherry juice intake in terms of the effect on DOMS in athletes.

4. Beetroot Juice

Red beetroot (*Beta vulgaris rubra*) is a functional food that contains high levels of nitrate and other phytochemicals, including bioactive compounds, such as betalain, ascorbic acid, carotenoids, phenolic acids, and flavonoids. Chronic and acute beetroot juice supplementation has been shown to improve blood pressure control, vascular function, and renal health [55]. Nitrate in the beetroot juice increases nitric oxide (NO) bioavailability, which subsequently improves vascular function, mitochondrial efficiency, glucose homoeostasis, and muscle contractility of type II fibers, thereby improving exercise performance [56], especially endurance exercise performance (in the range of 5–30 min) [57]. Therefore, nitrate is classified as a nutritional supplement that directly improves sports performance in the IOC consensus statement [6]. Moreover, beetroot juice may improve sprint and cognitive performance [58]. As for the timing of ingestion, beetroot juice needs to be ingested at least 90 min prior to the event [59]. On the other hand, betalain, the most potent antioxidant molecule found in beetroot, is thought to attenuate ROS scavenging and upregulate endogenous antioxidant enzymes. Nitrites have also been shown to inhibit radical formation and ROS production. Moreover, betalain is responsible for its analgesic effects via an anti-inflammatory related mechanism [60]. Therefore, beetroot juice is expected to accelerate the recovery of muscle damage by directly or indirectly reducing exercise-induced ROS production and DOMS. Previous paralleled and crossover design studies that examined the effect of beetroot juice on EIMD and DOMS markers are summarized below (Table 3).

4.1. Paralleled Design Studies

Clifford et al. assessed the effect of beetroot juice on EIMD and DOMS in a series of studies [61–64]. They examined the acute effect of beetroot juice [a higher dose (250 mL, ~250 mg of nitrate) and a lower dose (125 mL, the same composition as the higher dose beetroot juice, but provided half the dose)], and an isocaloric placebo drink (250 mL, with negligible nitrate content) consumed immediately (×3 bottles), 24 h (×2 bottles), and 48 h (×2 bottles) after 100-drop jumps in 30 physically active men. In this study, regardless of dosage, beetroot juice supplementation attenuated DOMS at 24, 48, and 72 h post-exercise, and reduced CMJ performance 72 h post-exercise. However, there were no significant differences in any of the cytokines assessed (IL-6, TNF-α, and IL-8) regardless of the amount of beetroot juice ingested [62]. Using the same drop jump protocol, a subsequent study by Clifford and colleagues reported that DOMS evaluated by pressure pain-threshold following 100-drop jumps was attenuated by beetroot juice ingestion (~210 mg of nitrate) compared to NO_3^- dose-matched sodium nitrate drink or placebo drink. Therefore, beetroot juice supplementation is more effective than sodium nitrate in attenuating DOMS associated with EIMD. The authors concluded that phytonutrients other than nitrate, such as betalains and phenolics, or interactions between them (or with nitrate), are likely responsible for its analgesic effects [64]. Clifford et al. also examined the effect of beetroot juice using two bouts of repeated-sprint exercise models [63]. In this study, beetroot juice ingestion (2 × 250 mL/day, ~251 mg/bottle of nitrate, 4 days) attenuated DOMS evaluated by pressure pain threshold and reductions in CMJ performance relative to placebo ingestion condition. However, beetroot juice did not affect the indirect oxidative stress markers (LOOH and protein carbonyls) and a direct marker of free radical production (ascorbyl free radical). Moreover, the same research group reported no effect of beetroot juice on responses after the marathon race [61]. Specifically, total blood leukocyte, neutrophil, and monocyte counts peaked immediately after marathon race, and responses did not return to pre-marathon values at day 2 post-marathon in both beetroot juice [total 6 bottles (250 mL/bottle, ~210 mg of nitrate) 3 days post-marathon] and an isocaloric placebo groups. Furthermore, the responses of cytokines (IL-6, IL-8, and TNF-α), CK, AST, CRP, and muscle soreness were not different between the two groups. Thus, beetroot juice does not appear to modulate inflammation or reduce muscle damage after prolonged endurance exercise.

4.2. Crossover Design Studies

Van Hoorebeke et al. (2016) reported that betalain-rich supplementation (100 mg/day for 6 days before the exercise trials and 50 mg on day 7), containing no sugars or nitrates, improved 5-km time trial performance and attenuated elevations in LDH from baseline compared to placebo ingestion in young competitive runners [65]. Montenegro et al. (2017), under similar supplementation conditions (dose and ingestion timing), reported that betalain-rich supplementation improved 10-km running time trial performance and 5-km time trial performance (performed 24 h after the 10-km time trial), as well as attenuating increased CK in competitive male and female triathletes [66]. Daab et al. (2020) reported that 7-day beetroot juice supplementation (2 × 150 mL/day, 3 days pre-exercise, day of test, and 3 days after intermittent damaging exercise) reduced muscle soreness and LDH, and improved the recovery of muscle function (CMJ, MVIC) after intermittent damaging exercise in soccer players [67].

Recently, although the order of intervention was not counterbalanced, long-term (4 weeks) beetroot juice supplementation (26 g/day freeze-dried beetroot) increased lipid peroxidation (i.e., MDA) in elite fencers. This result is unexpected because beetroot juice can decrease oxidative stress. The authors of a previous study speculated that beetroot juice consumption might have increased physical activity, ultimately increasing oxidative stress. Additionally, a significant increase in VO_{2max} was observed after ingestion of beetroot juice without attenuated muscle damage markers, such as CK and LDH [68].

Table 3. Effect of beetroot juice on EIMD and DOMS markers.

Reference (Year)	Population	Supplementation		Exercise	Outcome				
		Dose	Duration		Blood Damage Maker	Functional Performance Marker	DOMS, Pain	Inflammatory Marker	Oxidative Stress Marker
Paralleled design studies									
Clifford et al. (2016) [62]	Recreationally active males	H-BT: 250 mL of BTJ L-BT: 125 mL of BTJ PLA: 250 mL of placebo	3 d Ex-d (×3 servings), 24 h (×2 servings) and 48 h (×2 servings) post-Ex	Drop jumps	CK: ×	MVIC: × CMJ: ○ (H-BT)	PPT: ○ (H-and L-BT)	IL-6, TNF-α, IL-8: ×	
Clifford et al. (2017) [64]	Recreationally active males	BTJ: 250 mL of BTJ SN: 250 mL of sodium nitrate PLA: 250 mL of placebo	3 d Ex-d (×3 servings), 24 h (×2 servings) and 48 h (×2 servings) post-Ex	Drop jumps	CK: ×	MVIC, CMJ: ×	PPT: ○ (BLJ)	CRP: ×	
Clifford et al. (2016) [63]	Male team-sports players	500 mL of BTJ or a placebo	4 d (Ex-d, 24, and 48 h post-RST1 and 30-min post-RST2)	RST1: (first Ex) RST2: (second Ex)	CK: ×	MVIC, sprint: × CMJ, reactive strength index: ○	PPT: ○	CRP: ×	LOOH, PC, A•−: ×
Clifford et al. (2017) [61]	Runners, males and females	250 mL of BTJ or a placebo	3 d Ex-d (×3 servings), 24 h (×2 servings) and 48 h (×1 serving) post-Ex	Marathon	CK, AST: ×	MVIC, CMJ: ×	VAS: ×	IL-6, TNF-α, IL-8, CRP: ×	
Crossover design studies									
Van Hoorebeke et al. (2016) [65]	Competitive male runners	Betalain-rich concentrate capsule or placebo	7 d (D 1–6: 50 mg, twice/d; D 7: 50 mg pre-Ex	30 min of treadmill running followed by a 5-km TT	LDH (from baseline): ○ CK, LDH: ×	HR, RPE, lactate concentration,5-km TT duration: ○ Fatigue: ×	VAS: ×		
Montenegro et al. (2017) [66]	Triathletes, males and females	Betalain-rich concentrate capsule or placebo	7 d (D 1–6: 50 mg, twice/d; D 7: 50 mg pre- Ex	40 min of cycling followed by a 10-km running TT	CK: ○ LDH: ×	10-km TT duration, 5-km TT duration, Fatigue: ○ HR average, RPE: ×	VAS: ×		
Daab et al. (2020) [67]	Male soccer players	150 mL BTJ or placebo, twice/day	7 d (3 d pre-Ex, Ex-d and 3 d post-Ex)	LIST	CK: ○ LDH: ×	CMJ, MVIC, sprint: ○ Squat jump: ×	VAS: ○	CRP: ×	
Kozłowska et al. (2020) [68]	Elite fencers, males and females	Dietary recommendations with 26 g/day of freeze-dried BTJ or without BTJ	4 weeks	Fencing and general training	CK, LDH: ×	VO_{2max}: ○		IL-6: ×	MDA, GPx-1: ○ GPx-3, AOPP, 8-oxodG: ×

○, effective; ×, ineffective; DOMS, delayed-onset muscle soreness; IL-6, interleukin-6; IL-8, interleukin-8; TNF-α, tumor necrosis factor-α; CRP, C-reactive protein; CK, creatine kinase; AST, aspartate aminotransferase; LDH, lactate dehydrogenase; MVIC, maximal voluntary isometric contraction; CMJ, counter movement jump; VAS, visual analogue scale; PPT, pressure pain threshold; RPE, rate of perceived exertion; HR, heart rate; PC, protein carbonyls; GPx-1, glutathione peroxidase-1; GPx-3, glutathione peroxidase-3; LOOH, lipid hydroperoxides; MDA, malondialdehyde; AOPP, advanced oxidation protein product; 8-oxodG, 8-oxo-7.8-dihydro-2′-deoxyguanosine; A•−, plasma ascorbate free radical; PLA, placebo; BTJ, beetroot juice; SN, sodium nitrate; Ex, exercise; RST, repeated sprint test; VO_{2max}, volume oxygen consumption maximum; TT, time trial; LIST, Loughborough intermittent shuttle test.

4.3. Summary

One parallel study showed no effect on oxidative stress [63], whereas one crossover study showed that beetroot juice increased oxidative stress [68]. Previous studies demonstrated that beetroot juice had no effect on inflammatory responses (IL-6, IL-8, CRP, and TNF-α) following exercise modalities (sprint, plyometric, intermittent, and endurance exercise) regardless of parallel [61–64] or crossover [67,68] study design. From these results, it is thought that the antioxidant and anti-inflammatory effects of beetroot juice after exercise may be minimal based on the blood indices. However, blood markers may not directly reflect muscle conditions. Therefore, it remains to be elucidated whether beetroot juice modulate oxidative and inflammatory responses in muscles. Muscle pain, as measured by changes in pressure pain threshold, is alleviated by beetroot juice supplementation in a parallel study design; however, these studies by Clifford et al. did not employ a crossover study design. Muscle damage markers in blood, such as CK and AST, were not affected by beetroot juice intake in all parallel design studies wherein a drop jump, sprint, and marathon race were employed [61–64]. However, the CK and LDH levels were elevated following intense running or cycling, which was attenuated by beetroot juice intake in some crossover design studies [65–67]. Together, these findings suggest that the effect of beetroot juice on blood muscle damage indices is highly dependent on the study design, and crossover design studies suggest that beetroot juice may reduce muscle damage caused by endurance exercise. Meanwhile, most crossover studies have found that beetroot juice supplementation promotes faster recovery of sprint [67], CMJ [67], MVIC [67], time trial duration [65,66] and VO_{2max} [68] after muscle damage exercise. Furthermore, approximately half of the previous studies employing parallel designs detected positive effects on the aforementioned performance indices [62,63]. A possible reason for this improved performance may be related to increased electromyography amplitude during maximal isometric voluntary contractions, the improvement of neuromuscular efficiency, and improved cardiorespiratory performance, as suggested in a previous study [69,70], independent of muscle damage conditions. Therefore, the consumption of beetroot juice may be effective in improving the performance even under EIMD conditions.

5. Quercetin

Quercetin is a plant flavonoid found in green tea, red and white onions, apples, peppers, blueberries, and dark green vegetables. Quercetin has antioxidant and anti-inflammatory properties, as well as cardioprotective, anticancer, and hepatoprotective effects [71]. In addition, quercetin has antipathogenic activities [72] which may influence immune system and resistance to pathogens. Therefore, quercetin is classified as a nutritional supplement for immune health in athletes in the IOC consensus statement [6]. On the other hand, quercetin may possess potent antioxidant activity, as demonstrated in animal studies [73]. Moreover, studies using in vitro models demonstrated that quercetin attenuated the expression of the inflammatory cytokines TNF-α, IFN-γ, IL-6, and IL-1β transcripts in cultured human macrophages [74]. Human studies using a prolonged endurance exercise model (i.e., treadmill running or cycling) reported that chronic (3 weeks) pure quercetin supplementation did not protect against exercise-induced oxidative stress and inflammation [75]. However, when quercetin was consumed for 2 weeks alongside the co-ingestion of other components (e.g., epigallocatechin 3-gallate), supplementation was found to counteract inflammation [76]. In contrast, even if quercetin was combined with other components, acute (15 min before exercise) supplementation did not attenuate post-exercise inflammation [77]. Thus, the effect of quercetin appears to vary depending on the duration of intake and/or if another nutritional supplement is co-ingested. More recently, a study testing triathletes demonstrated that a quercetin supplement designed especially to increase quercetin bioavailability may reduce oxidative stress (i.e., d-ROMs) and muscle pain immediately after training, with an improvement in the total time in all the three single events (swim, bike and run) simulating a triathlon race [78]. Thus, any approach that increases the bioavailability of quercetin is important for increasing its effectiveness. Previous paralleled and crossover design studies that examined the effect of quercetin on EIMD and DOMS markers are summarized below (Table 4).

5.1. Paralleled Design Studies

Askari et al. (2012) showed that an 8-week supplementation of 500 mg/day quercetin combined with 200 mg/day vitamin C reduced plasma CK activity in male students [79]. In addition, Martin-Rincon et al. (2020) reported that a single dose of 140 mg mango leaf extract (Zynamite®) combined with 140 mg quercetin ingested one hour before 10-km running competition plus 100 drop jumps, followed by three additional doses (every 8 h thereafter for 24 h) attenuated muscle pain and the loss of jumping performance 24 h later compared with the placebo ingestion group in physically active male and female students [80]. In this study, the increases in the muscle damage marker in blood (Mb) following exercise were attenuated by quercetin supplementation in males only. Although CRP increased 24 h after exercise, quercetin supplementation had no effect on CRP at any point. On the other hand, O'Fallon et al. (2012) reported that 1000 mg/day (for 7 days before and 5 days after exercise) quercetin supplementation had no effect on markers of muscle damage (CK, muscle strength, soreness, resting arm angle, and upper arm swelling) or inflammation (IL-6 and CRP) after 24 eccentric exercises of the elbow flexors [81].

5.2. Crossover Design Studies

Bazzucchi et al. (2019) demonstrated the effect of 14-day quercetin supplementation (1000 mg/day) on neuromuscular impairment before, during, and after eccentric exercise of the elbow flexors in young active males [82]. Before exercise, quercetin supplementation increased isometric strength during MVIC compared to the baseline. During the eccentric exercise, the torque and muscle fiber conduction velocity decay were smaller in quercetin than in placebo ingestion. Immediately after exercise, isometric strength, the force–velocity relationship, and muscle fiber conduction velocity were lower in the placebo condition than in the quercetin ingestion condition. The authors concluded that quercetin supplementation seems to attenuate the severity of muscle weakness by sarcolemmal action potential propagation impairment [82]. A subsequent study by the same group using a similar design (the same quercetin dose, duration, and exercise protocol) demonstrated that 14-day quercetin supplementation (1000 mg/day) attenuated the increase in biomarkers of muscle damage (CK and LDH) associated with eccentric exercise [83]. Regarding these results, the authors speculated that 14 days of quercetin supplementation might have reduced lipid peroxidation and improved the redox status, ultimately increasing membrane resistance to mechanical stress [83].

Table 4. Effect of quercetin on EIMD and DOMS markers.

Reference (Year)	Population	Supplementation		Exercise	Outcome				
		Dose	Duration		Blood Damage Maker	Functional Performance Marker	DOMS, Pain	Inflammatory Marker	Oxidative Stress Marker
Paralleled design studies									
Askari et al. (2012) [79]	Male students	500 mg/day of quercetin with or without 200 mg/day vitamin C or placebo	8 weeks		CK: ○ (quercetin + vitamin C) AST: ×	Time to exhaustion: ×			
O'Fallon et al. (2012) [81]	Healthy subjects, males and females	1000 mg/day of quercetin or placebo	12 d (7 d pre- and 5 d post-Ex)	Eccentric Ex (elbow flexors)	CK: ×	Muscle strength, ROM, Swelling: ×	VAS: ×	IL-6, CRP: ×	
Martin-Rincon et al. (2020) [80]	Physically active students, males and females	140 mg of quercetin with 140 mg of Zynamite® or placebo	2 d (Pre-Ex, and every 8 h for 24 h)	Ran a 10-km race followed by 100 drop jumps	Mb: ○ (males) CK: ×	CMJ, mechanical impulse: ○	VAS: ○	CRP: ×	
Crossover design studies									
Bazzucchi et al. (2019) [82]	Moderately active males	500 mg of quercetin or placebo, twice/day	14 d (Pre-Ex)	Eccentric Ex (elbow flexors)	CK, LDH: ○	FV, MVIC, MFCV, ROM: ○ Circumference: ×	VAS: ×		
Bazzucchi et al. (2020) [83]	Low-to-moderate physically activate males	500 mg of quercetin or placebo, twice/day	14 d (Pre-Ex)	Eccentric Ex (elbow flexors)	CK, LDH: ○	FV, MVIC, MFCV, ROM: ○ Circumference: ×	VAS: ×		

○, effective; ×, ineffective; DOMS, delayed-onset muscle soreness; IL-6, interleukin-6; CRP, C-reactive protein; CK, creatine kinase; Mb, myoglobin; AST, aspartate aminotransferase; LDH, lactate dehydrogenase; MVIC, maximal voluntary isometric contraction; CMJ, counter movement jump; ROM, range of motion; FV, force–velocity relationship; MFCV, muscle fiber conduction velocity; VAS, visual analogue scale; PLA, placebo; Ex, exercise.

5.3. Summary

Quercetin ingestion does not provide anti-inflammatory effects after neither endurance nor local (e.g., elbow flexors and drop jumps) exercise in a parallel study design [80,81]. No crossover study has been conducted regarding the anti-inflammatory effects of quercetin. Several studies in which muscle damage was not assessed reported that quercetin supplementation enhances endurance exercise performance or anaerobic capacity as a result of improvement of mitochondrial biogenesis and antagonizing adenosine receptors [84,85]. In addition, quercetin may attenuate muscle strength loss following eccentric exercise or running [80,82,83] regardless of the research design. This ergogenic effect of quercetin may reflect an improvement of action potential propagation impairment due to the fact that the Ca^{2+} released from the sarcoplasmic reticulum or a blocking effect on the adenosine receptors, which may influence motor unit recruitment capacity. Most previous studies reported that quercetin attenuates muscle damage as assessed by blood markers (CK, LDH, and Mb), regardless of the study design, and independent of the physical activity [79,80,82,83]. The effect of quercetin on DOMS has been shown to be effective in a parallel study only [80]; thus, future crossover studies are warranted. The timing of quercetin intake may need to be considered because of the short half-life of quercetin (3.5 h) [86]. In addition, a clear anti-inflammatory effect has been reported in studies wherein quercetin was co-ingested with isoquercetin, n-3 polyunsaturated fatty acids (eicosapentaenoic acid and docosahexaenoic acid), and epigallocatechin 3-gallate [76]. As described in the aforementioned studies, a decreasing effect of quercetin on blood markers of muscle damage (CK and Mb) was observed when quercetin was co-ingested with vitamin C [79] or mango leaf extract [80]. Therefore, to maximize the effect of quercetin, the ingestion of additional nutritional supplements or the timing of quercetin intake may be important.

6. Isothiocyanate

All of the supplements reviewed herein, namely curcumin, tart cherry juice, beetroot juice, and quercetin, were classified as phenolic compounds. On the other hand, isothiocyanate, which is classified as an organosulfur compound, is an emerging phytochemical [87]. Isothiocyanate is found in vegetables, including those of the *Brassica* (Cruciferous) genus. For example, benzyl isothiocyanate and phenethyl isothiocyanate are found in cabbage and watercress, whereas sulforaphane is found in broccoli. Allyl isothiocyanate and 6-methylsulfinylhexyl isothiocyanate (6-MSITC) are present in wasabi (*Wasabia japonica*) which is a typical Japanese pungent spice. These compounds have cardioprotective and anticarcinogenic effects [88]. The common actions of isothiocyanate in organosulfur compounds have anti-inflammatory and antioxidant effects [87,89,90]. Therefore, isothiocyanate supplementation is expected to accelerate the recovery of EIMD and DOMS. However, very limited research regarding the effectiveness of isothiocyanate in improving EIMD is available in animal studies. 6-MSITC, a type of isothiocyanate, is known to be a potent Nrf2 activator and suppresses all three MAPK pathways, exhibiting anti-inflammatory and antioxidant properties [91,92]. In addition to these characteristics, a previous work reported that 6-MSITC might suppress calpain-1 activation, which is a Ca^{2+}-dependent protease [93], in the muscle tissue. Moreover, the same study demonstrated that 6-MSITC administration attenuates CK activity after forced swimming in mice [94]. The inhibition of calpain activity accelerates the force production restoration process after eccentric contractions in rats [95]. Based on these results obtained in animal studies, 6-MSITC intake is expected to accelerate the recovery process of reduced maximum muscle contraction after eccentric exercise in humans. A pilot study using a randomized, double-blind, crossover design examined the effect of 5-day 6-MSITC supplementation (9 mg/day) on EIMD and DOMS after eccentric exercise of the elbow flexors in young active males. In contrast to the hypothesis, calpain-1, muscle damage (MVIC torque, ROM, DOMS, CK, and swelling), and inflammatory markers (IL-8 and TNF-α) were not affected by 6-MSITC relative to those in the placebo-treated condition [96]. Given that this is the only human study assessing the effect of 6-MSITC, more human studies are needed to delineate the effectiveness of isothiocyanate in humans in the future.

7. Conclusions

7.1. Remarks

In the current review, dietary supplements with anti-inflammatory and antioxidant effects are discussed. Some positive effects mediated by curcumin, tart cherry juice, beetroot juice, and quercetin have been reported in EIMD and DOMS, although some of these results are not consistent among previous studies. These supplements may not only attenuate the aggravation of secondary muscle damage, but also improve performance by modulating cardiorespiratory and neuromuscular efficiency possibly in an interactive manner. It should be highlighted that exercise modality, physical fitness level, and study design need to be considered when interpreting the results of supplementation effects. Furthermore, the dose and duration of supplementation are important factors to maximize the effect of supplementation on EIMD and DOMS.

7.2. Future Perspectives

When using dietary supplements in competition or daily training to attenuate EIMD or DOMS, it is advisable for all individuals, including athletes, coaches, and experts, to interpret research outcomes. The dietary supplements presented in this review are included in the IOC consensus statements for high-performance athletes; however, the evidence is still limited and not well established for EIMD and DOMS. Moreover, we were unable to determine an appropriate dose and duration for each supplement for attenuating EIMD and DOMS, as the bioavailability and half-life of supplements can vary depending on their purification methods and forms. More studies are required to draw a firm conclusion regarding appropriate dose and duration. Moreover, further research is needed to identify the effectiveness of dietary supplements for EIMD and DOMS, especially in elite athletes [97].

In addition, we need to understand the differences between natural vs. purified products. We may need to take a large amount of natural products to increase the bioavailability necessary to attenuate EIMD and DOMS. It is also important to note that natural products may contain non-target ingredients which might modulate the action of supplements. Therefore, it is necessary to pay attention not only to the amount but also to the form of products.

Author Contributions: Conceptualization, Y.T. and K.S.; writing—original draft preparation, Y.T., N.F. and K.S.; writing—review and editing, Y.T., N.F. and K.S. All authors have read and agreed to the published version of the manuscript.

Funding: This research received no external funding.

Acknowledgments: This study was supported by the Scientific Research (A) (20H00574) from the Ministry of Education, Culture, Sports, Science, and Technology of Japan.

Conflicts of Interest: The author declares no conflict of interest.

References

1. Clarkson, P.M.; Nosaka, K.; Braun, B. Muscle function after exercise-induced muscle damage and rapid adaptation. *Med. Sci. Sports Exerc.* **1992**, *24*, 512–520. [CrossRef] [PubMed]
2. Tiidus, P.M. Radical species in inflammation and overtraining. *Can. J. Physiol. Pharmacol.* **1998**, *76*, 533–538. [CrossRef]
3. Proske, U.; Morgan, D.L. Muscle damage from eccentric exercise: Mechanism, mechanical signs, adaptation and clinical applications. *J. Physiol.* **2001**, *537*, 333–345. [CrossRef] [PubMed]
4. Peake, J.M.; Suzuki, K.; Coombes, J. The influence of antioxidant supplementation on markers of inflammation and the relationship to oxidative stress after exercise. *J. Nutr. Biochem.* **2007**, *18*, 357–371. [CrossRef] [PubMed]
5. Ji, L.L.; Gomez-Cabrera, M.C.; Vina, J. Role of nuclear factor kappaB and mitogen-activated protein kinase signaling in exercise-induced antioxidant enzyme adaptation. *Appl. Physiol. Nutr. Metab.* **2007**, *32*, 930–935. [CrossRef] [PubMed]

6. Maughan, R.J.; Burke, L.M.; Dvorak, J.; Larson-Meyer, D.E.; Peeling, P.; Phillips, S.M.; Rawson, E.S.; Walsh, N.P.; Garthe, I.; Geyer, H.; et al. IOC Consensus Statement: Dietary Supplements and the High-Performance Athlete. *Int. J. Sport Nutr. Exerc. Metab.* **2018**, *28*, 104–125. [CrossRef] [PubMed]
7. Rawson, E.S.; Miles, M.P.; Larson-Meyer, D.E. Dietary Supplements for Health, Adaptation, and Recovery in Athletes. *Int. J. Sport Nutr. Exerc. Metab.* **2018**, *28*, 188–199. [CrossRef] [PubMed]
8. Suzuki, K.; Tominaga, T.; Ruhee, R.T.; Ma, S. Characterization and Modulation of Systemic Inflammatory Response to Exhaustive Exercise in Relation to Oxidative Stress. *Antioxidants* **2020**, *9*, 401. [CrossRef] [PubMed]
9. Suzuki, K. Involvement of neutrophils in exercise-induced muscle damage and its modulation. *Gen. Intern. Med. Clin. Innov.* **2018**, *3*, 1–8. [CrossRef]
10. Cheung, K.; Hume, P.; Maxwell, L. Delayed onset muscle soreness: Treatment strategies and performance factors. *Sports Med.* **2003**, *33*, 145–164. [CrossRef] [PubMed]
11. Close, G.L.; Ashton, T.; McArdle, A.; MacLaren, D.P. The emerging role of free radicals in delayed onset muscle soreness and contraction-induced muscle injury. *Comp. Biochem. Physiol. Part A Mol. Integr. Physiol.* **2005**, *142*, 257–266. [CrossRef]
12. Australian Institute of Sport. 2021 AIS Supplements and Sports Food in High Performance Sport Framework. Available online: https://www.ais.gov.au/nutrition/supplements (accessed on 25 November 2021).
13. Nosaka, K.; Newton, M.; Sacco, P. Delayed-onset muscle soreness does not reflect the magnitude of eccentric exercise-induced muscle damage. *Scand. J. Med. Sci. Sports* **2002**, *12*, 337–346. [CrossRef] [PubMed]
14. Nosaka, K.; Clarkson, P.M. Variability in serum creatine kinase response after eccentric exercise of the elbow flexors. *Int. J. Sports Med.* **1996**, *17*, 120–127. [CrossRef]
15. Chen, T.C.; Chen, H.-L.; Lin, M.-J.; Yu, H.-I.; Nosaka, K. Contralateral Repeated Bout Effect of Eccentric Exercise of the Elbow Flexors. *Med. Sci. Sports Exerc.* **2016**, *48*, 2030–2039. [CrossRef]
16. Bloomer, R.J.; Falvo, M.J.; Schilling, B.K.; Smith, W.A. Prior exercise and antioxidant supplementation: Effect on oxidative stress and muscle injury. *J. Int. Soc. Sports Nutr.* **2007**, *4*, 9–10. [CrossRef]
17. Mohr, M.; Draganidis, D.; Chatzinikolaou, A.; Barbero-Álvarez, J.C.; Castagna, C.; Douroudos, I.; Avloniti, A.; Margeli, A.; Papassotiriou, I.; Flouris, A.; et al. Muscle damage, inflammatory, immune and performance responses to three football games in 1 week in competitive male players. *Graefe's Arch. Clin. Exp. Ophthalmol.* **2015**, *116*, 179–193. [CrossRef] [PubMed]
18. Suzuki, K.; Nakaji, S.; Yamada, M.; Totsuka, M.; Sato, K.; Sugawara, K. Systemic inflammatory response to exhaustive exercise. Cytokine kinetics. *Exerc. Immunol. Rev.* **2002**, *8*, 6–48. [PubMed]
19. Suzuki, K. Characterization of Exercise-Induced Cytokine Release, the Impacts on the Body, the Mechanisms and Modulations. *Int. J. Sports Exerc. Med.* **2019**, *5*. [CrossRef]
20. Newton, M.J.; Morgan, G.T.; Sacco, P.; Chapman, D.; Nosaka, K. Comparison of Responses to Strenuous Eccentric Exercise of the Elbow Flexors Between Resistance-Trained and Untrained Men. *J. Strength Cond. Res.* **2008**, *22*, 597–607. [CrossRef] [PubMed]
21. Perrone, D.; Ardito, F.; Giannatempo, G.; Dioguardi, M.; Troiano, G.; Russo, L.L.; DE Lillo, A.; Laino, L.; Muzio, L.L. Biological and therapeutic activities, and anticancer properties of curcumin. *Exp. Ther. Med.* **2015**, *10*, 1615–1623. [CrossRef] [PubMed]
22. Saeidinia, A.; Keihanian, F.; Butler, A.E.; Bagheri, R.K.; Atkin, S.L.; Sahebkar, A. Curcumin in heart failure: A choice for complementary therapy? *Pharmacol. Res.* **2018**, *131*, 112–119. [CrossRef] [PubMed]
23. Juszczyk, G.; Mikulska, J.; Kasperek, K.; Pietrzak, D.; Mrozek, W.; Herbet, M. Chronic Stress and Oxidative Stress as Common Factors of the Pathogenesis of Depression and Alzheimer's Disease: The Role of Antioxidants in Prevention and Treatment. *Antioxidants* **2021**, *10*, 1439. [CrossRef]
24. Marchesi, N.; Govoni, S.; Allegri, M. Non-drug pain relievers active on non-opioid pain mechanisms. *Pain Pr.* **2021**. [CrossRef] [PubMed]
25. Hasriadi; Wasana, P.W.D.; Vajragupta, O.; Rojsitthisak, P.; Towiwat, P. Mechanistic Insight into the Effects of Curcumin on Neuroinflammation-Driven Chronic Pain. *Pharmaceuticals* **2021**, *14*, 777. [CrossRef] [PubMed]
26. Sahin, K.; Pala, R.; Tuzcu, M.; Ozdemir, O.; Orhan, C.; Sahin, N.; Juturu, V. Curcumin prevents muscle damage by regulating NF-kappaB and Nrf2 pathways and improves performance: An in vivo model. *J. Inflamm. Res.* **2016**, *9*, 147–154. [CrossRef] [PubMed]
27. Basnet, P.; Skalko-Basnet, N. Curcumin: An anti-inflammatory molecule from a curry spice on the path to cancer treatment. *Molecules* **2011**, *16*, 4567–4598. [CrossRef] [PubMed]
28. Takahashi, M.; Suzuki, K.; Kim, H.K.; Otsuka, Y.; Imaizumi, A.; Miyashita, M.; Sakamoto, S. Effects of curcumin supplementation on exercise-induced oxidative stress in humans. *Int. J. Sports Med.* **2014**, *35*, 469–475. [CrossRef] [PubMed]
29. Chilelli, N.C.; Ragazzi, E.; Valentini, R.; Cosma, C.; Ferraresso, S.; Lapolla, A.; Sartore, G. Curcumin and Boswellia serrata Modulate the Glyco-Oxidative Status and Lipo-Oxidation in Master Athletes. *Nutrients* **2016**, *8*, 745. [CrossRef] [PubMed]
30. Delecroix, B.; Abaïdia, A.E.; LeDuc, C.; Dawson, B.; Dupont, G. Curcumin and Piperine Supplementation and Recovery Following Exercise Induced Muscle Damage: A Randomized Controlled Trial. *J. Sports Sci. Med.* **2017**, *16*, 147–153.
31. Tanabe, Y.; Maeda, S.; Akazawa, N.; Zempo-Miyaki, A.; Choi, Y.; Ra, S.-G.; Imaizumi, A.; Otsuka, Y.; Nosaka, K. Attenuation of indirect markers of eccentric exercise-induced muscle damage by curcumin. *Graefe's Arch. Clin. Exp. Ophthalmol.* **2015**, *115*, 1949–1957. [CrossRef]

32. Ashtary-Larky, D.; Kelishadi, M.R.; Bagheri, R.; Moosavian, S.P.; Wong, A.; Davoodi, S.H.; Khalili, P.; Dutheil, F.; Suzuki, K.; Asbaghi, O. The Effects of Nano-Curcumin Supplementation on Risk Factors for Cardiovascular Disease: A GRADE-Assessed Systematic Review and Meta-Analysis of Clinical Trials. *Antioxidants* **2021**, *10*, 1015. [CrossRef] [PubMed]
33. Drobnic, F.; Riera, J.; Appendino, G.; Togni, S.; Franceschi, F.; Valle, X.; Pons, A.; Tur, J. Reduction of delayed onset muscle soreness by a novel curcumin delivery system (Meriva®): A randomised, placebo-controlled trial. *J. Int. Soc. Sports Nutr.* **2014**, *11*, 31. [CrossRef] [PubMed]
34. Tanabe, Y.; Chino, K.; Sagayama, H.; Lee, H.J.; Ozawa, H.; Maeda, S.; Takahashi, H. Effective Timing of Curcumin Ingestion to Attenuate Eccentric Exercise-Induced Muscle Soreness in Men. *J. Nutr. Sci. Vitaminol.* **2019**, *65*, 82–89. [CrossRef] [PubMed]
35. Faria, F.R.; Gomes, A.C.; Antunes, A.; Rezende, K.; Pimentel, G.D.; Oliveira, C.L.P.; Antunes, B.M.; Lira, F.S.; Aoki, M.S.; Mota, J.F. Effects of turmeric extract supplementation on inflammation and muscle damage after a half-marathon race: A randomized, double-blind, placebo-controlled trial. *Graefe's Arch. Clin. Exp. Ophthalmol.* **2020**, *120*, 1531–1540. [CrossRef] [PubMed]
36. Nicol, L.M.; Rowlands, D.S.; Fazakerly, R.; Kellett, J. Curcumin supplementation likely attenuates delayed onset muscle soreness (DOMS). *Graefe's Arch. Clin. Exp. Ophthalmol.* **2015**, *115*, 1769–1777. [CrossRef]
37. Tanabe, Y.; Chino, K.; Ohnishi, T.; Ozawa, H.; Sagayama, H.; Maeda, S.; Takahashi, H. Effects of oral curcumin ingested before or after eccentric exercise on markers of muscle damage and inflammation. *Scand. J. Med. Sci. Sports* **2019**, *29*, 524–534. [CrossRef]
38. Drobnic, F. Curcumin reduces pain in DOMS. *Pain* **2016**, *157*, 2390–2391. [CrossRef]
39. Howatson, G.; McHugh, M.P.; Hill, J.A.; Brouner, J.; Jewell, A.P.; van Someren, K.A.; Shave, R.E.; Howatson, S.A. Influence of tart cherry juice on indices of recovery following marathon running. *Scand. J. Med. Sci. Sports* **2010**, *20*, 843–852. [CrossRef]
40. García-Lafuente, A.; Guillamón, E.; Villares, A.; Rostagno, M.A.; Martínez, J.A. Flavonoids as anti-inflammatory agents: Implications in cancer and cardiovascular disease. *Inflamm. Res.* **2009**, *58*, 537–552. [CrossRef]
41. Kelley, D.S.; Adkins, Y.; Laugero, K.D. A Review of the Health Benefits of Cherries. *Nutrients* **2018**, *10*, 368. [CrossRef]
42. Seeram, N.P.; Bourquin, L.D.; Nair, M.G. Degradation products of cyanidin glycosides from tart cherries and their bioactivities. *J. Agric. Food Chem.* **2001**, *49*, 4924–4929. [CrossRef] [PubMed]
43. Marzocchella, L.; Fantini, M.; Benvenuto, M.; Masuelli, L.; Tresoldi, I.; Modesti, A.; Bei, R. Dietary Flavonoids: Molecular Mechanisms of Action as Anti- Inflammatory Agents. *Recent Pat. Inflamm. Allergy Drug Discov.* **2011**, *5*, 200–220. [CrossRef]
44. Levers, K.; Dalton, R.; Galvan, E.; O'Connor, A.; Goodenough, C.; Simbo, S.; Mertens-Talcott, S.U.; Rasmussen, C.; Greenwood, M.; Riechman, S.; et al. Effects of powdered Montmorency tart cherry supplementation on acute endurance exercise performance in aerobically trained individuals. *J. Int. Soc. Sports Nutr.* **2016**, *13*, 22. [CrossRef] [PubMed]
45. Bowtell, J.; Kelly, V. Fruit-Derived Polyphenol Supplementation for Athlete Recovery and Performance. *Sports Med.* **2019**, *49*, 3–23. [CrossRef] [PubMed]
46. Lima, L.C.R.; Oliveira Assumpcao, C.; Prestes, J.; Sergio Denadai, B. Consumption of Cherries as a Strategy to Attenuate Exercise-Induced Muscle Damage and Inflammation in Humans. *Nutr. Hosp.* **2015**, *32*, 1885–1893. [CrossRef]
47. Bell, P.G.; McHugh, M.P.; Stevenson, E.; Howatson, G. The role of cherries in exercise and health. *Scand. J. Med. Sci. Sports* **2014**, *24*, 477–490. [CrossRef]
48. Bell, P.G.; Stevenson, E.; Davison, G.W.; Howatson, G. The Effects of Montmorency Tart Cherry Concentrate Supplementation on Recovery Following Prolonged, Intermittent Exercise. *Nutrients* **2016**, *8*, 441. [CrossRef]
49. Quinlan, R.; Hill, J.A. The Efficacy of Tart Cherry Juice in Aiding Recovery After Intermittent Exercise. *Int. J. Sports Physiol. Perform.* **2019**, *15*, 1–7. [CrossRef] [PubMed]
50. Lamb, K.L.; Ranchordas, M.K.; Johnson, E.; Denning, J.; Downing, F.; Lynn, A. No Effect of Tart Cherry Juice or Pomegranate Juice on Recovery from Exercise-Induced Muscle Damage in Non-Resistance Trained Men. *Nutrients* **2019**, *11*, 1593. [CrossRef]
51. Connolly, D.A.; McHugh, M.P.; Padilla-Zakour, O.I.; Carlson, L.; Sayers, S.P. Efficacy of a tart cherry juice blend in preventing the symptoms of muscle damage. *Br. J. Sports Med.* **2006**, *40*, 679–683. [CrossRef] [PubMed]
52. Bowtell, J.L.; Sumners, D.P.; Dyer, A.; Fox, P.; Mileva, K.N. Montmorency Cherry Juice Reduces Muscle Damage Caused by Intensive Strength Exercise. *Med. Sci. Sports Exerc.* **2011**, *43*, 1544–1551. [CrossRef]
53. Morehen, J.C.; Clarke, J.; Batsford, J.; Barrow, S.; Brown, A.D.; Stewart, C.E.; Morton, J.P.; Close, G.L. Montmorency tart cherry juice does not reduce markers of muscle soreness, function and inflammation following professional male rugby League match-play. *Eur. J. Sport Sci.* **2020**, *21*, 1003–1012. [CrossRef]
54. Abbott, W.; Brashill, C.; Brett, A.; Clifford, T. Tart Cherry Juice: No Effect on Muscle Function Loss or Muscle Soreness in Professional Soccer Players After a Match. *Int. J. Sports Physiol. Perform.* **2020**, *15*, 249–254. [CrossRef] [PubMed]
55. Mirmiran, P.; Houshialsadat, Z.; Gaeini, Z.; Bahadoran, Z.; Azizi, F. Functional properties of beetroot (*Beta vulgaris*) in management of cardio-metabolic diseases. *Nutr. Metab.* **2020**, *17*, 3. [CrossRef] [PubMed]
56. Peeling, P.; Binnie, M.J.; Goods, P.S.R.; Sim, M.; Burke, L.M. Evidence-Based Supplements for the Enhancement of Athletic Performance. *Int. J. Sport Nutr. Exerc. Metab.* **2018**, *28*, 178–187. [CrossRef] [PubMed]
57. Jones, A.M. Dietary nitrate supplementation and exercise performance. *Sports Med.* **2014**, *44* (Suppl. 1), S35–S45. [CrossRef]
58. Thompson, C.; Wylie, L.J.; Fulford, J.; Kelly, J.; Black, M.I.; McDonagh, S.T.; Jeukendrup, A.E.; Vanhatalo, A.; Jones, A.M. Dietary nitrate improves sprint performance and cognitive function during prolonged intermittent exercise. *Eur. J. Appl. Physiol.* **2015**, *115*, 1825–1834. [CrossRef] [PubMed]
59. Jones, A.M.; Vanhatalo, A.; Seals, D.R.; Rossman, M.J.; Piknova, B.; Jonvik, K.L. Dietary Nitrate and Nitric Oxide Metabolism: Mouth, Circulation, Skeletal Muscle, and Exercise Performance. *Med. Sci. Sports Exerc.* **2021**, *53*, 280–294. [CrossRef]

60. Reyes-Izquierdo, T.; Pietrzkowski, Z.; Argumedo, R.; Shu, C.; Nemzer, B.; Wybraniec, S. Betalain-rich red beet concentrate improves reduced knee discomfort and joint function: A double blind, placebo-controlled pilot clinical study. *Nutr. Diet. Suppl.* **2014**, *2014*, 9–13. [CrossRef]
61. Clifford, T.; Allerton, D.M.; Brown, M.A.; Harper, L.; Horsburgh, S.; Keane, K.M.; Stevenson, E.J.; Howatson, G. Minimal muscle damage after a marathon and no influence of beetroot juice on inflammation and recovery. *Appl. Physiol. Nutr. Metab.* **2017**, *42*, 263–270. [CrossRef]
62. Clifford, T.; Bell, O.; West, D.J.; Howatson, G.; Stevenson, E.J. The effects of beetroot juice supplementation on indices of muscle damage following eccentric exercise. *Eur. J. Appl. Physiol.* **2016**, *116*, 353–362. [CrossRef] [PubMed]
63. Clifford, T.; Berntzen, B.; Davison, G.W.; West, D.J.; Howatson, G.; Stevenson, E.J. Effects of Beetroot Juice on Recovery of Muscle Function and Performance between Bouts of Repeated Sprint Exercise. *Nutrients* **2016**, *8*, 506. [CrossRef]
64. Clifford, T.; Howatson, G.; West, D.J.; Stevenson, E.J. Beetroot juice is more beneficial than sodium nitrate for attenuating muscle pain after strenuous eccentric-bias exercise. *Appl. Physiol. Nutr. Metab.* **2017**, *42*, 1185–1191. [CrossRef]
65. Van Hoorebeke, J.S.; Trias, C.O.; Davis, B.A.; Lozada, C.F.; Casazza, G.A. Betalain-Rich Concentrate Supplementation Improves Exercise Performance in Competitive Runners. *Sports* **2016**, *4*, 40. [CrossRef]
66. Montenegro, C.F.; Kwong, D.A.; Minow, Z.A.; Davis, B.A.; Lozada, C.F.; Casazza, G.A. Betalain-rich concentrate supplementation improves exercise performance and recovery in competitive triathletes. *Appl. Physiol. Nutr. Metab.* **2017**, *42*, 166–172. [CrossRef] [PubMed]
67. Daab, W.; Bouzid, M.A.; Lajri, M.; Bouchiba, M.; Saafi, M.A.; Rebai, H. Chronic Beetroot Juice Supplementation Accelerates Recovery Kinetics following Simulated Match Play in Soccer Players. *J. Am. Coll. Nutr.* **2021**, *40*, 61–69. [CrossRef] [PubMed]
68. Kozłowska, L.; Mizera, O.; Gromadzińska, J.; Janasik, B.; Mikołajewska, K.; Mróz, A.; Wąsowicz, W. Changes in Oxidative Stress, Inflammation, and Muscle Damage Markers Following Diet and Beetroot Juice Supplementation in Elite Fencers. *Antioxidants* **2020**, *9*, 571. [CrossRef] [PubMed]
69. Flanagan, S.D.; Looney, D.P.; Miller, M.J.S.; Dupont, W.H.; Pryor, L.; Creighton, B.C.; Sterczala, A.J.; Szivak, T.K.; Hooper, D.R.; Maresh, C.M.; et al. The Effects of Nitrate-Rich Supplementation on Neuromuscular Efficiency during Heavy Resistance Exercise. *J. Am. Coll. Nutr.* **2016**, *35*, 100–107. [CrossRef] [PubMed]
70. Domínguez, R.; Cuenca, E.; Maté-Muñoz, J.L.; García-Fernández, P.; Serra-Paya, N.; Estevan, M.C.L.; Herreros, P.V.; Garnacho-Castaño, M.V. Effects of Beetroot Juice Supplementation on Cardiorespiratory Endurance in Athletes. A Systematic Review. *Nutrients* **2017**, *9*, 43. [CrossRef]
71. Yi, H.; Peng, H.; Wu, X.; Xu, X.; Kuang, T.; Zhang, J.; Du, L.; Fan, G. The Therapeutic Effects and Mechanisms of Quercetin on Metabolic Diseases: Pharmacological Data and Clinical Evidence. *Oxidative Med. Cell. Longev.* **2021**, *2021*, 6678662. [CrossRef] [PubMed]
72. Cushnie, T.P.; Lamb, A.J. Antimicrobial activity of flavonoids. *Int. J. Antimicrob. Agents* **2005**, *26*, 343–356. [CrossRef]
73. Meyers, K.J.; Rudolf, J.L.; Mitchell, A.E. Influence of dietary quercetin on glutathione redox status in mice. *J. Agric. Food Chem.* **2008**, *56*, 830–836. [CrossRef] [PubMed]
74. Overman, A.; Chuang, C.C.; McIntosh, M. Quercetin attenuates inflammation in human macrophages and adipocytes exposed to macrophage-conditioned media. *Int. J. Obes.* **2011**, *35*, 1165–1172. [CrossRef] [PubMed]
75. McAnulty, S.R.; McAnulty, L.S.; Nieman, D.C.; Quindry, J.C.; Hosick, P.A.; Hudson, M.H.; Still, L.; Henson, D.A.; Milne, G.L.; Morrow, J.D.; et al. Chronic quercetin ingestion and exercise-induced oxidative damage and inflammation. *Appl. Physiol. Nutr. Metab.* **2008**, *33*, 254–262. [CrossRef] [PubMed]
76. Nieman, D.C.; Henson, D.A.; Maxwell, K.R.; Williams, A.S.; McAnulty, S.R.; Jin, F.; Shanely, R.A.; Lines, T.C. Effects of quercetin and EGCG on mitochondrial biogenesis and immunity. *Med. Sci. Sports Exerc.* **2009**, *41*, 1467–1475. [CrossRef] [PubMed]
77. Konrad, M.; Nieman, D.C.; Henson, D.A.; Kennerly, K.M.; Jin, F.; Wallner-Liebmann, S.J. The acute effect of ingesting a quercetin-based supplement on exercise-induced inflammation and immune changes in runners. *Int. J. Sport Nutr. Exerc. Metab.* **2011**, *21*, 338–346. [CrossRef] [PubMed]
78. Riva, A.; Vitale, J.A.; Belcaro, G.; Hu, S.; Feragalli, B.; Vinciguerra, G.; Cacchio, M.; Bonanni, E.; Giacomelli, L.; Eggenhoffner, R.; et al. Quercetin phytosome(R) in triathlon athletes: A pilot registry study. *Minerva Med.* **2018**, *109*, 285–289. [CrossRef]
79. Askari, G.; Ghiasvand, R.; Karimian, J.; Feizi, A.; Paknahad, Z.; Sharifirad, G.; Hajishafiei, M. Does quercetin and vitamin C improve exercise performance, muscle damage, and body composition in male athletes? *J. Res. Med. Sci.* **2012**, *17*, 328–331.
80. Martin-Rincon, M.; Gelabert-Rebato, M.; Galvan-Alvarez, V.; Gallego-Selles, A.; Martinez-Canton, M.; Lopez-Rios, L.; Wiebe, J.C.; Martin-Rodriguez, S.; Arteaga-Ortiz, R.; Dorado, C.; et al. Supplementation with a Mango Leaf Extract (Zynamite®) in Combination with Quercetin Attenuates Muscle Damage and Pain and Accelerates Recovery after Strenuous Damaging Exercise. *Nutrients* **2020**, *12*, 614. [CrossRef]
81. O'Fallon, K.S.; Kaushik, D.; Michniak-Kohn, B.; Dunne, C.P.; Zambraski, E.J.; Clarkson, P.M. Effects of Quercetin Supplementation on Markers of Muscle Damage and Inflammation after Eccentric Exercise. *Int. J. Sport Nutr. Exerc. Metab.* **2012**, *22*, 430–437. [CrossRef]
82. Bazzucchi, I.; Patrizio, F.; Ceci, R.; Duranti, G.; Sgrò, P.; Sabatini, S.; Di Luigi, L.; Sacchetti, M.; Felici, F. The Effects of Quercetin Supplementation on Eccentric Exercise-Induced Muscle Damage. *Nutrients* **2019**, *11*, 205. [CrossRef]

83. Bazzucchi, I.; Patrizio, F.; Ceci, R.; Duranti, G.; Sabatini, S.; Sgrò, P.; Di Luigi, L.; Sacchetti, M. Quercetin Supplementation Improves Neuromuscular Function Recovery from Muscle Damage. *Nutrients* **2020**, *12*, 2850. [CrossRef] [PubMed]
84. Nieman, D.C.; Williams, A.S.; Shanely, R.A.; Jin, F.; Mcanulty, S.R.; Triplett, N.T.; Austin, M.D.; Henson, D.A. Quercetin's Influence on Exercise Performance and Muscle Mitochondrial Biogenesis. *Med. Sci. Sports Exerc.* **2010**, *42*, 338–345. [CrossRef] [PubMed]
85. Davis, J.M.; Carlstedt, C.J.; Chen, S.; Carmichael, M.D.; Murphy, E.A. The dietary flavonoid quercetin increases VO_{2max} and endurance capacity. *Int. J. Sport Nutr. Exerc. Metab.* **2010**, *20*, 56–62. [CrossRef]
86. Moon, Y.J.; Wang, L.; DiCenzo, R.; Morris, M.E. Quercetin pharmacokinetics in humans. *Biopharm. Drug Dispos.* **2008**, *29*, 205–217. [CrossRef] [PubMed]
87. Ruhee, R.T.; Roberts, L.A.; Ma, S.; Suzuki, K. Organosulfur Compounds: A Review of Their Anti-inflammatory Effects in Human Health. *Front. Nutr.* **2020**, *7*, 64. [CrossRef] [PubMed]
88. Kris-Etherton, P.M.; Hecker, K.D.; Bonanome, A.; Coval, S.M.; Binkoski, A.E.; Hilpert, K.F.; Griel, A.E.; Etherton, T.D. Bioactive compounds in foods: Their role in the prevention of cardiovascular disease and cancer. *Am. J. Med.* **2002**, *113* (Suppl. 9B), 71S–88S. [CrossRef]
89. Iciek, M.; Kwiecień, I.; Włodek, L. Biological properties of garlic and garlic-derived organosulfur compounds. *Environ. Mol. Mutagen.* **2009**, *50*, 247–265. [CrossRef]
90. Międkus, N.; Marszałek, K.; Podlacha, M.; Iqbal, A.; Puchalski, C.; Świergiel, A.H. Health Benefits of Plant-Derived Sulfur Compounds, Glucosinolates, and Organosulfur Compounds. *Molecules* **2020**, *25*, 3804. [CrossRef]
91. Uto, T.; Hou, D.-X.; Morinaga, O.; Shoyama, Y. Molecular Mechanisms Underlying Anti-Inflammatory Actions of 6-(Methylsulfinyl)hexyl Isothiocyanate Derived from Wasabi (*Wasabia japonica*). *Adv. Pharmacol. Sci.* **2012**, *2012*, 614046. [CrossRef]
92. Mizuno, K.; Kume, T.; Muto, C.; Takada-Takatori, Y.; Izumi, Y.; Sugimoto, H.; Akaike, A. Glutathione Biosynthesis via Activation of the Nuclear Factor E2–Related Factor 2 (Nrf2)–Antioxidant-Response Element (ARE) Pathway Is Essential for Neuroprotective Effects of Sulforaphane and 6-(Methylsulfinyl) Hexyl Isothiocyanate. *J. Pharmacol. Sci.* **2011**, *115*, 320–328. [CrossRef] [PubMed]
93. Zhang, B.T.; Yeung, S.S.; Allen, D.G.; Qin, L.; Yeung, E.W. Role of the calcium-calpain pathway in cytoskeletal damage after eccentric contractions. *J. Appl. Physiol.* **2008**, *105*, 352–357. [CrossRef] [PubMed]
94. Nabeshima, Y.; Abe, C.; Uto, Y.; Hiramatsu, R. Inhibitor of Muscle Damage or Muscle Fatigue. 11 October 2018. Available online: https://www.freepatentsonline.com/20180289660.pdf (accessed on 24 November 2021).
95. Kanzaki, K.; Watanabe, D.; Kuratani, M.; Yamada, T.; Matsunaga, S.; Wada, M. Role of calpain in eccentric contraction-induced proteolysis of Ca(2+)-regulatory proteins and force depression in rat fast-twitch skeletal muscle. *J. Appl. Physiol.* **2017**, *122*, 396–405. [CrossRef] [PubMed]
96. Tanabe, Y.; Akazawa, N.; Nishimaki, M.; Shimizu, K.; Fujii, N.; Takahashi, H. Effects of 6-(Methylsulfinyl)hexyl Isothiocyanate Ingestion on Muscle Damage after Eccentric Exercise in Healthy Males: A Pilot Placebo-Controlled Double-Blind Crossover Study. *J. Diet. Suppl.* **2021**, 1–15. [CrossRef]
97. Suzuki, K. Recent Progress in Applicability of Exercise Immunology and Inflammation Research to Sports Nutrition. *Nutrients* **2021**, *13*, 4299. [CrossRef]

nutrients

MDPI

Review

Prevalence of Dietary Supplement Use among Athletes Worldwide: A Scoping Review

Jana Daher, Moriah Mallick and Dalia El Khoury *

Department of Family Relations and Applied Nutrition, University of Guelph, 50 Stone Road, Guelph, ON N1G 2W1, Canada
* Correspondence: delkhour@uoguelph.ca

Abstract: Athletes represent a major part of dietary supplement users. This scoping review aims to explore the prevalence of dietary supplement use among athletes worldwide, most commonly used supplements, sources of information on dietary supplements and their reasons for use of these supplements. PubMed, CINAHL, MEDLINE, and PsycInfo were searched for original research articles. Studies were included if they involved athletes, identified the prevalence of dietary supplement use, and were published after 2017. A total of 26 articles were reviewed. Prevalence of dietary supplement use varied among articles, but sex-based differences related to the types of used dietary supplements existed. Generally, the findings were consistent in terms of reasons for use and sources of information. Unfortunately, the lack of homogeneity regarding the definition of dietary supplements, definition of use, reporting timeframes, and data collection methods complicates the attempt to compare the findings among studies.

Keywords: dietary supplements; athletes; prevalence; sports nutrition; reasons for use; sources of information

Citation: Daher, J.; Mallick, M.; El Khoury, D. Prevalence of Dietary Supplement Use among Athletes Worldwide: A Scoping Review. *Nutrients* **2022**, *14*, 4109. https://doi.org/10.3390/nu14194109

Academic Editor: Pedro L. Valenzuela

Received: 9 August 2022
Accepted: 29 September 2022
Published: 3 October 2022

1. Introduction

Natural health products, often referred to as dietary supplements, are naturally occurring substances intended to supplement the diet to restore or maintain good health [1]. These commercially available substances include, but are not limited to, proteins, herbs, botanicals, vitamins, and minerals [2]. The absence of consensus on a clear definition or categorization of dietary supplements [3–6] can complicate the attempts to provide an accurate overview of the current state of prevalence, posing multiple challenges to the interpretation of relevant research [7]. For example, the International Olympic Committee Consensus Statement defined dietary supplements as, "A food, food component, nutrient, or non-food compound that is purposefully ingested in addition to the habitually consumed diet with the aim of achieving a specific health and/or performance benefit", [8], and the National Institutes of Health defines dietary supplements as, "A product that is intended to supplement the diet; A dietary supplement contains one or more dietary ingredients (including vitamins, minerals, herbs or other botanicals, amino acids, and other substances) or their components; is intended to be taken by mouth as a pill, capsule, tablet, or liquid; and is identified on the front label of the product as being a dietary supplement" [9].

Substantial research has been conducted to study the prevalence of dietary supplement use and relevant practices around the world. Athletes were one of the most targeted groups of interest because they represent a major part of dietary supplement users [10]. Previous work has estimated the prevalence of dietary supplement use among athletes to be between 40% and 100%, depending on several factors including the level of competition, type of sport, and the definition of dietary supplement use [7].

This raises the concern of dietary supplement misuse and inadvertent doping (i.e., when a prohibited substance is unknowingly consumed) as they can expose users to harmful substances or precursors of prohibited substances. Initiated by the International

Olympic Committee in 1999, the World Anti-Doping Agency (WADA) was established, commencing the fight against doping in sports. Due to being classified as a subcategory of food, manufacturers of dietary supplements are not required to provide consumers with evidence of product safety or efficacy before marketing their products as they are exempt from Federal Drug Administration approval [7]. This means that manufacturing companies do not have to test their products for banned substances according to the WADA list. This can pose great risks to athletes' careers. For example, in September 2019, Carina Horn, a South African Olympic athlete, failed a drug test due to contaminated supplements and was sentenced to a 4-year ban. Luckily, Horn fought the claims against her in court and won her case. A scientist confirmed that the prohibited substances came from supplements Horn was consuming, more specifically, contaminated pre-and post-workout supplements. This incident of inadvertent doping caused Horn to miss the World Championships in 2019, and Tokyo's Summer Olympics in 2021 [11]. Similarly, in April 2019, Brandon Copeland, an American football linebacker, also failed a drug test due to contaminated supplements. Though unintentional, this incident resulted in a four-game suspension and a $745 fee to test each supplement to expose the contaminated product [12].

Contamination can occur either due to inadequate manufacturing procedures or can be intentional by manufacturers to increase the effectiveness of their supplements [13]. The most frequently reported undeclared contaminants of dietary supplements are anabolic-androgenic steroids and stimulants [14], which are mostly found in supplements targeted for enhancing athletic performance [13]. This amplifies the importance of purchasing third-party tested supplements. These are supplements tested for their safety and purity by third-party programs [15]. Unfortunately, many dietary supplements do not undergo third-party testing, and therefore, dietary supplements remain a great threat to competing athletes with the risk of contamination with doping-related substances [15].

Given that common sources of dietary supplement-related information come from fellow teammates, coaches, the internet, family and friends or their judgment [6], an educational intervention program is a possible way to improve dietary supplement knowledge among athletes to decrease the risk of dietary supplement misuse and inadvertent doping [16]. Considering the many risks associated with dietary supplement consumption, a food-first approach is often recommended to all populations when considering the use of dietary supplements. However, it is important to understand that this approach may not always be practical or appropriate, especially for athletes [17]. There are many reasons why the risk-benefit analysis may favor the consumption of dietary supplements. These include: (1) certain nutrients are difficult to consume through the diet in sufficient amounts, (2) some nutrients are limited to food items an athlete might not eat, (3) uncertainty of the number of ergogenic nutrients consumed due to high variability in food items, (4) larger doses of concentrated nutrients needed to correct deficiencies or other health implications, (5) whole foods may be impractical to consume before, during, or after physical activity and (6) dietary supplements may help when contamination of food hygiene is a concern [17]. Therefore, Close et al. (2022), suggest 'food first' should mean, "where practically possible, nutrient provision should come from whole foods and drinks rather than from isolated food components or dietary supplements". The International Association of Athletics Federations Consensus Statement [18] and the International Olympic Committee Consensus Statement [8] also acknowledge that a food-first approach may not always be practical, as the use of dietary supplements may be necessary for athletes to meet their nutritional needs when whole food consumption is impractical due to training schedules, preparation and storage issues and gut comfort [8,18]. Considering the emerging concerns regarding dietary supplements' safety, several studies have investigated their integrity and authenticity. Furthermore, the attempt to compare the prevalence of dietary supplement use and practices worldwide might not be so accurate due to inconsistent definitions among studies and a lack of differentiation between the general categories of dietary supplements, which complicates the attempts to compare specific trends, especially among athletes. This does not provide specificity to be able to compare studies on specific dietary supplements used by athletes. Currently, there are no recent rigorous research reviews that explore the prevalence of supplement use among athletes. Therefore, the purpose of this scoping review was to explore the prevalence of dietary supplement use among athletes worldwide from 2018 to 2022, most commonly used supplements, reasons for dietary supplement use and sources of information.

2. Materials and Methods

This scoping review was designed and conducted in accordance with the Preferred Reporting Items for Systematic Reviews and Meta-Analyses Extension for Scoping Reviews (PRISMA-ScR) guidelines (Table S1—Supplementary Materials) [19]. The review protocol can be obtained upon request from the corresponding author.

2.1. Eligibility Criteria

To be included in the review, peer-reviewed journal papers needed to (1) involve athletes, (2) identify the prevalence of dietary supplement use among athletes, (3) be published after 2017. Studies were excluded if they (1) investigated supplement use in gym users, (2) collected data before 2016. All the studies had to be fully completed and published; abstract-only, presentation-only, and unpublished studies were excluded.

2.2. Information Sources

Searches were conducted on the electronic databases of PubMed, CINAHL, PsycInfo, and MEDLINE for studies published from 2018 up until June 2022 (The last search was conducted in July 2022). The search was restricted to papers written or translated to English. Reference lists of all retrieved articles in addition to the profiles of authors with extensive experience in dietary supplement research were scanned for additional relevant articles.

2.3. Search Strategy

The search strategy involved a combination of keywords including (supplement OR product OR vitamin OR mineral OR protein OR ergogenic OR drink OR herbal OR amino acid OR nutraceutical OR bar), AND (athlete OR player OR physically active OR elite OR sport OR bodybuilder OR runner OR team OR football OR soccer OR swimmer OR weightlifter OR dancer OR triathlete OR baseball OR gymnastic OR ballet OR tennis OR sailor OR basketball OR hockey), AND (use OR consumption OR prevalence OR survey OR pattern OR report OR intake OR habit). The search was limited to results in which these keywords show in the title or abstract.

2.4. Selection Process

Studies were screened for eligibility by two of the authors. Any disagreements on study selection or data extraction were resolved by consensus or after discussion with the third author.

2.5. Data Charting and Items

The data charting table was developed by the first author and further improved and approved by the other two authors to finally include the authors' names, year of publication, country where each study was conducted, supplements of focus, type of sport, target population, age, sample size, data collection method, and results (prevalence of supplement use, most commonly used supplements, reasons for use, and sources of information).

3. Results

3.1. Selection of Studies

A total of 596 studies were identified through searching databases and other sources. After removing duplicates (n = 105), 491 articles were screened based on their titles and abstracts only, yielding 52 studies for full-text screening. Twenty-six articles were excluded, leaving a final pool of 26 studies that were eligible for inclusion in this scoping review (Figure 1).

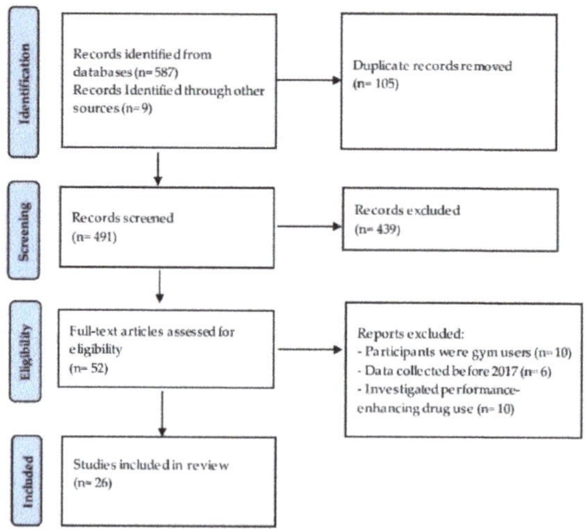

Figure 1. Selection of sources of evidence.

3.2. Characteristics of Studies

Figure 2 represents the studies' demographics. Studies were mostly conducted in Spain (31%) and the United States of America (27%) [15,20–33]. Some studies investigated supplement use in more than one country [34–37]. The twenty-six studies included a total of 17,342 participants. The sample sizes ranged from 20 [26] to 2113 subjects [24]. The majority of the studies included adult athletes, some included under 18 athletes [20,24,25,28,32,34,38–40], and none included older-adult athletes. Most studies included athletes from several sport categories [6,15,20–22,27,31,34,36–38,40], while others focused on one type of sport such as running [23,24], bodybuilding [41,42], football [32,35], rowing [26], sailing [25], rugby [30], fencing [28], handball [29], squash [33], and track and field [39]. Interestingly, one study focused on paralympic sports [34].

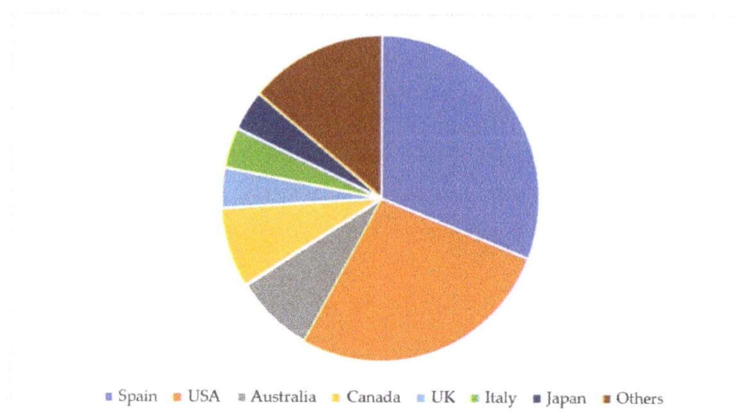

Figure 2. Summary of studies' demographics.

3.3. Data Collection Methods and Reporting Timeframes

All studies used self-reported questionnaires or surveys to collect data on dietary supplement use among athletes. Some studies have provided their questionnaire or survey in an online format [24,27,29,32,37,40,41]. However, the selected reporting timeframe varied across studies (Figure 3). Most of the studies investigated current use of dietary supplements, while other timeframes were the past year (n = 7), past six months (n = 2), past 3 months (n = 1), past month (n = 1), and past season (n = 1). None of the studies used qualitative or mixed-methods approach to research.

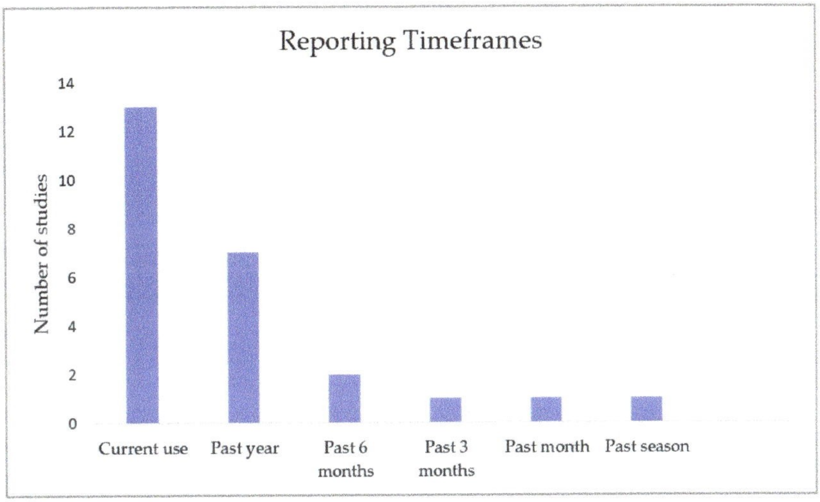

Figure 3. Reporting timeframes across studies.

3.4. Prevalence of Dietary Supplement Use among Athletes

The characteristics of each study, prevalence of dietary supplement use and most used dietary supplements are summarized in Table 1. It is worth highlighting that the defined use of dietary supplements differed among studies. A large number of the studies defined use as reporting using at least one dietary supplement in the chosen timeframe [6,15,20,21,23,29,30,35,40,43]. Other studies defined use as using at least one dietary supplement on two or more days per week [22,24,31]. The rest of the studies did not clarify how they defined dietary supplement use.

Table 1. Summary of studies with prevalence and most used dietary supplements.

Publication-Country	Target Population	Age Mean ± SD (Years)	Sex (Sample Size)	Data Collection Method (Time Frame)	Prevalence (Defined Use)	Most Used Supplements
Aguilar-Navarro et al. (2021) Spain [20]	Elite athletes (Individual & team sports)	15–66	Total: 504 M (n = 329) F (n = 175)	Questionnaire (preceding season)	62% M:65% F: 57% (reported using at least one DS)	M: Protein supplements. F: Multivitamins; Branched chain amino acids.
Baltazar-Martins et al. (2019) Spain [21]	Elite athletes (Individual & team sports)	NC	Total: 527 M (n = 346) F (n = 181)	Questionnaire (past year)	64% M: 67% F: 58% (reported using at least one DS)	Proteins; amino acids/ Branched chain amino acids; multivitamins.
Barrack et al. (2022) USA [22]	NCAA Division I athletes	NR	Total: 557 M (n = 298) F (n = 259)	Survey (past year)	45% (reported using at least one DS on 2 or more days per week)	M: Protein/amino acid supplements. F: Vitamin/mineral supplements.
Barrack et al. (2021) USA [23]	Elite collegiate endurance runners	18–22	Total: 135 M (n = 65) F (n = 70)	Survey (past 4 weeks)	79% M: 74% F: 83% (reported using at least one DS)	Multivitamin/minerals; iron. M: Amino acids; beta-alanine. F: Iron; calcium.
Barrack et al. (2020) USA [24]	Preadolescent endurance runners	13.2 ± 0.9	Total: 2113 M (n = 1255) F (n = 858)	Web-based Survey (past year)	26% M: 22% F: 33% (reported using DS on 2 or more days per week)	Sport foods; multivitamin/minerals. M: Creatine and sport foods. F: Multivitamin/minerals, vitamin D, calcium, iron, probiotic supplements, and diet pills.
Caraballo et al. (2020) Spain [25]	Elite sailors	12–17	Total: 42 M (n = 31) F (n = 11)	Questionnaire (General and current)	50% M: 55% F: 46%	M: Isotonic drinks; caffeine. F: Vitamin D; vitamin complexes.

Table 1. *Cont.*

Publication-Country	Target Population	Age Mean ± SD (Years)	Sex (Sample Size)	Data Collection Method (Time Frame)	Prevalence (Defined Use)	Most Used Supplements
Domínguez et al. (2020) Spain [26]	Heavyweight and lightweight rowers	23 ± 3	Total: 20 M (n = 16) F (n = 4)	Questionnaire (general and current—during the sports season)	100%	Iron; caffeine; β-alanine, energy bars; vitamin supplements; and isotonic drinks.
Graybeal et al. (2022) USA [27]	Endurance cyclists, runners, and triathletes.	39.4 ± 13.5	Total: 200 M (n = 92) F (n = 108)	Digital questionnaire (current use)	78%	Multivitamin; electrolytes; vitamin D; protein.
Hackett (2022) Australia [41]	Bodybuilders	≥18 years	Total: 235 M (n = 235)	Online survey (off season and 6 weeks before a competition)	96%	Creatine monohydrate; whey protein.
Hurst et al. (2020) United Kingdom [38]	Team and individual sports athletes	20.8 ± 4.5	Total: 557 M (n = 429) F (n = 128)	Survey (current use)	53%	Ergogenic supplements.
Jovanov et al. (2019) Serbia, Germany, Japan, Croatia [34]	Team and individual sports athletes	15–18	Total: 348 M (n = 174) F (n = 174)	Survey (current use)	82% M: 61% F: 39%	M: Whey protein, creatine, amino acids, caffeine, and NO reactor. F: Vitamins and mineral complexes.
Madden et al. (2018) Canada [43]	Wheelchair rugby athletes	36.3 ± 9.5	Total: 42 M (n = 33) F (n = 9)	Questionnaire (past three months)	M: 91% F: 78% (reported using at least one DS)	Electrolytes, sport bars, vitamin D, protein powder, and MVMM (multivitamin multimineral). M: Vitamin D, protein powder, and electrolytes. F: MVMM and vitamin D.
Mata et al. (2021) Spain [28]	Fencers	21.8 ± 5.9 years	Total: 49 M (n = 18) F (n = 31)	Questionnaire (General and current)	47%	Sports drinks, vitamin C, sport bars, caffeine. M: Sports drinks, sports bars, and iron. F: Sports drinks, sports bars, and caffeine.

Table 1. *Cont.*

Publication-Country	Target Population	Age Mean ± SD (Years)	Sex (Sample Size)	Data Collection Method (Time Frame)	Prevalence (Defined Use)	Most Used Supplements
Montuori et al. (2021) Italy [42]	Bodybuilders	>18	Total: 107 M (n = 73) F (n = 34)	Questionnaire/survey (general and current)	82% M: 66% F: 34%	NR
Muñoz et al. (2020) Spain [29]	Handball players	NR	Total: 187 M (n = 112) F (n = 75)	Online Questionnaire (current use)	60% (reported using at least one DS)	Sports drinks, energy bars and caffeine-containing products. M: creatine and L-carnitine.
Oliveira et al. (2022) Australia, Canada, Iceland, Netherlands, Norway and Portugal. [35]	Elite football players	Median age: 24	Total: 103 F (n = 103)	Questionnaire (past year)	82% (reported using at least one DS)	Vitamin D, omega-3 fatty acids, and protein (including whey protein and casein).
Roy et al. (2021) Canada [6]	Varsity athletes	20.5 ± 1.8	Total: 302 M (n = 92) F (n = 210)	Questionnaire (past 6 months)	58% M: 66% F: 53% (reported using at least one DS)	Protein, vitamins, minerals, and carbohydrate supplements. M: Amino acid supplements and stimulants. F: Prebiotics and probiotics.
Sánchez-Oliver et al. (2021) Spain [30]	Rugby players	M: 24.3 ± 5.0 F: 24.0 ± 4.9	Total: 144 M (n = 83) F (n = 61)	Questionnaire (general)	65% M: 77% F: 49% (reported using at least one DS on some occasion)	Whey protein, caffeine, sport drinks, energy bars, creatine monohydrate, BCAAs, and glutamine.M: Whey protein, creatine monohydrate, and glutamine.
Sassone et al. (2019) USA [31]	NCAA Division I athletes	18–26	Total: 557 M (n = 229) F (n = 258)	Survey (past year)	45% (reported using ≥1 dietary supplements ≥2 days per week)	Pre-workout & herbal supplements.
Sekulic et al. (2019) Croatia and Kosovo [36]	Professional team-sport athletes	22.11 ± 3.37	Total: 912 M (n = 556) F (n = 356)	Questionnaire (General and current)	13% (consumed DS regularly 36% (consumed DS occasionally)	Vitamins/minerals, isotonic drinks, energy bars, iron, recovery supplements, carbohydrates, proteins/amino acids.

Table 1. *Cont.*

Publication-Country	Target Population	Age Mean ± SD (Years)	Sex (Sample Size)	Data Collection Method (Time Frame)	Prevalence (Defined Use)	Most Used Supplements
Shoshan et al. (2021) USA [32]	Football players	16.9 ± 1.2	Total: 102 M (n = 98) F (n = 4)	Online questionnaire (general and current)	60% (protein supplements)29% (pre-workout supplements)	NR
Tabata et al. (2020) Japan [39]	Track and field elite athletes	Junior athletes: 17.7 ± 1.1 years Senior athletes: (25.2 ± 3.9 years	Total: 574 M (n = 314) F (n = 260)	Pre participation medical form (current use)	64% M: 60% F: 69%	Amino acids, vitamins, minerals, proteins. M: Protein, creatine. F: Vitamins, amino acids.
Vento & Wardenaar (2020) USA [15]	NCAA I collegiate student athletes	20 ± 1.6 years	Total: 138 M (n = 49) F (n = 89)	Questionnaire (Past year)	100% (reported using at least one DS)	Multivitamin and mineral supplements, and single vitamins or minerals. F: Vitamins and single minerals, exotic berries, herbs, maca root powder, ribose, ephedra, colostrum, and hydroxy-methyl-butyrate.
Ventura Comes et al. (2018) Spain [33]	National & international squash players	International players: 25.0 ± 6.2 National players: 35.6 ± 14.2	Total: 42 M (n = 29) F (n = 13)	Questionnaire—survey (General and current)	International athletes: 100% National athletes: 68%	Ergogenic aids C, sports food.
Waller et al. (2019) Australia [40]	Individual and team sports' athletes	20.4 ± 4.5	Total: 94 M (n = 39) F (n = 55)	Online questionnaire (past year)	87% (reported using at least one DS)	Sports drinks, caffeine, protein powder, and sports bars.
Wangdi et al. (2021) [a] 15 countries [37]	Individual and team sports' athletes	27.6 ± 9.8	Total: 80 M (n = 51) F (n = 27) did not disclose (n = 2)	Online questionnaire (current and previous use)	11% (reported current use)11% (reported previous use)	N/A

Percentages were rounded to the nearest whole number. DS: Dietary supplements; F: Females; M: Males; NR: Not reported; NC: Not clear; [a] This study investigated tart cherry use only.

The prevalence of dietary supplement use is presented in Table 1. The included studies covered a wide range of individual and team sports. Most studies included athletes from several sport categories, while others focused on one type of sport such as running, rowing, sailing, bodybuilding, rugby, fencing, handball, football, squash, and track & field.

Prevalence ranged from 11% [37] to 100% [15,26,33]. The use of dietary supplements among athletes was relatively high in the majority of the studies, but this can vary based on the breadth of the definition of a dietary supplement, reporting timeframe (i.e., past month vs. past year), data collection method and format, and definition of dietary supplement use (Table 1). In general, the consumption of dietary supplements was higher in males compared to females except for few studies [23,24,39]. Protein and vitamin/mineral supplements were among the most commonly used supplements reported by athletes. In most of the studies that presented the most commonly used supplements based on sex, it was clear that females were more likely to use vitamin/mineral supplements compared to males, while males were more likely to use protein supplements.

3.5. Reasons for Dietary Supplement Use

The reported reasons of dietary supplement use were generally consistent across studies (Table 2). The most frequently reported reasons are improving athletic performance, improving health, and accelerating recovery. Very few studies, among those that investigated motivations behind dietary supplement use, presented sex-based differences [22,25,34]. Females were more likely to use dietary supplements for health reasons, while males were more likely to report using dietary supplements to enhance performance.

Table 2. Reasons for dietary supplement use reported by athletes.

Publication	Reasons for Dietary Supplement Use (% of Participants that Reported the Reason *)
Barrack et al. (2020) [24]	M: Increasing strength/power, increasing muscle mass. F: Improving health
Carabello et al. (2020) [25]	M: Improving performance (65%) and physical appearance (15%). F: Improving health status (57%), preventing nutritional deficits (14%).
Domínguez et al. (2020) [26]	Improving recovery (80%), health reasons.
Graybeal et al. (2022) [27]	Improving performance and health, meeting nutrient requirements.
Jovanov et al. (2019) [34]	M: Improving athletic performance (19%) F: Improving health (18%)
Madden et al. (2018) [43]	Performance—medical/health
Mata et al. (2021) [28]	Improving performance (34%), improving health (29%)
Muñoz et al. (2020) [29]	Enhancing sports performance (54%), improving health (13%), and improving physical appearance (11%).
Oliveira et al. (2022) [35]	Staying healthy (66%), accelerating recovery (58%), increasing energy reducing fatigue (54%).
Roy et al. (2021) [6]	Maintaining good health (83%), increasing energy (71%), promoting recovery (69%), correcting or preventing micronutrient deficiencies (60%) and supplying convenient forms of energy and/or macronutrients (58%)
Sánchez-Oliver et al. (2021) [30]	Improving sport performance (62%), preventing nutritional deficits (14%)

Table 2. *Cont.*

Publication	Reasons for Dietary Supplement Use (% of Participants that Reported the Reason *)
Vento & Wardenaar (2020) [15]	Improving health and performance.
Waller et al. (2019) [40]	Enhancing recovery (63%), maintaining health (59%), and improving energy (50%)
Wangdi et al. (2021) [37]	Improving recovery (75%), sleep and immunity (30%), and general health (30%)

M: Males; F: Females; * Percentages were rounded to the nearest whole number; * Percentages were not reported for studies that split data into groups.

3.6. Sources of Information on Dietary Supplements

Sources of information on dietary supplements were investigated in most of the studies (Table 3). Health care professionals, coaches/trainers, the internet, and teammates were among the most commonly reported sources of information. It is apparent that males are more likely to rely on their coach/trainer, teammates, dietitian/nutritionist, and family and friends to receive information on dietary supplements, while females are more likely to rely on doctors/healthcare professionals, their coach/trainer, and family & friends.

Table 3. Sources of information on dietary supplements reported by athletes.

	Studies (% of Participants that Reported the Reason *)		
Source of Information	Reported by Males	Reported by Females	Reported by All Participants (In Case Sex-Based Differences Were Not Reported)
Doctor/health professional	Mata et al. (2021) [28] (50%);	Aguilar-Navarro et al. (2021) [20] (60%); Barrack et al. (2020) [24]; Sánchez-Oliver et al. (2021) [30] (16%);	Domínguez et al. (2020) [26] (50%); Graybeal et al. (2022) [27]; Montuori et al. (2021) [42] (64%); Muñoz et al. (2020) [29]; Oliveira et al. (2022) [35] (46%); Roy et al. (2021) [6] (59%); Vento & Wardenaar (2020) [15] (45%); Waller et al. (2019) [40];
Nutritionist/dietitian	Aguilar-Navarro et al. (2021) [20] (83%); Madden et al. (2018) [43] (52%); Sánchez-Oliver et al. (2021) [30] (19%);	Carabello et al. (2020) [25] (14%); Mata et al. (2021) [28] (22%);	Montuori et al. (2021) [42] (64%); Oliveira et al. (2022) [35] (43%); Vento & Wardenaar (2020) [15] (92%); Ventura Comes et al. (2018) [33] (21%);
Coach/trainer	Barrack et al. (2020) [24]; Carabello et al. (2020) [25] (42.3%); Madden et al. (2018) [43] (30%); Sánchez-Oliver et al. (2021) [30] (27%);	Aguilar-Navarro et al. (2021) [20] (85%); Mata et al. (2021) [28] (27%); Sánchez-Oliver et al. (2021) [30] (16%);	Domínguez et al. (2020) [26] (40%); Jovanov et al. (2019) [34] (41%); Muñoz et al. (2020) [29]; Oliveira et al. (2022) [35] (41%); Roy et al. (2021) [6] (39%); Vento & Wardenaar (2020) [15]; Ventura Comes et al. (2018) [33] (29%);
Internet/social media	Barrack et al. (2020) [24]; Madden et al. (2018) [43] (33%);	Madden et al. (2018) [43] (33%);	Graybeal et al. (2022) [27]; Jovanov et al. (2019) [34] (39%); Montuori et al. (2021) [42] (71%); Roy et al. (2021) [6] (48%); Waller et al. (2019) [40]; Wangdi et al. (2021) [37] (15%);
Teammates	Barrack et al. (2020) [24]; Carabello et al. (2020) [25] (23%); Mata et al. (2021) [28] (8%); Sánchez-Oliver et al. (2021) [30] (14%);	Madden et al. (2018) [43] (44%);	Roy et al. (2021) [6] (45%)

Table 3. *Cont.*

Source of Information	Studies (% of Participants that Reported the Reason *)		
	Reported by Males	**Reported by Females**	**Reported by All Participants (In Case Sex-Based Differences Were Not Reported)**
Family/friends	Carabello et al. (2020) [25] (19%); Mata et al. (2021) [28]; Sánchez-Oliver et al. (2021) [30] (17%);	Barrack et al. (2020) [24]; Carabello et al. (2020) [25] (43%); Mata et al. (2021) [28] (39%);	Roy et al. (2021) [6] (53%);
Self-education	Aguilar-Navarro et al. (2021) [20] (48%);	Aguilar-Navarro et al. (2021) [20] (28%);	Baltazar-Martins et al. (2019) [21]; Roy et al. (2021) [6] (48%); Sekulic et al. (2019) [36]
Scientific research			Graybeal et al. (2022) [27]; Wangdi et al. (2021) [37] (33%);

* Percentages were rounded to the nearest whole number. * Percentages were not reported for studies that split data into groups.

4. Discussion

The aim of this scoping review was to explore the prevalence of dietary supplement use among athletes worldwide in the past 5 years, most commonly used supplements, reasons for dietary supplement use and sources of information. Using rigorous scoping review methods, 27 studies were reviewed to examine the current breadth of knowledge of dietary supplement prevalence among athletes; no qualitative or mixed-methods studies were found. Given the increasing consumer interest in health and well-being that is well-reflected by the fast-growing dietary supplements industry, which is expected to reach around USD 278 billion by 2024, it is vital to examine the prevalence of dietary supplement use among athletes [44]. In this current review, the prevalence ranged between 11% [37] to 100% [15,26,33]. In general, the prevalence of dietary supplement consumption was higher in males compared to females except for few studies [23,24,39]. Additionally, there was minimal reporting on age-based differences, however few studies noted age as an influence on dietary supplement consumption, with older athletes consuming more dietary supplements than younger ones [20,27,39].

Currently, there is no universal definition of dietary supplements used within the scientific community, therefore, the definition used to define dietary supplements varied across studies. The broadness of definitions used to describe dietary supplements by studies affect their findings' comparability with other studies that define dietary supplements differently. Many authors studying this subject area also noted difficulty in comparing studies due to the lack of homogeneity between definitions and categorizations of dietary supplements [2,7]. The absence of a standard definition for dietary supplements creates an issue within the scientific community to accurately study trends between the results of different studies.

Furthermore, it is important to note that the reported prevalence by each study included in this review heavily relied on how they defined dietary supplement use. While some studies defined it as using at least one dietary supplement in a chosen time-frame [6,15,20,21,23,29,30,35,40,43], others defined it as using at least one dietary supplement on two or more days per week [22,24,31]. The remaining studies did not explicitly define dietary supplement use. Along with inconsistencies between defined dietary supplement use among studies, inconsistencies between used time frames also complicates the attempt to compare the prevalence of dietary supplement use among athletes. Current use of dietary supplements, use of dietary supplements in the past year, past six months, three months, past month, and past season were all timeframes used by studies. Similarly, lack of consistent methodology also hinders researcher's ability to compare studies. Interestingly, some studies have used online questionnaires/surveys to explore dietary supplement use, and all of these were conducted after 2019, which implies how the COVID-19 pandemic has affected this type of research, and might shape the format of similar future studies.

Most studies in this review focused on a wide range of dietary supplements, while only one focused on a specific dietary supplement such as tart cherry [37]. A possible reason dietary supplements may seem attractive to athletes is that they are continuously seeking ways to gain advantages over their competitors. Based on the studies included in this review, it appears the main reasons for dietary supplement use are improving athletic performance, improving health, and accelerating recovery. Fascinatingly, one study included in this review surveyed the attitudes of athletes who refrain from dietary supplement use, with the main reasoning being that they do not need them, and that they do not know enough about them [34]. In the few studies that examined sex-based differences, it was concluded that females were more likely to consume dietary supplements for health reasons and males were more likely to consume dietary supplements to enhance performance [22,25,34]. Another sex-based difference one study found is that females often used dietary supplements 'at times' rather than on a regular basis [43]. Potential false and misleading advertisement by companies in the dietary supplement industry coupled with lack of knowledge put athletes at great risk of inadvertent doping [32]. It is alarming that there is a large number of studies in which athletes reported that they rely on their coaches, teammates, the internet or family and friends for information on dietary supplements. Referring to a reliable source of information with regard to dietary supplements is critical in the athletic community, considering the probability of supplement contamination with prohibited substances and consequent health risks and anti-doping sanctions.

Determining the prevalence of doping amongst athletes was not within the scope of this review. However, considering the great risk of dietary supplement contamination with prohibited substances, athletes should consider all other options before obtaining nutrients from dietary supplements [7]. Consuming nutrients from whole foods provides greater benefits than the consumption of isolated nutrients [45]. Dietary supplements cannot excuse inadequate diets, and therefore, it is recommended that athletes optimize and prioritize their nutrient intake from whole foods. Of course, dietary supplement use cannot be fully disputed as there are circumstances where dietary supplement consumption is necessary [17]. Dietary supplements may be of great value to athletes who are vegan, vegetarian, or are treating deficiencies [17].

Despite the high prevalence of athletes consuming dietary supplements, there was minimal reporting on whether the dietary supplements were third party tested. Only one study reported information on this and found that while over 90% of participants believed it was vital to know whether the dietary supplement was third party tested, only 57% purchased third-party tested supplements [15]. Knowledge about nutrition and dietary supplement use is vital to athletes choosing to consume dietary supplements. Accurate information is needed to make informed decisions and protect against inadvertent doping and dietary supplement misuse. The integration of nutritional-knowledge programs may be highly valuable to increase the knowledge, beliefs and intentions of athletes who choose to consume dietary supplements [16].

A wide range of team and individual sports were included in the studies within this review. Interestingly, one study focused on wheelchair sport teams [34]. Aside from reasons for dietary supplement use, another sex-based difference observed was generally, dietary supplement consumption was higher in males than females. Only a few studies found contradictory results [23,24,39]. Gender minorities, including transgender individuals and gender non-binary individuals, were not included in this analysis, as no articles targeted this population. Future studies should include and study minority populations and paralympic sports to increase the generalizability of their results.

There are a number of limitations for the studies conducted to date on this topic. Firstly, a combined 58% of studies included within this review were conducted in Spain and the United States of America: mainly, by the same research team. Little research was conducted in the United Kingdom, East Asia and Middle Eastern countries. Moreover, there were no qualitative reviews on this topic. Qualitative studies provide a new perspective and can provide great insight that allows for better understanding and interpretation of results. Studies included in this review relied on self-assessment measures for dietary supplement intake information. Using self-reported data is subject to bias and is limited to the participants ability to assess themselves accurately.

This scoping review does have some limitations. First, our search was limited to articles written in or translated to English language, so there is a possibility that relevant articles written in other languages were left out. Additionally, the included studies were not assessed for risk of bias, which is critical to identify the quality of evidence. Nevertheless, this review provides a comprehensive overview of the recent prevalence of dietary supplement use among athletes.

5. Conclusions

In conclusion, the lack of homogeneity among studies regarding the definition of dietary supplements, reporting timeframes, and data collection methods complicates the attempt to compare the findings. Results from this review may contribute to future educational intervention program initiatives to increase the knowledge of users on dietary supplements, their benefits, and their risks and on the importance of their use under professional guidance. Given the higher prevalence of use of dietary supplements among athletes, more research and initiatives are indispensable in this population as proper nutrition is an extremely important factor in ensuring a high quality of life and optimum performance for athletes.

Supplementary Materials: The following supporting information can be downloaded at: https://www.mdpi.com/article/10.3390/nu14194109/s1, Table S1: Preferred Reporting Items for Systematic reviews and Meta-Analyses extension for Scoping Reviews (PRISMA-ScR) Checklist.

Author Contributions: Conceptualization, D.E.K. and J.D.; investigation, J.D.; resources, J.D. and M.M.; data curation, J.D. and M.M.; writing—original draft preparation, J.D., and M.M.; writing—review and editing, D.E.K., J.D., and M.M.; supervision, D.E.K. All authors have read and agreed to the published version of the manuscript.

Funding: This research received no external funding.

Institutional Review Board Statement: Not applicable.

Conflicts of Interest: The authors declare no conflict of interest.

References

1. Health Canada. Natural and Non-Prescription Health Products Directorate. Available online: https://www.canada.ca/en/health-canada/services/drugs-health-products/natural-non-prescription.html (accessed on 6 August 2022).
2. Knapik, J.J.; Trone, D.W.; Steelman, R.A.; Farina, E.K.; Lieberman, H.R. Adverse Effects Associated with Use of Specific Dietary Supplements: The US Military Dietary Supplement Use Study. *Food Chem. Toxicol.* **2022**, *161*, 112840. [CrossRef] [PubMed]
3. Diehl, K.; Thiel, A.; Zipfel, S.; Mayer, J.; Schnell, A.; Schneider, S. Elite Adolescent Athletes' Use of Dietary Supplements: Characteristics, Opinions, and Sources of Supply and Information. *Int. J. Sport Nutr. Exerc. Metab.* **2012**, *22*, 165–174. [CrossRef] [PubMed]
4. Knapik, J.J.; Steelman, R.A.; Hoedebecke, S.S.; Austin, K.G.; Farina, E.K.; Lieberman, H.R. Prevalence of Dietary Supplement Use by Athletes: Systematic Review and Meta-Analysis. *Sports Med.* **2016**, *46*, 103–123. [CrossRef] [PubMed]
5. Lun, V.; Erdman, K.A.; Fung, T.S.; Reimer, R.A. Dietary Supplementation Practices in Canadian High-Performance Athletes. *Int. J. Sport Nutr. Exerc. Metab.* **2012**, *22*, 31–37. [CrossRef] [PubMed]
6. Roy, K.-A.; El Khoury, D.; Dwyer, J.J.M.; Mountjoy, M. Dietary Supplementation Practices among Varsity Athletes at a Canadian University. *J. Diet. Suppl.* **2021**, *18*, 614–629. [CrossRef] [PubMed]
7. Garthe, I.; Maughan, R.J. Athletes and Supplements: Prevalence and Perspectives. *Int. J. Sport Nutr. Exerc. Metab.* **2018**, *28*, 126–138. [CrossRef]
8. Maughan, R.J.; Burke, L.M.; Dvorak, J.; Larson-Meyer, D.E. IOC Consensus Statement: Dietary Supplements and the High-Performance Athlete. *Int. J. Sport Nutr. Exerc. Metab.* **2018**, *28*, 23.
9. National Institutes of Health. Available online: https://ods.od.nih.gov/factsheets/WYNTK-Consumer/ (accessed on 13 July 2022).
10. Outram, S.; Stewart, B. Doping through supplement use: A review of the available empirical data. *Int. J. Sport Nutr. Exerc. Metab.* **2015**, *25*, 54–59. [CrossRef]
11. Daily Maverick. Available online: https://www.dailymaverick.co.za (accessed on 19 June 2022).

12. SNY. Available online: https://sny.tv/articles/brandon-copeland-opens-up-on-return-to-jets-after-frustrating-suspension (accessed on 19 June 2022).
13. Mathews, N.M. Prohibited Contaminants in Dietary Supplements. *Sports Health* **2018**, *10*, 19–30. [CrossRef]
14. Walpurgis, K.; Thomas, A.; Geyer, H.; Mareck, U.; Thevis, M. Dietary Supplement and Food Contaminations and Their Implications for Doping Controls. *Foods* **2020**, *9*, 1012. [CrossRef]
15. Vento, K.A.; Wardenaar, F.C. Third-Party Testing Nutritional Supplement Knowledge, Attitudes, and Use Among an NCAA I Collegiate Student-Athlete Population. *Front. Sports Act. Living* **2020**, *2*, 115. [CrossRef]
16. Daher, J.; El Khoury, D.; Dwyer, J.J.M. Education Interventions to Improve Knowledge, Beliefs, Intentions and Practices with Respect to Dietary Supplements and Doping Substances: A Narrative Review. *Nutrients* **2021**, *13*, 3935. [CrossRef]
17. Close, G.L.; Kasper, A.M.; Walsh, N.P.; Maughan, R.J. "Food First but Not Always Food Only": Recommendations for Using Dietary Supplements in Sport. *Int. J. Sport Nutr. Exerc. Metab.* **2022**, 1–16. [CrossRef]
18. Burke, L.M.; Castell, L.M.; Casa, D.J.; Close, G.L.; Costa, R.J.S.; Desbrow, B.; Halson, S.L.; Lis, D.M.; Melin, A.K.; Peeling, P.; et al. International Association of Athletics Federations Consensus Statement 2019: Nutrition for Athletics. *Int. J. Sport Nutr. Exerc. Metab.* **2019**, *29*, 73–84. [CrossRef]
19. Tricco, A.C.; Lillie, E.; Zarin, W.; O'Brien, K.K.; Colquhoun, H.; Levac, D.; Moher, D.; Peters, M.D.J.; Horsley, T.; Weeks, L.; et al. PRISMA Extension for Scoping Reviews (PRISMA-ScR): Checklist and explanation. *Ann. Intern. Med.* **2018**, *169*, 467–473. [CrossRef]
20. Aguilar-Navarro, M.; Baltazar-Martins, G.; Brito de Souza, D.; Muñoz-Guerra, J.; del Mar Plata, M.; Del Coso, J. Gender differences in prevalence and patterns of dietary supplement use in elite athletes. *Res. Q. Exerc. Sport* **2021**, *92*, 659–668. [CrossRef]
21. Baltazar-Martins, G.; Brito de Souza, D.; Aguilar-Navarro, M.; Muñoz-Guerra, J.; del Plata, M.M.; Del Coso, J. Prevalence and Patterns of Dietary Supplement Use in Elite Spanish Athletes. *J. Int. Soc. Sports Nutr.* **2019**, *16*, 30. [CrossRef]
22. Barrack, M.T.; Sassone, J.; Dizon, F.; Wu, A.C.; DeLuca, S.; Ackerman, K.E.; Tenforde, A.S. Dietary Supplement Intake and Factors Associated with Increased Use in Preadolescent Endurance Runners. *J. Acad. Nutr. Diet.* **2022**, *122*, 573–582. [CrossRef]
23. Barrack, M.; Fredericson, M.; Dizon, F.; Tenforde, A.; Kim, B.; Kraus, E.; Kussman, A.; Singh, S.; Nattiv, A. Dietary Supplement Use According to Sex and Triad Risk Factors in Collegiate Endurance Runners. *J. Strength Cond. Res.* **2021**, *35*, 404–410. [CrossRef]
24. Barrack, M.T.; Muster, M.; Nguyen, J.; Rafferty, A.; Lisagor, T. An Investigation of Habitual Dietary Supplement Use Among 557 NCAA Division I Athletes. *J. Am. Coll. Nutr.* **2020**, *39*, 619–627. [CrossRef]
25. Caraballo, I.; Domínguez, R.; Guerra-Hernandez, E.J.; Sánchez-Oliver, A.J. Analysis of Sports Supplements Consumption in Young Spanish Elite Dinghy Sailors. *Nutrients* **2020**, *12*, 993. [CrossRef]
26. Domínguez, R.; López-Domínguez, R.; López-Samanes, Á.; Gené, P.; González-Jurado, J.A.; Sánchez-Oliver, A.J. Analysis of Sport Supplement Consumption and Body Composition in Spanish Elite Rowers. *Nutrients* **2020**, *12*, 3871. [CrossRef]
27. Graybeal, A.J.; Kreutzer, A.; Willis, J.L.; Moss, K.; Braun-Trocchio, R.; Shah, M. Age Drives the Differences in Dietary Supplement Use in Endurance Athletes: A Cross-Sectional Analysis of Cyclists, Runners, and Triathletes. *J. Diet. Suppl.* **2022**, 1–19. [CrossRef]
28. Mata, F.; Domínguez, R.; López-Samanes, Á.; Sánchez-Gómez, Á.; Jodra, P.; Sánchez-Oliver, A.J. Analysis of the Consumption of Sports Supplements in Elite Fencers According to Sex and Competitive Level. *BMC Sports Sci. Med. Rehabil.* **2021**, *13*, 50. [CrossRef]
29. Muñoz, A.; López-Samanes, Á.; Domínguez, R.; Moreno-Pérez, V.; Jesús Sánchez-Oliver, A.; Del Coso, J. Use of Sports Supplements in Competitive Handball Players: Sex and Competitive Level Differences. *Nutrients* **2020**, *12*, 3357. [CrossRef]
30. Sánchez-Oliver, A.J.; Domínguez, R.; López-Tapia, P.; Tobal, F.M.; Jodra, P.; Montoya, J.J.; Guerra-Hernández, E.J.; Ramos-Álvarez, J.J. A Survey on Dietary Supplement Consumption in Amateur and Professional Rugby Players. *Foods* **2021**, *10*, 7. [CrossRef] [PubMed]
31. Sassone, J.; Muster, M.; Barrack, M.T. Prevalence and Predictors of Higher-Risk Supplement Use Among Collegiate Athletes. *J. Strength Cond. Res.* **2019**, *33*, 443–450. [CrossRef] [PubMed]
32. Shoshan, T.; Post, E. Prevalence of Protein and Pre-Workout Supplement Use among High School Football Players and Potential Product Contamination. *Glob. Pediatr. Health* **2021**, *8*, 2333794X2110312. [CrossRef] [PubMed]
33. Ventura Comes, A.; Sánchez-Oliver, A.; Martínez-Sanz, J.; Domínguez, R. Analysis of Nutritional Supplements Consumption by Squash Players. *Nutrients* **2018**, *10*, 1341. [CrossRef]
34. Jovanov, P.; Đorđić, V.; Obradović, B.; Barak, O.; Pezo, L.; Marić, A.; Sakač, M. Prevalence, Knowledge and Attitudes towards Using Sports Supplements among Young Athletes. *J. Int. Soc. Sports Nutr.* **2019**, *16*, 27. [CrossRef]
35. Oliveira, C.B.; Sousa, M.; Abreu, R.; Ferreira, Â.; Figueiredo, P.; Rago, V.; Teixeira, V.H.; Brito, J. Dietary Supplements Usage by Elite Female Football Players: An Exploration of Current Practices. *Scand. Med. Sci. Sports* **2022**, *32*, 73–80. [CrossRef]
36. Sekulic, D.; Tahiraj, E.; Maric, D.; Olujic, D.; Bianco, A.; Zaletel, P. What Drives Athletes toward Dietary Supplement Use: Objective Knowledge or Self-Perceived Competence? Cross-Sectional Analysis of Professional Team-Sport Players from Southeastern Europe during the Competitive Season. *J. Int. Soc. Sports Nutr.* **2019**, *16*, 25. [CrossRef]
37. Wangdi, J.T.; Sabou, V.; O'Leary, M.F.; Kelly, V.G.; Bowtell, J.L. Use, Practices and Attitudes of Elite and Sub-Elite Athletes towards Tart Cherry Supplementation. *Sports* **2021**, *9*, 49. [CrossRef]
38. Hurst, P.; Ring, C.; Kavussanu, M. Athletes Using Ergogenic and Medical Sport Supplements Report More Favourable Attitudes to Doping than Non-Users. *J. Sci. Med. Sport* **2021**, *24*, 307–311. [CrossRef]

39. Tabata, S.; Yamasawa, F.; Torii, S.; Manabe, T.; Kamada, H.; Namba, A.; Kato, J.; Kaneko, H.; Tahara, K.; Tsukahara, Y.; et al. Use of Nutritional Supplements by Elite Japanese Track and Field Athletes. *J. Int. Soc. Sports Nutr.* **2020**, *17*, 38. [CrossRef]
40. Waller, M.C.; Kerr, D.A.; Binnie, M.J.; Eaton, E.; Wood, C.; Stenvers, T.; Gucciardi, D.F.; Goodman, C.; Ducker, K.J. Supplement Use and Behaviors of Athletes Affiliated with an Australian State-Based Sports Institute. *Int. J. Sport Nutr. Exerc. Metab.* **2019**, *29*, 518–525. [CrossRef]
41. Hackett, D.A. Training, Supplementation, and Pharmacological Practices of Competitive Male Bodybuilders Across Training Phases. *J. Strength Cond. Res.* **2022**, *36*, 963–970. [CrossRef]
42. Montuori, P.; Loperto, I.; Paolo, C.; Castrianni, D.; Nubi, R.; De Rosa, E.; Palladino, R.; Triassi, M. Bodybuilding, Dietary Supplements and Hormones Use: Behaviour and Determinant Analysis in Young Bodybuilders. *BMC Sports Sci. Med. Rehabil.* **2021**, *13*, 147. [CrossRef]
43. Madden, R.; Shearer, J.; Legg, D.; Parnell, J. Evaluation of Dietary Supplement Use in Wheelchair Rugby Athletes. *Nutrients* **2018**, *10*, 1958. [CrossRef]
44. Elliott, C. Assessing vitamins, minerals and Supplements marketed to children in Canada. *Int. J. Environ. Res. Public Health* **2019**, *16*, 4326. [CrossRef]
45. Jacobs, D.R.; Gross, M.D.; Tapsell, L.C. Food Synergy: An Operational Concept for Understanding Nutrition. *Am. J. Clin. Nutr.* **2009**, *89*, 1543S–1548S. [CrossRef]

nutrients

Article

Analysis of Sport Supplement Consumption by Competitive Swimmers According to Sex and Competitive Level

Berta Moreno [1,2], Santiago Veiga [2], Antonio J. Sánchez-Oliver [3], Raúl Domínguez [3] and Esther Morencos [1,*]

1 Exercise Physiology Group, Exercise and Sport Sciences, Faculty of Health Sciences, Universidad Francisco de Vitoria, 28223 Madrid, Spain
2 Faculty of Physical Activity and Sports Sciences (INEF), Universidad Politécnica de Madrid (UPM), 28040 Madrid, Spain
3 Departamento de Motricidad Humana Rendimiento Deportivo, Universidad de Sevilla, 41013 Sevilla, Spain
* Correspondence: esther.morencos@ufv.es; Tel.: +34-91-709-1400

Abstract: Sports supplements (SS) are commonly used by athletes to improve their performance. SS use by competitive swimmers is reported to be prevalent but there is no evidence of such use by elite swimmers, either male or female. The objective of this research was to study the patterns of SS use by competitive swimmers based on sex and competitive levels (national and international); Methods: Using the categories of the Australian Institute of Sport (AIS), a total of 102 competitive swimmers (59 men and 43 women) completed a validated self-administered questionnaire on the use of SS; (3) Results: Overall, 86.9% of swimmers had consumed SSs with no differences observed between males and females (p = 0.247) or between competitive levels (p = 0.597). The SS that were most consumed by swimmers were caffeine (53.5%), sport drinks (52.5%), sport bars (51.5%), and vitamin C (43.4%). SSs categorized as medical supplements were consumed significantly more frequently by international swimmers (p = 0.012), with significant differences also found in the level—sex interaction (p = 0.049); (4) Conclusions: Compared to other sports disciplines, the prevalence of SS consumption is high in competitive swimmers regardless of performance level or gender. However, the consumption of medical supplements was greater in swimmers at a higher performance level.

Keywords: nutrition; swimming; ergogenic aids; performance; elite swimmers

Citation: Moreno, B.; Veiga, S.; Sánchez-Oliver, A.J.; Domínguez, R.; Morencos, E. Analysis of Sport Supplement Consumption by Competitive Swimmers According to Sex and Competitive Level. *Nutrients* **2022**, *14*, 3218. https://doi.org/10.3390/nu14153218

Academic Editor: Joerg Koenigstorfer

Received: 18 July 2022
Accepted: 4 August 2022
Published: 6 August 2022

1. Introduction

The main objective of competitive swimming is to complete a set distance (ranging from 50 m to 1500 m in official swimming pool events) in the shortest possible time using the front crawl, breaststroke, backstroke, or butterfly technique [1]. Swimming events can last from approximately 20 s to 16 min approximately, and depending on the characteristics of the event, the efforts require different energy systems, such as high-energy phosphagen, glycolytic and oxidative phosphorylation of carbohydrates, fats, or proteins [2].

The fact that swimming takes place in the water poses unique challenges for the swimmer, with the obligation to reduce drag forces and to maximize propulsive forces becoming a decisive factor in dictating the physiological and energetic demands rather than the duration of the test itself [3]. Training programs for elite competitors usually consist of a large amount of high-intensity training [4,5], although specific training demands depend on the characteristics of the sprint, middle-distance, or distance event. For example, the aerobic involvement in a 400 m front crawl event is 81%, while in the shorter events, such as 50 m and 100 m front crawl, the aerobic contribution is 15.3% [2]. This also has consequences on the different nutritional requirements for success in each discipline [2,6,7].

Previous studies have investigated strategies to increase performance by means of better recovery [2,3,8–10] through the use of nutritional measures, such as sports supplements [8,11,12]. The SSs should be considered as a supplement to the usual diet, which is consumed with the aim of achieving specific performance benefits [13]. Despite this, only a small portion of current SSs on the market have been shown to produce significant improvements in performance [13–16]. Some SS, such as sodium citrate or phosphate, have been reported to provide a negligible benefit to exercise capacity [17–19]. Thus, it is necessary to carry out a cost—benefit analysis based on the criteria for SS safety, efficacy, and legality [15] prior to introducing supplements, providing strategies that allow us to resist in the face of external agents [20].

Different international institutions periodically publish position stands that are elaborated to guide the practice of supplementation, such as the Australian Institute of Sport (AIS) which created the ABCD system, whereby each SS is classified according to the level of scientific evidence [21]: SSs in group A present a high level of scientific evidence; those in group B can have a positive effect in certain circumstances, but more evidence is necessary; those in group C are supplements for which evidence is lacking; and those in group D are prohibited substances. At the same time, SSs are subdivided into sports foods, medical supplements, and ergogenic aids. Several studies have reported the effects of supplementation in athletes based on this classification system [14,22–25], and athletes following a SS program under the AIS guide have displayed a greater consumption of SSs with a high level of scientific evidence [26].

The reported range of SS consumption in sports is very wide and comprises between 30–95% of athletes [23,25,27]. Sex and level of performance are among the most important variables for SS consumption, as SS consumption increases with the competitive level of athletes and in men compared to women [13,23,25,28]. A higher rate of SS consumption has been reported among swimmers (in comparison to other disciplines) as swimming was ranked among the top four sports in terms of the SS use prevalence at the 2000 Sydney Olympic Games [29,30]. The SS consumption patterns in competitive swimmers indicated that all 23 swimmers surveyed in Sri Lanka had consumed SSs and had a daily intake of 3.4 different supplements [26]. However, these data were collected from swimmers with a low competitive level, and, to the best of our knowledge, no other evidence on the SS consumption prevalence or SS characteristics in elite swimmers has been observed.

Therefore, the objective of this study was to analyze the use of SSs specifically in competitive swimmers (national and international levels) and to describe the consumption pattern according to sex and competitive level. It was hypothesized that swimmers of a higher level of performance and male swimmers would present higher SS consumption.

2. Materials and Methods

2.1. Participants

A total of 102 competitive swimmers (59 men and 43 women) voluntarily participated in this investigation. All participants belonged to a federated swimming club and were competing in national (n = 60) and/or international (n = 39) events at the time. Swimmers of international level had taken part in international-level competitions with the national team for at least two years. Three swimmers from the original sample were eliminated from the study because they did not have the required competitive national level; therefore, 99 swimmers were included in the final sample. All participants had an average of six days of training per week, four hours of training per day, and an average of three days per week of out-of-water training.

2.2. Instruments

The questionnaire used contained three main sections: the first one collected anthropometric, personal, and social data of the respondent; the second section covered the practice of the sport activity and included 10 questions about, for example, the number of years federated, the competitive level, years competing in the national team, the hours of water training by week, the sessions of water training by week or dry-land training sessions by week. The last and most extensive section was related to SS consumption. This section contained three questions on the type of diet the swimmers had, 12 questions on the use and consumption of SS (i.e., what supplements are taken, for what reasons are they taken, who advises to take them, when are they taken, what were the reasons or where can the supplements be purchased), and, finally, two questions on the use of banned substances. In addition, this part included the definition of sports supplements (SS) proposed by Knapik [28] and an updated list of SSs. The response options included a time frame such as whether swimmers took SSs for training, competition, or both and whether they took them before, during, or after training and/or competition.

The questionnaire was previously validated in terms of its content, application, structure, and presentation [31] and its quality was evaluated in a systematic review [28]. According to an eight-point scale that included assessments of sampling methods, sampling frame, sample size, measurement tools, bias, response rate, statistical presentation, and description of the participant sample, the quality of the questionnaire reached a 54% score (57 out of 164 questionnaires evaluated) and it was considered adequate to obtain accurate information on supplement use by athletes. It is worth noting its use in different studies that have analyzed the consumption of SS in athletes [14,24,25,27,32].

2.3. Process

All swimmers who participated in this research did so voluntarily and only had to complete a questionnaire on the use of supplements [31]. Swimmers completed the questionnaire between April and October 2019 in a web format that was prepared to facilitate its distribution (Google Forms, Google, Mountain View, CA, USA). The information recorded in the questionnaires did not allow the identification of the swimmers, all of whom remained anonymous. The participants were recruited with the help of the National Swimming Federation, which distributed an e-mail with instructions for completion and an online version of the questionnaire to all the teams with a national license. Thus, when the swimmers went to their usual training pool, the characteristics of the study were explained to them, and consent was obtained from all of them. The protocol complies with the Declaration of Helsinki for human research and was approved by the Ethics Committee of the local university committee.

2.4. Statistical Analysis

The Kolmogorov–Smirnov test and the Levene test were applied to check for normality and homoscedasticity. Quantitative variables were presented as an average (M) $\pm$ standard deviation (SD), while qualitative variables were in percentages. For the analysis of possible differences in the level of performance (international vs. national) and of the possible differences in sex with regard to the motivation, expectations, and contextualization of the use of SS, a chi-square test ($\chi 2$) was performed. If statistical differences were reported, an odds ratio (OR) was also performed. As to the total SSs ingested, a Student's T-test for independent samples was carried out to analyze possible differences between the levels of performance or between performance based on sex. The statistical level of significance was set at $p < 0.05$. The statistical analyses were performed using the Statistical Package for Social Sciences (version 18.0 for Mac, SPSSTM Inc., Chicago, IL, USA).

3. Results

The sample characteristics are reported in Table 1. Male swimmers presented as taller ($p < 0.001$) and heavier ($p = 0.005$) than female swimmers, although no anthropometric differences were reported for level or level—sex. Additionally, no statistically significant differences were found for the number of weekly training days or the number of strength training days in relation to the competitive level, sex, or level—sex ($p > 0.05$). However, national female swimmers performed more strength training days than did international female swimmers ($p = 0.044$). No differences were reported for level ($p = 0.522$) and sex ($p = 0.384$) in the years of federated swimming with 20.2% of the sample federate for less than 5 years, 39.4% between 5 and 8 years, and 40.4% for more than 9 years.

Table 1. Characterization of sample data divided by sex and competitive level (international and national).

Measure	Sex	International	National	*p*-Value Level	*p*-Value Sex	*p*-Value Level-Sex
Height (m)	Females	1.69 ± 0.06 $^{\lambda}$	1.68 ± 0.07 $^{\lambda}$	0.380	<0.001	0.809
	Males	1.80 ± 0.08 $^{\lambda}$	1.79 ± 0.07 $^{\lambda}$			
	Total	1.74 ± 0.09 $^{\lambda}$	1.75 ± 0.09 $^{\lambda}$			
Weight (kg)	Females	61.1 ± 5.5 $^{\lambda}$	58.1 ± 7.1 $^{\lambda}$	0.323	0.005	0. 014
	Males	70.2 ± 8.0 $^{\lambda}$	70.8 ± 9.4 $^{\lambda}$			
	Total	65.3 ± 8.1 $^{\lambda}$	66.4 ± 10.3 $^{\lambda}$			
Weekly training days	Females	5.9 ± 0.3	5.8 ± 0.5	0.594	0.936	0.839
	Males	5.9 ± 0.3	5.8 ± 0.8			
	Total	5.9 ± 0.3	5.8 ± 0.7			
Weekly strength training sessions	Females	3.5 ± 1.0 *	4.3 ± 1.7 *	0.084	0.244	0.213
	Males	3.5 ± 1.2	3.6 ± 1.4			
	Total	3.5 ± 1.1	3.9 ± 1.5			

Data expressed mean ± standard deviation (SD). $^{\lambda}$ Sex differences of the same competitive level; * Level differences of the same sex. Statistical significance fixed at $p < 0.05$.

3.1. SS Consumption Characteristics

In relation to SS consumption characteristics, 6.1% of the sample said they were against SS consumption in swimming, while 80.8% said they were in favor and 13.1% either did not know or did not answer, with no statistically significant differences observed according to sex ($p = 0.841$) or competitive level ($p = 0.417$). When asked if they had ever consumed SSs, 86.9% of the sample answered affirmatively, with no differences observed between men and women ($p = 0.247$) or between swimmers at international and national levels ($p = 0.597$). The main motivations for SS consumption were performance improvement (59.2%), health care (14.6%), or to cover dietary deficits (10.0%), with no statistically significant differences between sexes ($p = 0.109$) or between the level of swimmers ($p = 0.530$).

As shown in Figure 1, SSs were most frequently purchased at specialized SS stores (32.0%) and pharmacies (27.2%), followed by shopping centers (10.9%) and the Internet (10.9%), with no differences between sexes ($p = 0.193$). There were also no differences between swimmers at the national and international levels ($p = 0.822$).

As can be seen in Figure 2, the coach was the person who most frequently advised the consumption of SSs (40.3%), followed by the dietitian—nutritionist (20.1%), the physician (10.0%), the physical trainer (8.1%), family (6.7%), teammates (6.0%), friends (4.7%), or others (4.1%). No significant differences were observed between sexes ($p = 0.421$) or levels ($p = 0.227$).

Regarding when SSs were consumed within the season, most subjects reported consuming SSs during the competitive period (66.0%), followed by those who consumed them only during the training period (23.0%), throughout the year (7.0%), or at other times (4.0%), with no differences found according to sex ($p = 0.702$) or competitive level ($p = 0.838$). In addition, no differences were found between men and women ($p = 0.284$), although differences were observed according to level ($p < 0.001$). International level swimmers presented a greater mode of SS consumption before, during, and after exercise (39.5% vs. 18.6%), whereas national level swimmers had a greater SS consumption mode exclusively before (42.4% vs. 13.2%; OR = 2.56 [1.05–6.27]) or after (27.2% vs. 21.1%; OR = 1.29 [0.60–2.74]) exercise as compared to international level swimmers.

3.2. Type of SS Consumption

Group-level evidence of SSs (A, B, and C; see Table 2) showed no statistical differences in SS consumption for competitive level, sex, or level—sex ($p > 0.05$). As for the different subgroups of group A, a higher consumption of medical supplements was found in international level swimmers ($p = 0.012$), reaching statistically significant differences in men ($p = 0.001$) but not in women ($p = 0.709$). In addition, higher consumption was found in women at the national level as compared to men at the same competitive level ($p = 0.013$). Finally, the subgroup "sport performance" showed higher consumption for national level men as compared to national level women ($p = 0.036$).

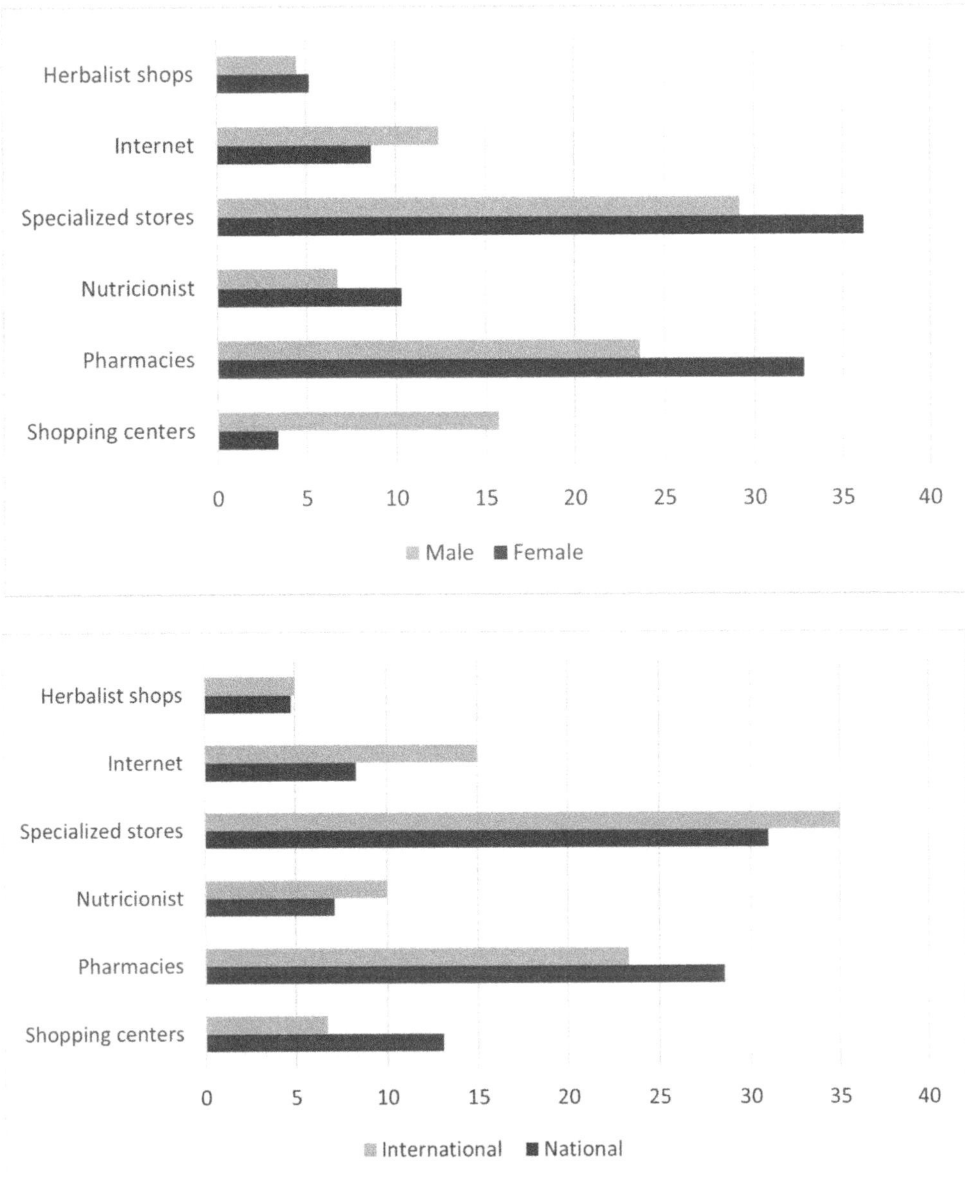

Figure 1. Main site of supplement purchase by elite swimmers according to sex (**up**) and competitive level (**down**).

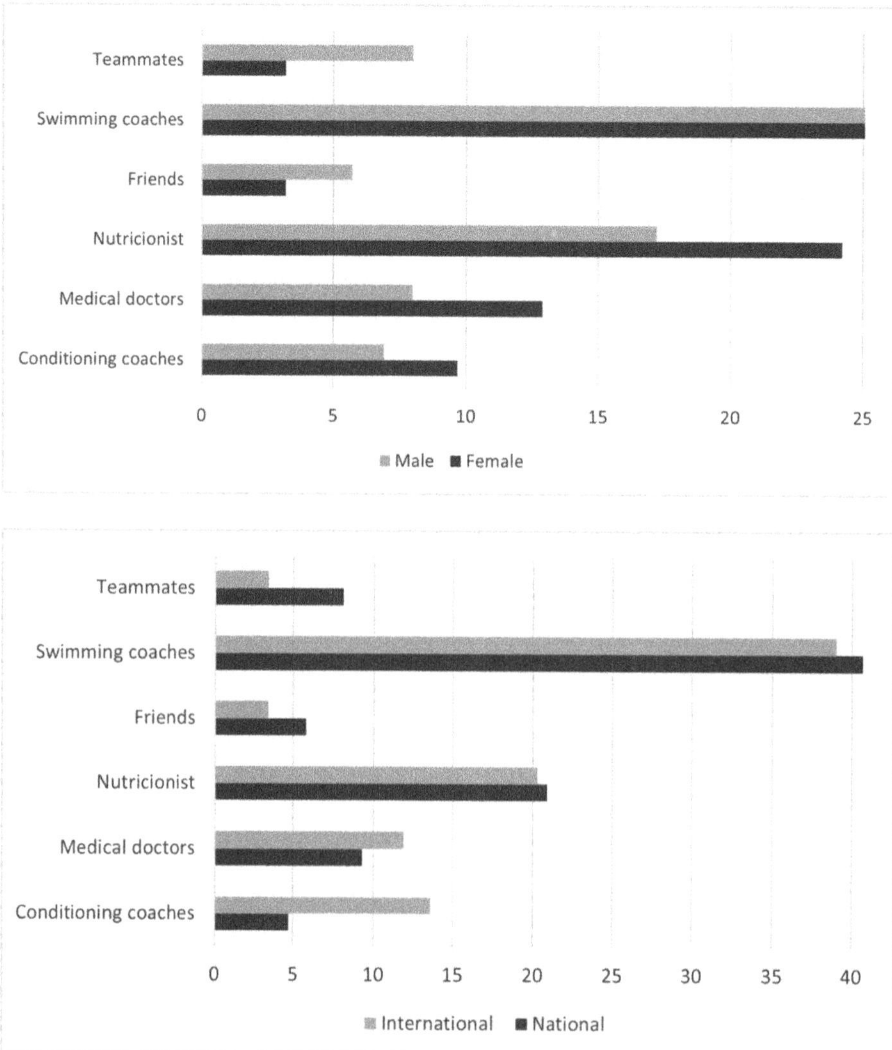

Figure 2. Sources of information or advice on the use of supplements by elite swimmers according to sex (**up**) and competitive level (**down**).

As can be seen in Table 3, there was a consumption rate higher than 10% for 17 SSs in total, with caffeine (53.5%), sports drinks (52.5%), sports bars (51.5%), and vitamin C (43.4%) as the most consumed substances. No differences were observed based on sex for supplements with a consumption rate of at least 10%. Males were observed to have significantly lower consumption of vitamin complexes compared to females ($p = 0.029$; OR = 0.33 [0.12–0.87]), but they had a higher consumption of creatine ($p = 0.041$; OR = 2.92 [1.10–7.72]), taurine ($p > 0.001$), and a trend toward significance in the case of whey protein ($p = 0.059$; OR = 2.77 [0.99–7.7]). On the other hand, international level athletes presented a greater iron intake ($p < 0.001$; OR = 5.77 [2.32–14.32]) than those at the national level.

Table 2. Number of SSs used by swimmers of both sexes and at different competitive levels according to AIS categories [21].

	AIS Categories	Sex	Total	International	National	*p*-Value Level	*p*-Value Sex	*p*-Value Level-Sex
	Total SS	Females	5.5 ± 3.5	6.4 ± 4.1	4.5 ± 2.4	0.091	0.841	0.600
		Males	5.4 ± 4.3	6.1 ± 4.8	5.1 ± 4.1			
		Total	5.4 ± 4.0	6.3 ± 4.4	4.9 ±3.6			
Group A	Sport foods	Females	1.4 ± 1.2	1.5 ± 1.4	1.3 ± 1.0	0.793	0.769	0.492
		Males	1.4 ± 1.2	1.3 ± 1.1	1.4 ± 1.2			
		Total	1.4 ± 1.2	1.4 ± 1.3	1.4 ± 1.1			
	Medical supplements	Females	1.0 ± 0.9	1.1 ± 0.89	1.0 ± 0.9 λ	0.012 *	0.210	0.049 *
		Males	0.7 ± 0.8	1.2 ± 1.0 #	0.4 ± 0.6			
		Total	0.8 ± 0.9	1.2 ± 0.9 #	0.6 ± 0.8			
	Sport performance	Females	1.0 ± 1.1	1.1 ± 1.2	0.8 ± 1.0 λ	0.979	0.160	0.190
		Males	1.4 ± 1.2	1.2 ± 1.0	1.5 ± 1.3			
		Total	1.2 ± 1.2	1.2 ± 1.1	1.3 ± 1.3			
	Total Group A	Females	3.4 ± 2.3	3.8 ± 2.6	3.1 ± 1.8	0.979	0.314	0.762
		Males	3.4 ± 2.5	3.7 ± 2.7	3.3 ± 2.4			
		Total	3.4 ± 2.4	3.7 ± 2.6	3.2 ± 2.2			
	Group B	Females	0.9 ± 0.9	1.1 ± 0.9	0.6 ± 0.9	0.132	0.713	0.302
		Males	0.8 ± 0.9	0.8 ± 0.9	0.7 ± 0.9			
		Total	0.8 ± 0.9	1.0 ± 0.9	0.7 ± 0.9			
	Group C	Females	1.2 ± 1.3	1.5 ± 1.4	0.8 ± 1.1	0.079	0.615	0.798
		Males	1.2 ± 1.9	1.6 ± 2.2	1.1 ± 1.8			
		Total	1.2 ± 1.7	1.6 ± 2.2	1.0 ± 1.6			

Data expressed mean ± standard deviation (SD). *: Significant difference for a determined factor; #: Significant difference between international and national of a same sex; λ Significant difference between males and females of a same competitive level; Statistical significance at $p < 0.05$.

Table 3. Most used supplements according to sex and competitive level based on AIS categories [21].

	AIS Categories	Supplement	Total	Sex				Level			
				Females	Males	*p*-Value	OR	International	National	*p*-Value	OR
Group A	Sport foods	Sport drinks	52.5%	46.2%	49.1%	0.542	0.72 [0.33–1.62]	46.2%	56.7%	0.410	0.66 [0.29–1.47]
		Sport bars	51.5%	45.1%	54.9%	0.685	0.80 [0.36–1.77]	43.6%	56.7%	0.223	0.59 [0.26–1.33]
		Whey protein	14.3%	31.6%	14.3%	0.059	2.77 [0.99–7.7]	33.3%	18.3%	0.099	2.2 [0.88–5.66]
	Medical supplement	Iron	33.3%	42.9%	26.3%	0.091	0.48 [0.20–1.11]	56.4%	18.3%	<0.001 *	5.77 [2.32–14.32]
		Vitamin D	27.3%	28.6%	26.3%	0.823	0.89 [0.37–2.18]	30.8%	25.0%	0.645	1.33 [0.54–3.27]
		Vitamin complex	22.2%	33.3%	14.0%	0.029 *	0.33 [0.12–0.87]	28.2%	18.3%	0.323	1.75 [0.67–4.55]
	Sport performance	Caffeine	53.5%	45.2%	59.6%	0.221	1.80 [0.80–4.01]	53.8%	53.3%	1.00	1.02 [0.46–2.29]
		Creatine	28.3%	16.7%	36.8%	0.041 *	2.92 [1.10–7.72]	25.6%	30.0%	0.820	0.81 [0.33–1.99]
		Bicarbonates	21.2%	14.3%	23.6%	0.214	2.14 [0.75–6.10]	15.4%	25.0%	0.319	0.55 [0.19–1.56]
		β-alanine	17.2%	21.4%	14.0%	0.421	0.60 [0.21–1.71]	20.5%	15.0%	0.587	1.46 [0.51–4.12]
	Group B	Vitamin C	43.4%	40.4%	47.6%	0.540	0.74 [0.33–1.66]	53.8%	36.7%	0.102	2.02 [0.89–4.57]
		Vitamin E	16.2%	14.3%	17.5%	0.785	1.28 [0.42–3.84]	-	-	-	-
		Carnitine	13.1%	16.7%	10.5%	0.386	0.59 [0.18–1.90]	15.4%	11.7%	0.762	1.38 [0.43–4.45]

Table 3. *Cont.*

AIS Categories	Supplement	Total	Sex				Level			
			Females	Males	p-Value	OR	International	National	p-Value	OR
Group C	Magnesium	20.2%	21.4%	19.3%	0.805	0.88 [0.33–2.36]	28.2%	15.0%	0.129	2.23 [0.82–6.01]
	Glutamine	20.2%	23.8%	17.5%	0.459	0.68 [0.25–1.82]	25.6%	16.7%	0.313	1.72 [0.64–4.63]
	Royal jelly	20.2%	26.2%	15.8%	0.217	0.53 [0.20–1.42]	25.6%	16.7%	0.313	1.72 [0.64–4.63]
	Taurine	12.1%	-	21.0%	0.001 *	-	7.7%	15.0%	0.355	0.47 [0.12–1.87]

* Statistical difference in the consume between groups ($p < 0.05$).

4. Discussion

The aim of this study was to analyze SS use in international and national level swimmers, describing the pattern of consumption according to sex and competitive level. Although previous studies [8,26,33–35] have examined SS consumption in competitive swimmers, to our knowledge, this is the first study to report on SS consumption in an extensive sample of elite level swimmers. The results of the present study show a high prevalence of SS use in competitive swimmers (86.9%) compared to other disciplines (30–95%), such as elite sailors (52%) [14] or rugby players (65.3%) [25]. These data support a higher use of SS in individual versus team sports (81% versus 58%) [36] and a prevalence similar to that of previous research on swimming [8,28,30,33,35,36].

4.1. Characteristics of SS Consumption in Competitive Swimmers

High training volume of competitive swimmers including the large number of weekly training sessions in and out the water [4] could explain the high prevalence of SS use in competitive swimmers. Contrary to expectations, no significant differences were observed between national and international level swimmers in the rate of SS consumption as has been shown in other studies [14,22]. This could be explained by the similar training volume of national and international caliber athletes, as defined by Mckay et al. [37] who distinguished the elite-international and the highly trained-national by the competitive standard. Finally, no differences were observed in the prevalence of SS use according to sex, contrary to other recent studies [14,25,36] but in line with similar training volume in swimming between gender.

The main reason for SS consumption in the present sample was to improve sports performance (59.2%), regardless of gender or competitive level. This motive for SS consumption is common (45–77.8%) among elite athletes in different sports [14,32,36,38], and it is consistent with the most used type of SS in the sample, that is, caffeine, which has previously been reported to improve sports performance [21,39]. The most frequent places of purchase of SS in this study, which were well beyond the rest, were specialized shops (32%) and pharmacies (27.2%), a finding that is consistent with a recent study of elite sailors by Caraballo et al. [14]. It is worth noting that online shopping, a current trend reported in some studies [25,36], was not one of the most frequent places of purchase considering the cases of biased and unreliable information, inclusion of undeclared pharmacological substances on the label, and lack of specific legislation [27,40–43].

Although the source of information about SS should be professionals in the field (sports doctors and/or dieticians—nutritionists), swimmers in the present research chose coaches as the main source of information (40.3%) as in a very recent study in gym users by Finamore [44] and the findings in a study of German athletes [45]. This demonstrates some areas of improvement in SS consumption by competitive swimmers, since athletes who receive advice from a professional have a higher consumption of SS for which there is a high level of evidence [25]. It is noteworthy that most of the SS consumed were of category A, which suggests that the coaches of our swimmers were very well informed and instructed to advise on responsible consumption of SS to elite swimmers.

Most subjects reported consuming SS during the competitive period (66.0%), regardless of gender or level of competition. This is related to the three most consumed SS substances of caffeine, sports drinks, and sports bars as they tend to be used during competitive periods. The timing of SS consumption coincided with data reported in similar studies of elite athletes [14], although differences were observed between international and national swimmers. Higher level competitive swimmers had higher SS intake during exercise compared with the higher pre-exercise SS intake of lower level swimmers. The social environment, training regimens, and competition place great demands on elite athletes [4]; perhaps for this reason, added to the demands of the competition itself, means that the highest-level swimmers decide to resort to supplementation as an aid at the moment of greatest sporting demand. This finding in the present investigation is interesting since none of the other studies on swimmers has measured the moment of SSs [2].

The amount of SS consumed in the sample of competitive swimmers (5.45) was higher than what has been reported on fencers (3.33) [23], rugby players (3.9) [25], and sailors (3.9) [14] but lower than studies conducted with squash players (8.4) [32], rowers (16.28) [22], all elite athletes. These data support the hypothesis that there is a difference in consumption depending on the sport or sport modality [13,28,31], although we did not detect a lot of differences in SS consumption by sex [25] or competitive level [28].

4.2. Type of SS Consumption in Competitive Swimmers

When dividing SSs according to the level of evidence (AIS classification), national level men in group A had higher consumption than did women. Although women consumed more SSs in medical supplement subgroup A (0.4 vs. 1.0), these differences in consumption could be explained by the biggest differences in the sport performance subgroup (1.5 vs. 0.8). On the other hand, within the medical supplement subgroup, higher consumption was observed at the international versus the national level for men and at the national level for women as compared to men. The reason for these differences could be the inclusion of iron in the medical supplement subgroup as it has been reported to be the most consumed supplement by elite athletes in different sports [22,23,28,32,36] and specifically by women [28,36]. Iron deficiency is one of the most prevalent nutritional deficiencies in the athlete population, especially in women due to the increased demand for iron during menstruation [46,47]; it is also prevalent at the end of the competitive period [48], which is more demanding for international athletes. In addition, this supplement requires individual dispensing and appropriate sports physician/scientist supervision, so it is reasonable that international swimmers would have a higher intake.

Regarding the most consumed SS in the sample, differences were found according to sex, with men consuming more creatine and taurine and showing a tendency in the case of whey protein, and women consuming more vitamin complexes. These findings are related to those obtained in previous studies in which iron and vitamin consumption were higher for women and protein supplements (including creatine) were higher for men [28,49,50]. It is worth noting that most of the SSs consumed in the present research belonged to group A (more than 10% prevalence), which may suggest that the sample of swimmers was well informed about the most effective supplements in their sport, even if coaches were the main advisers about SSs, as mentioned above. For this reason, a good coach's training-education in this subject (with documents such as the IOC, AIS, or ISSN [13,21,51]) could be a key aspect to correctly advise their swimmers at these levels.

Finally, the present study may present certain limitations that need to be noted for a better interpretation of the results. First, the questionnaire which was used to assess the consumption of dietary supplements in elite athletes collected information retrospectively, and this could lead to inaccurate information on the number and/or type of supplements reported. Even so, although the questionnaire collects the information retrospectively, a validated and reliable questionnaire was used to assess the use of dietary supplements in athletes, as was conducted in other studies of other sports with such a questionnaire [31]. These studies are proof that, despite these small limitations, such a questionnaire should not affect your answers, guaranteeing their accuracy. Second, it is possible that swimmers could have employed supplements but did not recognize their use at that time and, therefore, did not report their use in the questionnaire, resulting in a false negative.

The analysis of SS consumption in this study was analyzed per unit, not per quantity. The quantity should be subject to the weight of the athlete, so it is a very interesting topic for future studies.

5. Conclusions

The present study indicated a high prevalence of SS consumption in competitive swimmers compared to other disciplines, with caffeine, sports drinks, and sports bars being the most consumed SSs. Swimmers reported performance enhancement as the primary motivation for SS consumption and, consequently, SS intake was most common during the competitive period. Differences in SS consumption were observed according to the competitive level, with international level swimmers exhibiting (i) a greater consumption of SSs during exercise (and not only before or after exercise) and (ii) a greater intake of medical supplements (like iron) with a higher level of scientific evidence. In addition, differences were observed by gender in the consumption of certain SSs such as creatine and taurine or the vitamin complexes. These results provide the first evidence of SS consumption in elite swimmers and demonstrate some specific patterns according to the high demands of volume and intensity in the elite swimming training programs.

Author Contributions: Conceptualization, B.M., E.M., S.V. and A.J.S.-O., methodology, B.M., E.M., S.V., A.J.S.-O. and R.D., validation and formal analysis, A.J.S.-O. and R.D., investigation, B.M., E.M., S.V., A.J.S.-O. and R.D., data curation, B.M., E.M., S.V., A.J.S.-O. and R.D., writing—original draft preparation, B.M., E.M., S.V. and A.J.S.-O., supervision, E.M., S.V. and A.J.S.-O. All authors have read and agreed to the published version of the manuscript.

Funding: This research received no external funding.

Institutional Review Board Statement: The protocol complies with the Declaration of Helsinki for human research and was approved by the Ethics Committee of the local university committee.

Informed Consent Statement: Informed consent was obtained from all subjects involved in the study.

Data Availability Statement: The data presented in this study are available on request from the corresponding author. The data are not publicly available due to privacy restrictions.

Acknowledgments: The authors would like to thank the swimmers and coaches participating in the experiment for their valuable collaboration. The authors have no conflicts of interest to declare. The data sets generated during and/or analyzed during this study are not available to the public but can be requested from the corresponding author, who was the organizer of the study. The experiments comply with the laws in force in the country in which they were performed.

Conflicts of Interest: The authors declare no conflict of interest.

References

1. Morouço, P.G.; Marinho, D.A.; Izquierdo, M.; Neiva, H.; Marques, M.C. Relative Contribution of Arms and Legs in 30 s Fully Tethered Front Crawl Swimming. *BioMed Res. Int.* **2015**, *2015*, 1–6. [CrossRef]
2. Domínguez, R.; Sánchez-Oliver, A.J.; Cuenca, E.; Jodra, P.; Fernandes da Silva, S.; Mata-Ordóñez, F. Nutritional Needs in the Professional Practice of Swimming: A Review. *J. Exerc. Nutr. Biochem.* **2017**, *21*, 1–10. [CrossRef] [PubMed]
3. Pyne, D.B.; Sharp, R.L. Physical and Energy Requirements of Competitive Swimming Events. *Int. J. Sport Nutr. Exerc. Metab.* **2014**, *24*, 351–359. [CrossRef]
4. Hellard, P. Elite Swimmers' Training Patterns in the 25 Weeks Prior to Their Season's Best Performances: Insights Into Periodization From a 20-Years Cohort. *Front. Physiol.* **2019**, *10*, 16. [CrossRef] [PubMed]
5. Mujika, I.; Halson, S.; Burke, L.M.; Balagué, G.; Farrow, D. An Integrated, Multifactorial Approach to Periodization for Optimal Performance in Individual and Team Sports. *Int. J. Sports Physiol. Perform.* **2018**, *13*, 538–561. [CrossRef] [PubMed]
6. Cox, G.R.; Mujika, I.; van den Hoogenband, C.-R. Nutritional Recommendations for Water Polo. *Int. J. Sport Nutr. Exerc. Metab.* **2014**, *24*, 382–391. [CrossRef]
7. Mountjoy, M. FINA-Yakult Consensus Statement on Nutrition for the Aquatic Sports. *Int. J. Sport Nutr. Exerc. Metab.* **2014**, *24*, 349–350. [CrossRef]

8. Derave, W.; Tipton, K.D. Dietary Supplements for Aquatic Sports. *Int. J. Sport Nutr. Exerc. Metab.* **2014**, *24*, 437–449. [CrossRef]
9. Burke, L.M.; Mujika, I. Nutrition for Recovery in Aquatic Sports. *Int. J. Sport Nutr. Exerc. Metab.* **2014**, *24*, 425–436. [CrossRef]
10. Nédélec, M.; McCall, A.; Carling, C.; Legall, F.; Berthoin, S.; Dupont, G. Recovery in Soccer: Part II—Recovery Strategies. *Sports Med.* **2013**, *43*, 9–22. [CrossRef]
11. Heaton, L.E.; Davis, J.K.; Rawson, E.S.; Nuccio, R.P.; Witard, O.C.; Stein, K.W.; Baar, K.; Carter, J.M.; Baker, L.B. Selected In-Season Nutritional Strategies to Enhance Recovery for Team Sport Athletes: A Practical Overview. *Sports Med.* **2017**, *47*, 2201–2218. [CrossRef] [PubMed]
12. López-Samanes, Á.; Ortega Fonseca, J.F.; Fernández Elías, V.E.; Borreani, S.; Maté-Muñoz, J.L.; Kovacs, M.S. Nutritional Ergogenic Aids in Tennis: A Brief Review. *Strength Cond. J.* **2015**, *37*, 1–11. [CrossRef]
13. Maughan, R.J.; Burke, L.M.; Dvorak, J.; Larson-Meyer, D.E.; Peeling, P.; Phillips, S.M.; Rawson, E.S.; Walsh, N.P.; Garthe, I.; Geyer, H.; et al. IOC Consensus Statement: Dietary Supplements and the High-Performance Athlete. *Int. J. Sport Nutr. Exerc. Metab.* **2018**, *28*, 104–125. [CrossRef]
14. Caraballo, I.; Domínguez, R.; Guerra-Hernandez, E.J.; Sánchez-Oliver, A.J. Analysis of Sports Supplements Consumption in Young Spanish Elite Dinghy Sailors. *Nutrients* **2020**, *12*, 993. [CrossRef]
15. Maughan, R.J.; Shirreffs, S.M.; Vernec, A. Making Decisions About Supplement Use. *Int. J. Sport Nutr. Exerc. Metab.* **2018**, *28*, 212–219. [CrossRef] [PubMed]
16. Peeling, P.; Binnie, M.J.; Goods, P.S.R.; Sim, M.; Burke, L.M. Evidence-Based Supplements for the Enhancement of Athletic Performance. *Int. J. Sport Nutr. Exerc. Metab.* **2018**, *28*, 178–187. [CrossRef]
17. Carr, A.J.; Hopkins, W.G.; Gore, C.J. Effects of Acute Alkalosis and Acidosis on Performance: A Meta-Analysis. *Sports Med.* **2011**, *41*, 801–814. [CrossRef] [PubMed]
18. Brewer, C.P.; Dawson, B.; Wallman, K.E.; Guelfi, K.J. Effect of Sodium Phosphate Supplementation on Cycling Time Trial Perform—Ance and VO2 1 and 8 Days Post Loading. *J. Sports Sci. Med.* **2014**, *13*, 529–534.
19. West, J.S.; Ayton, T.; Wallman, K.E.; Guelfi, K.J. The Effect of 6 Days of Sodium Phosphate Supplementation on Appetite, Energy Intake, and Aerobic Capacity in Trained Men and Women. *Int. J. Sport Nutr. Exerc. Metab.* **2012**, *22*, 422–429. [CrossRef] [PubMed]
20. Yu, G.; Zhou, J.; Shen, J.; Tang, G.; Huang, F. Cationic Pillar[6]Arene/ATP Host–Guest Recognition: Selectivity, Inhibition of ATP Hydrolysis, and Application in Multidrug Resistance Treatment. *Chem. Sci.* **2016**, *7*, 4073–4078. [CrossRef]
21. AIS, A.I. of S. The AIS Sports Supplement Framework 2021. Available online: https://www.ais.gov.au/nutrition (accessed on 8 February 2022).
22. Domínguez, R.; López-Domínguez, R.; López-Samanes, Á.; Gené, P.; González-Jurado, J.A.; Sánchez-Oliver, A.J. Analysis of Sport Supplement Consumption and Body Composition in Spanish Elite Rowers. *Nutrients* **2020**, *12*, 3871. [CrossRef] [PubMed]
23. Mata, F.; Domínguez, R.; López-Samanes, Á.; Sánchez-Gómez, Á.; Jodra, P.; Sánchez-Oliver, A.J. Analysis of the Consumption of Sports Supplements in Elite Fencers According to Sex and Competitive Level. *BMC Sports Sci. Med. Rehabil.* **2021**, *13*, 50. [CrossRef]
24. Muñoz, A.; López-Samanes, Á.; Pérez-López, A.; Aguilar-Navarro, M.; Moreno-Heredero, B.; Rivilla-García, J.; González-Frutos, P.; Pino-Ortega, J.; Morencos, E.; Del Coso, J. Effects of Caffeine Ingestion on Physical Performance in Elite Women Handball Players: A Randomized, Controlled Study. *Int. J. Sports Physiol. Perform.* **2020**, *15*, 1406–1413. [CrossRef] [PubMed]
25. Sánchez-Oliver, A.J.; Domínguez, R.; López-Tapia, P.; Tobal, F.M.; Jodra, P.; Montoya, J.J.; Guerra-Hernández, E.J.; Ramos-Álvarez, J.J. A Survey on Dietary Supplement Consumption in Amateur and Professional Rugby Players. *Foods* **2020**, *10*, 7. [CrossRef] [PubMed]
26. de Silva, A.; Samarasinghe, Y.; Senanayake, D.; Lanerolle, P. Dietary Supplement Intake in National-Level Sri Lankan Athletes. *Int. J. Sport Nutr. Exerc. Metab.* **2010**, *20*, 15–20. [CrossRef]
27. Sánchez-Oliver, A.J.; Grimaldi-Puyana, M.; Domínguez, R. Evaluation and Behavior of Spanish Bodybuilders: Doping and Sports Supplements. *Biomolecules* **2019**, *9*, 122. [CrossRef]
28. Knapik, J.J.; Steelman, R.A.; Hoedebecke, S.S.; Austin, K.G.; Farina, E.K.; Lieberman, H.R. Prevalence of Dietary Supplement Use by Athletes: Systematic Review and Meta-Analysis. *Sports Med.* **2016**, *46*, 103–123. [CrossRef] [PubMed]
29. Shaw, G.; Boyd, K.T.; Burke, L.M.; Koivisto, A. Nutrition for Swimming. *Int. J. Sport Nutr. Exerc. Metab.* **2014**, *24*, 360–372. [CrossRef]
30. Corrigan, B.; Kazlauskas, R. Medication Use in Athletes Selected for Doping Control at the Sydney Olympics (2000). *Clin. J. Sport Med.* **2003**, *13*, 33–40. [CrossRef] [PubMed]
31. Sánchez Oliver, A.J. Suplementación Nutricional En La Actividad Físico-Deportiva: Análisis de La Calidad Del Suplemento Proteico Consumido. Doctoral Thesis, University of Granada, Granada, Spain, 2012.
32. Ventura Comes, A.; Sánchez-Oliver, A.; Martínez-Sanz, J.; Domínguez, R. Analysis of Nutritional Supplements Consumption by Squash Players. *Nutrients* **2018**, *10*, 1341. [CrossRef] [PubMed]
33. Shaw, G.; Slater, G.; Burke, L.M. Supplement Use of Elite Australian Swimmers. *Int. J. Sport Nutr. Exerc. Metab.* **2016**, *26*, 249–258. [CrossRef]
34. Dascombe, B.J.; Karunaratna, M.; Cartoon, J.; Fergie, B.; Goodman, C. Nutritional Supplementation Habits and Perceptions of Elite Athletes within a State-Based Sporting Institute. *J. Sci. Med. Sport* **2010**, *13*, 274–280. [CrossRef] [PubMed]
35. Shaw, G.; Slater, G.; Burke, L.M. Changes in the Supplementation Practices of Elite Australian Swimmers over 11 Years. *Int. J. Sport Nutr. Exerc. Metab.* **2016**, *26*, 565–571. [CrossRef]

36. Baltazar-Martins, G.; Brito de Souza, D.; Aguilar-Navarro, M.; Muñoz-Guerra, J.; Plata, M.D.M.; Del Coso, J. Prevalence and Patterns of Dietary Supplement Use in Elite Spanish Athletes. *J. Int. Soc. Sports Nutr.* **2019**, 16. [CrossRef] [PubMed]
37. McKay, A.K.A.; Stellingwerff, T.; Smith, E.S.; Martin, D.T.; Mujika, I.; Goosey-Tolfrey, V.L.; Sheppard, J.; Burke, L.M. Defining Training and Performance Caliber: A Participant Classification Framework. *Int. J. Sports Physiol. Perform.* **2022**, *17*, 317–331. [CrossRef]
38. López-Domínguez, R.; Sánchez-Oliver, A.J. Uso de suplementos nutricionales deportivos en remeros de elite: Diferencias entre nacionales e internacionales. *Retos Nuevas Tend. Educ. Física Deporte Recreación* **2018**, *34*, 272–275.
39. Spriet, L.L. Exercise and Sport Performance with Low Doses of Caffeine. *Sports Med.* **2014**, *44*, 175–184. [CrossRef]
40. Bjelica, A.; Aleksić, S.; Goločorbin-Kon, S.; Sazdanić, D.; Torović, L.; Cvejić, J. Internet Marketing of Cardioprotective Dietary Supplements. *J. Altern. Complement. Med.* **2020**, *26*, 204–211. [CrossRef]
41. Tian, H.H.; Ong, W.S.; Tan, C.L. Nutritional Supplement Use among University Athletes in Singapore. *Singap. Med. J.* **2009**, *50*, 165–172.
42. Jordan, M.A.; Haywood, T. Evaluation of Internet Websites Marketing Herbal Weight-Loss Supplements to Consumers. *J. Altern. Complement. Med.* **2007**, *13*, 1035–1043. [CrossRef] [PubMed]
43. Martínez-Sanz, J.; Sospedra, I.; Ortiz, C.; Baladía, E.; Gil-Izquierdo, A.; Ortiz-Moncada, R. Intended or Unintended Doping? A Review of the Presence of Doping Substances in Dietary Supplements Used in Sports. *Nutrients* **2017**, *9*, 1093. [CrossRef] [PubMed]
44. Finamore, A.; Benvenuti, L.; De Santis, A.; Cinti, S.; Rossi, L. Sportsmen's Attitude towards Dietary Supplements and Nutrition Knowledge: An Investigation in Selected Roman Area Gyms. *Nutrients* **2022**, *14*, 945. [CrossRef]
45. Wardenaar, F.C.; Ceelen, I.J.; Van Dijk, J.-W.; Hangelbroek, R.W.; Van Roy, L.; Van der Pouw, B.; De Vries, J.H.; Mensink, M.; Witkamp, R.F. Nutritional Supplement Use by Dutch Elite and Sub-Elite Athletes: Does Receiving Dietary Counseling Make a Difference? *Int. J. Sport Nutr. Exerc. Metab.* **2016**, *27*, 32–42. [CrossRef]
46. DellaValle, D.M.; Haas, J.D. Impact of Iron Depletion Without Anemia on Performance in Trained Endurance Athletes at the Beginning of a Training Season: A Study of Female Collegiate Rowers. *Int. J. Sport Nutr. Exerc. Metab.* **2011**, *21*, 501–506. [CrossRef]
47. Domínguez, R.; Sánchez-Oliver, A.; Mata-Ordoñez, F.; Feria-Madueño, A.; Grimaldi-Puyana, M.; López-Samanes, Á.; Pérez-López, A. Effects of an Acute Exercise Bout on Serum Hepcidin Levels. *Nutrients* **2018**, *10*, 209. [CrossRef] [PubMed]
48. Reinke, S.; Taylor, W.R.; Duda, G.N.; von Haehling, S.; Reinke, P.; Volk, H.-D.; Anker, S.D.; Doehner, W. Absolute and Functional Iron Deficiency in Professional Athletes during Training and Recovery. *Int. J. Cardiol.* **2012**, *156*, 186–191. [CrossRef]
49. Sánchez Oliver, A.J.; Miranda León, M.T.; Hernández, E.G. Estudio estadístico del consumo de suplementos nutricionales y dietéticos en gimnasios. *Arch Lat. Nutr.* **2008**, *58*, 221–227.
50. Sánchez Oliver', A.J.; Miranda León, M.T.; Guerra Hernández, E. Prevalence Ofprotein Supplement Use at Gyms. *Nutr. Hosp.* **2011**, *26*, 1168–1174. [CrossRef]
51. Kerksick, C.M.; Wilborn, C.D.; Roberts, M.D.; Smith-Ryan, A.; Kleiner, S.M.; Jäger, R.; Collins, R.; Cooke, M.; Davis, J.N.; Galvan, E.; et al. ISSN Exercise & Sports Nutrition Review Update: Research & Recommendations. *J. Int. Soc. Sports Nutr.* **2018**, *15*, 38. [CrossRef]

MDPI
St. Alban-Anlage 66
4052 Basel
Switzerland
Tel. +41 61 683 77 34
Fax +41 61 302 89 18
www.mdpi.com

Nutrients Editorial Office
E-mail: nutrients@mdpi.com
www.mdpi.com/journal/nutrients

www.ingramcontent.com/pod-product-compliance
Lightning Source LLC
Chambersburg PA
CBHW061516210926
51850CB00008B/1933
9783036577029